THE FOOD OF Spain

THE FOOD OF *Spain*

CLAUDIA RODEN

PHOTOGRAPHS BY JASON LOWE

ecco
ANNIVERSARY 40

An Imprint of HarperCollinsPublishers

HarperCollins books may be purchased
for educational, business,
or sales promotional use.
For information please write:
Special Markets Department, HarperCollins Publishers,
10 East 53rd Street, New York, NY 10022.

FIRST EDITION

Designed by Level, Calistoga, California

Library of Congress Cataloging-in-Publication Data has been applied for.

ISBN 978-0-06-196962-1

11 12 13 14 15 OV/QGT 10 9 8 7 6 5 4 3 2 1

For my children, Simon, Nadia, and Anna;

my grandchildren, Cesar, Peter, Sarah, Ruby, Nell, and Lily;

and also for Clive and Ros

CONTENTS

THE RECIPES

YOU WILL RETURN TO MY ORCHARD

AND ITS FIG TREE:

IN THE ALTITUDE OF BLOSSOMS YOUR SOUL

WILL FLOAT ON WINGS, COLLECTING

THE HONEY AND WAX OF THE ANGELIC HIVES.

—MIGUEL HERNÁNDEZ

from "Elegy"

THE FOOD OF Spain

THE FAINT AROMA OF
LEMON ZEST AND CINNAMON:
An Introduction

Recipes, I have come to understand, have a special place at the heart of Spanish identity. And they give the measure of a man. It was always so. In the early seventeenth century, Miguel de Cervantes began the first paragraph of *Don Quixote* by describing the gentleman who rode a scraggy horse, carrying a wooden lance and an ancient shield, as a man who ate lentils on Fridays, eggs on Saturdays, sometimes a pigeon on Sundays, and an occasional stew with more beef than mutton.

Spain figured powerfully in my life long before I first went there for the BBC television series *Claudia Roden's Mediterranean Cooking* in 1987. My grandmother Eugénie Alphandary spoke an old Judeo-Spanish language called Judezmo, or Ladino, which she said was old Castilian. She was from Constantinople (now Istanbul) and was descended from Jews who had been expelled from Spain in 1492 and went on to live in Ottoman lands. Her friends, who were mainly from Salonika, Smyrna, and Constantinople, were labeled Spaniolis in the Jewish community of Egypt that I grew up in. They were proud of their Spanish ancestry. They sang ballads about *hidalgos* (knights) and Moros (Moors), as Muslims were called in medieval Spain, and about princesses who became slaves. Some of their names—Toledano, Cuenca, Carmona, León, Burgos, Soria, Saragossa—were a record of the cities their ancestors came from. The dishes they clung to—*albóndigas* (meatballs), *almodrote* (vegetable flan), *maronchinos* (almond biscuits), *pan d'espanya* (sponge cake)—were their badge of identity.

1

As I traveled through Spain to research this book, the names of cities and streets conjured up in my mind the faces of my family and friends in Egypt. I recognized the names of vegetables and dishes. Traces of the old Muslim presence—arabesque carvings, blue and white tiles, a fountain spouting cool water in a scented garden—evoked nostalgic memories of the Arab world I was born in. At the sight of an old minaret, I imagined hearing the call to prayer of a *muezzin*. The streets lined with orange trees explained why my family makes orange cakes and crystallized orange peel, and why we put the distilled essence of orange blossom in so many of our desserts and pastries. The way people cook in Spain, the ingredients they put together, their little tricks, their turn of hand, are mysteriously familiar. A word, a taste, a smell, triggered memories I never knew I had. It is surprising how dishes can appeal directly to the emotions. They say that with food, as with music, you can touch people and even make them cry.

I am intrigued by how interested Spanish people are when they learn that I am a Sefardita (a Jew whose ancestors came from Spain). For centuries, the country had wiped its Muslim and Jewish past from national memory. The drama of the centuries-long Reconquista—the reconquest of their land from the Muslims—was the official and cherished feature of their history and self-image that was taught at school. But the legacies of the once huge population of Muslims and a significant minority of Jews, and the consequences of their expulsion or conversion, are now matters of scholarly research and public interest and discussion.

It is an exceptional time to be traveling and eating in Spain today. The country has changed dramatically in less than thirty years. After the horrors of the Spanish Civil War (1936 to 1939), when thousands died and parts of the country knew famine, and after a long period of oppression and hardship when food was rationed during General Francisco Franco's dictatorship, it is now a rich, modern, dynamic country, where everything, especially food, arouses great passions. And there has been a revolution in restaurant kitchens.

Spanish food had never until now received praise from foreigners. In the nineteenth century, although the French were fascinated with their neighbor, and accounts of their travels in Spain were immensely popular, they described the food with disdain. Writers such as Théophile Gautier, in *Un Voyage en Espagne;* Alexandre Dumas, in *Adventures in Spain* and *From Paris to Cádiz;* and Prosper Mérimée, in the novella on which the opera *Carmen* was based, complained that the food was poor and that too much oil and too much pork fat, too much garlic, and too much *pimentón* (paprika) made it unpalatable. Dumas sometimes insisted on cooking his own food in the hostels where he stayed. British writer Richard Ford's *Handbook for Travellers in Spain,* originally published in 1845, had nothing good to say about the food, nor did the hispanophile Gerald Brenan. At a recent dinner in Córdoba, I was asked politely if the food in England was all that good in Richard Ford's time. His comments obviously still hurt. In the mid-twentieth century, a bastardized tourist cuisine of the fixed-price menu and fake paellas arose during the massive expansion of cheap sand-sea-and-sun tourism. It is still there in parts, and tourists still complain, but Spain has transformed itself into the world's effervescent center of gastronomic creativity.

San Sebastián, in the Basque Country, has become the culinary capital of Europe, with the greatest concentration of Michelin three-star restaurants in Spain. Ferran Adrià at El Bulli in Roses, Catalonia, who is famous for using science and technology in his cuisine, is feted abroad as the greatest living chef. Food and travel writers rave about the extraordinary and fantastic *nueva cocina,* the new Spanish cuisine, and its star chefs are rightly acclaimed throughout the world. These avant-garde chefs use machines, cook *sous-vide* and with syringes, freeze-dry and caramelize, and create hot jellies, instant mousses, bubbling froths and foams, vapors, and explosions. They deconstruct traditional dishes and use exotic foreign ingredients. Their food is what they call an artist's *cocina de autor*—signed by the chef—and it is constantly changing.

There have been several phases in the gastronomic revolution over three decades. Among the other top influential chefs are Juan Mari Arzak, Pedro

Subijana, Andoni Luis Aduriz, Martin Berasategui, Sergi Arola, Dani García, Carme Ruscalleda, and Victor Arguinzoniz. Some things have been crazy, but the kitchen revolution has led to the development of an exquisite and refined professional *alta cocina* (haute cuisine) that Spain had never had before, and to an updating of the traditional culinary know-how that had been passed down the generations for centuries. The new ways of doing things—to grill, fry, and roast better, to boil and stew better, to present food better, and to make it more delicious and appealing—have reached home cooks. And there has been a new appreciation of traditional Spanish food as well—which is what this book is about.

Many of these innovative chefs now say that they have been inspired by their roots. They talk about their parents' and grandparents' cooking and about rescuing rural traditions and local ingredients that are in danger of disappearing. The revered Catalan chef Santi Santamaria, whose restaurant El Raco de Can Fabes is in San Celoni near Barcelona, says that cooking has to be sentiment as well as technique and that without "ideology," it is simply a matter of manual skills and technology. His ideology, he says, is rooted in the life of his peasant family and the progressive politics of his youth. He quoted the painter Joan Miró: "To be universal, you have to be local." The young Basque chef Andoni Luis Aduriz, of the restaurant Mugaritz in San Sebastián, spoke with touching intensity when he said that, apart from giving pleasure, his aim was to give "memories and emotions—even bad ones." This is the refrain today of most of the innovative chefs.

Despite the glamour of the innovators (in a cooking school I visited, all the students wanted to be like Ferran Adrià), a huge fraternity of chefs has stuck to traditional ways. In old-style *mesones*, informal restaurants or inns, and in grand establishments, they offer the food Spaniards have always known and loved. Because children now eat at school and men do not come home for lunch, because women work too and are busy (they cook on weekends or "just make pasta" and cook *a la plancha* [see page 121] or have Latin American or North African maids who also cook for them), restaurants and bars have become places where people go to find the traditional and regional home cooking they hanker after.

Throughout the country, there is a palpable feeling of nostalgia for the old rural life that was too quickly swept away by the booming tourist economy. It has translated into a newfound passion for regional cooking and products. During the Franco regime, regional cultures were suppressed and artisan products were discouraged in favor of industrial ones that could feed the population cheaply. When the autonomous communities (as the historic regions are now called) gained political recognition and the right to govern themselves in 1978, people felt free to celebrate their regional heritage and began to value their cuisines and their sometimes almost lost local products.

In a mood of regional nationalist hedonism, organizations have formed to preserve their culinary heritage by recording recipes. Such organizations have collected nine hundred recipes in Catalonia, six hundred in the Balearic Islands of Majorca and Menorca, and nine hundred in Galicia, and regional producers have rushed to defend their wines, their olive oils, their hams and charcuterie, their cheeses, beans, and honeys, and their indigenous breeds of cows, pigs, and capons. Many of them obtained *Denominaciones de Origen* (DOs)—designations of origin that specify geographical origin and time-honored traditional methods of production and guarantee quality. As Spaniards became more affluent and could afford to buy good wines and foods, it was worth investing effort and money in good quality. The European Union helped with subsidies, and the world has come to appreciate the results.

Like language and music, food in Spain is about local patriotism. The historic regions, now seventeen autonomous communities (nineteen with Ceuta and Melilla, Spanish enclaves on the Moroccan coast), each divided into provinces, were born out of the old medieval kingdoms. Each has its own history and culture, sometimes its own language, and a cuisine that springs from the land—the *comarca*, or *terroir*—and also reflects the past. The first thing you discover about Spain is its extraordinary geographical diversity. The greatest dif-

ference is between the very long, narrow coastal plains, with their string of vibrant port cities, and the vast empty interior—a high plateau and huge mountain ranges. Traveling through, you see endless flatlands and gentle hills, great rivers, mountain forests, marshlands, and deserts. There are seas of wheat and of rice, and endless landscapes carpeted with grapevines and olive trees. Until roads began to be built in the 1960s, the high mountains made internal transport difficult. Rural communities were isolated, and culinary styles developed separately. That is one reason why every province, every town, and every village has its own distinctive dishes or versions of a dish, and why every coastal region has at least three distinctive culinary styles; one of the sea, one of the rural coastal plain, and one of the mountains.

Regional cooking has survived because it is loaded with emotional associations and because Spaniards are attached to their roots. Until the mid-twentieth century, the majority of the population lived and worked on the land. Most people now live in towns or cities, but they regularly go back to the village where their parents or grandparents came from, and where there is usually a family home. What their grandparents cooked has become something to be proud of.

As I worked on this book and traveled throughout Spain, I asked everyone I met what their favorite foods were, how and where their parents and grandparents lived, and how they cooked. People were happy to give me old family recipes and to take me to bars and restaurants where I could taste their favorite dishes; some invited me to their homes. I had a few mentors who helped me and gave me contacts in different regions, and I talked with food writers and scholars, chefs and producers. I also spoke with fishermen who remembered when fish and seafood were regarded as poor food, with people who had once worked on the land as virtual serfs, with landed aristocrats, and with nuns who made pastries. I never studied Spanish formally, but I understood almost everything the people I met said, and they understood my mix of Italian, French, Judeo-Spanish, and the Spanish I gradually picked up. I taught myself to read Spanish and went through old and new cookbooks. My greatest mentor was Alicia Ríos, a food writer and historian and an olive oil expert, and when I stayed in her studio in Madrid, I had access to her huge library and archive of cookbooks.

The recipes in this book represent traditional home cooking from all the regions as it is cooked today. My aim was to feature the best dishes I could find, the most interesting and delicious, those I loved best and that I thought everyone would enjoy cooking and eating. Sometimes a dish was good, but the effort to make it was too big. I had a rule—because most of us are short on time—that there should be a balance between the effort of making a dish and the pleasure of eating it. This was the case for Catalan *canelones,* which I made when my granddaughters stayed the night, and they watched me prepare them. The stuffing is complex and intriguing, with many ingredients, and the process of filling the pasta, then making the sauce and baking the dish, is long and finicky. I had told them of my rule and that if a dish were really fantastic, it should go in the book no matter how difficult or time consuming it was to make. We all liked the *canelones,* but we agreed that, considering the time it took to make them, we did not love

them enough to give the dish a place in the book. There are dishes that you will not find in this book. For instance, I have only a few using salt cod, although there are dozens throughout Spain, because it is hard to find it in America and it is not part of our culture in the way that it is there. I do not feature many recipes with pigs' ears, feet, and offal for the same reason.

Most Spanish dishes were born in a rural world where there were no modern ovens or kitchen gadgets, when people worked hard and needed warming fatty foods that would give them energy for arduous toil in the fields. Things have changed so much. Peasant life as it was has disappeared. Now the work is done by immigrant workers. People have every kitchen gadget. They want to make things easier and are concerned with healthy eating, dishes that are quicker and lighter, with less fat and less frying. In many parts of the country where they once cooked exclusively with pork fat, they now mostly use olive oil (that is why I allowed myself to use olive oil rather than pork fat throughout the book). Fish and seafood are cooked much more quickly. Where people once preferred long-cooked vegetables, they may now prepare them slightly al dente. And they do not now always dredge everything in flour before frying it, as they once did.

But although traditional Spanish cooking has evolved, it has not lost its character and identity. As with poetry and music, cuisines have rhymes and tunes and recurrent themes that characterize them. Spain's signature tune is the *sofrito*, of fried onion and tomato, to which garlic and green peppers are often added.

Among its other themes are the bits of chopped cured ham that find their way into most dishes; the chorizo and blood sausage that are featured together in bean and chickpea stews; and the wine or sherry and brandy that go together in sauces. A *picada* of nuts crushed with garlic and fried bread tells you that a dish is Catalan. The gentle flavor of saffron tells you that you are on the Mediterranean coast or perhaps in the south. *Pimentón* or the faint aroma of lemon zest and cinnamon tells you that a dish is Spanish.

Part of the appeal of traditional

dishes is that they hold memories of the past. The Catalan chef Santi Santamaria wrote, "We are products of our history," and that the reference points of his cooking were the memories of his grandparents' generation and medieval Catalan cookbooks. In Spain, the past is always an intimate part of the present. I have found that history is a sensitive subject that arouses passions whenever I say that I am researching the history of Spain through its food. You can imagine that past against the background of Roman aqueducts, Moorish and Romanesque palaces, and medieval villages. At festivals, the taste for the spectacular and the macabre that Spain has kept from the Middle Ages is on show. During Semana Santa (Easter Week), when statues of the Virgin dressed in fine clothes are paraded through the streets, the men leading the processions are in the tall pointed hoods and robes worn by penitents during the public sentencing at the courts of the Inquisition (these were later adopted by the Ku Klux Klan). The popular festival of Moros y Cristianos is a costumed reenactment of the battles of the Reconquista.

Many old monasteries, castles, and palaces have been restored and transformed into state-run luxury hotels, called *paradores*. Their menus offer regional and "historic" dishes. A little booklet produced in 1998 to celebrate the seventieth anniversary of the first *paradores* explains that Spanish gastronomy is as varied as its history and gives recipes to illustrate the influences going back to Roman times. The stories behind what you eat in Spain are like pieces of a puzzle. Working on this book was for me a delicious and exciting way of finding all the fragments and putting them together to discover Spain.

At home in London, as I roast my red peppers and eggplants and sprinkle them with olive oil, as I caramelize onions or fry almonds with garlic and bread, wonderful aromas fill my house, and I remember the mountains and the olive groves, the old churches and convents. I miss the conviviality that Spaniards are so good at, but I re-create it with the friends who come to taste the dishes I have discovered. They are used to me calling to invite them just a day before. I tell them what is on the menu. When it was pigs' feet and ears, one or two said, "I'll pass on that." Over the past few years I have invited many friends and visitors from abroad to these tasting dinners. That too has been part of the pleasure of writing the book.

# of pigs and olive trees

{ *celts, romans, and visigoths* }

During a lunch with olive-oil men in Córdoba, Cristóbal Lovera Prieto said that there was a long controversy about Spanish culture that had lasted nearly thirty years. Was it Roman, or was it Arab? After a lot of argument, it was decided that it was Roman. At a dinner party in Madrid, when I said that I was researching the history and culture of Spanish food, the hostess, Antonieta, said, "You have to know that we are of Roman and Visigoth stock. Did you see the Roman aqueduct in Segovia?" She was angry, she said, at the way foreigners always noticed Moorish architecture and influences. "By the thirteenth century, almost all of the peninsula had been repossessed, and Muslims remained only in the small enclave of Granada." My reply, a rather earnest recitation of what I had just learned about the Muslim presence in Spain as late as the seventeenth century, must have made her feel that I was upset and perhaps that I saw her as prejudiced, because after dinner she put on a Moroccan belly dancing costume and showed me a recipe for hummus that she'd stuck on her fridge. Spaniards like to see themselves as Romans and Visigoths or Celts, or even Phoenicians. Obviously, these early civilizations have a place in this book.

Early on, possibly from the sixth century B.C., Phoenicians, Greeks, and Carthaginians established settlements along the Mediterranean coast of the Iberian Peninsula and on the Balearic Islands, while Celtic tribes coming over the Pyrenees settled in the north. The Phoenicians created salt pans (shallow pools where seawater is evaporated, leaving salt deposits) and introduced the techniques of preserving fish in salt for their overseas trade and the manner of baking fish in salt. The Carthaginians are said to have brought chickpeas with them. The Greeks cultivated grapevines and olive and almond trees. The Celts were swineherds. They venerated the indigenous oaks, which they believed had magical powers, and chestnut trees, and they fed their pigs acorns and chestnuts. Among their legacies are the cured pork products that have a hugely important place in Spanish gastronomy. They also reared cattle for dairy. When the entire Iberian Peninsula came under Roman rule (the Romans began their invasion in 206 B.C. and called it Hispania), the vineyards and olive groves were expanded, and wheat was established in the plains, reaffirming the classical Mediterranean triad of bread, wine, and olive oil on which Spanish food is based. The Romans also introduced peach, apricot, and lemon trees. But their lasting legacy is the Latin language, from which the languages spoken today in Spain (apart from the Basque language) derive.

When the Roman Empire began to crumble in the fifth century, pillaging Germanic tribes passed in waves until the Visigoths, whose ruling families of Germanic origin had been in the service of the Roman emperors, arrived at the end of the century. They established the capital of their kingdom in Toledo. Their king Recared converted to Catholicism in 587, and his successors continued to rule over a Roman Catholic Visigothic kingdom, which gradually covered all of the peninsula.

The Visigoths were stock-raising herders. They kept pigs and let them feed on acorns and berries in the woods and forests. They cooked with lard, not olive oil. They knew the art of salting and smoking meats. They raised geese, kept goats, and made cheese. They also made apple cider, and beer from fermented barley. Their conquered subjects continued as in Roman times, cultivating grapevines and olive trees; grains such as wheat, oats, barley, millet, and rye; broad beans, peas, chickpeas, and lentils; and vegetables such as cabbages and leeks. They had hazelnut and walnut trees, figs, pears, apples, and plums. They picked wild berries; collected snails; raised pigs, sheep, and goats; and hunted deer, wild boar, and small game such as rabbits and birds. Most of their fish came from rivers rather than the sea. There are no documents from Spain relating to the cooking of the time, but foreign travelers noted that it was rough and primitive, that pork was the most popular food, and that lard was preferred to olive oil.

cumin, pies, and eggplants

{ al-andalus }

Years ago, when I visited El Molino, a restaurant and center of gastronomic research outside Granada where they give courses on the history of Spanish food, I asked about the origins of the cooking. One of the teachers said, "Arab and Jewish," and gave me roast pork, which is forbidden to Jews and Muslims, as an example. He explained, "When the Muslims and Jews converted to Christianity, they cooked pork in the way they cooked lamb, which was to rub it with cumin seeds." Now you know why you may find cumin seeds on roast pork belly in Spain today. The Arab-Islamic presence had a huge impact on Spanish gastronomy, even in parts of the country where it was brief.

In 711, an Arab army crossed the Strait of Gibraltar with their North African Berber foot soldiers and vanquished the Visigoths. Except for a pocket of resistance in the north, all of the Iberian Peninsula fell under the rule of the Umayyad caliph of the Islamic Empire, who was based in Damascus, and became known as Al-Andalus. In 756, the entire Umayyad clan was massacred by the Abbasids, who relocated the capital of the empire to Baghdad. One Umayyad prince who escaped the slaughter, Abd-al-Rahman I, managed to regain Al-Andalus and founded an autonomous Islamic emirate under a new Syrian Umayyad dynasty. In 929, Abd-al-Rahman III declared himself caliph of a state independent from Baghdad, the Caliphate of Córdoba. Under the caliphs of Córdoba, a glittering culture flourished in Spain in many fields, including philosophy, poetry, music, medicine, science and mathematics, architecture, agriculture, and gastronomy.

The Muslims introduced irrigation techniques—a system of canals and the *noria*, a large waterwheel placed over a fast-flowing stream that carries a series of earthenware pots—and horticultural practices such as grafting. New crops were brought from all over the Islamic Empire, some indigenous to India and China. Among them were rice; a different species of wheat; sugarcane; vegetables such as artichokes, eggplants, spinach, and carrots; fruits such as bitter oranges, watermelons and other melons, dates, bananas, and quinces; new varieties of almonds; and saffron. The grapes of Jerez, which are used to make sherry, are said to have come from Shiraz in Persia. Lemons and pomegranates, which had disappeared after Roman times, were reintroduced. Market gardens and orchards sprang up around every city, and Moorish houses had private gardens and patios with a fountain and fruit trees.

New varieties of sheep, including the merino, prized for its wool, were brought over from North Africa, as were new species of pigeons, and dovecotes were set up. Libraries were full of works on botany and agriculture. Agronomists taught in mosques and markets when to plant, when to graft, when to harvest, what fertilizer to use, and how to predict the weather. The greatest medieval treatise on agriculture was written by a Muslim, Abu Zakaria.

Trade was heavy between Al-Andalus and the Islamic world and parts of India and the Far East. Muslim ships sailed across the Mediterranean, bringing back goods such as gems and silks as well as foodstuffs. Spices and aromatics were a mainstay of the trade. Muslim, Jewish, and Christian merchants grouped along ethnic lines, each group forming a kind of club, and Jewish traders controlled a major portion of the commerce, trading with Jewish communities around the Mediterranean. While Christians generally despised merchants, Jews and Muslims held them in high esteem.

The refinement of pleasure and the search for the most delicious foods became the preoccupation of the Muslim elite. A Kurdish lute player, Abu I-Hasan "Ali Ibn Nafi," known as Ziryab, who came from the court of Harun al Rashid in Baghdad and joined the Córdoban court, is credited with transforming the art of living in Al-Andalus. Apart from introducing new music, he taught people how to dress, how to wear makeup, how to cut their hair short, and how to dye their beards with henna. He also taught the refinements of cooking that emanated from Baghdad, as well as rules of etiquette, including table manners and table setting. He established an order for serving different courses, starting with cold appetizers, followed by meat and poultry, pastas, and rice dishes, and then soups, pies, puddings, and pastries. Before that, all the dishes had been put on the table at the same time.

By the eleventh century, the caliphate had declined and broken up into separate small rival kingdoms and principalities called *taifas*, which fought among themselves. In 1086, when the Almoravids, a puritanical fundamentalist Islamic Berber sect from Morocco, were called in to help fight off the Christians, they took over and reunited Al-Andalus. Another puritanical Berber dynasty, the Almohads, from the Atlas Mountains of Morocco, succeeded them, making the twelfth and thirteenth centuries a period of Berber influence and strict militant fundamentalist rule, which frowned upon good living.

THE RECONQUISTA

Within a few generations of the Arab occupation, the Christians began to fight back from their northern enclaves, pushing their frontiers southward. In the more-than-seven-centuries-long crusade known as the Reconquista, they fought to reconquer their land. They fought in a haphazard kind of way, grouping in separate kingdoms. Sometimes they fought among themselves, sometimes together, sometimes with the help of Muslim kings, sometimes for Muslim kings. By the time Alfonso VI conquered Toledo in 1085, the Christians had recaptured the central plateau, and by the mid-thirteenth century, almost all of the peninsula except for the enclave of Granada had been repossessed.

The marriage of Isabella of Castile and Ferdinand of Aragon in 1469 united the two most powerful kingdoms of Spain. In 1492, their armies entered Granada, and the Moorish king Boabdil handed over the keys of the city. The spot where he took his sad farewell, looking back at the city from which he had been banished forever, still bears the name Suspiro del Moro (sigh of the Moor).

The Reconquista was a holy war, a crusade against the infidel. It was also a continuous process of colonization of the land. Conquered territories were resettled by Christians from the north, who brought their own tastes with them—in particular, the use of pork and pork fat, forbidden by Muslims and Jews, which came to symbolize the Reconquista. Several characteristics of the Muslim agricultural revolution were reversed. The land fell into the hands of nobles and the ecclesiastical authorities, who used most of it for the production of cereal grains and for grazing sheep. Some of the new crops brought by the Arabs disappeared, such as bananas, sugarcane, and cotton.

CONVIVENCIA—LIVING TOGETHER

The story of the Muslims in Spain and the cultural interaction between the Christian, Jewish, and Muslim communities was recently opened up by scholars. For hundreds of years, Spain was a land where the three groups coexisted. The rich variety, the sensual character and complexity of Spanish cooking today is in part the result of that long *convivencia*, or "cohabitation," and the intermingling of the three cultures.

While the Reconquista was mostly over by the middle of the thirteenth century, the fact that an area had been reconquered by the Christians did not mean that the entire culture or population changed, but, rather, simply that a transfer of power had taken place. As the Christians moved south, there were usually not enough settlers to repopulate and cultivate the land, and Christians were not familiar with the type of agriculture there, so Muslims were allowed to remain. In Valencia, the Muslim population continued to work in the rice fields and in various crafts. The rural villages of central and southern regions of the peninsula remained predominantly tenanted by Muslims, who were allowed to keep their faith, customs, and laws. They were called Mudéjars. In the cities, they were mainly employed as craftsmen and in the building trades.

Throughout the centuries of Muslim occupation, there were ongoing wars and problems of coexistence, but there were also treaties and trade exchanges and long periods of peace. Christian knights served as mercenaries in Muslim armies and for *taifas,* and Christian troops were contracted out by their warlords to Al-Andalus in exchange for gold. There were constant migrations from the Muslim south to the Christian north of Christians who had kept their faith. These Christians, called Mozarabs, spoke Arabic, wore Moorish clothes, and cooked in the Moorish tradition. In parts under Muslim occupation, there was intermarriage (the caliphs' wives and mothers were often Christian women from the north of Spain) and numerous conversions of Christians to Islam. Christians who converted to Islam were called Muwallads. By the eleventh century, the majority of Christians in Al-Andalus had converted to Islam while keeping their ancestral identity. Muwallads could become lords and masters like Muslims, especially if they were descended from the old Visigoth nobility. When territories were reconquered, many Muwallads reconverted, sometimes en masse, and were reabsorbed into Christian society. Muslim converts to Christianity were called Moriscos.

During and after the Reconquista, there were many towns where Muslims lived among Christians and Jews. In reconquered towns under Christian rule, intermarriage (and sleeping together) was taboo, but the communities fraternized despite condemnation by the Church. They sometimes lived in the same neighborhoods, sometimes even in the same house. They did business together, they ate and drank together, sang and played games together, and invited each other to festivals and weddings. The style of cooking that had at first been rejected as part of the enemy Muslim culture by Christians was eventually assimilated by them. Its voluptuous character won over Castilian austerity.

Toledo in the time of King Alfonso X of León and Castile, known as Alfonso the Wise, was famously a tolerant world of cultural diversity, where large Muslim and Jewish communities lived in their own quarters among Mozarab Christians, and Christians who arrived from the north and from other countries. While the Castilian language was adopted there, Arabic remained the lingua franca for centuries.

Toledo is the center of Spain's marzipan industry, and there is a marzipan museum, where the delicacy is described as a product and symbol of the old intercommunal harmony. There is controversy today among historians as to whether coexistence was ever happy or even fruitful. It was certainly fruitful in the arts and sciences, and for food it was a great enrichment.

THE MORISCOS

The direct Muslim influence in the kitchen continued long after the fall of Granada and lasted into the seventeenth century through the Muslims who remained as Christians. King Boabdil had capitulated on terms that allowed the Muslims who remained in Spain to retain their faith, language, and property. But the terms were broken a few years later because of pressure from the clergy, and the Muslims were forced to convert or to leave. As converted Muslims, they suffered discrimination. They rebelled, and their revolts were brutally suppressed. In 1568, to prevent organized opposition, people of Muslim descent were forced to leave what had been the old kingdom of Granada and to disperse throughout Castile. Some fifty thousand, it is said, went in groups accompanied by soldiers to different parts of the country, where they were resettled in towns and mountain villages. They were originally artisans—weavers, dyers, masons, shoemakers—but became muleteers and street vendors. Dishes similar to those they would have sold as street food are now familiar in tapas bars all over Spain. Among these are *pinchos morunos* (small spicy kebabs), *fritura de pescado* (deep-fried fish and seafood), *empanadillas* (little pies), and chickpea and spinach stews. The *churros* (long fluted pieces of fried dough) sold for breakfast from stalls all over Spain

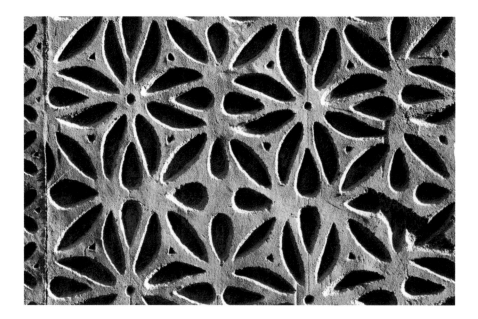

are the same as fritters found in North Africa today. Vendors who until recently went around villages by mule selling cheese, butter, honey, and the like, now go with vans, but they still wear a distinctive folk costume that some believe to be a version of the old Moorish dress.

Young Morisco girls worked in homes as domestic servants. They cooked for families, and their special dishes were appreciated. When wealthy and aristocratic Christian women remained unmarried, it was the custom for them to become nuns and to take their servants with them to the convent. Convents throughout Spain today specialize in Moorish-style pastries that are most likely a legacy of the Morisco maids. There were also prosperous Moriscos—silk merchants, skilled artisans, masons, physicians—still living in cities, whose families had integrated Christian society for generations. A report of 1588 from Seville described them as having great riches, dealing in food, and controlling the greater part of the bread trade.

Priests were sent to teach Moriscos to be good Catholics, while inspectors for the Inquisition knocked at their doors to make sure that they were not speaking Arabic, singing Moorish songs, dancing in their traditional manner, wearing Moorish-style clothes, or cooking Moorish dishes. Inquisitors could enter their homes at any time to check that they were cooking with pork fat and pork products—perhaps that is the time when the Spanish custom of putting little bits of ham in every possible dish, including vegetable and fish dishes, took root, as converted Muslims and Jews, as well as Old Christians, were forced to show proof of their allegiance to Christianity by eating pork. Back in 1514, one Íñigo López de Mendoza, count of Tendilla, captain general of the kingdom of Granada, and viceroy of Andalusia, sent a letter to the Catholic monarch, attacking the attempts of the Inquisition to force the Moriscos to abandon their customs. He wrote, "What clothing did we used to wear . . . what sort of food did we eat, if not in the Morisco style? Did the kings cease to be Christians and saints because of this?"

In Aragon and Valencia, the nobility depended on Morisco agricultural labor and so protected their peasants from the Inquisition, allowing them to observe their own religion in secret. Until the beginning of the seventeenth century, Moriscos represented about one-fifth of the population of Aragon, one-third in Valencia. The more Castile tried to force their cultural assimilation and integration, the more they held on to their identity. In 1609, all Moriscos were accused of conspiring against the Crown with the Ottoman Turks and with North African pirates, who were mostly Muslims who had left. Except for the few Moriscos certified by the clergy as true Christians, they were deported, and by the mid-seventeenth century, all descendants of Moors in the peninsula had officially been expelled from the country. Of course, some remained. You can sometimes tell that a person is of Moorish descent by their name, which denotes a trade such as stonemason or ironmonger and by the prefix "al." Alcaide (which means "the chief" in Arabic) is a common name in Spain. I met an Alcaide in Andalusia who said that there had been a handwritten book of recipes in Arabic in her family that was burnt by a great-aunt. The Inquisition may have tried to eradicate the Moriscos' cooking, but its impact is still striking today.

A HISPANO-MOORISH CUISINE

A new and unique culinary culture developed in Al-Andalus that mirrored the multicultural cosmopolitan society of people from various parts of the Muslim world together with Christians and Jews. The inhabitants of Granada, Toledo, Córdoba, and Seville and the Arab elites who established themselves in the major cities, in the south of Al-Andalus, and in the valley of the river Ebro followed the fashions and manners of Baghdad, including the high style of cooking that derived from Persia. Settlers from Shiraz in Persia founded the city of Jerez. Their culinary ways, together with those of settlers from Syria, Palestine, Egypt, Yemen, and North Africa, formed the basis of medieval Andalusian cooking. Poorer migrants, Berbers from North Africa, who were made to settle in the harsh rural mountain regions and in the marsh areas of Valencia, used basic methods to cook mainly chickpeas, rice, pasta, and couscous.

More than forty years ago I found a Spanish translation by Ambrosio Huici Miranda of a twelfth- or thirteenth-century Arabic culinary manuscript of Al-Andalus by an unknown writer at the British Library and tried some of the recipes. This same manual, entitled *Kitab al Tabikh fil Maghrib wal Andalus* (*Cookbook of the Maghreb and Al-Andalus*), translated into English and annotated by the American Charles Perry, has been published in *Medieval Arab Cookery*. Another work, Lucie Bolens's *La Cuisine Andalouse, un Art de Vivre: XIᵉ–XIIIᵉ Siècle* (*Andalusian Cooking, an Art of Living: Eleventh to Thirteenth Century*), which includes the same work and other sources, also gives an idea of the Moorish dishes of the time. Many of the recipes in these books are similar to those in a Baghdad manuscript of the same period by a certain Muhammad Ibn Al-Hasan Al-Baghdadi, translated and annotated by A. J. Arberry as *A Baghdad Cookery Book* (Islamic Culture, No. 13, 1939) and Charles Perry (Prospect Books, 2005), and another thirteenth-century manuscript from Damascus, *Wusla ila I-habib fi wasf al-Tayyibat Wa-al-tib* (*Book of the Bond with the Friend, or Description of*

Good Dishes and Perfumes), which the French sociologist Maxime Rodinson analyzed, both of which are published in *Medieval Arab Cookery*. The old Andalusian recipes make use of a long list of spices, including saffron, cinnamon, cumin, coriander, cardamom, mustard, nutmeg, cloves, allspice, aniseed, and ginger; and of herbs such as parsley, coriander, and mint. Sweet dishes are scented with orange blossom water and rose water. The favorite meat was lamb, but beef, kid, poultry, and game were also used. The Arab nobility famously hunted game birds—woodcock, partridge, pheasant, quail, and pigeon. They did not eat pork, but they did drink wine, which is also forbidden by Islam. Some of the old Moorish dishes disappeared when the Muslims left. In the seventeenth century, eating couscous was seen as an un-Christian activity to be despised, for which a person might be obliged to do penance.

Over the centuries, Arab cooking methods—the use of clay pots and skewers and the technique of preserving in vinegar or in sugar syrup—were adopted. Among the Moorish legacies are meats cooked with fruits, such as apples, pears, or quinces, and marriages of artichokes and fava beans and of eggplant and zucchini. Stuffed vegetables filled with ground meat or rice or a mixture of the two, grilled meats on skewers, and sauces thickened with ground almonds and hazelnuts are other legacies, as are garnishes of raisins and pine nuts. Meatballs, rice dishes, chickpea stews, rice pudding, fritters in syrup, almond pastries—all these and combinations of sweet and savory and of sweet and sour are legacies of that old mixed society of diverse cultures and identities.

You can hear the Arab influence in hundreds of culinary terms, such as *alboronía* (an eggplant dish), *almíbar* (syrup), *alcachofa* (artichoke), *albóndigas* (meatballs), *arroz* (rice), *escabeche* (foods marinated in vinegar), *fideos* (like very short spaghettini), and *aletría* (short macaroni). The tradition of salting and drying tuna roe to make *bottarga* came with the Arabs, as did the technique of alembic distillation for making brandies. The Arabs used spirits for medicinal purposes (the words *alembic* and *alcohol* are derived from the Arabic). Spanish alchemists (another Arabic word) and monks improved the techniques and the equipment for making brandy, and these were eventually passed on to France. Today many innovative chefs are inspired by the ancient cookbooks to explore their medieval gastronomic roots, and you might find couscous and *briks* (fried savories wrapped in paper-thin pastry) in some of the best Spanish restaurants.

Various versions of Spanish dishes are much loved in Arab countries today, particularly in North Africa, where the Muslims who had been expelled from Spain settled. In cities like Fez and Tétouan in Morocco, and in Tunisia, these dishes are described as Andalusian. A character in Cervantes's *Don Quixote*, a Morisco called Ricote, tells Sancho Panza, his former neighbor, that his people, condemned by the expulsion to wandering through the world in search of a new home, never stopped crying for Spain. But their dishes gave them comfort and started a culinary revolution in their new homelands.

almond cakes and
fried onion and garlic
{ jewish legacies }

When the Jews were banished from Spain in 1492, *they were given* the possibility of converting to Christianity and remaining in the country as converts, or Conversos, as they and their descendants were called. Sitting on a bench in a little square lined with orange trees in the Barrio Santa Cruz, the old Jewish quarter of Seville, I imagined my ancestors going about their lives in the labyrinth of narrow streets that wind their way around whitewashed houses with wrought-iron balconies. I had just bought pastries at the Convento de Santa Inés on Calle Doña María Coronel. The nun who sold them to me said that the convent had been founded by Doña María Coronel, a Sevillian noblewoman who poured boiling oil over her face to disfigure it, to avoid the persistent amorous advances of Pedro I the Cruel, who had had her husband executed. Her remains lie in a sepulchre in the convent. I was intrigued, because I knew a Jewish family called Coronel in Egypt, so I looked up Doña María and, yes, she was from a well-known Converso family. My friend Cuqui Gonzales de Caldas, who lives in Seville, says that the city has more churches and monasteries than any other in Spain because it had a large number of wealthy Jewish converts, and they and their descendants funded many of them to win acceptance and prestige.

There was a Jewish presence on the peninsula even before the Roman emperor Titus brought thousands of Jews back as slaves when he destroyed Jerusalem. After the Muslim occupation, large numbers of Jews migrated to Al-Andalus from different parts of the Islamic Empire. They spoke Arabic, dressed like Arabs, and cooked Arab foods, with a special Jewish touch. They prospered economically and culturally. It was here that they rediscovered and reinvented Hebrew as a literary language and here that the most beautiful Hebrew poetry was written. When the fanatic Almohads tried to convert them to Islam in the twelfth century, the Jews fled north to the Christian kingdoms, which is how some of the Moorish dishes spread to all parts of the peninsula.

The Jews settled in many cities, where they lived in quarters known as *aljamas* or *juderías*. There were artisans and physicians, scientists and scholars, merchants, moneylenders, and royal tax collectors. A few were bankers and courtiers who financed the wars against the Moors. (Conversos were later to finance Columbus's voyage.) Many rose to high ranks. But hostility against their perceived privileged status and relationship with the king resulted in riots and massacres and the forcible baptism of thousands of Jews in 1391.

The Tribunal of the Holy Office of the Inquisition, established in 1478 to ensure that Christians remained true to orthodox beliefs and practices, was used to pursue Conversos who kept up their Jewish faith in secret (it was abolished officially in 1834). In 1492, when Ferdinand and Isabella gave those who had not converted the choice to convert or to leave, in some towns, the entire Jewish community left; in others, the entire community converted. There were large numbers of Conversos in Castile, Aragon, Andalusia, and Valencia. Within a century, the majority had melted into the Christian population, but until the early nineteenth century,

they continued to be suspected of being secret Jews, or Marranos. If denounced, they were interrogated and then could be burned at the stake in an auto-da-fé (a ritual ceremony in a public square, of public penance of heretics and apostates), or they could be imprisoned and their property confiscated, and their families would be stigmatized for generations. Inquisitors came on Fridays to see if Conversos had put white tablecloths and candles on their tables to celebrate the Jewish Sabbath. The dreaded Torquemada, the notorious Grand Inquisitor, himself a Converso, would stand on a hill above a city on Saturdays to identify the houses where there was no smoke coming out of the chimneys (Jewish laws prohibit any work, including cooking and lighting a fire, on the Sabbath). Records of the Inquisition show that certain foods were used as evidence of practicing Judaism in secret when women were brought to trial. Because of the dietary laws, cooking was central to the Jewish identity. So as not to use pork fat, as Christians did for cooking, or clarified butter, which the Muslims used (the dietary laws forbid mixing meat with dairy products), Jews used olive oil exclusively for cooking. The smell of frying with olive oil became so strongly associated with them that even old Christians of non-Jewish descent avoided it for fear of being mistaken for secret Jews.

The traditional Sabbath dish *adafina,* a stew that was left to cook in a pot overnight in the ashes of a fire from Friday to Saturday (so that there was no need to light a fire on Saturday), was regularly cited as a sign of Judaizing. In it, meat, usually lamb and chicken, cut into large pieces, as well as ground meat rolled into large oval balls, was cooked with chickpeas, onions, and vegetables such as cabbage, spinach or chard, or eggplants. Sausages made of sheep's intestines stuffed with ground meat were also added to the pot, as were hard-boiled eggs in their shells, which were called *huevos haminados*. To prove their true conversion to the Catholic faith, Conversos added ham, pork sausages, and *morcilla* (blood sausage) to their stews. But the memory of *adafina* lives on in Spain's *cocidos* (see page 498), especially those of Madrid, Asturias, and Valencia, which contain chickpeas. In Asturias, there is a saying, *"Cocido de garbanzos guiso de Marranos"* ("Cocido with chickpeas is a stew of Marranos"; Marrano, meaning "pig," was used as a disparaging term for Conversos as well as for secret Jews). The *pelotas,* big balls of ground meat or chicken with bread, almonds, and pine nuts, sometimes wrapped in cabbage leaves, that go into the *cocidos* of Valencia, Murcia, and Catalonia today are similar to those in the Sabbath pots of North African Jews.

Conversos ate pork ostentatiously. In Majorca today, families of Converso origin are known as Xuetes (*xua* means "bacon") because in the past, they cooked and ate large quantities of bacon out of doors for everyone to see. Antonio Campins, author of *En un Fogón de La Mancha: La Ingeniosa Cocina de Don Quijote y Sancho* (In a Fireside Kitchen in La Mancha: The Ingenious Cooking of Don Quixote and Sancho Panza), sent me a story and a poem written in the fifteenth century by the Converso troubadour Antón de Montoro, known as El Ropero. One day when the troubadour went to the butcher, he found only pork, and that inspired him to write the following verses addressed to Córdoba's *corregidor* (mayor):

> One of the stalwarts of My Lord
> the King, a mighty bulwark, gave
> to the butchers reason and cause
> for my false oaths and perjury.
>
> To my sorrow I did not find
> one thing to kill my hunger, and
> they forced me to break holy vows
> made by my sainted ancestors.

Translated by Edith Grossman

Almodrote de berenjena, mashed eggplant baked with cheese and eggs, traditionally made on Friday to be eaten cold on Saturday, was a dish that, like *adafina,* compromised Jews and is mentioned in the papers of the Court of the Inquisition. Other Sabbath dishes were eggplant fritters; *fritadas,* baked omelets with vegetables; and *empanadas* and *empanadillas,* savory pies filled with ground meat. *Boronía* was a dish of fried eggplant, zucchini, and other vegetables. Sponge cake, almond pastries, marzipan, and *membrillo* (quince paste) were Sabbath sweets. Flourless cakes with almonds, eggs, and sugar, flavored with orange, were made for Passover, when Jews could not use flour. All these foods are still made in Spain and by Sephardi Jews all over the world.

Jews and Conversos were known for their overuse of ground meat to make *albóndigas* (meatballs) and stuffings for vegetables and pies. Eggplants, quinces, fennel, onions, and garlic were strongly associated with Jews and mentioned in plays and poems, usually by Conversos themselves, that secretly satirized and outed Conversos. Spices such as cinnamon, saffron, cumin, caraway, and coriander were also associated with their cooking. Jews were said to smell of onion and garlic and their homes to smell of frying onion and garlic. This duo became the basis of the ubiquitous Spanish *sofrito,* to which tomatoes from the New World were later added.

Laws of *limpieza de sangre* (blood purity) instituted under the Inquisition, which were in existence as late as 1865, excluded people with Jewish or Muslim ancestry from ennoblement, from certain professions, and from high office in institutions such as the Church and state or military orders. But some wealthy and influential Converso families (many of the Jews who decided to convert and stay were the wealthy ones who had a lot to lose) were able to hide their ancestry by using forged papers and paying witnesses. Some, fluent in many languages, became diplomats and ambassadors. Their international connections with relatives and other Jews of Spanish origin enabled them to make easy transfers of money and to trade around the Mediterranean and across the Atlantic. Some amassed immense fortunes and managed to buy land and titles, to enter into the Church and state hierarchies, and to marry into the impoverished aristocracy. The nobility, the clergy, and the kings came to depend on these Conversos for finance. They paid for the voyages of discovery and the military requirements of the empire. In the sixteenth century, two books appeared that provided evidence that a good part of the Spanish nobility, especially in Castile, had Jewish ancestry. This explains why Cervantes could have Sancho Panza argue that since he was a peasant who could brandish his "purity of blood," unlike the wealthy merchants, intellectuals, and nobles who had Converso blood ties, he had the right to be made a duke.

Foods that were once associated only with Jews are common today in many parts of Spain. Some of the pastries that nuns make in convents, such as the almond cakes of Santiago de Compostela, are of Jewish origin. In the early days of the Inquisition, having priests and nuns in the family was a way that Converso families protected themselves from persecution, and many nuns were of Jewish

descent (Saint Teresa of Ávila was one). That may be how Jewish pastries were taken up by the convents. Another pastry of Jewish origin is the famous coiled-snake-shaped *ensaimada* of Majorca made with lard (*saim*). A Jewish equivalent is made with butter or butter substitute. The roast baby lamb eaten in Castile and León with only a simple green salad was originally the ritual Passover lamb eaten with bitter herbs and lettuce dipped in salted water, representing the bitter tears of the Jews who were slaves in Egypt.

Spain's Jewish legacies are now celebrated after centuries of silence and denial. Something of a recovery of a collective historic memory is going on through conferences and music festivals. "Sephardi" dishes appear on restaurant menus. The government-sponsored Caminos de Sefarad (Sephardi Routes) link fifteen medieval cities with Jewish quarters and sites on a tourist itinerary. In Ribadavia, in Galicia, where the old Jewish community owned vineyards and produced wine and where today's Ribeiro wine is produced, they reenact a medieval Jewish wedding during the Fiesta de la História. It often happens that people I meet confide that they believe they are of Converso origin because of their names or family history, because their families lit candles in a secret room on Friday nights, or they hung their *jamón* outside (as once their ancestors would have done to prove that they had abandoned the Jewish faith), or cleaned the house on Saturday (showing ostentatiously that they were contravening Jewish laws). And they are probably right, as widely publicized recent studies on the DNA of the Spanish population have established that at least twenty percent has Jewish ancestry.

red and yellow in the kitchen

{ from the new world }

Although Spaniards use very few spices and very little black pepper, these feature prominently in national lore. The Iberian trade in spices, which began with the Phoenicians and the Romans and expanded hugely with the Arabs, stopped when the sea power of the Ottoman Turks and the North African pirates (most of them of Muslim Spanish descent) made traffic through the Mediterranean difficult. This hiatus provided the Genoese sailor Christopher Columbus with the goal of finding an alternate route to India and the Spice Islands. In 1492, Ferdinand and Isabella commissioned Columbus to explore the western seas. He sailed away and discovered the Caribbean Islands and the Americas. He was followed by Spanish conquistadores, who were mainly members of the lower nobility, and by other adventurers, entrepreneurs, and missionaries, who set out to conquer and colonize the New World. Peasants and artisans, mostly from Andalusia, Extremadura, and La Mancha, were sent off with cargoes of grain and breeding stock—chickens, pigs, sheep, goats, cattle, and horses—to settle the new lands. The conquerors brought Christianity and the Castilian language to their new empire. They built churches and palaces and sent home gold and silver.

At the same time, the Spanish kingdoms, with Castile at their head, acquired dominions in Europe through royal marriage. On Ferdinand's death in 1516, the throne of Castile and Aragon passed to his grandson Charles V, archduke of

Habsburg. He became Charles I of Spain, and the Spanish realms became partners in his dynastic rights to the Netherlands, Burgundy, the Duchy of Milan, and the Kingdom of Sicily. Charles's son Philip II inherited parts of France, the Netherlands, southern Italy, Sicily and Sardinia, a bit of Greece, and some of North Africa, as well as most of South and Central America, the Philippines, Ceylon, and several islands from Sumatra to the Azores. Then Portugal, with its Far Eastern and African possessions, and Brazil were added to his empire. Spain was thus the supreme imperial power in the world, and Toledo and Madrid became its centers of administration.

But Spain's glorious period of supremacy was brief. From about 1540 on, the cost of running the enormous empire was crippling, and constant wars to defend it drained its coffers. By the beginning of the eighteenth century, parts of the empire had been lost, Spain was impoverished, and the country was empty of people. Hundreds of thousands had died in wars and sea battles, while thousands more had emigrated to the New World to escape poverty. Plague epidemics and the expulsion of the Moriscos further contributed to the depopulation and falling agricultural production. By the early nineteenth century, almost all of the Latin American empire had been lost.

The discovery of the New World had an enormous influence, not just on the food of Spain. It was to revolutionize the diets of the Old and the New Worlds. The early colonists found the native inhabitants eating foods they had never seen. Among these were corn, potatoes, sweet potatoes, tomatoes, beans, and capsicum

peppers, which would become staples in the Old World, as well as Jerusalem artichokes, pumpkins, pineapples, papayas, guavas, custard apples, avocados, and peanuts. They saw the locals roasting and grinding corn and making tortillas. They tasted a chocolate drink and discovered the flavor of vanilla. They found turkeys and tobacco. On his return from his first voyage, Columbus made a triumphal show of the goods he had brought back at the court of Ferdinand and Isabella. Among the exhibits were gold and silver jewelry; a variety of animals, fruits, and vegetables; and ten "Indians." Pietro Martire d'Anghiera, an Italian cleric at the Spanish court, wrote at the time, "Something may be said about the [chile] pepper gathered in the islands and on the continent . . . but it is not pepper, though it has the same strength and flavor, and it is just as much esteemed. . . . When it is used, there is no need of Caucasian pepper."

Many of the colonists became farmers and used local Indians and Africans shipped from the West African coast as slaves. They planted wheat and other cereal grains, as well as grapevines and sugarcane brought over from Spain. They also grew local plants that were unknown in Europe. Franciscan and Jesuit missionaries were among the biggest landowning farmers. Potatoes, corn, and beans, the mainstays of the native peoples, were found to be the cheapest way to feed the slaves working in mines and fields. When the missionaries began to eat the foods themselves, they wrote that potatoes tasted "like cooked chestnuts when they [were] boiled" (they were probably sweet potatoes) and that sauces were made with peppers and tomatoes. When the priests and other colonists came home, they brought seeds, beans, and tubers to grow in their own gardens. They also brought back wild turkeys they had domesticated.

Turkey became the festive dish of the Spanish aristocracy, replacing the pigeon that had been the celebratory treat of the Muslim and Jewish communities, and turkey became associated with Christmas. The aristocracy and the clergy very quickly adopted chocolate as a drink. Beans were widely used. Spain already had black-eyed beans and fava beans, so the new varieties were easily accepted. Dried white and other types of beans including red and mottled beans became the food of the peasantry and of the urban poor; they were stewed with bits of cured pork or sausage to give them flavor. But other foods, such as potatoes and tomatoes, were slow in penetrating the Spanish diet.

Corn was taken up in the north, where it was used as animal fodder, and the rural poor turned it into flour to make bread, fried pancakes, and a kind of polenta porridge with milk. The peasants in the north also grew potatoes for themselves, but the Church, the nobility, the judiciary, and intellectuals despised them as "poor food," good only for hospitals, military barracks, and prisons. Records show that potatoes were bought as part of the regular budget by Seville's Hospital de la Sangre in 1573. Potatoes were not generally adopted in other parts of Spain or by the upper classes until the beginning of the nineteenth century, after the French agronomist Antoine-Augustin Parmentier popularized them in France.

Most Europeans at first thought tomatoes were poisonous. They were cultivated in the early sixteenth century in Seville, where the warm climate allowed them to thrive, but they did not come into general use until the eighteenth century. The first cookbook to mention them, *Lo Scalco alla Moderna* by Antonio Latini, was published in Naples in 1692, when the Italian south was part of the Spanish Empire. Less than a handful of recipes in the book contain tomatoes, and all of them are labeled "*alla spagnola*." A "coulis" of tomatoes with finely chopped onions and chile peppers, oil, vinegar, and salt is similar to descriptions of sauces that were found in the Americas at the time and very like dressings and sauces you encounter in Spain today. One complaint today of foreign travelers and also of Spanish restaurant critics about food in Spain is that tomatoes are used in almost everything. *Sofrito*, the tomato sauce with fried onions and garlic, is not only ubiquitous in Spain where nowadays it most often includes green peppers, but has become ever present in all Mediterranean cuisines.

Varieties of sweet bell and hot chile peppers spread quickly all over Spain. Chiles were first grown in monasteries, and the seeds were taken to all parts of Spain by traveling monks. Dried and crushed, or pulverized as *pimentón* (paprika), peppers and chiles became the favorite and ubiquitous flavorings, together with garlic. Spices and black pepper had been used all over Europe by the upper classes until they became rare when trade was interrupted. *Pimentón* eventually replaced them all in the Spaniards' affections.

The revolution in the Spanish diet caused by the discovery of the New World was slow, but in the end the combination of ingredients from the New and Old Worlds resulted in a rich and particularly colorful cuisine. Before peppers and tomatoes arrived, there had been nothing to eat that was red.

béchamel and *crema pastelera*

{ the french influence }

In the nineteenth century, the wealthy bourgeoisies of Catalonia and the Basque Country were in thrall to French haute cuisine, but the French influence on the cooking of its Iberian neighbor dates back a very long time. From the Middle Ages, France and Spain had fought each other and stolen colonies from each other; their royals also married each other, and they traded together and influenced each other culturally. In 778, Charlemagne, king of the Franks, invaded Catalonia and set it up as a buffer state to keep the Muslims out of France, and Catalonia remained culturally part of the Frankish world until the eleventh century. The kingdom of Navarre was under the control of French kings on and off through marriage and inheritance. French Occitania was a vassal of Catalonia-Aragon. The Languedoc, Provence, and Catalonia shared a similar language. Troubadours from Provence came to sing of love and the joys of life at the courts of northern Spain. The old Basque nobility, its merchant and banking families, clergy, and jurists, derived their wealth and titles from services to the king of France and Navarre. And the northern part of the Basque Country eventually became part of France.

Since the ninth century, French pilgrims had been making their way to the tomb of the apostle Saint James (Santiago el Mayor) in Santiago de Compostela, in Galicia. The oldest route, the Camino del Norte, was along the Bay of Biscay, through the Basque Country, Cantabria, and Asturias. The Camino

Francés, which was farther south; went through Navarre, La Rioja, Castile, and León. By the twelfth and thirteenth centuries, French shopkeepers, craftsmen, and innkeepers had set up along the pilgrims' routes. Whole quarters in towns such as Pamplona, Lograno, Burgos, León, Astorga, and Lugo were inhabited by Frenchmen, who were called Francos.

There was an early French presence throughout the entire peninsula. Religious orders such as the Burgundian Order of Cluny established a network of monasteries. Expeditions of soldiers headed by French nobles came to help in the crusade against the Muslims. The Knights Templars, a military order of monks led by French noblemen, helped the kings of Catalonia and Aragon and were rewarded with castles and a fifth of the conquered lands. In the mid-seventeenth century, French laborers were invited to settle in Spain to make up for the loss of agriculture workers that resulted from the forced departure of Moriscos. This early presence had an influence on the cooking of Spain, but the most important influence came directly through the royal kitchens.

The first sovereigns of the united kingdoms of Spain came from foreign dynasties through royal marriage; the Habsburgs from Austria, and the Bourbons from France. Throughout the Habsburg Dynasty (1516–1700), the kings and queens had separate kitchens. Foreign queens came with their own cooks. Philip IV's first wife, Isabel de Borbón, brought French cooks; Mariana de Austria brought pastry cooks from Austria. There were chefs at the palace from the Netherlands, Germany, Portugal, and Italy, but the majority were French. The seventeenth

century, a golden age of splendor and cultural flowering, was also a period of economic crisis, and the palace was forced to reduce its expenses; some of the cooks made redundant were taken on by the high nobility.

In the eighteenth century, French influences pervaded the palace kitchens under the Bourbons. Philip V of Spain was the grandson of Louis XIV of France. During Louis XIV's reign, the French had become accepted all over the world as the absolute arbiters on matters of style and taste. It was then, in the kitchens of Versailles and those of the French nobility who moved from the provinces to Paris, that the haute cuisine we know today developed, and that Paris was enshrined as gastronomy's international capital. Philip V used chefs trained at Versailles at his Palacio Real, and a cookbook by François Pierre de la Varenne entitled *Le Cuisinier François* (*The French Cook;* 1651), which codified the new cuisine, was used in the royal and noble kitchens of Madrid. The recipes reflected a sophisticated cuisine based on elaborate techniques, expensive ingredients such as foie gras and truffles, rich butter and cream sauces, and plenty of wine and brandy. To placate the Spanish cooks who felt displaced, there were always some Spanish dishes on the menu.

During and after the French Revolution, which began in 1789, French cooks who lost their employ crossed the border and found work with the high aristocracy and the new industrial bourgeoisie emerging in northern Spain. In the nineteenth century, French winemaking families settling in Majorca, La Rioja, and Cádiz brought their own particular regional cooking styles.

At the end of the nineteenth century, Mariano Pardo de Figueroa, writing under the pseudonym Doctor Thebussem, teamed up with several people, including a cook at the royal palace and a recipe writer, to discover, update, promote, and popularize a true Spanish national cuisine. It was a patriotic endeavor, a reaction against cosmopolitan and French influences. Together they wrote a book that featured recipes from fourteenth-century cookbooks and from a book by the royal cook Francisco Martínez Montiño, first published in 1611, entitled *Arte de Cocina, Pasteleria, Vizcoceria y Conserveria* (*Art of Cooking, Pastry and Cake Making and Preserves*).

But when they later researched what people were actually cooking, they found that their efforts had made no difference. French chefs had opened cooking schools for the upper classes and their cooks and taught from Carême and Auguste Escoffier's *Guide Culinaire*, while new cookbooks aimed at middle-class housewives featured mostly recipes translated from the French.

By the early twentieth century, there was a newfound fervor for all things

regional and traditional, and efforts were made to recover old recipes and to record rural ones. A cookbook by Countess de Pardo Bazán, published in 1913, is an example of that trend, but she too featured a great number of French recipes. In Catalonia, the prosperity generated by the industrial revolution brought about a cultural renaissance and the promotion of the Catalan language and Catalan artists, but French cuisine remained all the rage. The great food writer Simone Ortega's book *1080 Recetas de Cocina* (*1080 Recipes;* 1972) which was the bible of the middle classes for two generations, also contained in the original Spanish a majority of French dishes.

Some classic French dishes became Hispanicized, such as béchamel sauce, for which a chopped onion is cooked in butter or olive oil before the flour and milk are added and to which white wine or tomato paste is sometimes added. The *croquetas* you find in Spanish bars today, the *leche frita* (fried cream) that you can buy in supermarkets, the *crema pastelera* much used in pastries, the *crêpes* you find in northern Spain, and the *flan* that is common all over Spain are French dishes that have become an integral part of Spanish cuisine. As early as the eighteenth century, the elite started putting *bouquets garnis* in their soups, stews, and braises, but the bunch of bay leaves, thyme, and parsley tied with string took on a Spanish character when the local herbs growing wild were included. In Catalonia, the bunch of savory, thyme, and wild oregano wrapped in bay leaves is called *farcellets*. The ubiquitous combination of chopped onions, carrots, and leeks, called *mirepoix,* that is sautéed at the start of many stews is a French touch, as are the practices of flambéing, of caramelizing the tops of desserts, and of baking *au bain-marie* (in a water bath). Until the arrival of *nueva cocina,* anyone who aspired to cook grandly in Spain cooked French haute cuisine, and that is what was taught in cooking schools.

meat and game

{ the aristocracy }

In Sicily and southern Italy, there is what they call cucina povera, the "poor food" of the peasantry, and the *cucina nobile* of the nobility—an incredibly over-the-top style that you encounter today in banqueting rooms, at wedding parties, or on saints' days. Feasting there is a matter of keeping up appearances, *la bella figura,* and gastronomic extravagance can reach incredible heights. They call it *spagnolismo* and say that it is a legacy of Spanish rule. So I was expecting to find an equally grandiose haute cuisine in Spain, a land that once had the greatest number of nobles in the world, and that once reveled in ceremony and stately court etiquette. But all the people I asked about a noble aristocratic cuisine said there never was such a thing, that today's creative *nueva cocina* from star chefs is the first Spanish haute cuisine.

Up until the beginning of the twentieth century, the high aristocracy, the royal entourage at the Madrid court, had French cooks and ate mainly French food. They gave ostentatious banquets, serving many dishes buffet-style, in the French manner. But the vast number of landed nobility who lived in the countryside did not have sophisticated tastes. They simply ate a lot of meat, while their retainers who worked the land ate foods based on bread, legumes, and vegetables. The aristocratic culture of Spain was a culture of war. It was sober and austere. The Reconquista of the Middle Ages had created a social class whose raison d'être was war. For much of its history, Spain, and in particular Castile, was a society

constantly at arms, and the nobility was a fighting class. After the Muslims were finally vanquished, its armies fought converted Moriscos hiding in the mountains; they fought to take and to keep colonies across the sea; they fought in the Netherlands; they fought against England and France, and in Italy, Tunisia, and Algeria; they fought against Protestant heretics; and they fought at sea against the Turks and North African pirates. They also fought at home in the War of the Spanish Succession over being ruled by a Habsburg or Bourbon dynasty, when the Habsburg king Charles II died childless, having bequeathed his possessions to the grandson of his half sister and King Louis XIV of France.

The nobility of the Christian states was in part descended from the aristocrats of the Visigoth era and in part brought into being by their services to the sovereign. Private armies were recruited and maintained by nobles to serve the king. In recompense, the king gave the nobles immense domains, including entire villages, expropriated from the Muslims. The high nobility of grandees, the *grandes de España,* formed an exclusive caste at the top of a strict aristocratic hierarchy. Then came the *titulos:* dukes, marquises, and counts. When the king needed financial help, he named more *titulos* and distributed more land in return for money. A lower nobility of *caballeros* and *hidalgos* was distinguished from the plebeian population, the *pecheros,* by the title of "Don." Among them were soldiers who had fought valiantly and been knighted, and younger sons of nobles who had not inherited land but who served the crown in the hope of obtaining favors and property. City burghers wealthy enough to maintain horses and fight as knights also entered the ranks of the lower nobility. Small armies of these *caballeros* and *hidalgos* followed the kings and the great lords in battle. They were given small estates and sent off to fight on far-flung fronts and to conquer the New World. As the grandees and *titulos* kept buying up estates that brought them rents and profits, they came to control most of the land in the country. Some of the grand old families are still in possession of their ancestral estates and palaces. Some have wineries and produce olive oil. You will find their coats of arms on their *bodegas* (wineries).

Each kingdom had its own capital. Ferdinand and Isabella moved their courts from one town to another in different regions. Spain got its first capital in 1561, when the Habsburg king Philip II chose Madrid to be his residence, the seat of government, and the center of Spain's empire. When the royal palace at El Escorial was completed in 1584, the higher aristocracy of Castile and some of Aragon flocked to Madrid in search of royal favors and the pleasures of the court but kept their estates in the countryside. The lifestyle of the nobility was expensive, with large households and numerous retainers to sustain. Their residences were luxurious, with Flemish tapestries and family portraits on their walls. Their clothing was lavish, in satin and velvet, and silk brocade woven with threads of gold and silver. Thoroughbred horses and carriages were status symbols. There were theaters and fiestas and bullfights to attend, and huge amounts of money had to be set aside for dowries. Aristocrats were exempted from paying taxes, but they were expected to give the king money when he needed it for his wars and to supply armed soldiers for his armies. Serving the king could bring the grandees close to bankruptcy. In the sixteenth and seventeenth centuries, the nobility was in ongoing financial difficulty. For a time, however, they benefited from the silver and gold from the Americas and from the market for Spanish products in the Americas until other countries took over the trade with the New World.

In Castile and Aragon especially, the countryside was in the hands of noble warlords who owned land and controlled the rural economy and had the allegiance of thousands of peasants. Depending on where they had their estates, the great landowners produced and marketed grain, olive oil, or wine; some produced cork. Others drew income from mills or from hunting preserves, or they bred bulls for the *corrida*. Wool was Spain's main nonagricultural industry, and sheep farming was mostly in the hands of the nobility. Part of the motivation for regaining land from the Muslims was access to warmer winter grazing lands for the big flocks on the vast high central plateau that is noted for its long cold winters. As owners of

fields, roads, and villages, the nobility also lived on rents and dues paid by peasants, sometimes under a sharecropping contract.

The nobles ate so much meat that many suffered from gout. Eating a large amount of meat was a sign of status, and suckling pig, baby lamb, and veal were favorite foods. They also ate chickens, capons, turkeys, geese, guinea hens, and rabbits. They loved to hunt, and game was plentiful in the wilderness that belonged to them. Deer, wild boar, hares, and game birds such as partridge, pheasant, woodcock, pigeon, and wild duck, and migrating quail, were an important part of their diet. Apart from suckling pig, pork was eaten mostly in the form of cured meat. Away from the sea, they ate hardly any fish apart from salt cod and occasionally the grander freshwater fish such as salmon, eel, and trout. They shunned vegetables, which were considered poor food, but consumed plenty of fruit—pears, apples, figs, cherries, and oranges—and almonds and other nuts. They enjoyed pastries and confectionery, which they received as gifts from the convents they supported financially, and they drank wine and hot chocolate.

The very high nobility enjoyed French *haute cuisine*, but in general, the food eaten by the noble classes was simply cooked. They marinated game to tenderize the meat and cooked it in wine and brandy. Aromatics included garlic, saffron, cinnamon, cloves, bay leaves, oregano, and parsley. Condiments were oil, vinegar, mustard, and honey. Over the centuries, the large number of lesser nobility was mostly poverty-stricken. Unemployed in peacetime, they lived above their means, trying to keep up the high standards required of nobility without soiling their hands and losing status and honor by doing work or trade of any kind. Their situation is humorously depicted in one of the first picaresque novels, *La Vida de Lazarillo de Tormes*, published in 1554 by an unknown author and described as an autobiographical *novela de la hambre* (novella of hunger). It is the story of Lazarillo, a young lad who lives by his wits and serves many masters. In one chapter, his master is a proud impoverished nobleman who is starving but does not want the world to know. Rather than lose honor, he goes around town picking his teeth so that people will think he has just eaten meat. Not only is the nobleman not able to feed his servant, but the servant has to find ways to feed the master, for whom he has developed an affectionate respect.

The *hidalgos* who hung around the royal court in Madrid were held in popular ridicule for "speaking loudly of their honor while having scarcely a ducat to their names." "On the hidalgo's table," it was said, "there is much linen but little food." In certain circles, the table settings and adornments were more significant in establishing social distinction than was the quality of the food. This was the world satirized by Cervantes in *Don Quixote*, where serving king and Church was the ideal, and the prevailing ethos was one of chivalry, bravado, honor, and the love that conquers all. While Sancho Panza (*panza* means "belly") was always thinking about where he would get his next meal, Don Quixote gave food little thought and often managed to drag poor Sancho away from the table before he had finished eating, to set off on another mad adventure.

lenten dishes and pastries

{ of monasteries and convents }

The Catholic Church had a big influence on cooking traditions in Spain. For centuries it was one of the ruling forces, with the nobility and the military. Like the nobility, the Church financed private armies. It was immensely rich and powerful and, again like the nobility, was exempt from taxes levied by the Crown. While the material fortunes of the nobility deteriorated, the Church prospered, at least until the nineteenth century, when some of their lands were confiscated. Bishops, abbots, and cathedral chapters owned huge estates, given to them by the king, on land reclaimed from the Muslims. The clergy were at the top of the social hierarchy. They were divided into a rich and powerful aristocracy recruited from wealthy noble families and the multitude of minor clergy who served them. Families gained prestige if they had a priest or a nun as a relative.

The clergy were known for their appreciation of good food and their gargantuan appetites. Monasteries were famous for culinary refinement. The peasants who worked their vast lands gave the monks much of their produce in lieu of rent and maintained their vegetable and herb gardens. In the south, when monasteries took over Moorish palaces, they turned the interior patios into herb gardens. Monasteries were known for making wine, brandy, and cheese, and for growing uncommon vegetables such as artichokes, spinach, and asparagus, as well as a wide variety of herbs. Benedictine monks famously made chocolate.

The high clergy was very well educated and had French and Italian connections, and the food on their tables was more varied and refined than the mountains of meat on most aristocratic tables. The lower clergy cooked their meat and game with the brandy and wine they produced and the herbs they grew. King Charles V of Castile and Aragon, a renowned gourmand, chose to spend the years after his abdication in 1555 in the monastery of Yuste northwest of Madrid because, it was said, of the food. The Monasterio de Guadalupe in Extremadura, which provided daily meals for both monks and pilgrims, had a reputation for high gastronomy. The nineteenth-century chronicler Vicente Barrantes listed the New Year's fare given there to King Philip and his entourage as six baby deer, three large deer, two wild boar, a hundred ducks, a hundred partridges, a hundred pigeons, two hundred rabbits, four dozen hams, mountains of the best candied lemon peel and assorted confectionery, baskets of fruit, and gallons of wine.

The style of cooking had nothing to do with the locality, because the clergy came from different parts of the country and their orders moved them, together with their servants. Many of them had spent long periods with their orders in the New World and returned with new produce from there. Certain prestigious dishes and several cookbooks are associated with monasteries that became famous for their gastronomy. In the fourteenth century, the bishop of Tarragona's cook wrote *El Libre del Coch de la Canonja de Tarragona* (*The Cookbook of the Diocese of Tarragona*). *El Libre de Ventre* (*The Book of the Belly*) was written at the Ripoll monastery. The Franciscan Catalan writer and theologian Francesc Eiximenis devoted a book to the art of drinking and cooking and to the rules of

etiquette of the table. The most famous of these culinary manuscripts came from the monastery of Alcántara in Extremadura. It was discovered by the French general Jean-Andoche Junot when he sacked the monastery during the Peninsular War (1806–1814). He sent it to his wife, the future Duchess of Abrantès, who included some of the recipes in her memoirs. (Escoffier was later to comment that the manuscript was the only worthwhile French gain from the war.) One of the dishes, *faisán a la moda de Alcántara*, is pheasant stuffed with duck liver pâté and cooked in port wine with truffles (my version of this recipe is on page 386).

Nuns came to convents from different parts of Spain. They were from both the aristocracy and the peasantry. There was a strict hierarchy: rich women and the nobility were superior, and the others were servants and laborers. Many convents were founded by noblewomen for unmarried women of their own class. If the daughter of a landowner fell in love with someone inappropriate, such as a laborer or a retainer, she was forced to become a nun. The convents received enough wealth in dowries and bequests that their nuns could live in comfort. Some convents had dairy farms and produced all kinds of foods. Nuns in poorer convents offered cakes and pastries to show their gratitude to patrons who made their frugal existence possible.

The Church had a hold on the Spanish diet through the Office of the Inquisition, which was only formally abolished in 1834. The role of the Tribunal was to check on non-Catholic behavior, and that included eating meat on fast days. In La Rioja, at an eighteenth-century coach house converted into a hotel and restaurant I was shown a handwritten document, dated 1798, signed by two government representatives, a tax collector and a church inquisitor, who had come to inspect the inns in the village. They reported that everything was in order. People in the towns and in the countryside were obliged to abide by the rules of fasting and abstinence ordered by the Church during the seven weeks of *Cuaresma* (Lent), on every Friday, and, four times a year, at the beginning of the seasons, on Wednesday and Saturday as well. During these days dedicated to silence and prayer, meat was forbidden and only vegetarian and fish dishes were eaten. Traditional Lenten foods included salt cod and cured herring; legumes such as beans, chickpeas, and lentils; and eggs and dairy products, as well as a variety of vegetables, such as carrots, potatoes, turnips, leeks, spinach, peas, and fava beans. But pastries and chocolate were allowed—to compensate for the lack of meat.

In *Spanish Society 1400–1600*, the social historian Teofilo Ruiz quotes from the fourteenth-century *Libro de Buen Amor* (*Book of Good Love*) by Juan Ruiz, which describes the struggle between Don Carnal (Lord Carnality) and Doña Cuaresma

(Lady Lent). The former's armies, composed of succulent hams, bacon, cheeses, game, and abundant wine, are routed by Doña Lent's host of salted dried fish, beans, chickpeas, and other foods associated with vigils and fasting. Carnality was imprisoned and there began the metaphorical withdrawal from the world during the forty days preceding Easter Sunday.

In the early twentieth century, several cookbooks dedicated to making Lenten and fast dishes agreeable were published. Each began with an ecclesiastical permission and an introduction for the faithful explaining the divine obligation to fast, and the idea that fasting combats passions. One such book is the Catalan *Ayunos y Abstinencias* (*Fasts and Abstinence*, 1914) by Ignacio Doménech and F. Martí. A large chapter on soups for institutions (quantities are huge) gives substantial ones with legumes and vegetables, occasionally with a little salt cod added. They are flavored with herbs such as bay leaf, thyme, oregano, and parsley and sometimes with spices such as saffron and nutmeg. They all use stock cubes—Maggi or Knorr (yes!). The authors included recipes from several regions, as well as some foreign ones. "*Cocottes de guindas à la Rothschild*" is a pear compote with syrup perfumed with vanilla and Curaçao and sprinkled with chopped pistachios. The book, obviously, was not aimed at the peasantry or the urban poor.

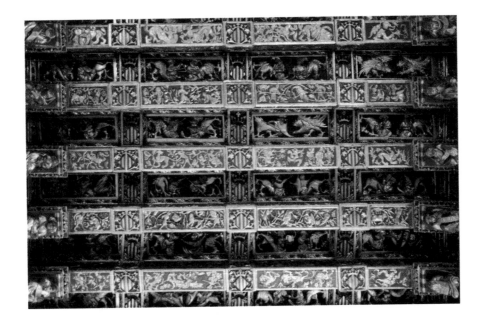

bread crumbs and *pimentón*

{ peasant food }

The real food of Spain was always the food of the peasantry, the campesinos. Until the mid-twentieth century, eighty percent of the population lived and worked on land owned by big landowners, for the most part the Church and the nobility. Nowadays, eighty percent lives in towns and cities. Mechanized farming methods changed the old ways in the countryside, and people left the land to work in tourist industries. Supermarkets and exporters offer such a low price for agricultural produce that it is no longer worth farming in a small way and producing a variety of crops.

Agriculture has become specialized and industrialized, and it is immigrants now—mostly North Africans, but also Latin Americans and East Europeans— who are the seasonal agricultural laborers. Huge areas concentrate on a single crop, such as grapes in Castile and olives in Andalusia. Foreigners are buying up the small farmhouses and cottages. Along the coasts, those who had a bit of land sold it to contractors who built golf courses, hotels, and holiday homes for tourists. Anybody who had a little plot by the sea could become a millionaire. (In the past, when families divided up their land, the eldest son would get the field; any land on the coast was not valued and was given to a daughter or the least-loved child.)

Though few Spaniards want to work the land today, they still love the land. Families keep old farmsteads as holiday retreats, where they have vegetable gardens and fruit trees. In towns and villages, they keep allotments—small plots they lease at a low rent from local authorities to grow vegetables and herbs. People are sentimental about the human landscape of the land, the traditional rural life that disappeared so quickly, in just a few decades. And the foods associated with that life, including those once shunned as "poor foods," are very popular today—that is, except with the young, who, as someone said, have gone from "poor foods" to fast foods.

In Spain, there was no middling landowning subsistence peasantry as there was in France. Peasant life and conditions varied from one region to another, but the overwhelming mass of the peasant population was poorly paid salaried laborers. The rest, small tenant farmers, were obliged by the old sharecropping system inherited from feudal times, which remained in effect until the 1950s, to pay crippling rents, sometimes in kind with much of the produce they grew, to their landlords and to do unpaid work for them. In return, they were allowed to cultivate a portion of the estate for their own benefit. In the distant past, the peasantry had also borne the burden of constant warfare in the form of taxation to fund those wars and were expected as well to go to war with their warlords.

In Andalusia, the peasantry was composed mostly of *jornaleros*, day laborers, who contracted for seasonal work by the day. In the north, especially in Galicia and Asturias, there were small proprietors and peasant farmers living on estates as sharecroppers. They handed over animals and crops to their landlords in lieu of rent, leaving little for themselves. Their smallholdings could barely support one family, and younger siblings had to emigrate to Latin America and Europe in

search of a living. In Catalonia and the Basque Country, there were some well-to-do farmers who paid rent and debts of allegiance to the lords of their lands. By the nineteenth century, landlords in those parts were sometimes city merchants or industrialists who had invested their newfound wealth in land because there was more status in owning land than in trade or industry.

The peasants ate what they grew. They grew grains and legumes for their landlords, to be dried and sold at the market or exported. They grew vegetables for their own use in the small private patches they kept. Beans and vegetables from the New World revolutionized the peasant diet centuries before they were adopted by the Spanish middle and upper classes, who viewed foods such as potatoes and vegetables as fit only for coarse palates. Potatoes, corn, and beans from the Americas replaced the grains and chestnuts that had been the mainstays of the peasantry. They used tomatoes and chiles as condiments and developed a predilection for dried and pulverized chiles, *pimentón*, both sweet and hot, which they sprinkled on almost everything. As early as 1560, there was scarcely a vegetable garden that did not have chiles.

The peasants kept chickens for their eggs, which they used to make dishes such as *tortillas* and to barter at the market for foods such as salt cod, sardines, and anchovies, or for rice and legumes if they did not grow them. In the woodlands, they foraged for chestnuts and mushrooms and gathered snails. Deer, wild boar, and other game were by law reserved for the noble landlords, but that did not prevent the peasantry from snaring rabbits and hares, poaching game birds, and catching migrating birds such as quail in nets hung between trees. In the mountain hinterland, they fished in the rivers when they could; they never had fresh fish from the sea, because of the lack of transport and refrigeration. In the north, they had milk from the solitary cows they kept and could turn it into cheese and butter; elsewhere, they made sheep's- and goat's-milk cheese. Before roads began to be built in the 1960s, there was no modern transport, and the high mountains and harsh terrain made it difficult to go to market by mule or horseback.

The culture of the pig had been important since the earliest times, and it came to symbolize the Christian Reconquista in the Middle Ages. By the middle of the eighteenth century, pork was an all-important part of peasant life throughout Spain. Those who could afford to buy a pig would feed it for nine months and then fatten it intensively for three more on their leftovers of beans, corn, potatoes, turnips, and cabbage, and sometimes fruit and chestnuts or acorns. Families killed their pigs in the coldest, driest, most windy months, usually November or December. They salted the hams and hung them to dry in airy lofts or, in wet rainy parts of the north, smoke-dried them in their kitchen hearth. They made sausages by chopping the meat with fat and seasonings, stuffing it into the scrubbed pig's intestines, and cured them. The fat was rendered to be used for cooking.

The *porcheria* (charcuterie) was made to last until the next *matanza* (the killing of a pig), and they didn't begin to eat it until the spring. It had to go a long way to feed a family. Only tiny pieces of sausage were used in stews and soups. Itinerant vendors went around villages "hiring" ham bones and chorizo for people to put in their bean stews, calling "*¡Sabor! ¡Sabor!*" (Flavor! Flavor!). The women ran out of their houses or called from the windows when they heard them, and they were charged according to the number of minutes they kept the bone or sausage in their soup and whether they were the first or the last to use it. Cured hams were a luxury, used as currency to pay the doctor. On the big estates in Andalusia, the landowning aristocracy killed many pigs each year to feed their peasant laborers with chorizo.

The pig is still the king of the Spanish kitchen, and it is used in its totality: you can see the feet, tail, snout, and ears at every butcher's market stall. Until the civil war, though, pork products were eaten almost exclusively by the peasantry. Today salted and smoked cured pork products and all manner of sausages are a prized part of Spanish gastronomy, and *jamón ibérico* is the jewel in the crown. Until recently, lard was the cooking fat used in many regional dishes, including sweet pastries. During Lent and periods of abstinence, *bacalao* (salt cod), "the pig of the sea," replaced cured pork in every kind of dish.

The only fresh meats the rural poor ate, apart from the small game and game birds they poached, were pork offal on the day of the *matanza* and lamb or chicken during festivals, saints' days, and events such as funerals, when the food was paid for by the community or offered by the rich (banquets were given as charitable legacies by rich people in their wills). Carnivals and other celebrations were dominated by food and drink. The way peasants ate and drank in excess on such occasions reveals their anxiety about and obsession with food. Their preoccupations and eating fantasies are reflected in mythical stories such as those about a land called Jauja, where the likes of partridges and hams flew through the air and landed in people's mouths. Paradise meant a stomach filled with delicacies that in real life were eaten only by the rich. In *Don Quixote*, Cervantes captured the dreams of the perpetually hungry peasants in his description of Camacho's wedding feast, a real orgy of excess: A whole ox, its belly stuffed with twenty-four tiny suckling pigs, is roasted on a spit over burning wood. Hanging on trees are skinned hares, plucked chickens, and a variety of game waiting to be cooked, as well as sixty wineskins, each filled with eight gallons of wine. Loaves of white bread and cheeses are stacked up like a wall. Sweet pastries are dropped into cauldrons filled with boiling oil, then lifted out and plunged into a pot of honey. A variety of spices are displayed in a huge chest. Sancho Panza asks a cook if he can dip a piece of bread into a simmering broth, and the cook ladles out three hens and two geese for him.

The preservation of food was an important part of rural traditions. Provisions were made in the summer to last over the winter. Chestnuts and fruits were dried in lofts or on rooftops. In northern regions, corn was dried and stored in stone or wood buildings called *hórreos*. Tomatoes and fruits such as apples, grapes, apricots, and plums were dried in the sun or in the hearth. Olives were cured. Tomato sauces were bottled in jars, as were roasted and peeled peppers. Vegetables were preserved in brine, and fruits in sugar syrup. People also made *escabeches* of fish, partridge, and quail by storing them in a vinegary marinade after cooking. Today these are commercial delicacies that people keep in their pantry.

In each region, there were two or three dishes that peasants ate almost every day, and these depended on what was available locally. Porridge, bread, and *tortas* (unleavened flatbreads) were made out of barley, millet, sorghum, wheat, and corn. Bread was the most important food and the basis of many dishes, such as *migas* (see page 476) and *sopa de ajo* (page 178). Soups and stews were made with fava beans, chickpeas, dried white beans, and peas and lentils. Chestnuts were among

the "poor foods" of Galicia, Asturias, and the Basque Country. The wealthy ate them only *confitades* (preserved in sugar syrup), as *marrons glacés,* or pureed with cream and sugar. In the wet regions of the north, apples, pears, plums, walnuts, and hazelnuts were grown. In the Mediterranean regions, many more vegetables, such as eggplants, zucchini, and pumpkins, and fruits were available.

In periods of economic crisis, corn was the main food of the poor. During the civil war, and the period of rationing after the war, eighty percent of the peasantry survived on corn. In Asturias, the exclusive diet of corn—as bread and as a kind of polenta with milk and butter—was responsible for the disease pellagra, referred to as *el mal de la rosa*. It was only in the 1950s that Spaniards started again making bread with wheat instead of corn flour; wheat had been too expensive before. They also ate *gachas,* a kind of gruel made with flour ground from grass peas (see page 478), beans, chickpeas, or wheat and oil and water.

The pastoral industry and the wool trade were all-important, especially in Castile. Transhumance, the annual migration of sheep from grazing lands in the north to winter pastures in the south and then back, was practiced. At one time a vast network of sheep tracks (*cañadas*) crisscrossed the whole of Spain. Shepherds packed their cooking pots on their mules. They made *migas* with fried bread crumbs flavored with garlic and *pimentón,* and they ate fried cheese with honey (page 161). Although shepherds were not permitted to eat the sheep in their charge, there are lamb dishes called *del pastor,* of the shepherd.

In the early twentieth century, peasants still worked simply to survive, and landowners did not invest in modernization to improve the yield of their land or the quality of their products such as grapes and olives. These were tumultuous times for Spain. There were peasant revolts, land seizures, miners' revolts in Asturias, and declarations of autonomy by Catalans and Basques. Anarchist and Marxist movements were born, and a leftist network of underground trade unions developed. The boundaries between the cities and the hinterlands became fluid, and there was a symbiotic relationship between the urban and rural worlds. People who lived in cities could be employed in agricultural work, and city elites—nobles, merchants, and others grown wealthy in trades such as wool, textiles, furniture, and mining—owned land in the countryside, often large estates, and lived there for part of the year.

With the huge migrations from the countryside to industrialized cities and from the poor south to the richer north that started in the late nineteenth century, peasant dishes began to appear in cities, usually with some modification. Some of these were saints' day specialties. Traditional peasant dishes were adopted by the middle classes, who simply added more meat. It was in the early twentieth century that regional peasant foods began to be discovered by food writers. One of the most influential of these was María Mestayer de Echagüe, whose two-volume *Enciclopedia Culinaria: La Cocina Completa*, published in 1933 under the pen name Marquesa de Parabere, featured many traditional Spanish recipes. Teodoro Bardají's *La Cocina de Ellas*, which came out in 1935, is now seen as the precursor of modern Spanish cuisine. Bardají was born in 1882 into a family of cooks and was sent as a boy to Madrid as an apprentice cook in a restaurant. He worked in several of the top establishments there and cooked for the Duke of Infantado for twenty years.

The civil war, which began in 1936, changed people's food habits. There was penury during the war and rationing after it, and Spaniards speak with deep emotion about the horrors of the war. Some are still haunted by how desperately hard life was. Hundreds of thousands died fighting or of starvation; others were executed after the war on the orders of General Franco. People were better off in the country than in the cities, where produce was scarce, but the breadwinners were fighting and agriculture was neglected. In the right-wing areas that had been on the side of the victorious Nationalists led by General Franco, people lived well; in the cities that had held out with the Republicans, they suffered most. Ignacio Doménech, who cooked for the high nobility and was a prolific writer about gastronomy, was the only author to produce a cookbook during the civil war. He wrote in the prologue, "The obsession in these last months of 1938 is food. . . . Everywhere all that people can think of is food." They dreamed of seeing markets full of fresh food and of feasts.

Don Quixote remarked that "there is no sauce in the world like hunger." Today it is the fond memories of the old life that is the sauce.

REGIONAL COOKING IN
A LAND OF MULTIPLE
LANDSCAPES AND STORIES

Because of its extraordinary geographic and ecological diversity and its dramatic patchwork history, Spain is a land of breathtaking gastronomic diversity. Every region has its own special style of cooking, and every coastal region has three different styles—one of the sea, one of the plains, and one of the mountains. But unlike in Italy, for example, cooking styles and dishes are not strictly contained within regional boundaries.

You can divide the country broadly into three gastronomic zones: wet and mountainous northern Spain, facing the Atlantic and the Cantabrian Sea; the dry central interior; and the Mediterranean coast and islands. But these are crisscrossed by other cultural zones. For instance, the great Ebro River and its fertile valley have brought Mediterranean crops and cooking from the coast deep into the northern interior, and the various regions that straddle the Pyrenees all have similar mountain dishes.

You have to look into the past to understand Spain's complex gastronomic map. Some dishes passed from one region to another through internal movements of populations. In the Middle Ages, as the Christian kings reconquered Muslim territories in the south, they gave them to aristocrats from the north who had helped them in battle, and northern peasants were encouraged to move south to repopulate the land. They brought with them their ways of making pork products, their beans, and their chestnuts trees. In the twelfth century, when the Berber

Cantabrian

La Corunna

Gijón

Santiago de Compostela

Oviedo

Asturias

Santander

Lugo

Galicia

Cantabria

Pontevedra

León

Vigo

Ourense

Castile and León

Burgos

Palencia

Zamora

Valladolid

Atlantic Ocean

Duero River

PORTUGAL

Salamanca

Segovia

Avila

Guadalajara

Madrid

Madrid

Alcántara

Tagus River

Cáceres

Toledo

Extremadura

Castile–La Mancha

Badajoz

Merida

Gudiana River

Ciudad Real

Gudalquivir River

Huelva

Córdoba

Seville

Jaén

Andalusia

Jerez de la Frontera

Antequera

Granada

Cádiz

Málaga

Almeria

Algeciras

Gibraltar

Mediterranean

Sea

Bay of Biscay

Miles

0   25   50   100   150   200

FRANCE

San Sebastián
Bilbao
Basque Country
Vitoria
Haro
Navarre
Logroño
La Rioja
Pamplona

Andorra

N

Tudela
Huesca
Soria
Zaragoza
Calatayud
Aragon
Ebro River
Lerida
Catalonia
Vic
Girona

Barcelona
Tarragona

Teruel
Cuenca

Balearic Sea

Castellón
Valencia
Majorca
Minorca

Valencia

Albacete

Ibiza

The Balearic Islands

Murcia
Alicante
Murcia
Cartagena

Canary Islands

Sea

Atlantic Ocean

Almohads tried to convert the Jews in Al-Andalus to Islam, they fled north en masse, with their Judeo-Moorish dishes. That is how their Passover almond cake (see page 30) came to be adopted as the iconic cake *tarta de Santiago de Compostela* (page 549). In the sixteenth century, Muslim converts to Christianity were forced to leave Andalusia and spread throughout the country. Many of them became vendors who sold their foods on the streets, and that is why *pinchos morunos*—marinated and spiced pork kebabs—are favorites on the tapas circuit. Clergy, who famously had a powerful influence on the diet of the peasantry, were moved around the country by their religious orders. They spread their ways of making brandy and cheese, and the nuns carried their famous pastry-making traditions from one convent to another.

Certain foods, such as *migas* (see page 476) made with bread crumbs, and the lamb stews referred to as *del pastor* (of the shepherd), can be found across the country along the old migratory routes of the seasonal transhumance of sheep that crisscrossed the country. A dressing of fried garlic, vinegar, and *pimentón* (paprika) and dishes called *al ajo arriero* (*ajo* means "garlic" and *arriero* means "mule driver") can be traced along the old routes traveled by the mules that transported salt cod between the seaports in the north and the interior. The muleteers also sold garlic, olive oil, and *pimentón*. Some dishes that appear in several different parts of the country arrived with Spanish returnees from colonies in the New World, Italy, and North Africa.

In more recent times, Spaniards became familiar with the foods of regions other than their own, and there was a certain homogenization of cooking traditions. From the nineteenth century on, there was mass migration from the poorer south to the industrial north and from the countryside to the cities. The many migrants from all over Spain who went to Madrid made that city a center of culinary diffusion. Until just over a couple of decades ago, agricultural laborers, sometimes with their entire families, traveled during harvest time from region to region to pick grapes, olives, and fruit and to harvest wheat and corn. They needed feeding, and the landlords who provided their meals sometimes adopted their dishes. The Spanish Civil War made many orphans, and so many young peasant girls needed work and a roof over their heads. After the war, most middle- and upper-class families took on two maids, one to clean and look after the children and one to cook. The cooks learned the style of the house and also brought the ways of their *comarca* (*terroir*). Now markets throughout Spain sell products from all over the country, and television programs encourage people even in small villages to cook specialties from different regions. Everyone makes tortillas, paella, gazpacho, *croquetas*, *fabada*, empanadas, and flan. They have become national dishes.

seafood and milk puddings

{ *the north* }

Northern Spain facing the Atlantic and the Cantabrian Sea is a wet "green" land of lush wooded mountains and vast pastures where cows graze. It is dairy country. They make cheese and milk desserts—custards, flans, fried cream, cheesecake, and rice pudding. Recently, indigenous breeds of cattle that had been neglected in favor of good milk producers have begun to be raised again. Apples and pears, walnuts, hazelnuts, and chestnuts grow here. The mountain forests have the widest variety of game, including deer and wild boar, rabbits, hares, and birds. The rivers that rush down the mountains are full of trout, salmon, and eels. The coast is dotted with fishing ports and villages where, despite the continuing depletion of fish stock, fishermen bring in a huge variety of fish and seafood—theirs are the best mollusks and crustaceans in Europe.

In this part of Spain, the peasantry was always poor but self-contained. They were tenant farmers and sharecroppers (*foreros*) who paid rent to the Church and the nobility who had owned the land since the early Middle Ages. In the nineteenth century, Church-held lands were expropriated by the state and became common lands. Smallholdings, small farms (*minifundios*) with little stone houses, each with its vegetable garden and grapevine trellises, are dotted around the mountains and valleys. Until very recently, every family kept one or two pigs, a solitary cow for milk and cheese, and chickens for eggs. They grew corn and rye alongside beans and potatoes, cabbages, turnips and carrots, leeks, peas, and fava beans. They cooked on the open hearth. For warmth in winter, it was usual for animals to sleep downstairs in the farmhouse while the family slept upstairs. In the northern regions, peasant families were known to look after their livestock with a kind of reverence. Pío Baroja, the Basque writer and radical Republican, wrote that in order to live well there, one had to be either a priest or a cow.

Transport was difficult over the high mountains, and rural life was hard. Most farms were too small to sustain more than one family. In Asturias, the Basque Provinces, and Catalonia, small farmsteads were passed to the eldest male on his marriage. In Navarre, parents chose the heir regardless of age or gender, while in León, peasants practiced equal inheritance. It was the custom for one of the remaining children to enter the Church, and another to join the army, and then the others would leave. In the past, the young emigrated in droves to the Americas. More recently, it was to France, Switzerland, and Germany. Nowadays young people can find work in their own cities, and emigrants are coming back.

The valley of the Ebro River, which cuts through the mountains of Navarre, La Rioja, and Aragon, has brought Mediterranean fruit and vegetables and Mediterranean styles of cooking, including the use of olive oil, to these landlocked northern regions. Cultural unity was the result of the pilgrim routes that run through all the northern regions to the shrine of Saint James in Santiago de Compostela in Galicia. After the relics of the saint were reputedly found there in the ninth century, Santiago became a place of pilgrimage as important as Rome and Jerusalem. For a long time, the French were the main pilgrims, and settlers on

the pilgrimage routes. That is one reason the north of Spain became early on a zone of French influence. In the nineteenth century, French haute cuisine was adopted by the newly rich mining and industrial bourgeoisie and by the *indianos*, as the returning emigrants grown rich in the American colonies were called. That is why you find crepelike pancakes, béchamel sauces, quichelike tarts, fried cream, flans, and *crema pastelera* there.

The stream of pilgrims to Santiago encouraged the building of churches, cathedrals, and monasteries along the way. The clergy were powerful landlords and had an important influence on what peasants grew. The priests and monks who traveled to the Americas with their religious orders were the first to bring back corn, potatoes, beans, and peppers when they were recalled to Spain in the sixteenth century, and these became local staples. The north is known as the zone of heartwarming bean and potato soups and stews.

Whereas wine has always been the drink of the Mediterranean coast, beer and cider were the traditional drinks on the Atlantic coast until a decade or so ago, when fine wines started to be produced there.

GALICIA

Galicia has its own language, which is similar to Portuguese, and is proud of its Celtic ancestry (they play bagpipes at events and festivals). Separated from the rest of Spain by high mountains, it was entirely isolated until recently. It was also the poorest region, and the only way out of poverty was emigration. That is why Galician dishes—boiled octopus (page 311), *caldo gallego* (page 182), and empanadas, large crusty pies—are among the most common dishes in cities all over Spain and as far away as Brazil, Mexico, Argentina, Venezuela, and Cuba, where Galician immigrants opened restaurants and bars. Now many of them are coming back, as life has changed with tourism. In cafés in Santiago, I heard groups of old men speaking with Latin American accents. They were there on holiday; their sons had returned there to work. Many, especially those from Argentina, have opened *churrasquerías* (steak houses). The meat, fabulous veal and beef from the indigenous blond *rubia gallega* cattle, is tender, juicy, marbled with fat, and full of flavor. Galicians have also brought back the indigenous Celtic pig, which looks a bit like a wild boar. The enormous succulent capons of Vilalba, which are fed on boiled corn, wheat, and potatoes or on chestnuts soaked in milk or wine, appear at markets all over Spain at Christmas time.

For centuries the cities of Galicia were under the control of bishops, and the countryside was shared by the cathedrals, the abbeys, and the secular aristocracy.

Together with Asturias, it was the region where peasants were more completely under the dominion of their landlords than elsewhere in the north. The rural population lived isolated in the hills and mountains in tiny farmsteads. They rented the land and owned the houses, which they built, and gave part of their produce to their landlord in payment of the rent. Families divided their land among all their children into ever smaller holdings.

Galicia, Asturias, Murcia, and the Canary Islands are the only regions in Spain today where corn is grown for human consumption as well as for animal fodder. In Galicia they make bread with cornmeal. Potatoes are the traditional staple, and apples and chestnuts are also used as a substitute for vegetables. The farmers give turnips to their pigs and eat the green tops. The green chile peppers from around the town of Padrón, called *pimientos del Padrón*, sweet but occasionally burning hot, are served in bars all over Spain, fried and sprinkled with coarse salt. Families who kept a pig had to cure the hams and other charcuterie indoors around the fireplace because of the wet weather (attics were damp). That is why the ham and the lard they use in some of their dishes give them a peculiar strong smoky flavor.

The Galician coast is known as the Costa del Marisco, the Seafood Coast, because of its magnificent seafood. Vigo is the largest fishing port in Europe, and Galicia has the largest fishing fleet. It also has shellfish farming and seafood processing industries. *Pulpo a la feria* (page 311), boiled octopus dressed with olive oil and *pimentón* and served with boiled potatoes, is Galicia's festive signature dish. The scallop shell is the symbol of Santiago de Compostela. Shells are

encrusted into the ground marking the Pilgrims' Way, and a relief in the shape of the shell is at the entrance of the great cathedral where the relics of the apostle Saint James are buried.

The region is known for its almond *tarta de Santiago* (page 549), its *marrons glacés,* and its cow's-milk cheeses, which are unusual in Spain. Most notable are the soft, creamy, mild-tasting Tetilla (its name means "nipple," and it is shaped like a woman's breast); San Simón, the strongly flavored smoked version; Arzúa-Ulloa; and Cebrerio. The Rías Baixas, an area of breathtakingly beautiful estuaries and fjords, produces some of the best white wines of Spain. The prestigious Albariños, crisp, dry, fresh, fruity, and aromatic, are made from Albariño grapes, which were brought to the region in the twelfth century by Cistercian monks from the Rhine and Moselle Valleys. The Monterei, Ribeiro, Rías Baixas, Ribeira Sacra, and Valdeoras wines also use local grape varieties. Ribeiro is the most popular with Galicians, the one that evokes nostalgic memories when they leave their Galicia homeland. The vineyards of the red Ribeiro wines belonged long ago to the Jews of Ribadavia, a former capital of Galicia. In one of their fiestas, they celebrate these Jewish roots by reenacting a Jewish wedding in costumes of the time. Orujo is a spirit distilled from the residue of crushed grapes. *Queimada* is a hot drink made by flaming orujo with lemon peel, cinnamon, sugar, and sometimes coffee beans in an earthenware bowl. The ritual preparation is said to have pagan origins and to keep away evil spirits. They believed in witches here, and they still sell amulets to protect you against evil.

ASTURIAS

According to legend, in 718, the Virgin Mary appeared in a cave at the top of a high mountain in the Asturian village of Covadonga, where the local leader, Pelayo, was taking refuge from the attacking Moors. She gave him a wooden cross that he used to fight off the Muslim armies, and he was crowned king of the first Christian kingdom of Spain. Asturias became a refuge for Christian nobility escaping Muslim occupation of the Iberian peninsula. In recognition of the place where the Reconquista began and of the role played by the nobles in the centuries-long war, the heir to the Spanish crown today has the title of Prince of Asturias, and Asturias is a principality.

This sensationally beautiful green and misty land of rugged towering mountains, fast-flowing rivers, and lakes is dotted with little farms (*caserías*) and apple orchards. It is renowned for its wide variety of beans, in particular for the large white ones called *fabes,* which go into the famous *fabada* (page 489). The region is also known for apple tarts, apple cakes, apple pancakes, and apple puddings, as well as for apple cider that is hard, dry, and still. In the cider houses, it is poured from on high so that it aerates as it splashes into glasses—and onto the floor. Cider is used for cooking fish and chicken and in desserts. Asturias is also a region of walnuts and walnut cakes. Corn is used to make bread and *tortos,* which are like deep-fried small Mexican tortillas. There are also thicker *tortos* that are cooked over a wood fire, and a creamy polenta called *fariñes* (page 481).

You see cattle, sheep, and goats grazing on farmsteads and in the high mountain range Picos de Europa, now a national park. Not long ago, foreign breeds of cows that produced lots of milk predominated; today the indigenous red Asturianas de la Montaña are raised for their meat. Game birds, especially woodcock (*becada*), are delicacies, and wild boar and deer are hunted. The wide variety of fish and seafood caught along the rugged coast is a splendid part of the local gastronomy. Hake and monkfish are favorites, as are crab and sea urchin. Salmon fishing in its many rivers makes Asturias the largest salmon-producing region of Spain.

In 1830, iron and coal were found, and mining and heavy industry caused a mini industrial revolution. At the same time, still-jobless young men left for Latin America. Many returned having made their fortunes. The exotic colorful Mexican-style colonial mansions they built, with domes and towers, pillars and balconies, are evident today in elegant cities, on mountainsides, and along the seacoasts. A palm tree in the front garden signifies that the original owner was a returnee from Cuba, Argentina, Uruguay, Mexico, or Venezuela. The *indianos,* as these overseas entrepreneurs were called, also adopted the French cuisine that was then fashionable with the local nobility and the new industrial bourgeoisie.

Asturias is the European region that offers the widest range of cheeses, and it is known as el Pais de los Quesos (the Land of Cheeses). Cow's, sheep's, and goat's milk are all used, sometimes on their own, sometimes in combination. The most famous cheese is the strong-tasting blue Cabrales, traditionally matured in mountain caves. Notable others are Los Beyos, Gamoneú, Peñamellera, Picón Bejes-Tresviso, and Afuega'l Pitu. But Asturias is the only region of Spain that does not produce wine.

CANTABRIA

Tiny Cantabria has had a special relationship with powerful Castile ever since it sent men to help King Ferdinand III conquer Córdoba and Seville in 1236. The capital, Santander, became Castile's way to the sea for its wool exports to northern Europe and for its trade with the New World. Because of its privileged trading position, it had early access to products such as olive oil from the south and the Mediterranean, which its neighbors did not have. In the nineteenth century, Santander, a port on the beautiful Costa Esmeralda (Emerald Coast), became the summer resort of the royals, which explains why some dishes have a touch of "class," and why olive oil has long been used for cooking instead of the traditional lard.

In the small mountain communities in the region that is known as La Montaña because of the steep Cantabrian mountain range, families kept a few cows, sheep, and goats. The cattle were looked after jointly by cowherds, while villagers took turns looking after one another's sheep and goats. Nowadays tourism has become more important than agriculture. In the valleys where grapevines and wheat, chickpeas, potatoes, and cabbages once grew, many fields have been given over to cattle grazing. The young pink meat of the indigenous breeds makes for splendid grills and for stews with beans and potatoes, as do venison and the meat of wild boar. It is a region rich in wild things: berries, chestnuts, walnuts, edible flowers, and herbs. On the coast, fish and seafood are cooked in simple ways, and salmon, trout, and eels are available from the rivers that fall from the mountains straight into the sea.

Like Asturias, Cantabria is an artisan cheese paradise, with a variety of cheeses. The most well known are the creamy blue Picón Bejes-Tresviso from a blend of cow's and sheep's milk, the fresh buttery cow's-milk Cantabria and Pasiego, the smoked Tresviso from Áliva, and the mild or smoked Liébana. Cóbreces is made with cow's milk by the Cistercian nuns of the monastery of the same name.

Apple cider is the traditional drink. The region also produces Chacolí, a light acidy white wine, and the sweet red Tostadillo. The region is famous for its canned red peppers (*pimientos de Isla*) and its anchovies preserved in salt or in oil.

San Sebastián has for some years now been a prime destination of food lovers from all over the world as the center with the greatest concentration of trail-blazing Michelin-starred chefs. Other gastronomic attractions are the lively bars offering both traditional and modern tapas—here called *pintxos*—and the famous men-only gastronomic societies, where members take turns cooking and vie to outdo one another. It is here that Spanish *nueva cocina* was born. In the 1970s, top restaurants only served French haute cuisine. They had been doing so since the late nineteenth century, when the beautiful seaside town was adopted as a retreat by Queen Regent Maria Christina and became the fashionable belle époque resort of the Spanish upper classes. After the discovery of iron and the development of heavy industries in the region, a wealthy Basque bourgeoisie that could afford expensive restaurants emerged. There was also an old aristocracy whose ancestors had been ennobled by the kings of Castile in recompense for helping them in the Reconquista and the conquest of the New World. French cooks found employment here when they came in large numbers after the French Revolution. Today, Spanish Basques also share dishes with the French Basques on the other side of the border, and they speak French as well as their own Basque language, Euskara.

When Paul Bocuse, the godfather of French nouvelle cuisine, came to speak at a conference in Madrid in 1976, he invited two young Basque chefs, Juan Mari Arzak and Pedro Subijana, to attend a course with him in Lyon. Back in San Sebastián, Arzak and Subijana, along with a group of enthusiastic chefs, began to develop *nueva cocina vasca*, Basque nouvelle cuisine. It was the start of what was to become a national movement to update traditional dishes and create new ones based on regional products, and eventually the first Spanish *alta cocina* (haute cuisine).

Basque culinary roots go back to the time before steel mills, factories, banking, and tourism enticed people away from the land, to when the mountain region was a world of farmers, shepherds, and fishermen, and when, as the Catalan traveler Mañe y Flaqué wrote one hundred and fifty years ago, "they look[ed] after their animals as if they were members of the family." Rural life has not entirely disappeared. Capons and turkeys are raised for festive occasions, the indigenous cattle for both beef and milk. Peas, green beans, and cauliflower are traditional vegetables still grown. Leeks and potatoes have a special place in the diet. The red bean of Tolosa is a favorite dried bean, and the white *pocha* bean is harvested very young and cooked fresh. At least thirty varieties of wild mushrooms can be found in fields and woodlands. The pickled spicy green *guindilla* peppers of Ibarra are served as tapas, and the elongated peppers from Guernica are used in many dishes including the famous *piperada* (page 198). Many Basque dishes including *piperada*, squid cooked in its ink (page 307), and *gâteau Basque*, are similar to those of their neighbors in Navarre and La Rioja.

More than anything, Basques love fish and seafood. Life on the Cantabrian coast was once all about fishing. Men went out in their boats at night, their women ran to meet them on the beach in the morning with baskets on their heads, and they went off to sell the catch at the market. For centuries, fishermen went out on the high seas for long periods to catch whales and cod, which they dried and salted on the boats. They fetched the salt from salt pans in Cádiz. Now there is large-scale commercialization and mechanization of the fishing industry and small fishing fleets are depleted, but fish and seafood are appreciated more than ever, as are tiny elvers from the rivers.

Local wines are the slightly acidic white Txacolí, or Chacolí, which is good with seafood and as an aperitif, and the sparkling red Rioja Alavesa. Cider, the traditional Basque drink, is sweeter and fizzier than Galician cider. Idiazabal, the great Basque sheep's-milk cheese, is buttery, with an intense piquant, slightly acidic flavor. Shepherds used to make it when they grazed their sheep on the mountains and lived in small huts nearby during spring and summer. Their Gaz-

tazzara is a strong-tasting, spreadable sheep's-milk cheese.

The Basque language is said to be the oldest in Europe, and DNA tests have confirmed that Basques are descendants of a race that had inhabited the Western Pyrenees along the Bay of Biscay since ancient times. The Basques sought autonomy from Spain in the nineteenth century, but the separatist movement was crushed during the civil war. It was rekindled after Franco's death, and there are still militant separatists who campaign for complete independence.

Basques are as passionate about

food as they are about politics and music. Theirs is a society of cooks and gourmets and of singers, and they sing lyrical Basque folk songs. The members of a men's gastronomic society where I was a guest have their own choir.

NAVARRE

The landscape in Navarre ranges from the misty wet Pyrenees, with vast forests of pine, chestnut, and hazelnut trees, to meadows with sheep and cattle grazing on their slopes, the desertlike Bardenas Reales near Tudela, and river valleys, vineyards, orchards, olive groves, and vegetable gardens in the wide Ebro Valley. There, irrigation systems originally installed by the Arabs allow the land to produce a succession of crops each year, including sugar beets and a huge variety of vegetables. The region is famous for its asparagus, artichoke, cardoon, and borage dishes and for the small fresh white beans called *pochas*.

The little pointed red peppers of Lodosa in southwest Navarre called *pimientos del piquillo*, which we can now get in cans and jars, roasted and peeled, have long been popular in tapas bars and restaurants all over Spain, usually stuffed with fish or seafood or with ground pork.

Navarre has no coast, but the rivers have trout and salmon. The region shares produce and dishes with neighboring La Rioja and Aragon. Many are an exciting mix of Mediterranean, French, and Arab influences.

Navarre, called Pamplona at the time, was inhabited by Basque tribes when

Muslims conquered the Ebro Valley in 714. In 824, a Basque chieftain named Iñigo Aritza was made king of Pamplona, which later became the kingdom of Navarre. The Christian kingdom coexisted with the small Muslim *taifa* kingdoms of Zaragoza and Tudela. Navarre passed by marriage to the counts of Champagne and then to the French crown in 1305, and it remained, on and off, under a French king until it was annexed by Castile in 1515. Basque and French are spoken here along with Castilian Spanish.

There are more heraldic crests and coats of arms on the stone houses in

Navarre than in any other part of Spain. During the heyday of the kingdom, twenty percent of the population was of noble family. At the turn of the twentieth century, many wealthy *indianos* returned from the Americas to their ancestral villages, bringing new wealth to the region. Navarre's noble heritage is reflected in its refined cooking. Game braised in rich wine sauces, sometimes containing chocolate (see page 374), is common in mountain villages. There is wild boar, rabbit, and hare, and birds such as quail, partridge, and pigeon. The veal from local calves varies from pink to red, with a fine marbling of fat, and makes for splendid grilled dishes cooked over charcoal embers and heartwarming mountain stews. The region is also famous for lamb and goat: *chuletitas*, baby lamb chops, and roast suckling lamb are local specialties. Pork, both fresh and cured, is popular. Local sausages include *la chistorra* and a chorizo of Pamplona made with a mix of beef and pork. The *longaniza* of Navarre is made of pancetta. Newer products are duck foie gras and duck confit.

Navarre produces two great cheeses with sheep's milk: the soft, aromatic, slightly sharp and piquant Roncal, and a strong-tasting aged or smoked Idiazabal that is similar to the Basque version. Navarre wines are like those of La Rioja, made with similar grapes and similar methods of production; the rosés are delightful. Pacharán is a liqueur made by macerating sloe berries and coffee beans in an anise-flavored spirit.

LA RIOJA

La Rioja, the great wine region of Spain, is a land of rolling hills and valleys surrounded by mountains, with a climate that varies from cool and wet to warm and humid to dry. La Rioja is still all about wine. Towns are packed with *bodegas* (wineries), some venerable and aristocratic, others small and family-run, and some corporate and industrial; a few were built by world-famous architects. The Romans made wine here, then the local monks took it up. Old monasteries abound in the mountains and forests. Some have been converted into hotels, a few into wineries. It is said that the Castilian language was born in one of the oldest monasteries, Yuso, where the first texts written in an early form of Castilian were found. There is a continuous history of Christianity in the area that flourished even through Muslim rule, and the pilgrims' route to Santiago passes through. It was a place of settlement for knights and nobles. They formed a wine nobility that has left many small palaces and mansions in the honey-colored wine-making hamlets. You see noble heraldic shields everywhere, even on village houses.

Much of the broad Ebro Valley and the valleys of six of its tributaries, including the river Oja, from which La Rioja got its name, are covered with vineyards. The Rioja DOC includes an area that stretches into parts of the Basque Country and Navarre. Until a little over fifteen years ago—before many other regions started producing really good wines—people all over Spain knew only Rioja apart from their own local wine. La Rioja became prominent after phylloxera devastated the French vineyards in the second half of the nineteenth century and vintners from Bordeaux came to plant grapes free of the disease and to make their wines there. For years, French Cabernet and Merlot grapes were grown in La Rioja. When phylloxera destroyed the Spanish vineyards too, and French and Spanish vineyards were replanted with phylloxera-resistant rootstocks from America, the French went back home and the Riojans went back to their indigenous Tempranillo, Garnacha, Mazuelo, Graciano, and Viura grapes. But they kept the French ways of vineyard management and wine-making techniques, including the aging of wine in oak barrels. They have now gone further and adopted new technology. Winemakers used to buy their grapes from farmers, but now they have their own vineyards. While La Rioja is known for its excellent aged red wines, it also has good whites and rosés, as well as brandies and liqueurs.

As with all fine wine areas, La Rioja is also a gastronomic region. *Bodegas* offer both traditional and innovative tapas to accompany wine tastings. Grand restaurants serve innovative cuisine; family-run inns and unpretentious traditional *casas de comidas* (literally, eating houses) offer home cooking. Riojan home cooking has much in common with that of neighboring Navarre, Aragon, and León. It is simpler than that of many other regions and relies on the quality of the local produce. In the valleys and plains of the river Ebro and its tributaries, there are extensive wheat fields and potato and sugar beet plantations, as well as olive tree groves. Peaches, pears, and cherries grow. Market gardens are full of vegetables, including artichokes, asparagus, cardoons, borage, Swiss chard, eggplant, and zucchini. Small and fiery red chile peppers, *alegrías riojanas,* add a piquant flavor to many dishes. Mediterranean-style cooking with olive oil coexists with French ways of cooking with butter and cream and thickening soups and sauces with roux. As you would expect, there is a lot of cooking with wine and brandy: desserts are often fruits poached in wine. And pastries are made with walnuts or almonds.

The mountains of La Rioja have their own separate food culture. Pigs are kept. All kinds of cured products—a delicious sweet blood sausage made with rice, chorizo, and salami-like *salchichón*—go into stews rich with red beans and the mottled *caparrones,* which are like borlotti beans. Wild boar, deer, partridge, hare, and quail are hunted in the woodlands. Sheep, goats, and cattle graze on the hillsides. A favorite way of cooking meat—especially baby lamb chops, *chuletitas,* and large T-bone steaks, *chuletones*—is grilling it over smoldering grapevine prunings. Lamb and goat are spit-roasted. Potatoes and wild mushrooms are common garnishes. Trout and salt cod are popular. Riojans serve their fresh salty, slightly acidic Camerano goat cheese as a tapa with caramelized onions.

ARAGON

When the Kingdom of Aragon was united with Catalonia through the marriage of the count of Barcelona to Petronila of Aragon in 1137, the joint Crown went on to acquire eastern Spain and a whole empire in the Mediterranean. It is a beautiful story that is told in the Catalan section, on page 102. In 1469, the union of King Ferdinand of Aragon and Isabella of Castile brought the two most powerful kingdoms of the peninsula together and led to the creation of a united Spain.

In this large, landlocked area, which ranges from mountain glaciers and forests to rich pasturelands, arid desert steppes, and verdant river valleys, there are at least two major Aragonese food cultures. One is typical of the fertile valley of the Ebro River that cuts through the mountains. It is a cosmopolitan Mediterranean style that makes much use of vegetables, fruits, and olive oil. Wheat, barley, and rye are important crops. Olives from lower Aragon are used to produce sweet, fruity, and aromatic extra virgin oils. Market gardens provide peppers, tomatoes, green and white beans, zucchini, sweet onions, asparagus, cardoons,

and borage. The fruits of Aragon—plums, pears, apples, cherries, and especially peaches—are much admired throughout Spain. Rivers provide freshwater crab, and crayfish, trout, and salmon. Among Aragonese sweets are peaches in wine (page 527) and candied and chocolate-covered fruit.

The white truffles that once abounded in the wild are now being farmed. Some of the local dishes testify to the tastes of the Muslims who were allowed to stay on as Moriscos (Christian converts) until the seventeenth century, to irrigate the land and nurture the fruits and vegetables. The northern part of the region is on the border with France, and some dishes have a French touch and make use of butter and cream.

Game, meat, cured pork, and cheese belong to the food culture of the mountains, where cattle, sheep, and goats graze in lush pastures. Lamb is the traditional meat, and popular dishes such as *migas,* made with bread crumbs, remind you of the old transhumant life of shepherds. Teruel, in southern Aragon, is renowned for its pork products from indigenous pigs. The hams are cured with very little salt and have a delicate flavor and creamy fat. The blood sausage is made with rice and onions. Partridge, quail, rabbit and hare, and big game like deer and wild boar are hunted. Not many cheeses are made here. Their creamy Tronchón, a mix of sheep's milk and goat's milk, was mentioned in Cervantes's *Don Quixote.*

Aragon is an old wine-producing land. In the past, much of its traditional harsh, highly alcoholic wines went to France for blending, but the region is now producing some fine reds, whites, and rosés with native and foreign grape varieties. Its Cariñena and Somontano have been reborn. And Aragon also makes fruit liqueurs and brandies with berries, cherries, and nuts.

bread and chickpeas

{ central spain }

The vast Spanish interior that encompasses Castile and León, Castile–La Mancha, Madrid, and Extremadura is a high plateau, the Meseta, bordered and divided into two by mountain ranges and crossed by great rivers. Before roads were built a few decades ago, it was difficult to enter—travelers came by horse or mule—and empty of people. It is the "dry Spain," with the typical continental climate of extremely cold winters, unbearably hot summers, and hardly any rain, with no sea to soften the harshness. The predominant vegetation is treeless wild entanglements of thorny scrub, but there are grasslands in the river basins, and the mountains are cloaked in dense woodlands. The Romans planted wheat and barley on the plains and grapevines on the hillsides and valleys, making the Meseta a land of bread and wine. Agriculture consists mostly of small family farms that raise barley, wheat, grapes, sugar beets, and legumes. Chickpeas, lentils, and beans that need little water are major crops. Many also raise poultry and livestock, and almost all farm families have at least one or two pigs. Fruit and vegetables are grown in irrigated areas by the rivers.

Although central Spain covers a huge area, there is little culinary diversity. Centuries of struggle against the Muslims had a profound effect on its culture and gastronomy. The area was the frontier zone during the eight-centuries-long struggle between the Christian kingdoms of the north and the Muslim kingdoms of the south. It was constantly at war: castles and fortified cities were won and lost, and kings were always on the move. Conquered lands were given over to the noble warlords and religious military orders on whom the kings depended for waging their wars. In such a world, ranching of sheep, cattle, and horses, which could be moved easily to new frontier settlements, was the primary activity. As new land was conquered and resettled, because of the new settlers' inexperience in agriculture and the shortage of Muslim labor, cultivated lands were given over to sheep farming, and wool production became by far the most important part of the economy, providing the merino wool that was sold to Europe.

Because of the arid environment, flocks and herds had to be moved huge distances from pasture to pasture. The necessity of driving the sheep and cattle from the north to the grasslands of La Mancha and Extremadura in the south was an important part of the push to conquer more territory from the Muslims. In the thirteenth century, a sheep-breeders' guild, the Mesta, was formed by small sheep owners and a few great landlords and monasteries to organize the movement of the flocks that migrated seasonally and to ensure their protection from Muslim raids by knights and religious military orders. Large monasteries, many of which are now *paradores* (state-run hotels), are a reminder today of the warrior monks—the Knights Templars and Hospitalers, the orders of Calatrava, Alcántara, and Santiago—who fought for and then colonized the new frontiers for the Castilian kings. Like the huge and ever-growing nobility, they raised sheep, but they also had a strong interest in horticulture. They had vegetable gardens, orchards, and vineyards; they kept bees; and they made honey, wine, and cheese.

As territory was regained, pork, forbidden in Muslim times, became the popular meat, and hog raising was taken up in a big way, especially in Extremadura, around Salamanca, and in the Andalusian interior. Pigs were left to forage on mushroom and acorns in the oak forests (*dehesas*) prevalent in these parts, giving the meat its distinctive flavor. Families without land were allowed to bring their pigs to feed on royal or common lands.

The ascetic life and attitudes born under the hard frontier conditions

and inhospitable climate changed little over the centuries. Life for shepherds and peasants was especially harsh. The simple and austere dishes they survived on are still with us; they are mainly winter stews. Elegantly restrained dishes of roast lamb and pork—the grandest being roast suckling pig and baby lamb, which are still offered today—were the status foods of the nobility and grandees. The wildlife, like the land, belonged to the nobility. The small game—partridge, pheasant, pigeon, quail, hare, and rabbit that inhabited the scrub and fed on wild herbs and berries—and the deer and wild boar of the woodlands were all theirs (though poachers had access to them). Shepherds and peasants got the "ignoble cuts"—feet, ears, heads, brains, tails, tripe. They cooked them with chickpeas, lentils, and beans. While central Spain is characterized as "the Spain of the roast," *España del asado,* the festive peasant foods are stews, *platos de cuchara* (literally "spoon dishes"), that you eat with a spoon. Today these and the iconic foods of shepherds and peasants based on bread crumbs, *migas,* are extremely popular.

In the seventeenth century, when famine spread throughout the peninsula, and wool was no longer in demand, the sheep breeders took up cereal farming. Pasturelands were given over to grain, and the sheep began to be bred for their meat and cheese rather than for wool. They were raised on the stubble of the cereal grasses and on barley, oats, and vetch. The migration of sheep (transhumance) became unnecessary. But still today, in celebration of the long sheep-walks (*cañadas*) and the rights granted to the Mesta in the fifteenth century, flocks cross the center of Madrid once a year.

There is in parts of central Spain an exotic culinary heritage that is a legacy of the Muslims and Jews. Christians met them at the market, bought their food, and enjoyed their hospitality. Many Muslims and Jews remained after the expulsion of 1492, as converts to Christianity, and the Jews in particular melted into the population. The *pistos* and eggplant dishes, the *cocidos,* the liberal use of garlic, roast baby lamb cooked in a clay dish accompanied only by a green salad, almond sweets, and cheese served with honey are all part of the cosmopolitan culture the Castilians encountered when they first moved into Toledo.

CASTILE AND LEÓN

The ancient kingdom of León, which once encompassed Galicia, Asturias, Cantabria, and Castile in the north, took up the torch of the Reconquista from the Asturian kings. Castile was a province of León. Its name derives from the vast number of castles that were built to defend the land. Castile split from León in the early eleventh century, and the two kingdoms were often at war and periodically united by conquest or royal marriage, until they were finally reunited in 1230. Today the region of Castile and León is studded with enchanting medieval cities, each with a Gothic cathedral and scores of Romanesque churches and monasteries, a reminder that those wars were about defending Christianity.

Castile and León, also known as Castilla la Vieja (Old Castile), is a vast unending plain on the northern Meseta, a silent and austere landscape of rolling wheat fields and scrub, surrounded by the Montes de León in the north and the Sistema Central range in the south, with fertile valleys watered by the Duero River and its tributaries and lakes. The climate is dry, baking hot in summer, freezing cold in the long winter. But in the north in the mountains of León, it is rainy and green.

Wheat is the main crop, and bread is the symbol of Castile, which was known as the breadbasket of Spain. Bread was the basis of the food of shepherds and peasants. Among these dishes are *sopa de ajo*, a soup of bread and garlic (page 178), and an endless variety of *migas*, bread crumbs with ham, chorizo, bacon, or blood sausage (see page 476). Communal bread ovens, where townspeople could bring their breads to be baked, were used into the twentieth century. No other region produces as many and as wide a variety of legumes: white, red, and black beans; lentils; and chickpeas. The small *pedrosillano* chickpeas are the most common ingredient in peasant stews, which also include cabbage. The huge white *la granja* beans (*granja* means "farm") from around Segovia are the region's most prized beans, famously cooked with pig's ears and sausages (page 497). Soups and stews with beans or chickpeas and pork products—sausages, pig's ears and feet—are now still everyday meals in the long winter months.

Castile and León is pastoral ranching country. The Morucha breed of cattle, originally raised for the plow and the bullring around Salamanca, is now primarily raised for beef, while Ávila is famous for the veal from its indigenous Avileña black breed of cows. The two most common breeds of sheep are the Churra and the Castellana. Their meat has a distinctive and delicious taste, and cheeses from their milk include the intensely flavored, slightly sharp and salty Zamorano and Castellano and the Pata de Mulo (the name means mule's leg). The fresh bland Burgos and Villalón are a mix of cow's and sheep's milk; their Del Tietar is goat cheese.

The region is also one of Spain's important hog-breeding areas. The dry, cool air of the highlands means that the *jamón serrano* from white pigs requires only a light salt cure. Salamanca is famous for its magnificent ham and sausages from the small black Ibérico pig, variously known as *pata negra* (black foot) or *de bellota* if the pigs are fed on acorns (*bellotas*) in the woodlands. The *morcilla* (blood sausage) of Burgos, made with rice and onions, is particularly delicious. *Farinato* is a white sausage made with ground pork, bread crumbs, lard, and seasoning. The dishes that Castile and León is most famous for are roast suckling pig (*cochinillo*) and baby lamb (*lechazo*). It is said that baby lamb is at its meltingly tender best within the triangle of the cities of Segovia, Soria, and Burgos, and suckling pig is at its best in the area between Segovia, Arevalo, and Peñaranda de Bracamonte.

The region is also hunting and shooting country. Wild boar is found in the mountain forests, roe deer in the national game preserve. Partridge, quail, hare, rabbit, and duck can be shot at game club reserves and on thousands of game estates. Partridge is the main Castilian game bird; its numbers are kept high by re-population. Tender baby pigeons (squabs) are a traditional delicacy. You can still see curious *palomares* (dovecotes) in wheat fields, where the grains once provided ready seed for thousands of the birds.

Except in León, there is not much culinary diversity in this largest of Spanish regions. You find similar dishes in all the towns—roast baby lamb served with green salad; bean and lentil stews; lamb with chickpeas (*olla podrida*); chicken in almond sauce (*pollo en pepitoria*) (page 357); partridge or quail in *escabeche;* rabbit or chicken with garlic. Among the many convent sweets, the *yemas de Santa Teresa* (page 575) made with egg yolk and sugar alone from Ávila are the most famous (see page 570).

León, in the mountainous north, on the pilgrims' way to Santiago, a route once lined with dozens of hostels for pilgrims, has more gastronomic variety, with dishes similar to those of Galicia. La Margatería is the mountain homeland of the

mysterious Maragatos, the muleteers who transported salt cod and other goods between the sea and the interior and who are whispered to be descendants of converted Muslims. They have distinctive dishes, and cherries in orujo, a powerful spirit, is a specialty.

Astorga was one of the first places to manufacture chocolate in Europe, and it still does today. The cheeses of León are a strong-tasting goat's-milk cheese called Armada and a blue cheese from Valdeón that is similar to the Asturian Cabrales.

The region of Castile and León produces some of Spain's best wines from vineyards along the river Duero. The prestigious red Ribera del Duero are delicious young and can age into splendid Gran Reservas. The majority of wineries use the native Tempranillo grape. A few mix in a small percentage of other grapes, such as Cabernet Sauvignon and Merlot. Other top-quality local wines are the fruity red Toro, the Bierzo, the Cigales rosés, and the Rueda whites.

MADRID

Madrid, in the center of Spain, was a province of Castile–La Mancha until it became an autonomous community in 1983. The countryside is an area of changing landscapes, with cereal fields, mountains covered with forests, and rivers, lakes, and valleys. There are vineyards and wine villages, and wine-making is an old tradition. The purple-red Vinos de Madrid are very good fruity wines. A mature sheep's milk cheese called Campo Real is produced here.

The Fortress of Mayrit was reconquered from the Muslims in 1083 by King Alfonso VI of Castile, who took Toledo two years later. In 1561, the city of Madrid (which took its name from the fortress) was chosen by the Habsburg king Philip II to be the seat of his court and the permanent capital of Spain. Different quarters of the city reflect various periods of its history. The old medieval and Renaissance town center is the Madrid de los Austrias, built during the reign of the Habsburgs. The eighteenth-century Madrid de los Borbones (of the Bourbons) is luxurious, with grandiose monuments and Baroque and neoclassical palaces of the old aristocracy (some have been turned into hotels). There is the Romantic nineteenth-century Madrid Isabelino, and now a new ultramodern Madrid.

As the capital of Spain, the city has drawn migrants from all the regions. In the past, it had attracted the aristocracy around the court. Today the inhabitants come from all over and their presence is evidenced by the huge number of restaurants representing every region. Overseas immigrants, mostly from Latin America, now form about one-sixth of the population. On warm weekend days, you can see some of these newer residents in the Párque del Oeste, where they set up stalls selling their homemade foods.

Madrid is a city of civil servants, bankers, service providers, and painters. The old aristocracy is still there, too, so one might expect a sophisticated cuisine. But the region shares dishes with the rest of central Spain and has only a few of its own. The most famous is *cocido madrileño,* of pork and chicken with chickpeas, potatoes, cabbage, turnips, marrow bones, bacon, chorizo, and blood sausage (page 498). It is said to be a legacy of the wealthy Conversos (converted Jews) who married into the Castilian aristocracy—an old Sabbath dish into which the Jewish converts piled all kinds of pork to show that their conversion was real. Another specialty is *callos a la madrileña,* a "poor food" of tripe with tomato sauce.

A Christmas specialty that is now cooked throughout the year and is also found elsewhere in the country is baked sea bream with slices of lemon embedded in cuts and a sprinkling of bread crumbs and parsley (page 323). And cafés and street vendors sell *churros* (crunchy ribbed strips of fried dough) and extra-thick hot chocolate (page 586).

CASTILE – LA MANCHA

The province of La Mancha covers most of the region of Castile–La Mancha, in the southern Meseta. It is the setting of Miguel de Cervantes's *Don Quixote,* and the landscape is as Cervantes described it: rolling plains and low hills, for the most part desolate, arid, treeless, and covered with thorny scrub, but in parts

mountainous with vast oak and pine forests, green pastures, rivers, and lakes. The climate is harsher and more extreme than that of the northern plateau, with intensely hot summers, very cold winters, and hardly any rain. Yet the region has always been an important agricultural zone, which still produces most of Spain's wheat and half of its wine, and also olive oil. The old windmills that were used to grind flour, the kind that Don Quixote mistook for giants, dot the wide-open plains. Other crops are barley and corn, chickpeas and lentils, and beans and peas. La Mancha's eggplants are famously delicious; its purple garlic is considered the best in Spain; its honey gets its flavor from the wild aromatic plants in the scrub; and its saffron, the dried stigmas of the *Crocus sativus*, is of the highest quality. The region also grows sugar beets, and sunflowers for their oil.

The area was reconquered from the Muslims by the twelfth century. Castile's frontiersmen, noble warlords, and military monastic orders were all big sheep owners, and sheep raising for merino wool became the pillar of the region's economy. Sheep, shepherds, and cheese feature regularly in Don Quixote and Sancho Panza's adventures. Today sheep are reared for meat and cheese, and the local Manchego is Spain's most famous cheese. It ranges from fresh and creamy to mature and hard, slightly salty, and piquant. There is also Oropesa and Valle de Alcudia. Montes de Toledo is a goat's-milk cheese.

The wildlife includes deer, wild boar, rabbits and hares, partridges, and quail. The marshlands in the Guadiana River Basin are a stopping place for migratory and water birds. In the province of Toledo, where the red-legged partridge breeds, the most appreciated item on menus is *perdiz* (partridge). There are trout, barbel, and pike in the rivers.

The cooking is like that in the rest of central Spain, featuring meat, offal and giblets, bread, and beans, and reflects the old medieval ascetic lifestyles. The grand status dishes—roast lamb, braised venison, and braised or stewed wild boar—are elegantly sober. Quail and partridge are prepared in simple ways, sometimes in *escabeche*, in a vinegary marinade, so as to preserve them. Only the *gazpachos* or *galianos* are over-the-top grandiose stews that include rabbit, hare, and pigeon all together in a bell pepper and tomato sauce; they are served on thin disks of fried unleavened bread with bits of fried dough to soak up the sauce. *Pisto* (page 254) is a combination of sautéed onions, peppers, eggplants, zucchini, and tomatoes, to which potatoes, ham, and eggs are sometimes added. *Asadillo* (page 236) is roasted red peppers simply dressed with garlic, tomato, and oil. Marinated eggplants can be found everywhere in central Spain, at fairs and taverns. *Mojetes* are potatoes sautéed with garlic, paprika, and tomatoes, to which an egg is sometimes added. Toledo's marzipan (page 572) and almond pastries such as *marquesas* (page 574) are famous.

La Mancha is the most extensive grapevine-growing region in Spain, perhaps in the world. Old photographs show peasants harvesting the grapes and carrying them in carts, treading them, dancing and laughing. They had a good time and it provided them with a living, but the wine they produced was characterless, in some cases plain awful, bulk wine. Now La Mancha produces some good wines at very competitive prices. Their whites from the old much-maligned Airén grapes are now crisp, light, and tasty. A number of fine reds are made with the indigenous Tempranillo grape (here also called Cencibel), with Monastrell and Garnacha Tintorera, mixed with Cabernet Sauvignon, Syrah, or Merlot. Valdepeñas, also known as Aloque and Clarete, are a reborn classic, made by mixing white and red grapes.

EXTREMADURA

Extremadura shares the southern plateau with Castile–La Mancha. It produces *jamón ibérico*, an incomparable delicacy and Spain's greatest gastronomic treasure, from the small black Ibérico pig, which feeds on acorns in the oak woodlands. The hams are air-dried in the special microclimate of the Sierra de Montánchez for up to four years. The region also produces my very favorite

Spanish cheese, the creamy, almost liquid Torta del Casar, made from the milk of merino sheep, which has a delicious slightly salty taste. You eat it with a spoon, first slicing a piece off the thin crust on the top, then putting it back on like a lid. Other high-quality products are extra virgin olive oils, honeys, and the famous smoked *pimentón de la Vera*, which comes in mild (*dulce*), bittersweet (*agridulce*), and hot (*picante*) varieties.

Extremadura was never an independent kingdom. The Romans found silver mines there and the Muslims built fortified towns. When the area was reconquered in the thirteenth century, it became a province of Castile. The land was given over to nobles from Castile, León, and Galicia and to the knights of Santiago and Alcántara, the monastic military orders who organized its colonization. In the sixteenth century, because opportunities at home were limited in comparison with those in Castile, men of ambition left in great numbers for the Americas. The most famous conquistadores—Pizarro, Cortés, and Balboa, among others—as well as the majority of the early emigrants to the New World, came from Extremadura. Many who returned brought back riches and built mansions and palaces, emblazoned with their heraldic coats of arms. It is said that Extremadura was the first place that had chiles brought back from the Americas and that the monks were the first to grow them in their monastery vegetable gardens. In the mid-nineteenth century, farmers started to grow different varieties (from mild to hot) on a large scale. They dried them in barns heated by holm oak fires, which gave them a smokey flavor, then pulverized them into *pimentón*, the Spanish paprika that flavors chorizos and so many regional Spanish dishes.

In this land of rolling plains, with fields of wheat, barley, corn, and chickpeas, great wooded mountains, and fertile valleys, sheep and pig farming was early on the most important part of the economy. Nobles owned extensive estates of agricultural and grazing lands. They sold their wool to Castilian merchants and rented their pastures in the winter to northern stock raisers. Small farmers could rent common lands owned by towns and villages for grazing animals and growing grapevines, fruits, and vegetables. They also had access to the royal lands, particularly the mountain woodlands that provided the sweet acorns that fattened their pigs. Monasteries and convents owned vineyards and olive groves in the hills. While the cooking of the region is serious and austere, known for pastoral and peasant dishes, with lamb, pork, and offal, the monasteries always had a reputation for fine cooking.

Along with Torta del Casar, other good cheeses of Extremadura are the merino sheep's-milk Cañarejal and La Serena and the goat's-milk Ibores and Cabra del Tiétar. Like all Spanish regions, Extremadura has an old wine-making tradition. Ribera del Guadiana was one of the first wine areas in Spain to use modern refrigeration equipment to combat the extremely high summer temperatures. Their new fruity reds made with Tempranillo grapes and whites with Paradilla grapes are extremely reasonable. In some villages, such as Montánchez, the local Pitarra wine is fermented in clay pots called *tinajas* and kept in family cellars.

rice and vegetables

{ mediterranean spain }

Mediterranean Spain is the Spain of the deep blue sea, luminous sky, and fragrant air. It is dry, with hot summers and mild winters, with occasional bursts of rain. People promenade and meet in open-air cafés. It is the Spain of the *alegría de vivir* (joy of living). Gastronomically, it is the colorful sensuous Spain of strong flavors and aromas. The Mediterranean has been my world since I holidayed in Alexandria when I was a child, and it has been my "patch" since I started writing about food. I feel at home here.

The Spanish Levant: Catalonia, Valencia, Murcia, and the Balearic Islands, and Andalusia, too, share a culinary culture with the countries around the Mediterranean, most particularly with southern France, Italy, and Morocco. Catalonia had a major role in creating and spreading that distinctive food culture; for hundreds of years, it was the undisputed "Queen of the Mediterranean" as a great seafaring mercantile nation, and it was the dominant partner in the Catalan-Aragonese kingdom, which had an empire around the Mediterranean Sea. Before Catalonia and Aragon were united by royal marriage in 1137, a count of Barcelona had acquired Provence and part of the Pyrenees through marriage to the heiress of Provence. The Catalans, in the name of the joint Crown, took Valencia and the islands of Majorca and Menorca from the Muslims, and received Sicily through marriage. The Pope granted James II of Aragon sovereignty over Sardinia and Corsica, and the joint Crown went on to acquire Naples, Macedonia, parts of Greece, the North African island of Jerba, and the French Roussillon and Cerdagne. It also established trading posts or consulates in port cities as far away as Alexandria. The old Catalan lands, as they were called, of Valencia and the Balearic Islands, were largely repopulated by Catalans when the Muslims left. This explains why the people there today speak a Catalan language and have many dishes in common. You can see why the *coca* is like pizza and the Provençal *pissaladière*, why *samfaina* is like ratatouille, and why the Spanish tomato sauce is the ubiquitous signature sauce of Mediterranean cooking.

Despite the similarities, every region, province, and village on the long coast and on the islands has its own take on the Mediterranean style. It is a style rich in grains, vegetables, fruit, and nuts as well as fish, and olive oil is the main cooking fat. The Romans planted wheat, olives, and grapevines; the Arabs introduced rice and a large number of vegetables and fruits; and many more fruits and vegetables came from the New World. Mediterranean vegetables include zucchini, eggplants, peppers, tomatoes, broad beans, spinach, asparagus, green beans, artichokes, and pumpkins, among many others. The fish stock in the Mediterranean has been much depleted, but the Spanish coast boasts the most glorious fish and seafood dishes.

CATALONIA

Catalan cuisine is the richest, most complex, and most sophisticated of Spain. The fish and seafood dishes are magisterial. Catalonia has a new foie gras industry and more wild mushrooms than anywhere else in Spain. Catalans are known for mixing savory with sweet and sweet with sour, for pairing meat with fruit and seafood with meat. A dish of chicken and lobster is an example of the *mar i muntanya*, or "sea and mountain," style. Raisins and pine nuts are common garnishes. Wine and brandy are much used in cooking, and chocolate appears too.

Catalans describe some of their dishes as *barroco e sabroso* (baroque and tasty). Many dishes begin with a *sofregit* (*sofrito* in Castilian), a sauce of fried onion, garlic, and just a little tomato. *Picada*, a garlic, parsley, and almond or hazelnut paste, is often added at the end of cooking to thicken stews. *Romesco* (page 143), a nutty sauce made with almonds or hazelnuts, garlic, tomato, and dried sweet red peppers, all blended to a thick cream, accompanies all kinds of dishes. *Alioli*, or *allioli* in Catalan (page 141), is a garlicky olive oil sauce. A mix of olive oil and pork fat is the traditional cooking fat (goose and duck fat were also used), but now most people have dropped lard, for health reasons and because today's commercial lard is not as good as the one peasants once lovingly produced for their own use. Catalonia's fruity extra virgin olive oils, in which Arbequino is the predominant olive, are among the finest of Spain. The *frutado,* a fruitier oil made with green olives, has a hint of apple and a slight bitter-almond flavor; the *dulce,* made with ripe black olives, is yellow, sweet, and mild. Some of Catalonia's olive trees are the oldest in Spain. There is one in Tarragona that is said to be more than a thousand years old.

Along the narrow coastal plain and in the wide valley of the river Ebro, the produce and the cooking are Mediterranean, but the Catalan interior is all high mountains with a gastronomic culture of the Pyrenees. Cows and goats are raised for butter and cheese, and intensive pig farming provides a huge variety of *embotits* (sausages and salamis). The city of Vic is famous for its fresh *botifarres,* salami-type *salchichón,* the spiced *longaniza,* and *fuet* (see page 494).

Catalans have always been hardworking and proud of their industrial and trading activities, which resulted in the growth of a wealthy bourgeoisie that had no counterpart in Castile, where that type of work was never seen as compatible with an aristocratic lifestyle. It was a bourgeoisie that aspired to live well and eat well. In the nineteenth century, the manufacture of cotton cloth from fibers imported from Latin American plantations started an industrial revolution. Other industries included the production of wine and brandy, which were exported to Europe. Spaniards who had grown wealthy in Cuba, the *indianos,* came back to start manufacturing businesses, and Andalusian peasants from the south came

to work in the mills. Barcelona become the hub of Spain. The Catalan language, which hadn't been taught in school since the Bourbons, regained its literary nobility, and the glorious imperial Catalan medieval past was celebrated.

But Catalan gastronomic traditions were neglected in favor of French haute cuisine. The dispossessed French aristocrats and cooks who had flooded in from the start of the French Revolution profoundly influenced the new Barcelona bourgeoisie, which adopted French ways in the kitchen. Italian immigrants arrived at the same time and opened the first inns. Many French and Italian dishes were Hispanicized: béchamel made with fried onions and tomato paste and Spanish *canelones* (cannelloni) are two examples. By the end of the nineteenth century, a large number of exclusive, flamboyant French-style restaurants had opened in cosmopolitan Barcelona. Catalan chefs learned French haute cuisine by working with French chefs and in cooking schools. The wealthy Catalan elite expected its home cooks to make the exquisite and sophisticated French-style dishes that became its *cuisine bourgeoise*.

It wasn't until the late twentieth century, after Franco's crushing of the culture and the growth of industrialized food products, that Catalans began to value their own rural and popular home cooking. The prolific writer and gastronome Manuel Vázquez Montalbán (1939–2003) was one of the first to begin chronicling "the signs of resistance of Catalonia's gastronomic identity." If it was a priority to save the language, it was also, he believed, important to save the cuisine. In

1977, he published *L'Art del Menjar a Catalunya* (*The Art of Eating in Catalonia*). But by 1994, it was clear that *nueva cocina* was threatening Catalan cooking traditions. Although proud that the most innovative cuisine in history, which put Spain on the gastronomic map and created demand for its products, came from their own superstar Ferran Adrià, at his restaurant El Bulli in Roses, Catalans also saw it as a tragedy, because young chefs in thrall to Adrià only wanted to make mousses, gelatins, foams, and terrines of everything and to appear on television. As a result, a group of food historians, gastronomes, nutritionists, sociologists, and others got together with chefs to form the Fundació Institut Català de la Cuina (Catalan Culinary Institute) in 1996, dedicated to researching the history and roots of Catalan cooking and to collecting and recording recipes from both professionals and home cooks in every town, village, and fishing port before the recipes disappeared. Over five years, with the help of four hundred chefs and many home cooks, they collected nine hundred recipes and organized them alphabetically in a heavy tome, *Corpus de la Cuina Catalana*, intended to be the bible of classic Catalan cooking. They are also encouraging chefs to revisit and update traditional Catalan dishes by making them lighter and simpler. My friend Pepa Aymami (see page 267) has been involved in the project from the start. When I stayed with her in Barcelona, she invited some of her colleagues to lunch. They talked passionately about the food of Catalonia and its history.

Many Catalan dishes go back to the Middle Ages and the Renaissance, when there was a court cuisine and Catalans were rich from trading and from their Mediterranean empire. For centuries, their cooks were the most highly regarded and influential in Europe, and recipe collections written in Catalan are proof that medieval Catalan cuisine achieved widespread fame in the fourteenth and fifteenth centuries. I had a taste of that medieval cuisine many years ago at the home of the late Rudolf Grewe, who was translating from ancient Catalan a now-famous anonymous Catalan cookbook, *Libre de Sent Sovi*, presumed to have been written in the fourteenth century, and researching its background. When Rudolf had come to London earlier and consulted me about medieval Arab cooking, I cooked dishes for him from the thirteenth-century Arabic culinary manual known as *A Baghdad Cookery Book* (see page 22). And when I was in New York City, where he lived, he invited me to eat dishes from *Libre de Sent Sovi*. A giant crucifix bought from an old church hung on a big white wall over the table. Rudolf made a *sofregit* of slowly fried onions with garlic, and an almond sauce, both quintessential cornerstones of Catalan cooking today; baby eggplants stuffed with a herby goat's cheese; and fried fish *escabeche*, followed by chicken with almond sauce. For dessert, we had fresh cheese with rose water and honey.

Another medieval Catalan cookbook, *Libre del Coch*, was written by Ruperto de Nola, who was head cook to Alfonso V, count of Barcelona and king of Aragon, who became king of Naples in 1443. Nola also later cooked for Alfonso's son, King Ferdinand. His sumptuous dishes symbolized the cultural apogee of the old Catalan lands. Some of his recipes claim to be in the style of Genoa, Venice, Lombardy, and France. Some are recognizably Arab in that they mix sweet with sour, savory with sweet, and marry meat with fruits such as pears and quinces. They use ground almonds, rose and orange blossom water, and sour pomegranate juice and are garnished with raisins and pine nuts. Almond pastries and fritters with sprinklings of sugar and cinnamon are among the sweets. There is an early *crema catalana*.

Many Spanish chefs today cite *Sent Sovi* and *Libre del Coch* as sources of inspiration. A few have even based menus on them. Chef and food writer Josep Lladonosa, who was for many years head chef at the famous restaurant Set Portes in Barcelona, was one of the first to use these old books and to popularize the old dishes. He told me how well they were received and how quickly they were adopted by other establishments.

Catalans are extremely proud of their cheeses and wines. Among their well-known cheeses, Garrotxa is a firm but creamy slightly tangy goat's-milk cheese covered by a light blue-gray mold; Montcerda is a semi-hard aromatic cow's-milk cheese; Serrat, a sheep's-milk cheese, has an intense piquant flavor; and Mato, from cow's or goat's milk, which is soft, fresh, and unsalted, is great with honey. A creamy curd called Tupi, made from sheep's milk, is sold in little clay pots and served as a dessert. In the Basque Country, it is called *mamia;* elsewhere it is called *cuajada*, which means "curd."

Catalan wines are among the most varied and exciting in Spain. Priorat's rich, complex, and full-bodied fruity reds are outstanding. The Penedès region makes wonderful red and white wines and is famous for its cava, made with local grapes

by the Champagne method into sweet, semisweet, dry, extra dry, brut, and extra brut sparkling wines. Alella produces good dry and sweet whites, and Conca de Barberà produces rosés. Other good vineyards are Terra Alta, Montsant, Coster de Segre, Empordá, Tarragona, Pla de Bages, and Catalunya. Rum; *anis,* an anise-flavored liqueur; and *vin ranci,* a type of fortified wine like sherry, are much used in cooking.

VALENCIA

Valencia is a land of oranges and rice fields and market gardens that produce vegetables all year round. Roman legionnaires from southern Italy founded the city of Valencia in 137 B.C. One of the Roman legacies is the outdoor stone ovens that many people have in their gardens today. Some local products, like dried salted fish and vegetable preserves, are said to have been introduced by the Phoenicians, Greeks, or Romans. When James I conquered Valencia from the Muslims in 1238, he made it an autonomous kingdom within the Crown of Aragon and colonized it mainly with Catalans, the reason why the region has many dishes in common with Catalonia. But a large part of the population remained Muslim, of mainly Berber descent. When they were forced to convert to Christianity in the sixteenth century, the nobility protected them because they depended on their labor. Their eventual mass expulsion in 1616 caused a catastrophic economic decline of the region.

Village names in rural areas beginning with *beni* ("son of" in Arabic) conjoined with names of Berber tribes are evidence of the spread of North African settlements, which also left a mark on the agriculture. Their systems of irrigation from rivers and springs allow the production of several harvests a year on the coastal plain and in river valleys. Even today a "water court," the Tribunal de las Aguas, set up by the Muslims to resolve conflicts about water, meets every Thursday in the center of Valencia. The Arabs planted rice in the watery marshlands and lagoons, or *albuferas.* You can still see the traditional houses, *barracas,* made from wood, reeds, clay, and mud, where the workers slept on the first floor, while the owner and his family lived on the floor above, where the grain was also kept.

Valencia has the widest repertoire of rice dishes in Spain: paella was born here. *Fideuà,* essentially a seafood paella with pasta instead of rice, is relatively new. Fish and seafood are cooked on a grill or a griddle and served with *alioli,* or simmered in the soups and stews called *cassolas, sucs,* and *suquets.* There is chicken and rabbit, wild game from the scrublands, and duck from the lagoons and marshlands. Vegetables are roasted or simply boiled and dressed; they are also stuffed or used in omelets. Among the region's distinctive dishes are the pizza-type *cocas* and *empanadas,* savory pies. In the countryside and mountain hinterland, meat stews made with lamb (there are no cows), chicken, cured pork and sausages, chickpeas, beans, and vegetables are festive specials. What makes them different from the stews in the rest of Spain are their large meat or chicken dumplings, called *pilotes* or *pelotas.*

The usual dessert is fresh or dried fruit. Apart from the Moorish convent pastries, Valencians make sweets with fruits and vegetables: sweet potatoes, a kind of squash called *cabello de angel* (angel's hair), like spaghetti squash, that falls apart into threads, oranges, and pumpkin. They also have delicious ice creams with almonds (page 518) and with the nougatlike *turrón* (page 514).

Every province of Valencia has a special product. Black truffles are found in the Maestrazgo mountains, and the Marina Alta district produces honey. Jijona (or Xixona) is the world capital of *turrón,* made with ground almonds and honey. La Vila Joiosa is famous for its chocolate. Other mountain products include the long thin pork sausage *llonganissa, botifarra* (blood sausage), a white sausage called *blanquet,* peppery chorizos, and the soft paprika-flavored spreadable pork sausage *sobrassada.* The region's cheeses made from goat's or sheep's milk or a mix are bland, soft, and fresh. They include Servilleta, Cassoletta, and Blanquet. They are eaten with honey as a dessert.

Valencia's best-quality wines are Utiel-Requena, Valencia, and Alicante. There are white, red, and rosés, as well as sweet Moscatels; the Alejandría Moscatel is well known. Famous local drinks are the very refreshing milky tiger nut *horchata* (page 587), which I adore, and *agua de Valencia* (Valencia water), which is cava or other sparkling wine mixed with Cointreau and orange juice (page 585).

MURCIA

Murcia is a small mountainous region with fertile river valleys, a coastal plain, and a saltwater lagoon called the Mar Menor (Small Sea). It has the same semi-arid Mediterranean climate as its neighbor Valencia, and the two share an early history of Roman settlement and a long Muslim presence. But the Catalan influence on the cooking is missing, because the Castilians conquered the Muslim kingdom in 1243, before the Catalans and Aragonese got there. The land was divided among military orders and knights from Castile and the north, and as in Valencia, the Muslims stayed on to work the land.

Dishes here are less flamboyant than in Valencia or Catalonia. Murcia is known as the *huerta* (vegetable garden) of Spain and has more vegetable dishes than any other region. Vegetables are cooked with rice and are put into omelets, pies, soups and stews, and salads. They are also stuffed. The region is famous for the high quality of its rice, particularly in Calasparra (see page 440). Murcia's rice dishes, like its game dishes, with rabbit and hare, partridge and quail, are hearty, herby, and full of flavor. Baby lamb and kid are the grand festive dishes. *Caldo con pelotas*, a Christmas special, is a stew made of turkey or chicken with meatballs as big as oranges. The Mar Menor yields lobsters and prawns and a rich variety of fish. Fish baked in a salt crust—a Phoenician legacy—is one of the specialties.

Murcia is full of orange and lemon groves, and it also grows melons and watermelons, apricots, plums, and pomegranates. In the almost-desert areas, there are prickly pears. The region has industries of crystallized fruit, fruit preserves, marmalade, jams, and honeys. The goat's-milk cheeses are soft, bland when fresh; cured, they have a slightly stronger flavor. Murcia al vino is a matured cheese that has been soaked in wine. Three wines—Jumilla, Yecla, and Bullas—that are made with a mix of local grape varieties and French ones are very pleasing.

THE BALEARIC ISLANDS

The undulating hills, rugged coastline, and sandy beaches of the main Balearic Islands—Majorca, Minorca, Ibiza, and Formentera—have been attracting people from all over the world since the mid-nineteenth century. Until tourism

expanded, most of the population lived in the interior, away from the sea, in fear of pirate raids. Now it is concentrated along the coast and in the big cities, where the work is.

Majorca grew rich on Mediterranean trade. The land was divided among nobles descended from the Catalans who conquered the islands in 1229. Today their mansions in the hills, and Mudéjar (Hispano-Muslim)-style town houses built around patios, have been turned into hotels or have become the holiday retreats of international celebrities. Many of the old peasant houses scattered around the countryside have gone to painters, writers, and hippies. In village squares where women once washed their laundry and pigs were slaughtered, hordes of tourists sit in the cafés. I stayed in Palma de Majorca with my cousin Steve Afif, who is an artist. I can understand why he lives there: it is the good life.

What surprised me is that researchers have recorded no less than six hundred regional dishes in the archipelago of islands. Although the islands are small, they are strategically located and were an important trading center. Settlers and occupiers have been coming for centuries, and the islands have always been open to foreign influences. The gastronomy, like the culture, is primarily Catalan—*cocas*, *suquets*, toasted bread smeared with tomato, *alioli*—but the Arab influence is important. You can feel the old Arab presence in the poultry stuffed with almonds and dried fruit just as you do when you see the old waterwheels and mills.

The islands are fantastically rich in products of the land and sea. A hundred years ago, the Catalan painter Santiago Rusiñol described the vegetation in these

words: "The fruit trees spread themselves. . . . Everything grows, blossoms, and fructifies as if to relieve its heart of some burden, and to bestow homage and gifts on the little houses around." Apart from the usual wheat, grapes, and olives, there are apricots, peaches, pomegranates, figs, and carobs. Peasant dishes are based on vegetables: eggplant is a favorite. Rabbits, hares, and partridges inhabit the islands, quails stop there on their migrations, and there are sheep, but the most important dishes are fish and seafood. Majorca's *caldereta de langosta* (page 345) is a stupendous lobster stew. Mayonnaise accompanies many dishes, and there are theories that claim it was born in Mahón.

As in Catalonia, olive oil and lard have an important role in cooking and pastry making. Balearic oils are more astringent and bitter than the Catalan. Rusiñol described the oldest olive trees as "twisting themselves into such intricate knots and rolling about in such hysterical convulsions that they could hardly be called trees"; they were, he said, more like epileptics. The main varieties of olives are Empeltre, Arbequina, and Picual.

The English occupied the island of Minorca in 1708, and they stayed for almost eighty years. They brought Friesian cattle over from England, and the fresh Minorcan cow's-milk cheese *queso de Mahón* is used to make a cheese tart called *flaó* (page 520). The aged semi-hard variety has a delicious strong, slightly salty flavor. *Flor de sal,* sea salt harvested by hand from salt flats along the coast, is a new product of the island.

The foremost Majorcan specialty is *sobrasada,* an orange-colored semi-cured pork sausage that is a soft, spreadable paste, flavored with *pimentón* and other spices. There is a mild variety and a hot one. The paste is pressed into pigs' intestines or into large bladders. The traditional meat used is from a special breed of fat black local pigs with long ears called *porc negre* (these are not the *ibérico pata negra*). The paste is eaten on toasted bread, often with something sweet and fruity such as quince paste or honey, or ripe figs. It is also fried with eggs. For the Majorcan peasantry, *sobrasada* was the main, and for some the only, source of meat. The sausages are described in Spanish documents of the seventeenth century, when they were already a major product.

Majorca is also famous for a fabulously light, melt-in-the-mouth yeast-based puff pastry called *ensaimada,* made with lard (*saim* in the local dialect). Small *ensaimadas* are eaten for breakfast and with drinks, and a huge coiled-serpent-like *ensaimada* stuffed with custard is eaten as a dessert. I could eat it every day.

In the nineteenth century, the Majorcan aristocracy sent their cooks to France to learn the art of confectionery. They came back with chestnuts in brandy syrup, meringues called *baisers* ("kisses" in French), and almond cakes covered with chocolate. The island has the sweetest, tastiest almonds, and tourists arrange visits to coincide with the blossoming of the almond trees because the sight and fragrance are such a wondrous experience. The almonds go into traditional Moorish pastries, and there is an almond cake and an almond ice cream (page 518).

Majorca is the only one of the islands to produce wine. Binissalem and Pla i Llevant are made from native grapes—Manto Negro and Callet for red wines and Moll for whites. Palo de Mallorca is a celebrated digestive made from cinchona bark (a native of the Western Andes of South America), brown sugar, cinnamon, and nutmeg. The English introduced gin in Minorca, where it is distilled from fermented grape skins and seeds and flavored with juniper berries and aromatic herbs. *Pellofa* is gin with a dash of soda and lemon peel; *pomada* is a mix of gin and lemonade. Ibiza makes a strong herb liqueur that must be watered down with ice. The islands' hot *sangrí* is a punch with red wine, lemon or orange peel, and a dash of nutmeg; it is served over toasted bread. *Punys* is rum or brandy diluted with water, with added sugar and lemon peel.

ANDALUSIA

Orange trees line the streets of Andalusia, and the scent of jasmine is in the air. It is the home of bullfighting, flamenco, and Gypsies, and it is where the tapas tradition was born. It was as the imperial Roman province of Baetica that it produced grains, wine, and olive oil for the Roman Empire. But it is the ghosts of Al-Andalus that haunt the land, with its Moorish castles and palaces, its mosques and white-washed villages that the Muslims left behind. Ziryab, a lute player and poet who came from the court of Harun al Rashid (the Abbasid Caliph who was immortalized in *The Thousand and One Nights*) in Baghdad in 822 and revolutionized the cooking at the court of Córdoba, would be smiling to find that lamb with honey and fish with raisins and pine nuts are on the menus of fashionable restaurants here, and that the nuns make the greatest variety of Moorish pastries in all of Spain. No other region so captures the allure of the old Muslim presence.

But Andalusia has many faces. Most of the region is wild and mountainous, with huge *sierras* (mountain ranges) covered with scrub or chestnut and oak forests. The sierras are pig country, with the ideal conditions for curing pork in the cold, dry winter air. The prestigious cured ham *jamón ibérico* is produced here from the famous black *pata negra* pigs, which feed on sweet acorns in the oak forests. Trevélez, in Las Alpujarras in the Sierra Nevada, and the village of Jabugo, in the Sierra de Aracena, are renowned for their exquisite *jamón ibérico*. Mountain cheeses are mainly goat cheeses, from the milk of the Málaga breed of goats. Grazalema, from a blend of sheep's and goat's milk, is slightly spicy.

Rice grows in the desertlike stretches and in wetlands with freshwater lagoons. Irrigation and a brilliant sun allow areas on the coast and the huge basin of the great Guadalquivir River to produce a fantastic abundance of vegetables. Seville, on the banks of the river, was the gateway and port for goods arriving from the New World in the sixteenth century and so was the first city to receive the new vegetables and fruits. Almond groves dotted around the countryside are important to confectionery and pastry production throughout Spain.

Between the river valley and the mountains, gently rolling hills are covered by seas of wheat and sunflowers, orange and lemon groves, and vineyards. As one drives from Granada toward Jaén, they all eventually give way to olive trees, line after line, as far as the eye can see and however far you travel. Olives and olive oil are the culinary symbols of Andalusia, and the province of Jaén is the greatest producer of olive oil in the world. Its extra virgin oils, made from Picual olives, are fruity and fragrant. Three sensational Andalusian extra virgin oils, mainly from Picual and Hojiblanca olives, are the fruity, mildly bitter, and slightly pungent Priego de Córdoba, the slightly bitter Sierra Mágina, and the intense Sierra de Segura.

With both Atlantic and Mediterranean coasts and an extraordinary variety of fish and seafood from the two waters, it's not surprising that the cooking of the

sea represents some of the region's greatest dishes. Andalusians are famous for deep-frying fish and seafood, but they also have many other coastal specialties. Among them are sea bream Cádiz-style with sherry (page 332) and fish in onion and saffron sauce from Málaga (page 333).

Andalusia has always been a region of great wealth and extreme poverty. The majority of the population was illiterate until the mid-twentieth century. As the land was gradually reconquered at the end of the fifteenth century, it was shared among warrior nobles from Castile, Galicia, and Asturias and the Church, and divided into large estates called *latifundios*. Peasant families from Asturias who came to work on the land brought with them the culture of chestnuts, as well as the culture of the pig, from the north.

Most of today's big estates date from the nineteenth century, when the land held by the Church and the municipalities was put up for sale. At the same time, landowners began to sell some of their land to the workers who lived on their estates. All the members of peasant families worked and saved up to buy a plot. Generations spent most of their life economizing, and those who emigrated sent money from abroad to help their families.

The landless rural poor lived in small villages and were taken on as day laborers; they would hang around the village square to be picked. They depended on the charity of the Church and the philanthropy of the elite. Peasant revolts and uprisings did not change their conditions. Their mass migration to the cities, to the industrialized north and abroad, began in the nineteenth century. But some have come back to buy their dream bit of land and to plant olive trees. Today tourism provides seasonal work, and it is migrant workers who do the laboring in the fields. The old life of the peasants has only recently disappeared, and their *gazpachos* (page 170), *salmorejos* (page 172), and *ajo blancos* (page 177) have become famous around the world.

Sherry and locally brewed lager beers are the favorite aperitifs of Andalusia. Its sherry, now officially called Jerez-Xerez-Sherry, is one of the most well-known wines of the world. It is made in the area lying between Jerez de la Frontera,

Puerto de Santa María, and San Lucar de Barrameda in the province of Cádiz. It is fortified, after fermentation, with grape-distilled brandy. The juice of mainly Palomino grapes is fermented and left to age in oak barrels. What is unique about sherry production is the *solera* system, by which wines from different harvests are blended and aged at the same time: rows of barrels are stacked in at least three layers, the ones with the oldest wine at the bottom and the ones with the newest at the top. Wine ready to be bottled is drawn off from the bottom-row barrels, the *solera,* which contain the oldest blend. Then each barrel is topped up with wine from the row above.

Several different styles of sherry are produced. For fino, the driest and palest, a natural yeast called *flor* is allowed to grow on the surface to protect the wine from oxidation, and this affects the taste. Pale, crisp, and moderately dry manzanilla sherry is also aged with *flor.* Oloroso is fortified to a higher strength, in which the *flor* cannot survive. Aged oxidatively for a very long time, it becomes a dark-gold rich and mellow wine with a caramel undertone. Amontillado is aged first under a cap of *flor* and then exposed to oxygen, which produces an amber wine, lighter than oloroso, with a slightly sweet, nutty flavor. Sweet and medium sherries have added sweet wine from Pedro Ximénez or Moscatel grapes that are dried in the sun. Cooking with sherry characterizes Andalusian dishes. Every kind is used—fino, manzanilla, oloroso, amontillado, and Pedro Ximénez.

Other Andalusian denominations that produce both dry fortified wines and sweet wines are Montilla-Moriles, Málaga–Sierra de Málaga, and El Condado de Huelva. Sweet wines made from Pedro Ximénez (also labeled PX) are often dark-coffee-black, intensely sweet and syrupy, with raisin flavors. Those made from Moscatel grapes are white and have orange blossom aromas. The best are from Málaga.

Andalusia also produces most of Spain's brandies, which are drunk as digestives and much used in cooking; they are sweeter than French Cognac. An anise-flavored spirit, *aguardiente de anis,* that can be sweet or dry is used in pastry making.

A variety of vinegars are made here too. Dark brown sherry vinegar, *vinagre de Jerez,* is strong and complex in flavor. There are also sweet vinegars from Pedro Ximénez and Moscatel grapes. A new product, Pedro Ximénez Wine Reduction, is the wine reduced to a dark thick syrup. It is added to vinegar in dressings and drizzled over desserts and ice cream.

# of wrinkly potatoes and hot sauces

{ the canary islands }

The Canary Islands are different from the rest of Spain. These seven volcanic islands and six islets lie in the Atlantic Ocean off the coast of Africa, near the border between Morocco and Western Sahara. They were conquered by the kingdom of Castile during the fifteenth century, and settlers from the peninsula started occupying the land that had been inhabited by the Guanche, people of Berber origin. They built cities and planted sugarcane and grapevines initially using native slave labor. The islands became a stopping point on the way to and from the New World and a place for foreign merchants to trade.

Today the main economy of the islands is tourism. The fantastical landscape, which ranges from volcanic desolation to green jungle, and the eternal spring weather attract millions of holidaying Europeans, along with workers from the Spanish mainland, South America, and Africa. Dishes with Spanish, North African, and Latin American influences appear in the Canary kitchen. The settlers were quick to plant products from the New World like the potato (they have twenty different varieties), corn, tomatoes, and chile peppers. The islands are famous for their *papas arrugatas*, or wrinkled potatoes (page 279), and for the Moroccan-style spicy sauces—green, red, and peppery *mojos* (page 280)—that accompany potatoes, vegetables, fish and seafood, and meat. *Gofio*, a porridge of ground barley, wheat, chickpeas, or corn, or sometimes a combination, was the staple food of the Guanche and is still an important part of the local cuisine.

The subtropical climate allows the cultivation of oranges and lemons, apricots, peaches, almonds, wheat, barley, and corn. There are huge plantations of extra-sweet dwarf bananas, which were introduced in the mid-nineteenth century. More recently, the islanders have started to grow exotic fruits such as avocados, papayas, mangoes, kiwis, and pineapples. Palm honey is a rich golden syrup made from the sap of palm trees. Goats are a source of meat and of a variety of good cheeses. *Almogrote* is a soft paste of aged goat cheese with garlic, chile pepper, and olive oil, served on toast.

The Canaries produce red and white wine. Their sweet Malmsey (Malvasia) wines were popular in England long ago—Shakespeare mentioned them often. They also make a high-quality rum from sugarcane.

kitchen utensils

In Spain, people always kept their cooking utensils and passed them on to their children—and some still do. Gypsies used to travel around the country sharpening knives, repairing pots and pans, and making baskets. They would bang a tune on a frying pan to announce their annual arrival in each town. The Fiesta de Caldereros (Tinkers' Festival) in Tolosa in February commemorates the tradition with a reenactment of the old activities in Gypsy dress.

I love seeing Spaniards crushing garlic with a pinch of salt in a mortar, grating tomatoes, passing sauces through a conical sieve, and cooking in clay dishes, but at home I have my own ways of performing these tasks. Traditional Spanish utensils are nice to use and look beautiful on the table, but you do not need them to cook any of the dishes in this book, except, perhaps, if you want to make a large paella.

- The *paella*, a large shallow two-handled pan with slanting sides, used for cooking the dish of the same name, is sold in many sizes. The wide shallow pan allows for even evaporation of the liquid and keeps the different ingredients from disappearing in the rice. Huge paella pans are used for cooking outdoors over a wood fire or on a large gas ring set on a tripod over a butane canister. A heavier pan distributes the heat more evenly when cooking over a conventional stove burner. (According to my friend Lourdes, a specialist in rice and paella, the pan is wrongly called and sold as a *paellera*, though some people use that term.)

- A *cazuela* is a shallow fired-clay dish with a glazed interior. It can be used in the oven and over direct heat on a gas burner (a few good brands can also be used on an electric burner). It distributes and retains heat well. It should last for a few years if treated properly; it may crack eventually, but it is cheap to replace. Before you use a *cazuela* for the first time, you must soak it in water for at least 6 hours, then drain it, fill it almost entirely with water, and bring the water slowly to a boil over low heat. Let the water simmer very gently until it has almost evaporated. When cooking in a *cazuela* over a burner, it is important to always start on low heat and then turn it up gradually once the rim begins to feel warm. Very high heat is not advisable. You can make soups, stews, braises, and rice dishes in a *cazuela*.

- *Cocotes* are tall clay pots with straight sides and lids.

- *Ollas* are tall stewing pots with curved sides and lids. Most are metal, but some are made of clay. *Pucheros* are tall metal pots with straight sides and lids. Traditional stews are called *ollas* and *pucheros* after these pots.

- A *mortero* is a mortar and pestle. These are much used in Spain for crushing garlic and parsley, almonds and other nuts, and fried bread, and to make sauces such as *alioli* and romesco. The traditional Spanish *mortero* is made of heavy porcelain and has a beautiful yellow glaze, but marble ones are equally good. A blender or food processor and an electric hand mixer can do many of the same jobs very well. A *dornillo* is a large wooden mortar used in Andalusia.

- A *plancha* is a heavy metal two-handled flat griddle. It can also be a flat-top plate that is part of the stove.

- A *chino* is a conical sieve (a *chinois*) with a wooden pestle traditionally used to strain sauces. Today in Spain it is more common to blend sauces to a smooth cream by using an immersion blender straight in the saucepan.

- A *salamandra* is a heavy metal disk mounted on a long handle. It is heated over a flame and used to caramelize the top of *crema catalana* and other desserts. But mini blowtorches are now widely available and just as effective as the traditional salamander.

STOCKS AND BASICS

Nowadays in Spain, people buy ready-made meat, chicken, and fish stocks. We too can now buy good stocks, and it is fine to use them as a base. Bouillon cubes can also be used to strengthen flavors. (I have even seen boxes of these kept under kitchen tables in Spanish restaurants.) But good homemade stocks are worth making if you have the time.

cooking from this book

I hope the recipes in this book will inspire you and that you will get a lot of pleasure from cooking and eating Spanish dishes. Here are some general suggestions for achieving good results.

- Always buy good ingredients, the best you can afford—very fresh fish, good meat, and, if possible, free-range organic chickens and eggs.

- Use sea salt and freshly ground black pepper, unsalted butter, and whole milk.

- Buy unwaxed lemons when you will be using the grated zest or strips of peel.

- Wash your vegetables and fruits. I wash and rub my chickens with lemon juice— a measure of hygiene learnt in Egypt—but now I hear that there is no need even to wash them, as any bacteria would die after a good time in a hot oven.

- Cooking is about pleasure, about pleasing yourself and pleasing others. You have to like what you cook. When you follow these recipes, you must also follow your instincts and use your good sense. When you cook, you have to look and touch and smell, and you have to adjust seasonings and flavorings to your own taste. The time needed to fry a chopped onion, for example, varies depending on its size, the type and amount of oil, the size of the pan and whether it is heavy or light, and the heat. You have to decide how soft you like it and how golden. What is low heat for you might be medium-low for someone else. If your tomatoes are tasteless or too acidic, you will need to add a little more sugar. The heads of garlic that you get might be bigger than the one I get, so use as much as you like.

- Ovens vary, and their heat is not always accurate. Cooking time also depends on whether a dish was cold from the refrigerator when it went in. So look in the oven and take the food out a little before time or leave it in the oven for a little longer if necessary.

- Spanish cooking does not have strict rules like French haute cuisine. In Spain, everyone feels they can have their own way of doing things—and so should you. You will acquire skills by cooking the same recipe over again, but do always feel that if a dish tastes good to you, that is how it should be.

chicken stock

{ caldo de pollo }

I often roast chicken because it is my grandchildren's favorite food, and then I use the carcasses and juices to make a delicious and easy stock that can be used for clear soups, rice, and vegetable dishes. The secret is slow simmering—and don't add salt until the end or the stock may be too salty after it is much reduced.

MAKES ABOUT 1 QUART

Carcass of 1 roast chicken, with the wings, plus the juices and fat from the roasting pan

1 carrot, sliced

1 onion, halved

1 celery stalk, sliced

2 bay leaves

A small bunch of parsley stems

4 to 5 black peppercorns

About 8 cups water

Salt

Put the chicken, including the juices and fat from the roasting pan, vegetables, bay leaves, parsley stems, and peppercorns in a large pot, add water to cover, and bring to a boil. Skim off any scum, reduce the heat, and simmer very gently for 3 hours, skimming every so often and adding water as necessary to keep the carcass covered.

Strain the stock through a fine sieve into a saucepan and simmer until reduced to about 4 cups. Add salt to taste.

Let the stock cool before ladling off the fat that floats to the top, or remove it with paper towels (see Note). Or chill the stock in the refrigerator and lift off the fat when it has solidified. The stock can be refrigerated for 2 to 3 days.

Note: Do not remove the fat if you are using the stock to cook rice or a bean soup or stew.

fish stock

{ caldo de pescado }

It is not easy for us to find the types of rockfish that give fish stocks in Spain their fabulous flavor, but we can make a more than acceptable one. Use only the bones and heads of fresh white fish (most fishmongers give them away); do not use oily fish such as salmon, sardines, tuna, or bluefish, as they would give the stock an unpleasant taste. The best results I have had were with crustacean shells—shrimp, lobster, or crab shells—and with whole tiny shrimps.

MAKES ABOUT 1 QUART

2 pounds fish bones and heads,
    or 3 cups raw shrimp shells,
    or 2 cups tiny raw shrimp

1 onion, sliced

1 large carrot, sliced

1 celery stalk, sliced

1 leek, sliced

A small bunch of parsley stems

5 cups water

Salt

Wash the fish bones and heads or crustacean shells thoroughly under cold running water. Put all the ingredients except the salt in a large pot and bring to a boil. Skim off any scum, then reduce the heat and simmer for 20 to 25 minutes (any longer, and the flavor of the stock becomes unpleasantly bitter). Strain through a fine sieve, return to the pot, and reduce a little for a more intense flavor. Add salt to taste.

to clean and cook clams

Discard any clams that are chipped or broken, as well as those that are too heavy (which will be full of mud) or too light (which will be dead). Also discard any open clams that do not close when they are tapped on the sink or dipped in ice-cold water; they should be tightly closed. Store them in a cool place where they can breathe, such as in a bowl in the refrigerator, covered with damp paper towels.

Clam farms put the clams through a process that washes them, but you may still need to scrub them with a stiff brush in a bowl of cold water. Some sand will remain inside; leave the clams in fresh cold water for 20 minutes—as they breathe, they will push the sand out of their shells. Then lift them out and rinse in one or two more changes of water.

To steam clams open, put them in a large pan with just a finger of water, cover the pan, and set over high heat. Take off the heat as soon as they open, about 3 to 5 minutes—they will be cooked. Discard any that remain closed.

Alternatively, you can cook clams on a flat griddle over high heat.

to clean and cook mussels

Proceed as for clams, but pull off the beards when you scrub the mussels.

to clean and prepare squid

Pull the head of each squid away from the body and discard the soft innards that come out with it. Discard the insides of the body: the ink sac, if any, the icicle-shaped translucent bone, and any soft innards. Leave the tentacles in their bunches, but remove the eyes and the small round beak (cartilage) at the base of the tentacles by cutting them away with a sharp knife just below the eyes (be careful so that ink doesn't squirt out at you from the eyes). Rinse thoroughly.

to roast bell peppers

Choose fleshy bell peppers. Put them on a sheet of foil on a baking sheet and roast them in a preheated 375°F oven for 30 to 45 minutes, turning them once, until they feel soft when you press them and their skins blister and begin to blacken.

Alternatively, cook them under the broiler, about 3½ inches from the heat, or on an outdoor grill, turning them occasionally, until their skins are blistered and blackened all over.

Put them immediately in a plastic bag and twist it closed, or put them in a pan with a tight-fitting lid, and let stand for 10 to 15 minutes—this helps to loosen the skins further. When the peppers are cool enough to handle, peel them and remove the cores and seeds. You can keep the juices—strain them to remove the seeds—to use as part of a dressing.

Note: Canned or jarred *piquillo* peppers (see page 151), which have been roasted, peeled, and seeded, can be used as an alternative to roasted bell peppers in many recipes.

to prepare dried *ñora* peppers

There are several ways of preparing these sweet peppers for cooking:

- Simmer them in water to cover for 10 minutes, then leave for 30 minutes and drain. Remove the stems and seeds and mash or blend them to a paste.

- Pour boiling water over them in a little bowl and let soak for 30 minutes. Cut the peppers open, discard the stems and seeds, and scrape the flesh from the skin with a spoon.

- Remove the stems and seeds, and fry them in a little oil.

Alternatives: If *ñora* peppers are not available, you can use *pimentón dulce,* or sweet Spanish paprika (*ñoras* or other similarly sweet dried peppers are used to make *pimentón dulce*). The thick red *choricero* paste sold in jars, made from the soaked pulp of dried *choricero* peppers, can also be used.

to peel tomatoes

In Jaén, in Andalusia, my friend Manolo peels tomatoes with a knife or turns them briefly under the broiler and then pulls off the skin. In Catalonia, they cut them crosswise in half, grate the flesh through the large holes of a box grater until they get to the skin, holding on to the skin to keep it intact, then discard the skin. This way, the tomatoes are already very finely chopped.

Here is how I peel tomatoes: I pierce them with the point of a knife in two or three places, put them in a bowl, and pour enough boiling water over them to cover them entirely. I leave them for 3 to 4 minutes, until I can see the skin crack where I have pierced it, then quickly drain them and pull off the skin when they are cool enough to handle.

to prepare small artichoke hearts

With a small sharp knife, cut off the stem of each artichoke. Cut away or pull off the tough outer leaves until you are left with the pale inner leaves. Slice off the tough ends of these, then open them with your fingers and scoop out the prickly inner choke with a pointed spoon. Drop the artichokes into water acidulated with lemon juice or vinegar to prevent the exposed parts from darkening.

to prepare artichoke bottoms

Use medium or large globe artichokes. Cut off the stem of each one at the base. Pull off the outer leaves and, with a small sharp knife, trim the base, cutting around it at an angle to remove all the leaves. Scrape away the chokes. Drop the artichokes into acidulated water (see above) as you go.

to peel and chop garlic

To peel and chop garlic cloves, cut off the root ends, lay them on a board, place the flat side of a large knife on top, and thump it with your fist. The papery skin will come away easily. Then chop with an up-and-down motion, holding the tip of the knife against the board.

three ways to crush or mash garlic to a paste

1. It is common in Spain to pound garlic and a little salt in a mortar with a pestle and then mash it to a paste with a rotating motion.
2. A way popular with chefs here is to put the peeled cloves on a wooden board and roughly chop them with a large knife. Then add a pinch of coarse salt and crush the garlic with the flat side of the knife, holding it at a 45-degree angle and pressing down with force. Continue with a back-and-forth motion until you have a paste.
3. Use a garlic press. Some cooks don't use them because they are difficult to wash—but it is easy with a nail brush.

to make fresh bread crumbs

Fresh bread crumbs are used in stuffings and meatballs. Use a loaf of dense country-style white bread, a day old or older. Cut away the crust and cut it into thick slices, then into pieces. Turn them into crumbs in the food processor. They will keep for a long time in a plastic bag in the refrigerator.

to peel chestnuts

Make a long slit on the flat side of each chestnut and put them under the grill, turning them over to brown both sides, then peel them while still hot.

DRESSINGS AND SAUCES

{ aliños y salsas }

Within Spain, Catalonia and the rest of the Mediterranean coast are considered the "zone of sauces." These are cold sauces and dressings that make fabulous accompaniments to all kinds of dishes, especially meats, fish, and cooked vegetables. With their subtle or strong flavors, they lift the poached or grilled foods people like to make in hot weather. They also create an exciting spectacle for the table, in little bowls to pass around, with their bright or gentle colors. Green salads are simply dressed with extra virgin olive oil and lemon juice or vinegar, but other more substantial salads are dressed with *vinagretas* embellished with tiny bits of chopped ingredients, such as tomatoes, herbs, capers, olives, onions, and hard-boiled eggs. *Vinagretas* are less vinegary than the vinaigrettes of France. Spain now produces a wide variety of superb extra virgin olive oils (see page 229) and wine and cider vinegars (see page 136) that are well worth discovering.

The people of the island of Minorca claim that mayonnaise was born there, in the port town of Mahón, and that the original name was *mahonesa*. Their story is that it was adopted by the French after the Duke of Richelieu took the city from the English in 1756. The sauce has a huge importance in the cooking of Mediterranean Spain, where it appears in many guises and accompanies many dishes. Mayonnaise and *alioli* are eaten in other countries around the Mediterranean, but those of Catalonia are especially notable—there are different and unique versions, such as *alioli* with quinces, apples, or pears, or with honey. *Romesco,* Catalonia's iconic nut sauce, named after a pepper, was born in Tarragona at the end of the nineteenth century, when it was called *salsa vermeilla* (red sauce)—it is orangy red from tomato and the red pepper.

The Canary Islands in the Atlantic off the coast of Morocco have a range of splendid sauces, several of them based on garlic, herbs, peppers, and olive oil, which they call *mojos.*

In Catalonia and northern Spain, there are a number of Spanish versions of béchamel sauce, several of which you will find within the recipes of this book, such as in ham croquettes (page 166), eggplant with béchamel and cheese (page 253), and fish and seafood in a saffron béchamel (page 337). The most symbolic Spanish sauce, though, is the fresh tomato sauce that became the signature tune of Mediterranean cooking (see page 145).

spanish vinaigrette

{ *vinagreta* }

You can also add capers, chopped olives, cucumbers, and/or other chopped herbs to this vinagreta. *My friend Lourdes March uses it with boiled vegetables and grilled or poached fish.*

SERVES 6

7 tablespoons extra virgin olive oil

2 tablespoons white or red wine vinegar or sherry vinegar, or 2 tablespoons sherry vinegar plus 1 tablespoon Pedro Ximénez or other sweet wine

Salt and pepper

1 tablespoon chopped flat-leaf parsley

1 small red or sweet white onion, finely chopped

1 hard-boiled egg, finely chopped

Using a fork, beat the oil and vinegar with salt and pepper to taste in a small bowl, then add the remaining ingredients and mix well.

VARIATIONS

- Use the juice of ½ to 1 lemon, or to taste, instead of the vinegar and add the grated zest of ½ lemon.

- Add 1 tablespoon chopped herbs, such as tarragon and oregano.

vinegar

{ *vinagre* }

Spain produces a variety of vinegars. There are red *crianza* vinegars aged in oak barrels and varietal ones made from single grapes, such as Cabernet Sauvignon, Chardonnay, and Garnacha. Makers of cava, the sparkling white wine, produce a white wine vinegar, and cider houses (*sidrerías*) in northern Spain make cider vinegar. Pedro Ximénez is a sweet dark vinegar. A pale yellow sweet-and-sour Moscatel vinegar is made from Muscat grapes.

Vinagre de Jerez, made from sherry in wineries in Jerez, can be young or aged for at least six months in casks of American oak. Vinagre de Jerez Reserva is aged from two to five years. Some of these are amber colored, some are very dark, some are strong and powerful (you need only a drop), and some are sweet. There are vinegars whose *solera* (the aging process; see page 115) is a hundred years old that can be drunk straight.

Apart from being used in dressings for salads, vinegar is used in Spain in cold soups such as gazpacho and *ajo blanco;* in hot soups and in stews to cut the richness of pork fat; in *escabeche;* and to deglaze the juices in a roasting pan or sauté pan. An aged sherry vinegar mixed with a sweet Pedro Ximénez makes a sublime caramel-colored sweet-and-sour pan sauce.

tomato vinaigrette

{ vinagreta de tomate —catalonia }

*This Catalan dressing (*vinagreta de tomàquet *in Catalan) is wonderful with fish and seafood salads and with boiled or steamed vegetables.*

SERVES 4 TO 6

4 to 5 tablespoons extra virgin olive oil

1 tablespoon red or white wine vinegar or fresh lemon juice

Salt and pepper

2 medium tomatoes or 1 large tomato (about 5 ounces), diced or chopped (see variations)

With a fork, beat the oil with the vinegar or lemon and salt and pepper to taste in a small bowl, then mix in the tomatoes.

VARIATIONS

- For a sweet-and-sour Andalusian version, add 2 teaspoons honey.

- Add 4 finely chopped scallions or 1 crushed garlic clove plus 1 tablespoon chopped flat-leaf parsley.

- Instead of chopping the tomatoes, cut them crosswise in half and grate them on the large holes of a vegetable grater, leaving the skin behind.

tomato and onion dressing

{ salmorreta — valencia }

Serve this simple fresh dressing with grilled or poached fish. The secret, according to my friend Lourdes March, is cooking the tomato under the broiler so that it acquires a roasted flavor, but in my view it is equally good if the tomato is raw (quarter it and leave the skin on).

SERVES 4 TO 6

1 large tomato

½ large sweet onion,
    cut into pieces

1 to 3 garlic cloves,
    crushed to a paste (optional)

½ red chile pepper, deseeded and
    finely chopped

2 tablespoons chopped flat-leaf
    parsley

6 tablespoons extra virgin olive oil

2 tablespoons red or white wine
    vinegar

Salt and pepper

Roast the tomato under the broiler, turning it a few times for about 20 minutes, until it softens a little and the skin comes off easily. Pull off the skin, quarter the tomato, and remove the core.

Blend the onion, garlic, chile, and parsley to a paste in a food processor, then add the tomato, oil, and vinegar and blend thoroughly. Season to taste with salt and pepper.

green sauce with parsley

{ mojo de perejil—canary islands }

In the Canary Islands, they make a series of wonderful garlicky sauces called mojos. *You will find two more accompanying the "wrinkly" potatoes in the chapter on vegetables (page 279). This one is a beautiful fresh-tasting accompaniment to fish and meat and keeps well in the refrigerator. It is difficult to give an exact measure for the amount of parsley to buy, as the thickness and weight of stems in bunches vary, but the large bunch I used weighed 6 ounces with stems, and the leaves filled a little more than a cup.*

SERVES 8 OR MORE

A little more than 1 cup flat-leaf
  parsley leaves

5 garlic cloves, crushed to a paste

¾ cup mild extra virgin olive oil

2 to 3 tablespoons white or
  red wine vinegar

Salt

Blend all the ingredients to a creamy consistency in a blender or food processor.

mayonnaise

{ mayonesa—mediterranean spain }

It is worth learning to make mayonnaise and acquiring confidence, as it is the basis of many other sauces. The eggs should be fresh, and if possible free-range and organic. All the ingredients, including the egg yolks, must be at room temperature. And the bowl should be warmed with hot water and thoroughly dried. All this is very important.

Extra virgin olive oil makes mayonnaise too strong for most tastes. Chefs I spoke to in Spain used sunflower oil or refined (not extra virgin) olive oil, or a mixture of sunflower and extra virgin olive oil. I use a mix of two-thirds sunflower oil and one-third mild extra virgin olive oil. But you should do it to your taste.

SERVES 4 TO 6

2 large egg yolks

¼ teaspoon salt, or a pinch more

2 to 4 teaspoons fresh lemon juice or white wine vinegar

1¼ cups oil—about 2:1 parts sunflower and mild extra virgin olive oil

Take the eggs out of the fridge well before you need them—it will help keep them from curdling.

Put the yolks in a warm mixing bowl, add the salt and lemon juice or vinegar, and beat with a whisk or an electric mixer for about 1 minute, until smooth. Add the oil (first the sunflower oil, then the olive oil) to the egg yolks drop by drop at first, whisking constantly. When the mixture begins to thicken (within a minute, after you've added about 4 tablespoons oil), you can add the oil a little faster, but not too fast, as the egg yolks can only absorb the oil at a certain pace. Allow the oil to be absorbed each time before adding more. When all the oil is incorporated and you have a thick, smooth, firm mayonnaise, taste and add a little more salt and/or lemon or vinegar if necessary, whisking all the time. If it is too thick, whisk in a tablespoon of water.

Put the mayonnaise, covered, in the fridge until you are ready to use it. It keeps well for a few days.

Note: Mayonnaise can suddenly curdle, meaning it will become quite thin and the oil will start to separate and float to the top. If this should happen, you can easily save it: Put another room-temperature egg yolk into another warm bowl, then start whisking in the curdled mayonnaise, a teaspoon at a time to begin with, until it re-emulsifies.

garlic mayonnaise

{ alioli con huevo — catalonia,

valencia, balearic islands }

This creamy white, garlicky sauce is a traditional accompaniment for fish and seafood, grilled meats and poultry, rice, pasta, and potatoes. There are many versions of alioli. *A tiny bit of honey is sometimes added, as are mashed tomatoes and purees of salt cod or of fruits such as quinces, apples, and pears; see the variations that follow.*

The Catalan spelling is allioli. *It means "garlic and oil," and the original sauce is an emulsion of garlic and oil alone. Garlic is mashed to a paste in a large mortar, then extra virgin olive oil is added drop by drop, and stirred in vigorously with the pestle—always in the same direction—until it becomes a stiff sauce. Unless you are an old hand at it, it is not easy to succeed. All the people I asked in Spain said that these days nearly everyone makes it with egg yolks, like the Provençal aioli, a garlicky mayonnaise. It is easier to make, and most Spaniards have come to prefer a lighter flavor. One chef does not use raw garlic—she roasts or blanches it first so that the flavor is more gentle. The Catalan writer and gastronome Josep Pla famously said that the original* alioli *was to the milder garlic mayonnaise what "a lion is to a pet cat." Now, it seems, even Catalans have come to love cats.*

SERVES 4 TO 6

2 large egg yolks

3 to 5 garlic cloves

1¼ cups oil—about 2:1 parts
    sunflower and mild
    extra virgin olive oil

Follow the *mayonesa* recipe, but do not add the lemon or vinegar. Add 3 to 5 garlic cloves, depending on the size and how garlicky you want the *alioli* to be. Cut the cloves open and remove the green shoots in the middle, then pound and mash them to a paste with a pinch of salt (see page 130). Add the paste to the egg yolks in the bowl and proceed as on page 140.

VARIATIONS

- For *alioli* made with store-bought mayonnaise, put 1 cup mayonnaise in a bowl and beat in 3 to 4 garlic cloves that have been crushed to a paste and 3 tablespoons extra virgin olive oil. Add salt if necessary. This makes 1⅓ cups. Be sure to use good-quality mayonnaise for this. It is cheating, but then many Spaniards cheat.

- For Catalan *allioli de mel* (with honey), add ½ tablespoon, or to taste, of orange blossom or another aromatic honey.

quince alioli

{ alioli de membrillo — catalonia }

I make this gently fruity aromatic sauce with store-bought mayonnaise. If the quince has little flavor, it is best to use apples or pears as in the variations.

MAKES ABOUT 2 CUPS

1 small quince
  (about 8 to 10 ounces)

3 to 4 garlic cloves,
  crushed to a paste

¼ cup extra virgin olive oil

One 14-ounce jar (about 1¾ cups)
  good-quality store-bought
  mayonnaise

Put the whole quince in a saucepan of water to cover and cook over low heat until it is very soft. Depending on its ripeness and quality, it can take 30 minutes or quite a bit longer, but watch that it does not fall apart. (If you have other food in the oven, you can roast it instead.)

Cut the quince in half and remove the core. Then peel it and mash the flesh to a smooth puree in a small bowl. Beat the garlic and olive oil into the puree with a fork, then beat in the mayonnaise thoroughly.

VARIATIONS

- For an apple *alioli*, use 2 tart apples, such as Granny Smiths (about 10 ounces total), instead of the quince. Peel and core them and cut them into thick slices. Put them in a small pan with about ⅓ cup of water and cook with the lid on over low heat for about 15 minutes, until they are soft; they will cook in the steam. Remove the lid and cook over medium heat to evaporate any remaining liquid. Mash or blend the apples to a puree and proceed as above.

- For a pear *alioli*, use 2 pears instead of apples.

almond, dried pepper, and tomato sauce

{ *salsa de romesco—catalonia* }

Romesco is the star at festivals in the ancient Roman port of Tarragona, where it was born, and there are competitions for the best one. It is made with ground almonds or hazelnuts or a mixture of the two, tomatoes, and, traditionally, a mild, sweet dried pepper called romesco *or* cuerno de cabra *(goat's horn), because of its curved shape. But these peppers are very expensive, so it is the small, round, wine-red Murcian* ñoras *(*nyoras *in Catalan), also mild and sweet but with a taste of their own, that are more widely used today.*

The sauce is simple, but there are many versions. Ingredients can be toasted or fried, and proportions vary so that it is more or less thick. A variant of romesco is the salsa salvitjada *(*salvitxada *in Catalan) served at* calçotadas—*the famous Catalan festivals where* calçots, *a type of scallion grown in a special way to become extra fat, are grilled in the open. And the sauce is* xató *when it is used as a dressing for a mixed salad of escarole with salt cod or anchovies called* xatonada. *In the beginning, fishermen made romesco with bread, while people in the country-side who grew almond trees made it with almonds.*

Ñora peppers have just started to appear in specialty shops outside Spain, and you can buy them online. You can substitute other mild dried peppers, and you can also make a perfect romesco simply using* pimentón dulce *(sweet paprika), which is the same dried pepper in pow-dered form.*

Everybody has their own way of making romesco sauce, and nowadays chefs improvise with all kinds of ingredients. The archive collection of the Institut Català de la Cuina (Catalan Culinary Institute) gives this very basic recipe, and the variations are a matter of "do you fry or toast and do you add fried bread or not." The quantities are to your taste.

Romesco traditionally accompanies fish, vegetables, or meat. Use it for grilled prawns and fish and for roasted vegetables including large shallots or medium onions.

>>>

2 *ñora* peppers or other mild dried peppers (see the variations)

½ head garlic, in its skin

6 small tomatoes (about 1 pound)

½ cup whole blanched almonds or hazelnuts, or ¼ cup of each, lightly toasted

2 to 3 teaspoons wine vinegar, or to taste

¼ cup extra virgin olive oil, or to taste

Salt

Cut the peppers open and remove the seeds and stems. Soak in boiling water for at least 30 minutes, or until soft; drain.

Meanwhile, put the garlic and tomatoes on a foil-lined baking sheet and cook under a hot broiler until the garlic feels soft and the tomato skins come off easily, 20 to 25 minutes. Pull the skins off the tomatoes, and squeeze the garlic out of the skins.

Blend the drained pepper, the garlic, and the almonds and/or hazelnuts to a paste in a food processor. Add the tomatoes and blend to a light rough cream (the nuts give it a rough texture). Add the vinegar, oil, and salt to taste.

VARIATIONS

- Instead of roasting them, fry the peeled garlic cloves, cut in half if large, in a little oil until soft and lightly brown; and fry the nuts in oil instead of toasting them.

- For a thicker version, add a slice of fried white bread.

- For a thinner sauce, use more olive oil.

- Use 2 teaspoons *pimentón dulce* (or sweet paprika) instead of the dried peppers.

- Add a piece of fresh hot chile or a pinch of cayenne to the processor along with the garlic.

tomato sauce

{ salsa de tomate }

The great Catalan writer Josep Pla complained that the rural world had an ancestral obsession with putting tomatoes into everything, and that they invaded every food and made Spanish cooking monotonous. Tomato sauce is certainly ubiquitous, and there are many versions. A commercial version called tomate frito *is a pureed tomato sauce with a flavor of fried onions and garlic. (Pla also called garlic the "Genghis Khan of the kitchen.") This is a basic tomato sauce without garlic. According to old Spanish tradition, it should be made with enough oil to cover the bottom of the skillet by almost half an inch, but I have seen it made with much less oil, and that is how I prefer it.*

SERVES 6

1 large sweet onion, finely chopped

¼ cup olive oil

2 pounds ripe tomatoes, peeled and chopped

2 teaspoons sugar, or to taste

Salt

Fry the onion in the oil in a large skillet over low heat, stirring often, until it is soft and beginning to color. Add the tomatoes and cook for about 25 minutes, or until the sauce is reduced and jammy, stirring occasionally so that it doesn't stick and burn. Add the sugar and salt to taste toward the end, as their flavor will get concentrated when the sauce is reduced.

VARIATIONS

- Traditionally the sauce was passed through a food mill; now you can use an immersion blender if you want to blend it right in the pan.

- Add 2 to 3 finely chopped garlic cloves to the onion.

- The Riojan *fritada* version of this tomato sauce made with green peppers is now popular throughout Spain. It accompanies meat, fish, and vegetables, which are sometimes cooked in the sauce. Add 1 cored, seeded, and diced green pepper to the onion when it is slightly soft.

- For the Catalan *salsa de tomàquet*, omit the onion. Cook the tomatoes in a little oil until they are reduced to a thick sauce, then add salt and, if necessary, a little sugar. Some versions add a little chopped garlic at the start.

TAPAS

One of the pleasures of life in Spain is the tapas tradition: visiting bars and meeting friends before lunch or dinner for a glass of wine, beer, or sherry accompanied by little plates of food. You meet, chat, and have fun. My friend Alicia remembers the time, not long ago, when women would always hurry back home after church to prepare lunch while the men got together at the local bars, drinking and eating tapas as they waited for the meal to be ready. Now the women go too.

Some large cities, like Seville, San Sebastián, Barcelona, and Madrid, have "tapas zones"—streets packed with *tabernas*, also known as *tascas*, where you eat and drink standing up, and bars and *cervecerías* (beer houses), where you can sit down. It is usual to go on a *tapeo*, or tapas crawl, from one place to another. The bars get so full that patrons spill out into the street. In Basque cities, the tradition of moving from bar to bar with friends is called *poteo*, from *potes*, the heavy wineglasses once used in the area, or *txikiteo*, after the coin that once represented the price of a glass of wine.

Tapas originated in Andalusia, and Seville is the capital where the custom is supposed to have begun. The word *tapa*, which means "cover" or "lid," is said to have referred in early days to the slice of ham or cheese that was laid across the tops of narrow sherry glasses, *cañas*, by innkeepers when they handed them to stagecoach drivers—to keep them sober and, it is said, to keep insects out of the wine. The salty tidbits also kept clients thirsty.

The world of tapas is complex. The simplest are the *tentempiés*—nibbles such as olives, fried almonds, fried peppers *del Padrón*, bits of cheese, slices of *jamón*, sausages. Standard tapas include potato omelets cut into little squares, croquettes, baby eels sizzling with garlic, fried squid, prawns fried with garlic and parsley, small deep-fried fish, grilled blood sausage, chorizo cooked in wine or cider, boiled octopus with potatoes, meatballs in a sauce, mushrooms with garlic, oxtail stew, chickpea and bean stews, and *empanadillas* (little savory pies). Some bars specialize in certain kinds of tapas, and every region has its own specialties: in the north, it is seafood; on the Mediterranean coast, it is vegetables; and in the south, it is deep-fried fish.

Raciones are larger portions of tapas that are meant to be shared. *Cazuelas* are stews and foods with a sauce that are served in small earthenware dishes of the same name. In the north of Spain, there are *pinchos*, bite-size offerings on toothpicks. If the toothpicks are wrapped in colored paper, looking like the barbed batons used in bullfights, the tapas are called *banderillas*. *Montaditos* are canapés on toast or savory tartlets. Some bars in San Sebastián and Bilbao offer *modern* creative upscale *pinchos* (*pintxos* in Basque) such as tartlets of foie gras with sautéed apple and Calvados, fried Moroccan *brik* (little savory parcels wrapped in paper-thin pastry), and blood sausage *caramelos* wrapped like bonbons in filo pastry. It is usual for *pinchos* to be set out on the bar counter for patrons to help themselves.

Tapas belong to the world of bars and taverns—people do not serve tapas at home. Instead, they offer *aperitivos* before a meal. These consist of foods that don't need to be cooked. In the past, during long formal meals both at home and in elegant restaurants, platters of cured ham, sausage, olives, and other foods were left on the table throughout the meal for people to nibble on between courses. Today the usual appetizers offered with drinks before a meal, apart from bread with tomato (page 154), which is de rigueur in Catalonia and Majorca, are platters of charcuterie with bread. Platters of preserved fish and seafood or a few cheeses are sometimes offered. There may also be olives, fried salted almonds, and pickled vegetables in brine or in olive oil. It has become fashionable in America to entertain casually by serving four or five cooked dishes laid out like tapas on the table at the same time. You will find inspiration for these throughout the book, but if you want to follow the Spanish way, here are some ideas to inspire you.

a platter of charcuterie

Choose two or more of the following. Take them out of the fridge about 20 minutes before they are to be eaten, so they can come to room temperature. Serve them with a sliced baguette or other good bread. For more about the cured hams, see page 163; for more about sausages, see page 492.

- *Jamón serrano*—the name means ham "from the mountain," or *sierra*, where it is dry, cool, and breezy enough to air-cure it.

- *Jamón ibérico* is dry-cured ham from the native Iberian black pig. The quality *de bellota*, produced from pigs fed on acorns, or *bellotas* (see page 164), is the best in the world, with a fabulous taste and aroma and a soft, silky texture. It is extremely expensive.

- *Lomo* is dry-cured pork loin, trimmed of fat, marinated in a paste of garlic, *pimentón*, oregano, and olive oil, and encased in a sausage skin.

- *Chorizo* is a brownish-red cured pork sausage flavored with garlic and *pimentón*. There are infinite regional variations: thin or fat, sweet or spicy, coarse or smooth-textured, air-dried or smoked, cured or semi-cured. Choose one that does not need to be cooked.

- *Salchichón* is a hard salami-type sausage. The best are produced around the Catalan town of Vic, seasoned simply with salt and pepper. There is also one with wine and one with local black truffles. *Fuet,* from Vic, is a thin small *salchichón.*

- *Sobrasada,* a specialty of Majorca, is a very soft red paste of pork and fat, flavored with garlic and *pimentón,* encased in a sausage skin. It can be spread on slices of dense bread and is good accompanied by *membrillo* (quince paste), *fruta confitada* (crystallized fruit), or sliced figs or grapes. When it is good it is great, but I have tried some that are not worth eating.

- *Cecina,* salt-cured beef with lacy fat, has a strong meaty flavor. Once the food of the rural poor, when it was made from the meat of cattle, goats, horses, or mules that had died on the farm, it is now a great delicacy, produced exclusively from high-quality beef. It should be sliced paper-thin.

a platter of seafood in cans or jars or cured seafood

Choose two or more of the following:

- Mussels (*mejillones*), clams (*almejas*), or cockles (*berberechos*). Serve them with a dribble of extra virgin olive oil and, if you like, a drop of vinegar.

- *Boquerones,* white anchovies marinated in vinegar and packed in olive oil. Tuna (*atún*), anchovy fillets (*anchoas*), mackerel (*caballas*), or sardines (*sardinas*) in olive oil.

- Baby eels/elvers (*angulas*), prawns (*gambas*), or baby squid (*chipirones*). Heat a generous amount of olive oil in a pan until it is sizzling hot. Add some crushed garlic and the elvers, prawns, or tiny squid and quickly heat through, turning them once. If you like, add a sprinkling of flat-leaf parsley and serve sizzling hot.

- Octopus (*pulpo*). Serve it with a dribble of extra virgin olive oil and a dusting of sweet or spicy *pimentón* (or paprika).

- *Mojama*, the salt-cured and dried tuna loin. Cut it into thin slices and serve it with a dribble of extra virgin olive oil, accompanied by chopped tomatoes.

- *Botarga* (or *bottarga*), the salt-cured, pressed and dried roe of gray mullet (*huevas de mujol*) or of tuna (*huevas de atún*). (It is very expensive.) Serve very thinly sliced on bread or toast with a dribble of extra virgin olive oil and perhaps a drop of lemon juice.

---

other spanish delicacies in cans or jars that can go with the platters above

- Snails (*caracoles*). Serve sizzling hot in olive oil with crushed garlic and finely chopped flat-leaf parsley.

- Olives. There are many choices—see page 153.

- Capers (*alcaparras*) and caper berries (*alcaparrones*). Those preserved in brine need to be rinsed. Those preserved in salt must be soaked in water for at least 1 hour; change the water three times.

- *Piquillo* peppers (*pimientos del piquillo*). These roasted and peeled small pointy red peppers are good cut into ribbons and mixed with chopped anchovy fillets. Or stuff the peppers with crabmeat or tuna mashed with olive oil and lemon juice.

- Small green mildly spicy chilies, *Ibarrako piparrak*, also called *guindillas de Ibarra*, from Ibarra in the Basque Country.

- Soft fat white asparagus (*esparragos blancos*) from Navarre (they are white because they are grown covered by soil). These are delicious with mayonnaise. Tiny baby artichokes (*alcachofas*), wild mushrooms, cardoons (*cardos*), borage stems (*borraja*), chard (*acelgas*), green garlic shoots (*ajetes*), small white beans (*alubias*), and / or baby fava beans (*habitas*). All these need only a dribble of olive oil and a little salt or a *vinagreta* (page 135).

suggestions for canapés for a drinks party

Some tapas bars specialize in bite-sized finger foods—*pinchos*, served on toothpicks, and *montaditos*, or canapés.

Quimet i Quimet, a little bar and wine shop in Barcelona known as the culinary king of canned foods, serves enchanting combinations of preserved products on small pieces of toasted brioche-type bread or in little tartlet shells, such as mussels with caviar on a bed of tomato confit; anchovies, capers, and chopped cornichons on olive paste; and Manchego cheese with fig paste. Make up your own marriages of little delicacies and embellish them with a dollop of mayonnaise, olive paste, or salsa verde, or a trickle of extra virgin olive oil and a sprinkling of chopped flat-leaf parsley.

---

cooked *morcilla* and chorizo

- *Morcilla* is blood sausage. (Be sure you use a Spanish one, as others are quite different.) Cut it into good slices and panfry them in olive oil, or grill or broil them for about 3 minutes on each side. Accompany them, if you like, with apple slices sautéed in butter or olive oil.

- Chorizos that are semi-cured need to be cooked. They can simply be cut into pieces and fried in just a drop of oil, as they release their own fat. Or they can be cooked whole or cut into slices in a pan of red or white wine, sherry, or cider for 20 to 30 minutes. They can also be wrapped in foil with a little wine or cider and baked in the oven. Or grill them, then pour brandy or rum over them and set it alight: these are called *chorizos al infierno* (hell). *Chistorra*, a long chorizo-type sausage from Navarre and the Basque Country, is grilled or fried or cooked in wine or cider.

olives

{ *aceitunas* }

Spain is a leading producer and exporter of olives, mostly green olives. On the tree, olives are first yellowish, then pale green, and they gradually turn from pink to purple to black as they ripen. Spaniards prefer them when they are still green and their oils have not fully developed. Following the Sevillian style of processing, they are washed, soaked in an alkaline solution for about five to seven hours to remove their bitterness, and then washed again and left to ferment in brine. Every region has its own traditional way of flavoring its olives, with garlic and herbs such as bay leaves, thyme, oregano, and/or fennel. In Andalusia, they add a little vinegar. The production of mechanically pitted olives stuffed with anchovies, almonds, or roasted red pepper and canned or jarred is a major industry.

The Manzanilla olives from Seville and southwest Spain are the most popular green table olives. Large and oval, pale green with tiny white dots, they are aromatic and mildly bitter. A whole family of olives—the black Cacereña, the green and black Carrasqueña, the Aloreña, the Campo Real, the Morona—is descended from the Manzanilla, either through adaptation to different environments or through grafting. Other popular green olives are the Gordal Sevillana, as big as a quail egg, fleshy, and sweet, and the fruity and aromatic Hojiblanca of Córdoba. The small, very tasty, violet-green Arbequina is a specialty of Catalonia. Among the less common olives are the green Cornicabra of La Mancha; the almost black, oily, strong-tasting, and bitter Empeltre from Aragon; the sweet, oily Cuquillo of Valencia; the aromatic Picual of Jaén; and the Verdial of Huelva, which is darkened by oxidation.

catalan tomato bread

{ pan con tomate—catalonia }

*In Catalonia, I was offered bread rubbed with tomato (*pa amb tomàquet*) at all times of day, especially for breakfast and before a meal. The orthodox way is for the bread to be rubbed on both sides with tomato, but I always got bread rubbed on one side only, which seems the best way, as then you do not need a knife and fork—you can just pick it up with your hands.*

FOR EACH SERVING

2 thick slices good
    country-style bread

½ large ripe tomato

Mild extra virgin olive oil

Salt

Toast the bread lightly. Rub one side of each toast with the cut side of the tomato so that the bread is well imbibed with the juices. Drizzle a little olive oil on top and sprinkle with a little salt.

VARIATIONS

- *Pan con tomate* can serve as the base for slices of cured ham or sausage, Pyrenean cheese, or preserved anchovies or sardines.

- A Majorcan version, called *pamboli amb tomàtiga,* is topped with black olives and capers.

- An Andalusian way is to blend the tomatoes to a puree in the food processor and spread it on thickly. You can blend them without peeling, although the local cooks will tell you to peel them. They cut away the peel with a knife.

cheese

{ *queso* }

It is not the custom in Spain to serve a cheese platter after dinner, but some top restaurants have now started to offer tastings of artisanal cheeses at the end of the meal. Cheese is eaten as a *tapa* or an *aperitivo* with wine, beer, or cider. It is sometimes accompanied by the quince paste called *membrillo* or *codoñate*, and it is also served with grapes.

Enric Canut, the author of *Los 100 Quesos Españoles* (*The 100 Cheeses of Spain*), who, with others, rescued, helped to rejuvenate, and continues to champion traditional artisanal cheeses, gave our little group of British journalists in Barcelona a tasting of cheeses and a fascinating talk. The huge variety of cheeses in Spain is due to centuries-old customs and lifestyles—shepherds made cheese when they moved with their sheep and when they spent a lot of time alone with their goats in the mountains—and to the great diversity of *comarcas* (*terroirs*).

Sheep's- and goat's-milk cheeses are still the most common. The harsh climate of the vast semi-arid plains of the interior suits the foraging habits of sheep, while goats are happy even in rocky mountainous areas. Cow's-milk cheeses are produced only in the wet northern areas, which have green pastures, and in Minorca, where Friesian cows were brought over from England during a period of English occupation. What is peculiar to Spain is the blending of two and sometimes three types of milk in a single cheese.

In 1960, when Spain's economy was suffering under Franco's government, a decree was issued requiring cheese producers to process a minimum of 10,000 liters of milk per day. Cheese counters soon filled with industrially processed cheeses, and most of the artisanal ones became illegal. After 1984, when the decree was repealed, artisan cheese makers could sell their craft again. It is only in the last twenty years that many great artisan cheeses have become available outside their regions, and some have earned a *Denominación de Origen* (DO) label. A few are becoming known abroad. You will find more about these in the chapters on the individual regions.

The lovely Spanish custom of eating cheese with honey is worth adopting. In the past, honey vendors on mules would go from village to village with barrels of cheese, honey, and *arrope*, a sweet syrup made from boiled-down grape juice. They were called *mieleros* (*miel* means "honey") and wore special clothes. Now they travel around in vans, but they still wear the same type of clothes. *Mel y mató* is a popular Catalan dessert of *mató*, a fresh unsalted cheese made from cow's or goat's milk (you can substitute fresh ricotta, although it won't be as good) with a dribble of honey (*mel* in Catalan). In other parts of Spain, a traditional shepherd's snack of fried or grilled cheese—a medium-young Manchego, a sheep's-milk cheese, or a goat's-milk cheese will do—with scented honey has become popular (see page 161). An old custom is to put cubes of Manchego in a jar with extra virgin olive oil and dried herbs such as thyme, marjoram, or rosemary and let it marinate for a month.

sweet roasted tomatoes

{ *tomate confitado — andalusia* }

These tomatoes have a deliciously intense flavor. Serve them hot or cold as an appetizer or an accompaniment to meat or fish. It is best to use plum tomatoes. Although the tomatoes take a long time to cook, you can cook them well ahead, even days in advance, as they keep well in the refrigerator.

SERVES 6 TO 8

12 ripe but firm plum tomatoes

Olive oil

3 tablespoons sugar

Salt and pepper

Cut the tomatoes in half through their stem end and remove any hard green bits. Place a piece of foil on a baking sheet and brush it with olive oil. Arrange the tomatoes cut side up on it. Sprinkle with the sugar and salt and pepper and give each one a little dribble of olive oil. Bake in an oven preheated to 275°F for 3½ to 4 hours, until shriveled and shrunken.

salt cod fritters

{ buñuelos de bacalao }

I tried several versions of these fritters, some with the fish mixed with a batter of flour and water or flour and milk, some just with potatoes and egg. These are fluffy and slightly moist. You may be able to buy desalted salt cod, vacuum-packed or frozen. If not, make these with fresh cod.

**MAKES ABOUT 23
SMALL FRITTERS**

1 to 2 baking potatoes (about
    9 ounces), peeled and quartered

½ pound desalted bacalao
    (salt cod; see page 338),
    or skinless fresh cod fillet

Salt and pepper

2 large eggs, lightly beaten

2 garlic cloves, crushed to a paste

2 tablespoons all-purpose flour

½ teaspoon baking powder

4 to 5 tablespoons beer

2 tablespoons finely chopped
    flat-leaf parsley

Olive or sunflower oil for
    deep-frying

Boil the potatoes in salted water until soft; drain and mash them.

Remove any skin and bones from the desalted salt cod, if using it, and poach it for 2 minutes, then drain. When it is cool enough to handle, finely shred it with your fingers. If you are using fresh cod, simply poach it for 3 minutes, or until it just begins to flake.

Mix the fish and potatoes in a bowl, and add salt and pepper to taste; even salt cod might need some salt if it has been desalted excessively. Add the eggs, garlic, flour, baking powder, beer, and parsley and beat very well. Leave the creamy paste to rest for about 2 hours covered in the fridge.

Heat ½ inch of oil in a wide skillet until a small piece of bread sizzles when you drop it in but does not brown too quickly. Drop small portions—about 2 tablespoons worth—of the cod mixture into the oil, in batches, and cook over medium heat until the little fritters are golden, turning them over once. Drain on paper towels.

bread

{ *pan* }

Bread has always been an important part of a Spanish meal. I telephoned Rosa Tovar, who wrote a book about bread, to find out more about it. In Cervantes's *Don Quixote*, there is a scene where Sancho Panza says that he has seen Dulcinea eating bread that was "not very white," which implied that she was poor. Today the most common traditional breads are big round loaves made with wheat flour. The *libreta* (from *libra*, pound, because it weighs one pound) is the finest and whitest. The *hogaza*, a country bread, is rougher and not quite white. Bakeries (*panaderías*) and markets in Galicia, Asturias, and the Basque Country sell corn and rye breads, as well as their usual wheat loaves. Catalans and others in Mediterranean Spain eat dense, coarse-textured round loaves cut in thick slices, which they sprinkle with extra virgin olive oil or rub with tomatoes. But the most common bread now throughout the whole of Spain is a crusty baguette-style loaf that is a bit denser than a French baguette. It is called *pistola* in Madrid and *pan de barra* elsewhere.

fried goat cheese with honey

{ queso de cabra frito con miel—andalusia }

The combination of a slightly salty goat cheese and fragrant honey is surprising and exquisite. I first tasted it in Andalusia, but it is also served elsewhere. Use a firm goat's-milk cheese.

SERVES 4

Fine matzo meal

2 large egg yolks

4 slices firm goat cheese,
about ⅓ inch thick

2 tablespoons olive oil for frying

A pot of orange blossom or other
fragrant honey to pass around

Put a good layer of matzo meal on a plate. Lightly beat the egg yolks in a shallow soup plate.

Working in batches, turn the slices of cheese in the egg yolks, using your fingers to cover them well and being careful not to break the slices. Lay the cheese on top of the matzo meal and sprinkle with more matzo meal so that the slices are well covered.

Fry the slices in medium-hot oil in a nonstick skillet, turning them over very carefully with a spatula, until golden on both sides, about 1 to 2 minutes on each side. Lift them out and serve them immediately. Pass the honey around for people to help themselves to a heaping teaspoonful or so.

cured ham

{ jamón }

Pig rearing in Spain is as old as antiquity. It's always been part of the rural tradition, providing meat for the peasantry, and adding flavor to their otherwise bland food. After the pig was slaughtered, the meat was dry-cured to last. Peasant families kept at least one pig and then lived off the ham and sausages for an entire year. The hams were usually heavily salted to make sure that they would not spoil. The best ones were made in the mountain areas, where the cold, dry climate was ideal for curing. The hams were hung to dry on rooftops and in attics with open windows. In rainy regions, hams were dried in the kitchen fireplace, where they acquired a smoky flavor.

In the nineteenth century, pork products were still seen as the food of the rural poor and the lower classes; the upper classes found them "indigestible." It was only during the Spanish Civil War, when food was scarce, that they came to appreciate cured pork products.

Jamón, dry-cured ham, is now the best-loved food in Spain and the undisputed king of Spanish gastronomy. Consumption of cured ham and sausages has grown at a huge rate over the last two decades, triggering a rush of investment in modern production facilities with state-of-the-art technology that the European Union has helped to fund. Today Spain is the world's leading producer of dry-cured pork.

Two broad types of cured ham are made from different breeds of pigs. The most typical, which accounts for about eighty percent of all cured ham in Spain, is *jamón serrano—serrano* means "from the *sierra,"* or mountain range. These hams are produced from the meat of the European white (really pink) pig, which is mostly crossbred commercially. The other, *jamón ibérico,* from the meat of the indigenous black Ibérico pig, amounts to only about ten percent of the total production. White pigs are quicker to fatten and more fertile, producing bigger litters than black pigs, which makes their hams cheaper.

Jamón serrano is now commercially produced all over Spain. Conditions similar to those of the *sierras* are created with technology that controls temperature, humidity, and airflow in curing plants. The raw hams—the best come from the hind legs—are covered with a layer of moist coarse sea salt for about two weeks, during which time much of their moisture is drawn out and the meat acquires some saltiness. The salt is washed off and the hams are hung on racks to rest for a month. Then they are moved to *secaderos*, or drying rooms, where the temperature is gradually raised and the humidity lowered in a drying and aging process that lasts about seven months; it causes the fat to infiltrate the muscle and a distinctive flavor and aroma to develop. Finally, the hams are transferred to the cooler *bodegas* (caves) to mature for another two months. The best *serrano* hams come from Trevélez in the Sierra Nevada and from Teruel in Aragon.

Jamón ibérico comes from the Ibérico pig, which lives mostly in southwest Spain. It is descended from a Mediterranean wild boar and has a dark skin, long legs, and a pointy snout. It is also known as *pata negra* (black foot). Ibérico products are protected by four *Denominaciones de Origen* (DO). One controls the breeds: there are one-hundred-percent-pure Ibérico pigs and crossbreeds that are at least seventy-five percent Ibérico. Three other grades are determined by the hogs' feed. The finest is *de bellota*, indicating that the pigs are allowed to roam free in a *dehesa*, or *terroir*, of holm and cork oak tree woodlands to feed on acorns (*bellotas*) for a few months before slaughter. The next-best quality, *de recebo*, is

produced from pigs that are pastured and fed on a mixture of grain and acorns. The third grade, variously called *de pienso*, *cebo*, and *campo*, is from pigs fed entirely on grain.

The oak *dehesas* are protected natural parks, mainly in the mountains of Andalusia and Extremadura, as well as Salamanca. Year-old pigs are taken there four months before slaughter, when the acorns start to fall—from October on. Ibérico pigs know how to crack open the acorns, eat the insides, and spit out the shells. During this period, they put on a huge amount of weight and the fat infiltrates the muscles. The curing, aging, and maturing of the hams is done according to centuries-old traditions, with the help of the latest technology, and the process takes more than two years. As they age, a particular flora forms on the hams, which is supposed to add to their aroma.

Jamon ibérico de bellota is the jewel in the crown of Spanish charcuterie and one of the great foods of the world. Names such as Jabugo, Aracena, Cáceres, Badajoz, Huelva, Ciudad Real, Seville, Córdoba, and Guijuelo are associated with the best ham. Believe me, it is irresistible—dark red, soft, and silky, marbled with fat, and with a delicious, lingering sweet, barely salty flavor and a beautiful aroma. Apparently an added advantage is that the fat resulting from the acorn diet increases the meat's level of oleic acid, the unsaturated fat that lowers "bad" cholesterol and raises "good" cholesterol. It is the best ham I have ever eaten. On one occasion when I had the chance to eat as much as I liked, I honestly could not stop eating it.

The ham should be eaten on its own accompanied only by bread and wine. It is at its best carved off the bone in extra-thin slices down the length of the bone and served at room temperature on a warm plate. For carving, the entire ham is mounted horizontally on a wooden stand, with the trotter held in a clamp, and a long, thin, flexible knife is used to slice the meat.

Ibérico pigs have very small litters; the breeding, handling, and curing are labor-intensive; and the process is seasonal. That is why the hams are so expensive. Because a whole ham would last too long for today's small households, and young people do not have the skill to slice by hand, the majority of these hams are sold boned and vacuum-packed, ready for slicing by machine in a shop, or packaged in slices. To experience the best texture, flavor, and aroma of vacuum-packed slices, take them out of the fridge at least twenty minutes before you are ready to eat.

ham croquettes

{ croquetas de jamón }

*Different types of croquettes—made with ham, chicken, salt cod, and seafood, or even cheese—
are served in every tapas bar and restaurant. The one with ham is the* reina de las croquetas, *the
queen of croquettes. I tried many different recipes that were very elaborate and difficult; this one is
extremely simple and works perfectly well. It is creamy inside with a good strong flavor.*

*Angelita García de Paredes, a Franciscan missionary nun in a convent in Seville (see page 214),
gave me the recipe. She makes the béchamel in a particular way, and it is thicker than in other*
croqueta *recipes. When the batter is chilled, it firms quite a bit, making it easier to shape, and
when it is fried, it becomes creamy inside with a thick crisp crust. You can prepare the* croquetas
for frying the day before and keep them in the refrigerator.

MAKES ABOUT 30 *CROQUETAS*

6 tablespoons (¾ stick) unsalted
    butter

1 medium large onion, finely
    chopped

7 ounces sliced *jamón serrano* or
    prosciutto, finely chopped (in
    the food processor if you like)

Pinch of nutmeg

3 cups whole milk

1 cup all-purpose flour

Salt if necessary

Fine matzo meal or fine dry bread
    crumbs

Medium matzo meal or dry bread
    crumbs

2 large eggs

Sunflower or olive oil for
    deep-frying

Melt the butter in a large saucepan over low heat and
gently sauté the onion until it is soft. Add the ham and
cook, stirring, for a minute or so. Stir in the nutmeg and
1½ cups of the milk and bring to a boil.

With an electric mixer, beat the flour with the remaining 1½ cups milk in a bowl until any lumps have disappeared. Pour into the pan, stirring vigorously, and cook,
stirring constantly, for 8 to 10 minutes, until the béchamel
is a thick paste that comes away from the bottom of the
pan. Add salt if necessary—it may not need it because the
ham is salty. Scrape into a bowl, cover with plastic wrap,
and chill for at least 2 hours, or overnight.

To make the *croquetas,* cover a large plate with plenty of
fine matzo meal or bread crumbs and a second plate with
medium matzo meal or bread crumbs. Beat the eggs lightly
in a soup plate.

Most Spanish cooks use two large spoons greased with
oil to shape the *croquetas* into ovals; Angelita uses a pastry bag to squeeze out tubular pieces. But you may find it
easier, as I do, to take lumps of the béchamel paste the size
of a walnut and roll them into balls between the palms of

your hands. You can rub your hands in oil to keep the paste from sticking. Drop the *croquetas* as you make them, in batches, into the fine matzo meal or bread crumbs. Roll the balls in the fine matzo meal to cover them well all over, then roll them in the beaten egg and then in the medium matzo meal. This will give them a nice thick crust.

Heat the oil in a deep skillet until it is only medium hot (until a piece of bread dropped in sizzles immediately but does not turn dark quickly). Lower the *croquetas* into the oil, in batches, and fry over medium-low heat for 5 to 6 minutes, until lightly browned, turning them once. (If the oil is too hot, they will burst.) Lift them out with a slotted spoon and drain on paper towels. They are best eaten right away, but they can be reheated in the oven.

VARIATION

For *croquetas de bacalao*, with salt cod, or for *croquetas* with fresh cod, boil 7 ounces desalted salt cod (see *Bacalao*, page 338) or fresh cod fillets for 3 to 5 minutes in water or milk, until the flesh begins to flake when you cut into it, then drain. When the cod is cool enough to handle, remove and discard any skin or bones and shred the flesh with your fingers, then mix it into the hot béchamel. Add salt to taste, a pinch of nutmeg, and some finely chopped flat-leaf parsley, and proceed as above.

SOUPS

{ sopas }

Soups were the comfort everyday foods of the peasants and shepherds. Those based on fried bread and garlic sustained the shepherds of central Spain. The cold gazpachos of Andalusia were made by laborers in the fields. Spain's fish soups are said to be fishermen's soups, although I doubt that fishermen put in the wine and brandy that go in most of them today. You will find these in the chapter on fish, because they are substantial and can be served as the main meal.

Potajes, hearty vegetable soups with beans, chickpeas, and lentils, are from the Castilian interior and the mountains of northern Spain. They were everyday meals that turned into festive stews when *jamón,* chorizo, *morcilla* (blood sausage), pig's ears and trotters, and spareribs were added. You will find some of these celebratory dishes in the chapter on bean and chickpea stews.

Delicate broths resulting from a *cocido,* a pot of boiled meats (page 498), with added vermicelli or rice, bits of ham or chicken, and chopped hard-boiled eggs, are popular everywhere. And cream of vegetable soups are found in parts of Spain where they have luscious vegetable gardens.

Cold Tomato Soup with Chopped Hard-Boiled Eggs and Ham, page 172.　　**169**

gazpacho

{ *gazpacho rojo de tomates—andalusia* }

This famous cold soup is the best thing to have on a hot day in the summer when tomatoes are sweet and full of flavor. It was born in the province of Seville, where tomatoes were first grown in Spain. It was the meal agricultural laborers made when they worked in vegetable gardens. They brought with them a dornillo *(large wooden mortar and pestle) to pound the ingredients that grew on the spot; some olive oil, salt, and vinegar to dress them; and bread. Years ago, when I went to Spain to do a BBC TV series, the gazpacho was pounded by hand in the old way and the result was like a finely chopped and mashed salad of tomatoes, cucumbers, and peppers. Nowadays gazpachos are pureed in a food processor or blender.*

There are many versions of gazpacho. My friend Manolo (see page 173) makes his with just tomatoes, garlic, and his own olive oil and vinegar. He makes quantities that he pours into large Coca-Cola bottles so that he and his sister and any friends who happen to be around can have some at any time of the day. I have used the following recipe for years. I do not peel the tomatoes—if you use a food processor, the skin all but disappears. You can make this hours in advance, even the day before. If it is a very hot day, add an ice cube to each bowl when you serve. The garnish is optional. In Andalusia, they use green bell pepper because they like the peppery taste, but I like it with the sweeter red pepper.

1 thick slice white bread,
    crusts removed

2¼ pounds ripe plum tomatoes

1 red or green bell pepper, cored,
    seeded, and cut into 4 pieces

2 to 3 garlic cloves,
    crushed to a paste

2 tablespoons sherry vinegar or
    wine vinegar, or more to taste

6 tablespoons extra virgin olive oil,
    or to taste

Salt and pepper to taste

1 teaspoon sugar, or more to taste

FOR THE OPTIONAL GARNISH

½ cucumber, finely diced

½ red onion or 4 scallions,
    finely chopped

½ red or green bell pepper,
    finely diced

1 to 2 slices of white bread,
    cut into small cubes and lightly
    toasted

Dry the slice of bread under the broiler, without browning it, turning it once. Break it up into pieces.

Quarter the tomatoes and remove the hard white bits at the stem end.

Blend the bell pepper to a paste in a food processor. Add the rest of the soup ingredients and blend to a light cream. Add a little cold water if necessary to thin the gazpacho—about ½ to ⅔ cup. Pour into a serving bowl and chill in the refrigerator, covered with plastic wrap, for at least an hour or for up to a day.

Check the seasoning, and serve the gazpacho in soup bowls, accompanied, if you like, by the garnishes. Pass them around, each type in a separate little plate or in four piles in a large serving plate.

VARIATION

Add ½ cucumber, peeled and cut into pieces, and blend with the rest of the ingredients.

cold tomato soup with chopped hard-boiled eggs and ham

{ salmorejo cordobés con huevos y jamón — andalusia }

Salmorejo, *a thick, dense, creamy version of gazpacho made with more bread, is a Córdoban specialty. It is served at all flamenco* cantes *(festivals) and at other festive occasions, together with a glass of wine. You find it in every bar and tavern in Córdoba, topped with chopped hard-boiled eggs and bits of* jamón serrano. *Some recipes have as much bread as tomatoes. In Antequera and the area south of Córdoba, they call it* porra *and add bits of canned tuna with the garnish. In Córdoba, I had a discussion about peeling the tomatoes with a group of people on a bus. Most said you have to peel them, but a couple who had food processors admitted they did not. I do not peel them.*

SERVES 4

5 to 7 ounces (6 to 7 slices) crustless white bread, preferably day-old

1½ pounds tomatoes

2 to 4 garlic cloves, crushed

½ cup extra virgin olive oil

1½ to 2 tablespoons red or white wine vinegar

½ to ¾ teaspoon superfine sugar

Salt and pepper

FOR THE GARNISH

2 tablespoons extra virgin olive oil

2 hard-boiled eggs, chopped

¼ pound sliced *jamón serrano* or prosciutto, chopped

Put the bread in a food processor and process it into fine crumbs. Pour into a serving bowl.

Cut the tomatoes into quarters and remove the hard white bits at the stem ends. Blend in the food processor until the peel shows only as tiny specks of red in the pink cream. Add the rest of the ingredients except the bread crumbs, tasting to decide how much garlic and vinegar you want, and blend well. Add the bread crumbs and mix well. Refrigerate until chilled.

Serve in bowls, garnished with a sprinkling of the olive oil and the chopped eggs and ham.

VARIATION

For a *porra* that was once the mainstay of the peasantry of Antequera, blend 1 pound bread, soaked in water, with 1 pound tomatoes, quartered; 1 green bell pepper, cored, seeded, and cut into 4 pieces; 4 to 5 crushed garlic cloves; ¾ cup extra virgin olive oil; and salt and red or white wine vinegar to taste. Garnish with chopped eggs and *jamón* and flaked canned tuna.

MANOLO EL SERENO

{ *peasant life on an andalusian* cortijo }

Manuel Ruiz López, known as Manolo el Sereno, worked on an estate in Jaén, Andalusia, from the age of seven until he was drafted into the Spanish Army of Africa. His ten siblings were all placed in work when they were seven years old, the girls with families in town. Manolo worked with the mules. In Castile and northern Spain, oxen were the main work animals, but in Andalusia, it was mules. In the winter, Manolo and the other resident laborers slept with the mules, horses, and donkeys to keep warm.

Manolo returned from the army to find work as the *sereno,* night watchman, in Frailes, a village in the province of Jaén, deep in the interior of the Sierra Sur. Today his official job is to measure the rainfall and the height of the river. He is also the president of El Dornillo, the gastronomic guild of the province (a *dornillo* is the huge wooden mortar that peasants took to the fields to make gazpacho).

When the travel writer Michael Jacobs (see page 390) chaired a panel on the Moorish influence on food in Spain at the Hay Festival in Granada in 2008, Manolo and a group of friends arrived with olive branches, vegetables, fruits, herbs, and kitchen utensils—an entire installation—as props for our panel. Then Manolo took me and my copanelist Alicia Ríos back to stay in his house, which he shared with his disabled sister (she has, sadly, passed away since then). Downstairs it was a modest but comfortable traditional village house; upstairs, it was grand. In the living room, there was a shelf filled with books all inscribed to Manolo. Later he told us that he never formally learned to read and write and had depended on people he met to teach him. He now writes with the most beautiful hand, and his greatest joy is giving hospitality to writers. As the days went by, I felt extremely lucky and happy to be a writer on the receiving end of his enormous generosity. I stayed in a room with a super-glamorous en-suite bathroom, where Sara Montiel, a megastar of the 1950s, slept when she came a few years before for the showing of one of her films at the long-abandoned local mini cinema. Her photographs—one with Manolo—are pinned on the walls.

Around the house are fruit and nut trees—apricot, quince, fig, pear, almond, pistachio, chestnut—and a vegetable garden. There are also chickens and rabbits. There is an outdoor space with stone tables and lighting—the kind you might get on a nightclub terrace—where Manolo entertains friends. In another part of the yard is a playground for his friends' children.

On many occasions, I sat with Alicia, Manolo, and his sister Carmelita at a little round table covered by a heavy blanket, under which was an electric brazier. I asked him, while we picked at food, what life was like on the *cortijo* when he was growing up. *Cortijos* are the complex of farm buildings around a courtyard that are at the center of the old Andalusian estates. Vegetables and fruit were cultivated in an area around the *cortijo*. Part of the estate was given over to wheat, barley, and other crops such as lentils, beans, and chickpeas. Some of it was grazing land for sheep and goats. Horses and fighting bulls were also raised on some estates. *Haciendas* were grander versions of the *cortijo*, combining a farm and a stately country house.

Landowners had overseers to manage their estates, and *caseras*, housekeepers, to look after the house. They rented parts of their land to *labradores*, peasant farmers; the poorest, most arid, and most distant bits of the estate went to *peletrines*, small sharecroppers. While the women cultivated their gardens and kept chickens, the men got work plowing with their own draught animals on the estate. Day laborers, *braceros* or *jornaleros*, who lived in villages and towns, sometimes far away, were employed on a seasonal basis, and during harvest time, they were put up on the estate. As many as a hundred men slept on the floor of a long barn. Entire families were put up in tiny outbuildings. The women and children picked chickpeas, beans, and lentils. Manolo was one of those who lived permanently on the estate as servants. Although his main job was tending the mules, sometimes he helped the woman who cooked for the laborers. They made gazpacho, *cocidos*, *potajes*, and *ajo blanco* (with bean flour, not almonds). Every morning the men made *migas* with leftover bread. When the *jornaleros* were working in the fields, they organized feasts. They danced and sang and played flamenco music (some *jornaleros* were Gypsies).

Manolo is the most popular man in Frailes because during his time as a watchman, he saw everything and knew everything that was going on, and he helped everyone (he says he stopped burglars from breaking into houses but let them off). He also worked at the pharmacy with his sister and assisted the doctor, giving injections. Despite being eighty, he is still immensely strong. I thought he was short when I first met him, but most people in Frailes are smaller still. He took us to visit friends of his. The Rosales had *arroz caldoso* with rabbit and chicken simmering in the fireplace and invited us to eat. José Velasco Serrano, who used to work as a cook during the season in Palma de Majorca and now caters for hundreds of people at festivals, talked about recipes of the Balearic Islands. Beautiful Mercedes, a social worker who lives in a large new house with her teacher husband and two children, talked nostalgically of the times when she moved with her parents and siblings around the country to do the harvest, and went grape picking for the *vendimias* in La Mancha and in France.

Now the land in this part of Andalusia has been given over entirely to olive trees. It has been divided many times among children of landowning families. Over the last two to three decades, many of the small sharecroppers and old laborers bought bits of land from the old estates from their savings earned abroad. They bring their olives to a cooperative for pressing. Their oil represents sixty percent of the production of Jaén, the bit of Spain that is the greatest producer of olive oil in the world. Many *cortijos* have been sold to English people, as have the little peasant houses and the barns where the work animals used to sleep. Manolo says Spain has changed more in the last twenty-five years than it had in centuries. While the young eat fast foods and sandwiches, older people still cook the things that were part of the old life. Many of Manolo's recipes and those of his friends are in this book.

cold almond soup with garlic and grapes

{ *ajo blanco con uvas — andalusia* }

*This splendid soup (*ajo blanco *means "white garlic"), also called* gazpacho blanco, *is widely popular. Proportions vary — some cooks use as much bread as almonds. The soup is usually served with peeled and seeded muscat grapes or, less commonly, with small melon balls. You can use any sweet grapes. I used to peel them, but I stopped doing that and found the result just as pleasing. You can make the soup hours ahead or even the day before.*

In Frailes, I helped Manolo (see page 173) make enough soup to fill a dozen super-size Coca-Cola bottles for a celebration of the Jaén Gastronomic Association. We made it with almonds picked from his trees, which we soaked overnight and then peeled (they popped out easily from the skin). We used the oil from his olives, which he presses in an old converted washing machine — the smallest oil press in Spain. At the feast in Valdepeñas de Jaén, our ajo blanco *was served in small plastic glasses followed by charcuterie, a great paella, and pastries. A band of old men played flamenco and people got up and sang of the pain and the joys of those who worked on the land.*

SERVES 6

9 ounces (about 2¼ cups)
    blanched whole almonds

3 ounces (about 3 slices) crustless
    white bread soaked in water for
    a few minutes, until soggy

3 garlic cloves, or to taste,
    crushed to a paste

½ cup extra virgin olive oil

2 drops — no more — almond
    extract (optional)

About 3 cups cold water

Salt

2 to 3 tablespoons sherry vinegar
    or white wine vinegar, to taste

36 or more seedless white grapes

Grind the almonds very fine in a food processor. Add the bread, garlic, and oil and blend well. Add the almond extract if you like. With the motor running, gradually pour in enough water to give the soup a light creamy consistency. Season to taste with salt and vinegar. Transfer to a bowl, cover with plastic wrap, and chill for at least 2 hours. To serve, ladle the soup into bowls, drizzle with oil, and drop 6 or more grapes into each.

VARIATION

Loli Flores of Seville gave me her recipe for an *ajo blanco de piñones*, made with pine nuts instead of almonds. Grind 8 ounces (1⅔ cups) pine nuts with 2 slices day-old white bread, crusts removed, and 2 crushed garlic cloves in a food processor. Add 6 tablespoons extra virgin olive oil, 2 to 3 tablespoons vinegar, salt to taste, and about 3 cups water and blend to a light creamy consistency. Serve chilled, garnished with muscat or other grapes.

garlic soup

{ s o p a d e a j o — c a s t i l e }

You find versions of sopa de ajo *in Aragon, Extremadura, and Andalusia along the routes that shepherds with their sheep once traveled in search of fresh pastures. Originally the soup consisted only of garlic and bread fried in lard or olive oil, with water poured over. The soup was largely responsible, together with* migas *(see page 476), for the bad image of Spanish food acquired by travelers in the past who encountered platefuls of soggy bread in inns and taverns. In a grander form, with an egg added, garlic soup was on the menus of Madrid cafés frequented by artists, writers, and other bohemians. I never felt like trying it until I saw it on the menu of the restaurant in the elegant boutique hotel Orfila, a small nineteenth-century palace in Madrid that serves traditional foods in an exquisite modern style; see the variation below.*

SERVES 2

2¼ cups chicken stock or water

2 garlic cloves

2 tablespoons olive oil

1 slice dense white bread or
   ¼ pound baguette, broken
   into small pieces

½ teaspoon *pimentón dulce*
   (or sweet paprika)

Salt

2 large eggs

Bring the stock or water to a boil in a saucepan. Meanwhile, lightly brown the garlic in the oil in another saucepan over medium-high heat. Add the pieces of bread and stir vigorously for a few seconds, until lightly browned. Stir in the *pimentón* (or paprika), then pour in the boiling stock or water. Add a little salt and simmer for 5 minutes.

Just before serving, break the eggs into the soup and simmer briefly until the whites set. Ladle into bowls, putting an egg in each bowl.

VARIATIONS

• Fry some chopped *jamón* with the garlic.

• For a sophisticated Madrid version, use fine bread crumbs and only the yolks of the eggs. They should still be almost liquid.

• For a Málagan version, add a chopped peeled tomato.

• For Seville's version, add ¼ teaspoon cumin.

chicken broth with
sherry and ground almonds

{ consomé al jerez y almendras—andalusia }

Serve this elegant silky soup in cups. Make the chicken stock on page 125, or buy a good-quality one.

SERVES 2

1 cup chicken stock

⅓ cup dry or medium-dry sherry

¼ cup ground almonds

Salt

3 large egg yolks

Bring the stock and sherry to a boil in a saucepan. Stir in the almonds and a little salt, taking into account the saltiness of the stock, and simmer for 2 minutes.

Just before serving, bring the soup back to a simmer. Beat the egg yolks in a small bowl, beat in a ladleful of the broth, and then pour back into the pan, stirring vigorously. Continue to stir for a few seconds over low heat; do not let the soup boil, or the yolks will curdle.

clear broth with ham
and chopped hard-boiled eggs
{ sopa de picadillo—andalusia }

The caldo, *or broth (the literal meaning of* caldo *is "hot"), is considered by some the best part of a big* cocido *(page 498). According to a Spanish proverb,* "El caldo de gallina, a los muertos resucita" *(Broth from an old hen can resuscitate the dead). Another saying is that* "caldo sin jamón ni gallina no vale una sardina" *(broth without ham and a hen is not worth a sardine). Nowadays in Spain people can buy good broths or stock, and so can we—either make the chicken stock on page 125, or buy a good-quality beef or chicken stock. Do not use bouillon cubes for this soup.*

Vermicelli is more often used than rice. Crush vermicelli into small pieces with your hands. Sherry gives the broth an intriguing flavor; see the variation below.

SERVES 3 TO 4

4½ cups beef or chicken stock

½ cup crushed vermicelli or
⅓ cup rice

Salt

4 slices *jamón serrano* or
prosciutto, finely chopped

1 hard-boiled egg, finely chopped

Bring the stock to a boil in a saucepan. Drop in the broken vermicelli or rice and simmer until tender, just a few minutes for vermicelli, about 18 minutes for rice. Add a little salt and stir in the ham.

Ladle into bowls and pass the chopped egg for everyone to sprinkle some on.

VARIATION
Add ½ cup amontillado sherry with the vermicelli, or if using rice, add it a few minutes before the rice is done.

potato, cabbage, and bean soup

{ *caldo gallego — galicia* }

Galicians make this soup with what they grow in their vegetable patch—beans, potatoes, cabbage, and turnip greens. (They feed the turnips to their pigs.) Their cabbages grow very big and long. They use them young and small for this soup; when the cabbages get big and tough, they boil them for their animals. Smoked salt pork fat, called unto, *gives the soup a distinctive flavor. Because the climate was too wet to cure the pork in the attics of their little farmsteads, peasant farmers cured it in their fireplaces, and that is why a smoky flavor is one of the characteristics of many Galician dishes. Cristobo Ramírez, a journalist on* La Voz de Galicia *who writes about gastronomy, said that when he was young, they ate* caldo *every day. These days, grand versions are made with chicken, veal, or ham broths rather than the traditional water. I loved the one I ate at the Hostal de las Reyes Católicos, the* parador *opposite the great Cathedral of Santiago de Compostela that has lodged pilgrims since 1499.*

SERVES 6

8 cups chicken or ham stock
   (or 8 to 9 cups water plus
   2 bouillon cubes, and a ham
   bone if you have one)

8 thin slices smoked bacon

2 baking potatoes, peeled and cut
   into 1-inch pieces

½ pound green cabbage leaves,
   spring greens, or turnip tops,
   cut into 2 to 3 pieces each

Salt and pepper

One 14-ounce can small white beans

Put the stock, bacon, potatoes, and cabbage, greens, or turnip tops in a large saucepan and bring to a boil. Add salt and pepper to taste and simmer gently, covered, over low heat for 30 minutes, or until the vegetables are tender.

Add the beans and cook for 5 minutes more.

lentil soup

{ potaje de lentejas — castile and león }

Most regions of central Spain have a lentil soup that can become a substantial stew if chorizo is added. They use green or brown lentils of different sizes. Lentils do not need to be soaked in advance, but, depending on their provenance, they may need checking for tiny stones, and you do need to rinse them in cold water.

SERVES 6 TO 8

2 cups large green or brown lentils,
    picked over and rinsed

¼ cup olive oil

1 large onion, chopped

1 large carrot, chopped

3 garlic cloves, finely chopped

3 ounces sliced *jamón serrano* or
    prosciutto, chopped

1 large beefsteak tomato or
    2 medium tomatoes,
    peeled and chopped

1 teaspoon *pimentón dulce*
    (or sweet paprika)

Pepper

4 cups beef or chicken stock
    (or 4 cups water plus
    2 bouillon cubes)

½ cup amontillado sherry (optional)

3 bay leaves

Salt

2 tablespoons red or
    white wine vinegar

Put the lentils in a medium pot with 5 cups of water and bring to a boil. Remove any foam and simmer for 15 minutes.

Meanwhile, heat the oil in a large skillet. Add the onion and carrot and cook over low heat, stirring often, until the onion is soft and golden. Add the garlic and *jamón* or prosciutto and stir well, then add the tomatoes, *pimentón* (or paprika), and pepper, and cook until the tomatoes soften.

Pour this into the pan with the lentils, add the stock (or water and bouillon cubes), sherry, bay leaves, and salt, and cook, covered, for 20 to 30 minutes, until the lentils and vegetables are soft. Add water if necessary— you need a good amount of liquid. Stir in the vinegar just before serving.

VARIATIONS

- For a substantial main dish, add 8 thick slices cooked chorizo and 8 thick slices cooked *morcilla* (Spanish blood sausage) at the end of cooking. To cook these sausages, boil a whole chorizo in water for 20 minutes. Add a whole *morcilla* and cook for 10 minutes. Drain.

- Use a dry white or a sweet Moscatel wine instead of the sherry.

- Just before serving, stir in 1 to 2 garlic cloves crushed with 1 to 2 tablespoons chopped flat-leaf parsley in a mortar (this is called *pesto*).

spinach and chickpea soup

{ potaje de garbanzos y espinacas—castile }

This is a Castilian version of a thick soup that is eaten in many parts of Spain during Lent, when it is known as garbanzos de vigilia *(meaning "chickpeas of abstinence"). During Lent, bits of salt cod are sometimes added; at other times, bits of ham or bacon may go in. It is delicious and satisfying, with a rich texture and an intriguing flavor that comes from the mashed paste of fried bread, garlic, and spices that is stirred in at the end. It is a complex dish, but not a difficult one.*

These days supermarkets usually sell baby spinach with very thin stems. If you buy spinach at a farmers' market, you will need to pull off the tough stems and wash the leaves carefully.

SERVES 6

3 medium waxy potatoes,
   peeled and cut into quarters

Two 14-ounce cans of chickpeas,
   drained

5½ cups vegetable or chicken stock
   (or 5½ cups water plus 1 bouillon
   cube)

1 pound fresh spinach or
   frozen spinach, defrosted

1 tablespoon red or white wine
   vinegar

Salt

2 hard-boiled eggs

¼ cup olive oil

4 to 5 garlic cloves

2 slices bread, crusts removed

1 teaspoon *pimentón dulce*

1 teaspoon ground cumin

Pinch of pure ground chile powder

Put the potatoes and chickpeas in a large saucepan with about 4 cups of the stock and simmer, covered, for 10 minutes. Add the fresh or frozen spinach and cook, covered, for 5 minutes.

Add the vinegar and some salt and cook for 10 minutes more.

Meanwhile, remove the hard-boiled egg yolks and reserve them. Chop the egg whites and reserve them.

Heat the oil in a small skillet and fry the garlic cloves and bread over medium-high heat, turning them, until golden brown. Watch closely, as they will brown quickly. Drain on paper towels.

Put the garlic and bread in a food processor, add the *pimentón dulce*, cumin, and chile powder, and blend to a fine paste. Add the hard-boiled egg yolks and blend well. Gradually pour in the remaining stock and blend to a thin cream.

Pour this garlic mixture into the soup, stir well, and check the seasoning. Cook for another 10 minutes, then stir in the egg whites. Add some water if necessary to thin the soup a little—but it is meant to be thick.

watercress soup

{ *potaje de berros — canary islands* }

This hearty green soup has a slightly piquant flavor. It is quick to make and also good without beans.

SERVES 6

6½ cups chicken stock
(or 6½ cups water plus
2 bouillon cubes)

1 to 2 baking potatoes
(10 to 14 ounces),
peeled and diced

6 slices rindless bacon,
cut into small pieces

1½ tablespoons olive oil

4 to 5 garlic cloves, chopped

5 ounces watercress, stems
included, coarsely chopped

One 14-ounce can small white
beans, drained

Salt

Bring the chicken stock (or water and bouillon cubes) to a boil in a pot. Throw in the potatoes and cook until tender.

Meanwhile, fry the bacon in the oil in a skillet, turning occasionally until it is cooked but not brown.

Add the garlic and stir until it just begins to color. Add the bacon and garlic to the potatoes, then add the watercress, beans, and some salt. Simmer briefly, until the watercress is soft but still retains a little crunchiness and its color.

cream of asparagus soup

{ crema de espárragos—navarre }

The cultivation of asparagus was introduced by the Arabs in the valley of the river Ebro in Navarre. Nowadays the main production is of the fat all-white asparagus, which are grown covered with earth, without exposure to the sun. But this lovely soup is made with green asparagus that grow naturally.

SERVES 6

1¼ pounds asparagus

1 large baking potato (about 8 ounces), peeled and cut into ¾- to 1-inch cubes

4½ cups chicken stock (or 4½ cups water plus 2 bouillon cubes)

1 to 1½ cups whole milk

Salt

Cut off the asparagus tips and set them aside. Cut the asparagus stalks into 4 pieces each, discarding the hard bottom ends.

Put the potatoes and stock (or water and bouillon cubes) in a large pan, bring to a boil, and cook for 10 to 15 minutes, until the potatoes are tender. Add the asparagus and cook for 10 minutes, or until soft.

Blend the soup to a cream with an immersion blender or in a food processor and return to the pan. Bring to a boil, adding enough milk to thin it to a light cream. Season to taste with salt, drop the asparagus tips into the soup, and cook for 2 to 3 minutes more, until they are tender.

VARIATION

Instead of the 4½ cups stock, use 2¼ cups water and 2¼ cups dry white wine.

vegetable soup with peas

{ puré de guisantes }

Cream of vegetable soups are popular throughout northern Spain and Andalusia. Some people still pass them through a chino, *a conical sieve, with a wooden pestle, but usually they are blended with a hand blender or food processor. I found this soup, based on peas, in* Tía Victoria's Spanish Kitchen, *by Victoria Serra (translated by Elizabeth Gili—see page 261). It has a wonderful, delicate flavor and an appealing texture.*

SERVES 4

½ large onion, chopped

2 tablespoons butter

1 tablespoon olive oil

1 medium baking potato,
    peeled and cut into small pieces

1 or 2 carrots, cut into small pieces

4½ cups chicken or vegetable
    stock (or 4½ cups water plus
    2 bouillon cubes)

1⅔ cups fresh peas or defrosted
    frozen baby peas

Salt

Fresh cream for serving (optional)

Sauté the onion in the butter and oil in a large saucepan, stirring until soft. Add the potato, carrot, and stock (or water and bouillon cubes), stir well, bring to a boil, and simmer, covered, for about 20 minutes, or until the vegetables have softened.

Add the peas and cook until they are tender, 5 to 10 minutes. Blend the soup to a creamy consistency with an immersion blender or in a food processor. Add salt (taking into consideration the saltiness of the stock) and water if you want it thinner.

Pass the cream around, if desired, for people to help themselves.

cream of pumpkin soup

{ crema de calabaza — asturias }

I have collected versions of cream of pumpkin soup from several regions. This recipe is for a soup I tasted in Asturias. Serve with fresh cream. Pass it around for people to help themselves.

SERVES 6

One 2-pound wedge pumpkin or
   1 medium butternut squash

2 carrots

1 leek, white part only

1 onion

5 tablespoons olive oil

4½ cups chicken stock
   (or 4½ cups water plus
   2 bouillon cubes)

Scant 1 tablespoon fresh lemon
   juice, to taste

Salt and pepper

1 teaspoon sugar (optional)

Remove the seeds and fibers from the pumpkin, or halve the squash lengthwise and remove the seeds and fibers. To remove the peel, cut the pumpkin or squash into chunks and slice the peel away with a large heavy knife.

Chop the carrots, leek, and onion (you can do this all together in a food processor). Sauté the vegetables in the oil in a pot over low heat until slightly browned, stirring and turning them often.

Add the pumpkin or squash and enough of the stock or water with the bouillon cubes to just cover, then add the lemon juice, salt and pepper to taste, and, if you like, the sugar. Bring to a simmer and simmer for about 20 minutes, until the pumpkin or squash is soft.

Let the soup cool a little before blending to a cream with an immersion blender or in a food processor. Add the remaining stock or water (plus more water if you like the soup thin). Bring to a boil, stirring, and serve very hot.

VARIATIONS

- A simple alternative is to cook the vegetables together, in the boiling stock, then blend the soup to a cream with the olive oil.

- For another very simple version, put about 1 pound cubed pumpkin or squash in a pan with ¾ cup water, put the lid on, and steam for 20 to 30 minutes, until it is soft. Add 1¼ cups whole milk, season with salt, and bring to a boil. Blend to a cream, adjust the seasoning, add a tiny bit of sugar if you like, and serve with a sprinkling of cinnamon.

EGG DISHES

{ *h u e v o s* }

Peasant families always had eggs because they kept hens, and many people still keep them in their town gardens. They use the eggs to make all kinds of omelets or scramble them. They put hard-boiled eggs, cut into quarters, in salads and stews, or chop them to garnish many dishes. And they thicken sauces with egg yolks. You will find examples in different chapters of the book, but here are a few of the most popular egg dishes.

Potato Omelet, page 196.

potato omelet

{ *tortilla de patatas* }

This is also known as tortilla española *because you find it everywhere, in every region, in tapas bars and in homes. Some like it with potatoes only, some add onions. Some like it moist, others prefer it firm and dry. Some slice the potatoes, some cut them into small dice. I like it with onions and slightly creamy. I will not pretend that it is easy to make. On the contrary, making* tortilla española *is an art that has secrets and tricks and requires skill and intuition. In trying to make a large one, I failed twice, partly because I did not have the strength to turn a tortilla from a heavy skillet onto a large platter without most of the uncooked part spilling out. Finally I called my friend Alicia in despair. She sent me five pages of "secrets" for getting it right.*

For years, I had been making an Arab-style potato omelet, by boiling the potatoes, then slicing them, and finishing the omelet under the broiler. Alicia said, "No! No! No!" to that. She advised me to make two small omelets rather than one large one. She said to use a very light nonstick skillet and a slightly concave pan lid larger than the skillet to catch any liquid running out from the overturned omelet before returning it to the skillet. The shape of the lid is important. I have been told by people that a lid for making tortilla *is something you hand down in the family.*

Through Alicia, I met a young chef who taught at a cooking school; he said that they used sunflower oil because it is cheaper than olive oil. Alicia kept silent, but when we were alone, she said, "No! Anyway, with olive oil you can use it again and again, so it actually works out to be cheaper than other oils."

SERVES 4

½ pound new or waxy potatoes, peeled, cut into ½-inch dice, and patted dry

1¼ cups olive oil, or enough to cover the potatoes

1 medium onion, cut in half and thinly sliced

Salt

6 large eggs

Dry the potatoes on a dish towel or paper towels as soon as you have sliced them. Heat the oil in a nonstick skillet just large enough to contain all the ingredients (I use one with a base 6½ inches in diameter) over medium heat. Add the potatoes and onion, and cook, covered, over low heat (in this way they are stewed rather than fried) for 20 to 30 minutes, until the potatoes are tender when you prick them with the point of a knife. Move them occasionally with a fork and do not let them color. Drain them in a colander, reserving the oil. Spread on paper towels and sprinkle lightly with salt.

Beat the eggs lightly with a fork in a bowl, adding a little salt. Add the potatoes and onions, and mix gently.

Pour 1 tablespoon of the reserved oil back into the skillet and heat until it almost begins to smoke. Pour in the egg and potato mixture, turn down the heat to low, and cook for 3 to 4 minutes, until the eggs set at the bottom; shake the pan occasionally with a gentle circular movement so that the omelet doesn't stick.

Place a slightly concave lid larger than the pan on top of the pan and flip the pan over quickly, inverting the omelet onto the lid. Heat another tablespoon of the oil in the skillet (you can keep the remaining oil to make another omelet) over high heat, then slide the omelet gently into the pan, uncooked side down, lower the heat, and cook for 2 minutes more or until just set.

Run a wooden spoon around the edges of the omelet to give it a tidy look and turn out. Serve warm or at room temperature.

VARIATIONS

- I have put the tortilla under the broiler to finish it instead of turning it over, and I recommend it to those who find it difficult to turn the tortilla over.

- In Navarre, there is a *tortilla al horno,* cooked in the oven. Boiled potatoes cut into little squares are mixed with chopped flat-leaf parsley and beaten eggs and seasoned with salt and pepper, poured into a greased dish, and baked at 325°F for 45 to 60 minutes.

- For a *tortilla de cebolla,* with onions alone, fry 2 large onions halved and thinly sliced in 3 tablespoons oil until golden. Mix them in a bowl with 8 lightly beaten eggs, season with salt and pepper, and proceed as above.

peppers and tomatoes with eggs

{ piperada vasca — basque country }

When I was a girl at boarding school in Paris, we often had the French Basque piperade *for dinner. The fried onions, peppers, and tomatoes with eggs mixed in at the end looked a mess but tasted good. Modern Basque chefs roast the peppers and deconstruct the dish to make it more presentable and appetizing. That means more pans to wash, but it is worth it. And you can more easily double the quantities. Serve it with slices of toasted or fried bread.*

SERVES 2 TO 3

1 large onion, cut into
    ½-inch-thick slices

2 tablespoons olive oil

2 garlic cloves, sliced

1 small chile pepper, seeded
    and chopped

3 medium tomatoes,
    peeled and chopped

½ teaspoon sugar

Salt and pepper

1 red bell pepper, roasted (see
    page 128), peeled, seeded, and
    cut into ½-inch-wide strips

1 green bell pepper, roasted (see
    page 128), peeled, seeded, and
    cut into ½-inch-wide strips

1 tablespoon butter

4 large eggs, lightly beaten

3 or more slices *jamón serrano* or
    prosciutto for garnish (optional)

Fry the onion in the oil in a large skillet over low heat, stirring often, until soft and golden. Add the garlic and chile pepper and stir for a few seconds, then add the tomatoes. Add the sugar and salt and pepper to taste and cook for about 10 minutes, until the tomatoes have collapsed and the liquid has evaporated. Stir in the peppers. (You can do this well in advance and reheat the *piperada* when you are ready to serve.)

Just before serving, melt the butter in a small skillet. Add the eggs, with a little salt. Let the eggs set slightly at the bottom over medium heat before gently turning and stirring them with a wooden spoon or spatula. Turn off the heat while there are still some runny parts—the eggs will continue to cook and will be done by the time you serve. They have to be creamy. Serve the *piperada* with the scrambled eggs on the side and the *jamón*, if using, heated under the broiler.

creamy salt cod omelet

{ tortilla jugosa de bacalao — basque country }

Traditionally, it was the custom to visit cider makers in the hills of the Basque Country to taste the new vintage and stock up on provisions. Today cider houses still open for a few months of the year, from mid-January through the end of April, and offer local dishes in their tavernlike restaurants with communal wooden tables. Hard cider runs out of taps from enormous barrels as people line up to have their glasses replenished. A moist-creamy salt cod omelet is one of the specialties. Basques are crazy about salt cod, but if you can't get salt cod, use hake fillets or fresh cod (for how to make it taste like salt cod, see Bacalao, page 338).

SERVES 2

8 thin scallions or 4 fat ones, trimmed and thinly sliced

½ green bell pepper, chopped

3 tablespoons olive oil

Salt

4½ ounces salt cod, desalted (see Bacalao, page 338)

4 large eggs

1 tablespoon finely chopped flat-leaf parsley

Sauté the scallions and bell pepper in 1 tablespoon of the oil in a 12-inch nonstick skillet, stirring occasionally and adding a little salt, until they are soft.

Put the cod in a pan of cold water and bring it slowly to a boil, then barely simmer for 3 minutes. Lift out the fish, and when it is cool enough to handle, remove any skin and bones and break it up into small pieces. Beat the eggs lightly with a fork in a bowl, adding a little salt. Add the scallions and peppers, fish, and parsley and mix well.

Clean the skillet with paper towels, and pour in the remaining 2 tablespoons oil. Heat over high heat until the oil is almost smoking, then pour in the egg mixture, tilt the pan so that it spreads evenly, and reduce the heat to medium. The trick now is to stir for only a few seconds to allow some of the liquid at the top to reach the bottom of the pan and set. Shake the pan so that the omelet does not stick. In less than a minute, when there is still some liquid in the center, using a spatula, fold one side of the omelet over to the center, then fold the other side to overlap. You will have an elongated oval. Cut the omelet in half—it should be runny in the middle—and slide onto your plates.

VARIATION

Instead of the scallions and green pepper, use a chopped onion and a little chopped chile pepper.

vegetable omelet

{ *tortilla de la huerta—murcia* }

Murcia is known as the vegetable garden of Spain. They grow all kinds of vegetables that turn up in omelets. This one makes a good vegetarian dish.

SERVES 2 TO 3 AS

A STARTER

1 red bell pepper, cored, seeded, and cut into ¾-inch squares

1 small eggplant, cut into ¾-inch dice

¼ cup olive oil

4 garlic cloves, crushed

3 medium tomatoes, peeled and chopped

Salt

4 large eggs

Sauté the bell pepper and eggplant in 3 tablespoons of the oil in a wide skillet, stirring and turning them, for about 12 minutes, until tender. The eggplant will absorb the oil very quickly but will release it again as it becomes soft. Stir in the garlic, and after a few seconds, when it just begins to color, add the tomatoes and some salt. Cook, stirring, until the tomatoes are reduced to a jammy sauce.

Beat the eggs in a bowl with a little salt, then stir in the vegetables. Pour the remaining tablespoon of oil into an 8-inch nonstick skillet. (The pan should be small so that the omelet is thick.) Pour in the egg mixture, and cook gently over medium-low heat until the bottom is set. Put it under the broiler and cook until the top is just set.

VARIATION

You can add some chopped *jamón serrano* or bacon at the beginning when you fry the vegetables.

scrambled eggs with asparagus and shrimp

{ revuelto de espárragos con gambas—andalusia }

This is made with the thin wild asparagus called trigeros, *after the word* trigo, *which means "wheat," because they grow wild in wheat fields. I ate it in a restaurant in Jaén, where they also had scapes in the dish—these are the young tender garlic shoots or stalks of the flowers of the garlic plant (*ajetes *in Spanish) that are harvested just as they begin to grow in a curl, before they straighten into a stem. They are also known as garlic spears. They are discarded by farmers in most of the United States, but you can find them in farmers' markets. Theirs is a mild garlicky taste. Serve the* revuelto *with thin toast.*

SERVES 4

½ pound thin asparagus

¼ cup olive oil

4 garlic shoots (scapes), cut into
    1-inch lengths, or garlic cloves,
    sliced

Salt

½ pound small shrimp, peeled

4 large eggs, lightly beaten

2 tablespoons chopped
    flat-leaf parsley

Cut the asparagus into 1-inch pieces and discard the tough ends. Boil them in salted water until they are soft; drain.

Heat the oil with the garlic in a large skillet over medium heat. Before the garlic begins to color, add the asparagus and sauté for ½ minute, stirring and turning them and adding a little salt. Add the shrimp and cook, turning once, just until they turn pink. Pour in the eggs, add the parsley and a little salt, and stir for a few seconds—the eggs should still be slightly liquid. They will turn creamy off the heat.

VARIATION

Fry 4 slices bacon, coarsely chopped, in the oil in the skillet, then add the garlic and the asparagus and continue as above.

scrambled eggs with wild mushrooms

{ revueltos con setas — basque country }

This simple way of serving wild mushrooms makes a sumptuous first course. The traditional wisdom is to clean off any soil with a soft vegetable brush or to wipe them gently with a damp cloth, but washing them under the cold water tap and shaking off the water does not spoil their taste, and absorbing a little water makes them less porous to oil when they are cooking. Trim off the earthy base of their stems, rinse them, and dry them with a kitchen towel; cut large ones in half or into quarters and leave small ones whole. Be ready to eat, with your toast, when you start scrambling the eggs: they should be moist and creamy.

SERVES 4

¼ cup mild extra virgin olive oil

14 ounces mixed wild mushrooms, such as cèpes (porcini), chanterelles, and morels

Salt and pepper

2 tablespoons unsalted butter

8 large eggs, lightly beaten with a fork

4 slices good country bread, lightly toasted

Heat the oil in a large skillet. Add the mushrooms and cook for 7 to 10 minutes, over high heat to start with, then over medium heat; season with salt and pepper and stir, turning the mushrooms until they are tender and lightly brown in parts.

Meanwhile, heat a large nonstick frying pan. Put in the butter, and when it is almost melted, add the eggs and sprinkle with a little salt. Let the eggs set slightly at the bottom before gently turning and stirring them with a wooden spoon or spatula so that the liquid part at the top runs underneath. Turn off the heat when there are still some runny parts—the eggs will continue to cook and will be done by the time you serve.

To serve, spoon some scrambled eggs onto each toast and cover with the sizzling mushrooms.

VARIATION

You can use cultivated cremini mushrooms in the same way.

SAVORY PIES AND TARTS

{ coques, empanadas, y empanadillas }

Empanadas, *large savory pies, are a symbol of Galicia, while* empanadillas, small turnovers, are a specialty of the Balearic Islands and Valencia. Savory pies feature prominently in medieval Arabic manuscripts of Al-Andalus and are an Arab legacy. Pizza-type open tarts called *coques* (*coca* in the singular), which came into the Spanish repertoire much later, are a specialty of Catalonia, Valencia, and the Balearic Islands. They are made with a bread dough and a variety of pastry doughs made with olive oil and lard or butter, sometimes with eggs, or with puff pastry. All kinds of ingredients are used as toppings and fillings, from vegetables and preserved fish (anchovies, tuna, sardines) to chorizo and other sausages, as well as olives and pine nuts, but hardly ever cheese. Sweet *empanadillas* and *coques* are associated with festivals. Creamy tarts belong to northern Spain.

Little Pies with a Tomato, Pepper, and Tuna Filling, page 218.

coca with roasted peppers and eggplants

{ *coca de recapte—catalonia and valencia* }

In Catalonia the most common coca, *which is sold in bakeries, has a thin bread-dough base and a topping of roasted peppers and eggplants (the region's beloved* escalivada*; see page 243) and onions and tomatoes. They say this* coca *was born in the area of Lleida and Tarragona. It is eaten cold (I like it hot too).* De recapte *here means "what you have in stock," because you can add the kind of things that are normally on hand in the Catalan kitchen—see the variations.*

SERVES 4 TO 8 AS A STARTER; 2 AS A MAIN DISH

FOR THE DOUGH

2¾ cups bread flour, or as needed

1 teaspoon salt

2 tablespoons olive oil

2 teaspoons active dry yeast

About ¾ cup plus 2 tablespoons warm water

¼ teaspoon sugar

FOR THE TOPPING

2 eggplants (about 1 to 1½ pounds)

3 red bell peppers

2 large onions, chopped

5 tablespoons olive oil

2 tomatoes, peeled and chopped

1 teaspoon sugar

Salt

Put the flour in a large bowl and sprinkle in the salt and oil. Put the yeast in a measuring cup with about ½ cup of the warm water and the sugar and stir well.

When the yeast mixture begins to froth, pour it into the flour, then very gradually pour in the remaining warm water, adding only just enough to make a soft ball that sticks together, stirring it in first with a fork, then working it with your hands.

Knead the dough in the bowl for 10 minutes, adding more water by the tablespoon if it is too dry or a little flour if it is too sticky, until smooth and elastic. Grease the bowl with about ½ tablespoon oil, then turn the dough in it, coating it well with oil, so that a crust will not form when it rises. Cover the bowl with plastic wrap and let the dough rise in a warm place for 1 to 2 hours, until doubled in volume.

For the topping, put the eggplants and peppers on a sheet of foil on a baking sheet, and prick the eggplants in a few places with a pointed knife. Put the tray in a preheated 350°F oven and bake, turning once, until the peppers are soft and the skins have blistered and the eggplants are soft, 30 to 45 minutes (the eggplants will take quite a bit longer than the peppers).

While the peppers and eggplants are in the oven, fry the onions in 3 tablespoons of oil in a large skillet,

>>>

covered to begin with, stirring often until soft. Add the tomatoes, sugar, and some salt, and cook, stirring occasionally, until most of the liquid has evaporated.

When the peppers are soft, put them in 1 or 2 sturdy plastic bags, and twist to seal them. Leave them for about 10 minutes to steam and cool. Pull off the skin from the peppers, remove the stems and seeds, and cut the peppers into ½- to ¾-inch squares.

Peel the eggplants, put them in a colander, and press slightly to let the juices drain away. Then cut them into similar-size pieces. Mix the eggplants and peppers together and toss with salt to taste and the remaining 2 tablespoons of oil so that they are well coated.

Brush two large baking sheets with oil. Punch the risen dough down and knead for a couple of minutes. Divide it into 2 balls. Roll each one out on a floured surface with a floured rolling pin into an oblong or oval about 11 by 15 inches. Lift up each sheet of dough by wrapping it around the rolling pin and unwrapping it onto a baking sheet.

Spread the onion and tomato sauce evenly over the dough, then dot with the peppers and eggplants.

Bake on the upper and lower racks of a preheated 350°F oven, switching the position of the baking sheets halfway through, for about 30 minutes, or until the edges of the crust are crisp and brown. Serve warm or at room temperature, cut into 4 or 8 pieces.

VARIATIONS

- Cut the vegetables into ¾-inch-wide strips instead of into squares or pieces.

- Spread among the vegetables a can of anchovy fillets in oil, or of tuna or sardines, drained and broken into pieces, before baking.

- Add 8 fresh pork sausages, lightly fried and cut into slices, to the topping.

- Add about 12 slices bacon, cut into strips and lightly fried.

- Add 1 pound mushrooms, sliced and briefly sautéed in oil.

coca with peppers, tomatoes, and onions

{ coca de trempó—majorca }

A journalist from the Catalan newspaper La Vanguardia, *Lydia Larrey, called to ask me about pizza-type foods in Mediterranean countries. After we talked, I asked her to e-mail me her favorite* coca *recipe, and she sent me this one. It is from her native Majorca, where it is sold in pastry shops. The name comes from the local salad of diced tomatoes, green peppers, and onions, called* trempó, *which is used as the topping.*

The dough contains no yeast. After I had made it, I e-mailed Lydia, and she confirmed that it was as it should be, with the pastry very thin and crisp.

SERVES 6 AS A STARTER

FOR THE TOPPING

4 medium tomatoes

1 medium onion

1 green bell pepper (in Majorca
  they use a light green pepper
  called *rubio*)

1 to 2 teaspoons sugar (optional)

Salt

3 tablespoons extra virgin olive oil

FOR THE DOUGH

½ cup olive oil

½ cup lukewarm water

½ teaspoon salt

About 1¾ cups all-purpose flour,
  or as needed

For the topping, cut the tomatoes, onion, and green pepper into small pieces. Put them in a bowl, season with a little sugar and some salt, and mix well. Let stand for 1 to 2 hours.

Meanwhile, for the dough, mix the olive oil, water, and salt very well in a bowl. Gradually stir in the flour, mixing with a fork and then with your hand; add just enough flour to form a smooth soft ball that does not stick to your fingers. Wrap in plastic wrap and let rest at room temperature for 30 minutes.

Divide the dough in half. Spread each half into a round or rectangle on a large baking sheet, pressing it into a very thin layer with your fingers and the palm of your hand. Form a low rim around the edges of each one if you like. Bake for 10 minutes in a preheated 350°F oven to set the pastry.

Drain the topping thoroughly, so that the pastry does not get too soggy, and toss with the extra virgin olive oil. Cover the pastry entirely with the topping and bake for 45 to 60 minutes, until the pastry is crisp and the topping soft. If the topping starts to brown before the pastry is crisp, cover the *cocas* with foil.

Serve warm or at room temperature, cut into squares or wedges.

>>>

- Add black olives or capers to the topping.

- For a *coca de pimiento*, with a red pepper topping, roast 5 red bell peppers (see page 128). Peel and seed them, and cut them into thin strips. Toss them with 2 crushed garlic cloves mixed with 3 tablespoons extra virgin olive oil, 1 tablespoon vinegar, salt, and ½ teaspoon cumin.

- Instead of the oil-based pastry, you can use the dough from the *Coca de Recapte* on page 209. Use half the quantity, and roll it out very thin.

onion coca

{ coca de cebes — valencia }

I love this coca. *It is easy to make.*

SERVES 6 AS A STARTER

FOR THE TOPPING

4 large Spanish onions (about
    2 pounds), cut in half and sliced

¼ cup olive oil

Salt and pepper

12 anchovy fillets

About 12 black olives, such as
    Kalamata, pitted or not

FOR THE DOUGH

2 large eggs

⅓ cup olive oil

⅓ cup water

½ teaspoon salt

1 teaspoon baking soda

About 3⅓ cups all-purpose flour

½ egg white, lightly beaten

Cook the onions in the oil in a wide skillet, covered, over low heat for 40 minutes, until very soft and beginning to color, stirring and turning them often. Uncover 10 minutes before the end, and add a little salt and pepper.

Meanwhile, for the dough, beat the eggs vigorously with a fork in a large bowl. Gradually beat in the oil and water, then the salt and baking soda. Add the flour a little at a time, mixing it in first with the fork and then with your hands, adding only just enough to make a soft, smooth dough. Wrap the dough in plastic wrap and let rest for 30 minutes.

Roll the dough out into a large thin rectangle, and line a lightly greased 12-by-16-inch baking sheet with it. Pinch and lift the dough slightly around the edges and brush the top with the egg white. Bake in a preheated 350°F oven for 10 minutes to seal the crust and prevent it from getting soggy.

Spread the topping all over the dough, and arrange the anchovies and olives on top. Bake for another 30 minutes, or until the pastry around the edges is golden brown. Serve warm or at room temperature.

VARIATION

To make this with store-bought puff pastry, use a 17¼-ounce package (2 sheets) of pastry. Roll each piece out as thin as you can on a floured surface with a floured rolling pin, and transfer to an oiled 16-by-12-inch baking sheet. Brush the tops with the egg white and bake in a preheated 375°F oven for 30 minutes, or until puffed and golden. (The pastry will flatten when you spread the topping on it.) Spread the onions evenly over the pastry, and arrange the anchovy fillets and olives on top.

ANGELITA GARCÍA DE PAREDES BARREDA

My croquetas *kept bursting and falling apart. My friend Alicia told me her sister-* in-law Angelita's always worked. I called her and she explained the recipe on the phone—it worked perfectly (see page 166). Then I went to see her in Seville. Angelita García de Paredes Barreda is an eighty-four-year-old Franciscan missionary nun who for many years worked in different cities of the United States, helping out poor immigrants from South America, Puerto Rico, and Cuba. She also spent time with an Indian tribe in Mexico. She stopped wearing a habit when she realized that people opened up to her more when she wore regular clothes. She is from an illustrious military family. Her ancestor Diego García de Paredes from Trujillo, in Extremadura, was a noble and daring officer who fought for the Castilian kings in Granada, Flanders, and Italy in the late fifteenth and early sixteenth century. His son, also Diego García de Paredes, founded the city of Trujillo, a provincial capital in Venezuela, where he became viceroy.

Angelita was one of ten children. Her father was a colonel in the Spanish army. Her grandmother was educated at the Irish Sisters of Loreto's Institute of the Virgin Mary school in Gibraltar, where the bishop was a relative. The order went on to open schools in Spain, known as Las Irlandesas. Angelita and her twin sister first attended their day school and later went to their boarding school in Castilleja de la Cuesta, a small town in the province of Seville. When they finished in Castilleja and returned home, an English tutor, a governess for the González Byass sherry family, came to the house every day for English conversation with the girls of the family. Many of the Jerez elite had an English education. Some were descended from families who had come from England in the eighteenth century. They introduced the custom of tea with toast and biscuits and some English dishes.

Angelita showed me around Seville and the great cathedral, which is the largest Gothic cathedral in the world. We stopped at the little chapel that holds the sepulchre of her father's ancestors, the Jácomes, an illustrious Converso family. Angelita's community of retired Franciscan nuns lives very frugally. Angelita loves cooking, and when it is her turn to cook, she manages to prepare inexpensive but exquisite meals—I know they are delicious, because she described them to me. But the huge pile of recipes she gave me, some handwritten, some typed, reflect the grand style of her family as well as their Italian connection—her great-grandmother on her mother's side was from Italy.

Angelita is a highly educated and intellectual nun, she speaks four languages, and is very sociable and cheerful. She joined me and some friends in tapas bars and restaurants of Seville and walked with us in the early hours of the morning through the city. *Empanada de atún* on the following page is one of her recipes.

angelita's tuna pie

{ empanada de atún — galicia }

SERVES 6 TO 8

FOR THE PASTRY

1 large egg

1 teaspoon baking soda

½ cup olive oil

½ cup dry white wine or hard cider

½ teaspoon salt

About 2¼ cups all-purpose flour

1 egg, separated

FOR THE FILLING

1 large onion, chopped

1 red bell pepper, cored, seeded, and cut into small pieces

2 tablespoons olive oil

One 14-ounce can chopped tomatoes

1 teaspoon sugar

Salt

About 14 ounces canned tuna in oil, drained and flaked

20 to 24 olives, such as Kalamata, pitted and chopped

2 hard-boiled eggs, chopped

For the pastry, beat the egg lightly with a fork in a large bowl. Beat in the baking soda, oil, wine, and salt. Gradually work in enough flour to make a soft, malleable dough, stirring it in with a fork to begin with, then working it in with your hands. Roll the dough into a ball, wrap it in plastic wrap, and let it rest at room temperature for an hour.

Meanwhile, for the filling, fry the onion and bell pepper in the oil in a large skillet, stirring often, until soft. Add the tomatoes, sugar, and a little salt and cook over medium heat for about 15 minutes, until the sauce is jammy. Stir in the tuna, olives, and chopped eggs.

Grease a pie pan about 11 inches in diameter with oil. Divide the dough into 2 pieces, one slightly less than twice as big as the other. Roll out the larger piece (keep the remaining dough in plastic wrap) on a smooth work surface—do not flour the surface or the rolling pin; the dough will not stick, because it is oil-based. Roll it out so that it is large enough to come over the edges of the pan, and carefully transfer the dough to the pan by rolling it up onto the rolling pin, then unrolling it gently into the pan. Without stretching the dough, ease it into the corners. Trim the edges to a ½-inch border. Lightly beat the egg white, and brush it all over the dough. Bake in a preheated 350°F oven for 10 minutes, then let cool. (Leave the oven on.)

Spread the filling evenly in the pie shell. Roll out the remaining dough to a large circle and lay it carefully on top of the filling so that it covers the edges of the bottom crust. Brush with the egg yolk mixed with 1 teaspoon water. Bake for 35 to 40 minutes, until the crust is lightly browned. It is good hot or cold.

little pies with a tomato, pepper, and tuna filling

{ empanadillas de atún y pimiento —

valencia and majorca }

Empanadillas *developed from the Arab savory pastries called* sanbusak. *They have a variety of fillings, but the most common is tomatoes, peppers, and tuna. Some cooks add chopped hard-boiled eggs or pine nuts. The doughs also vary. This one is very easy to make and to work with.*

The pies can be fried, but I prefer them baked. They are good to serve at parties, as they can be picked up with the fingers. They are best eaten warm but are also good cold.

MAKES 16 TO 20 EMPANADILLAS

FOR THE DOUGH

½ cup olive oil

½ cup warm water or dry white wine

½ teaspoon salt

About 2⅓ cups all-purpose flour

For the dough, mix the oil, water or white wine, and salt in a bowl, beating with a fork. Gradually work in enough flour to make a soft, smooth, malleable dough that does not stick to the bowl or to your hands; begin by stirring the flour in with a fork, then work it in with your hands and knead briefly. You can use the dough right away or keep it for as long as a day, covered in plastic wrap, but keep it at room temperature, not in the refrigerator.

For the filling, fry the onion in the oil in a large skillet until very soft, stirring often. Add the tomatoes and cook over medium heat until the liquid has disappeared and you can see the oil sizzling. Season to taste with salt and pepper. Add the tuna, shredding it with your fingers, the roasted pepper, olives, and parsley. Mix well, and let cool.

To make the *empanadillas,* divide the dough into 4 or 6 pieces (it is easier to roll out small amounts). Roll each piece out as thinly as you can and cut into rounds with a 4-inch pastry cutter (or use a small saucer as a guide); you do not need to flour the surface or the rolling pin, as the

FOR THE FILLING

½ large onion, finely chopped

2 tablespoons olive oil

3 medium tomatoes,
    peeled and chopped

Salt and pepper

4 ounces canned tuna, drained

1 red bell pepper, roasted (see
    page 128), peeled, seeded,
    and cut into ⅔-inch pieces

14 green or black olives,
    pitted and chopped

2 tablespoons chopped
    flat-leaf parsley

2 large egg yolks, lightly beaten
    with 1 teaspoon of water,
    for the glaze

dough is oily and will not stick. Reserve the scraps and roll them into a ball, then roll out again and cut into rounds; do not waste any dough. Fill each batch of pastry rounds as you cut them. Brush the edges with some of the egg yolk, put a generous tablespoon of filling in the middle, bring two opposite sides of the pastry up to meet over the filling, making a half-moon-shaped pie, and pinch the edges together, then lay the pie down and press the edges with the tines of a fork to seal it.

Place the *empanadillas* on a baking sheet lined with foil lightly greased with oil. Brush the tops with the remaining egg yolk, and bake in a preheated 350°F oven for 30 minutes, or until golden. Serve warm.

meat pie

{ pastel de carne — murcia }

The Murcian meat pie is celebrated as an important part of the local culture, with regional festivals dedicated to it, and it is also famous in other parts of Spain. It is said to be of Arab origin (for me, the cinnamon is the clue). Bakeries and pastry shops make these pies with two different types of lard pastry: a short-crust base and a puff pastry top. The top is crafted in a curious way, with tightly coiled ribbons of thin dough, which come out of the oven as amazing crisp, golden, spiky pastry spirals. Some bakers add crumbled morcilla (blood sausage), some chopped chorizo; more rarely there is a touch of something sweet like raisins. The artistry did not work in the same glorious way with my store-bought puff pastry, so I made my second pie with a flat top. You can serve it hot or cold.

SERVES 6 TO 8

1 pound store-bought pie dough

¾ pound store-bought puff pastry

1 egg yolk, lightly beaten with a
    drop of water

FOR THE FILLING

1½ pounds ground veal
    (there should be a little fat)

1 garlic clove, crushed to a paste

Salt and pepper

1 teaspoon cinnamon

¼ pound sliced *jamón serrano*
    or prosciutto, finely chopped

2 ounces cooked chorizo, chopped

4 hard-boiled eggs, cut into
    thin wedges

Butter a 10-inch tart pan or mold. Roll out the pie dough on a floured surface with a floured rolling pin so that it is large enough to line the mold or pan. Trim the excess dough by cutting around the edges with a knife.

For the filling, put the veal in a bowl. Add the garlic, some salt and pepper, the cinnamon, and the *jamón* or prosciutto and mix well, working it with your hands into a soft paste. Spread the filling evenly in the dough. Sprinkle with the chopped chorizo, arrange the hard-boiled eggs on top, and dust lightly with salt.

Roll out the puff pastry dough on a floured surface with a floured rolling pin to a round about 10½ inches in diameter. Lift it up by rolling it onto the rolling pin, then unroll it over the filling. Trim the edges with a knife and press the edges of the top and bottom crusts together. Brush all over with the egg yolk, and cut a small steam hole in the middle with a pointed knife.

Bake for 50 to 60 minutes in a preheated 400°F oven; cover the pastry with foil after about 30 minutes, when the top is golden brown and the pastry puffed up.

creamy leek tart

{ tarta de puerros — basque country }

Basques love leeks, and you find them in many of their dishes. This tart makes an elegant first course that can be served hot or cold.

SERVES 8 AS A STARTER

FOR THE PASTRY

1⅔ cups all-purpose flour

¼ teaspoon salt

8 tablespoons (1 stick) unsalted
   butter, chilled and cut into
   small pieces

1 large egg, lightly beaten

1 to 2 tablespoons milk
   (if necessary)

½ egg white, lightly beaten

FOR THE FILLING

1 pound leeks, trimmed, washed,
   and cut into 2-inch-long pieces

Salt

4 large eggs

1 cup heavy cream

For the pastry, put the flour and salt in a bowl. Rub in the butter with your fingertips until the mixture becomes like damp sand in texture. (You can also do this very well by putting them through the food processor, then transfer to a bowl.) Add the egg, mix well, and then work very briefly with your hands until the dough holds together in a soft ball, adding a little milk if necessary. Wrap the dough in plastic wrap and refrigerate for 1 hour.

Before using the dough, let it warm up and soften a little so that it becomes easier to work.

Grease an 11-inch tart pan or flan mold. Line the bottom and sides with the dough by flattening lumps in the palms of your hands and pressing them into place. Then smooth the seams. Brush the dough with the egg white and prick it in a few places with a fork.

Bake in a preheated 350°F oven for about 20 minutes, until the pastry is lightly colored. Remove from the oven and let cool.

For the filling, cook the leeks in boiling salted water for about 10 minutes, until soft. Drain well and chop them, not too fine, in the food processor. Drain again to get rid of the water.

Lightly beat the eggs with a fork in a bowl, then beat in the cream. Stir in the leeks and add salt to taste. Pour into the baked crust and bake in a preheated 350°F oven for 40 to 45 minutes, or until the filling is set and the top golden.

SALADS AND VEGETABLES

{ ensaladas y verduras }

Vegetables and salads are served as entreméses *or starters in Spain.* Salads can be very simple—a few tomatoes with a sprinkling of chopped sweet onions; a bowl of crisp lettuce; sliced oranges with a few black olives; or diced tomatoes, peppers, and cucumbers—or they can be complex and represent a light snack. An English friend who has had Spanish au pairs complained that they "could never leave vegetables alone," and it is true. Spaniards do not boil vegetables for a plain side dish; they turn them into something that can be enjoyed as a dish in itself.

An enormous variety of vegetables grows in Valencia, Murcia, Catalonia, Andalusia, and in the valleys of the great rivers of Spain. There are only a few Spanish vegetables that we cannot easily get in America. These include tiny tender baby artichokes that can be eaten whole and *pochas,* a type of white bean that is grown on family farms in La Rioja and Navarre and is eaten fresh. Most of the vegetables in our supermarkets come from far away and have not ripened in the sun. Some, such as artichokes, peas, and spinach, are frozen in a way that preserves their flavor and texture, so do not feel unhappy about using them if fresh ones are not available.

Vegetables were once dismissed in Spain as "poor food," belonging to the vegetable patches of the peasantry. It is only since the middle of the twentieth century that they have become truly appreciated. And now star chefs of the *nueva*

Vegetables with Tomato and Hard-Boiled Egg Vinaigrette, page 228.

cocina have elevated them to a rank equal to that of foie gras and caviar on their menus—or at least that is what they say. These chefs do produce fantastic delicacies with them that are a take on what their grandmothers used to make. The peasant families who were the source of the old vegetable dishes lavished love and attention on their preparation, as vegetables were all they had. They sometimes added chickpeas and dried beans or chestnuts, sometimes almonds or pine nuts and raisins, and most often tiny bits of home-cured ham. This last tradition came about at the time when agents of the Inquisition often visited at mealtimes, obliging everyone to prove their Catholicism in an obvious way. During Lent, and on the many days of abstinence from meat throughout the year, ham was never included in a dish because it could leave you open to accusations of heresy and to punishment. But Lent made little difference to the urban poor anyway, as they lived on bread and vegetables alone. Monasteries famously devised special vegetable dishes to be cooked during Lent. They added herbs and sometimes substituted salt cod for ham.

One of the best things that the innovative chefs have done is to put grilled or roasted vegetables—which is the way peasants prepared them out in the fields—and lightly boiled vegetables on their menus, thereby making them trendy. *Hervido* (or *bollit* in Valencian Catalan), an assortment of boiled vegetables that represents the traditional evening first course in Valencia and Murcia, has spread to other parts. On my arrival in Madrid, my friend Alicia served up a platter of hot steamed tiny artichokes, tender wide green beans, and asparagus. I dressed the vegetables on my plate with sweet fruity extra virgin olive oil and a sprinkling of sea salt. It was all I could wish for. New or waxy potatoes and vegetables such as zucchini, leeks, scallions, chard, and spinach are all served in this way. Some like to add a little vinegar with the olive oil.

If you are vegetarian, you will find a huge choice of dishes here. You will also find vegetable dishes in other chapters, combined with rice, in fillings for pies, as toppings for pizza-type *cocas,* and in soups and omelets. They make perfect starters, and sometimes main dishes too.

orange salad

{ *e n s a l a d a   d e   n a r a n j a — a n d a l u s i a* }

The Arabs introduced bitter oranges to the Iberian Peninsula, and in the early sixteenth century, sweet orange trees from China were planted. Sweet oranges are used in a variety of salads. A tablespoon of sweet wine or port mixed with sherry vinegar in the dressing adds an intriguing touch to this one.

SERVES 4

2 oranges

1 small head romaine lettuce

½ sweet red onion,
    finely chopped

3 tablespoons extra virgin olive oil

1 tablespoon sherry vinegar

1 tablespoon sweet Pedro Ximénez
    wine or port

Salt

Peel the oranges so that no pith is left, and cut them into slices crosswise. Cut the lettuce into wide strips. Arrange the lettuce and oranges on a platter and sprinkle on the onion.

Just before serving, beat the olive oil, vinegar, wine or port, and a little salt with a fork and pour over the salad, then gently toss the salad.

vegetables with tomato and hard-boiled egg vinaigrette

{ *verduras de la huerta con la salsa vinagreta—murcia* }

This simple dish of boiled vegetables makes a light and refreshing, as well as an elegant, start to a meal. It can be served hot or at room temperature, and the vegetables can be prepared in advance. All kinds of vegetables may be used. You can substitute or add others, such as carrots, runner beans, green beans, and cauliflower. The main thing is to give each the right cooking time. Leeks have to be very well cooked and soft, while asparagus are best a little crunchy.

SERVES 4 TO 6

4 leeks, trimmed, washed, and cut into 3 pieces each

About 1 pound new or small waxy potatoes, peeled and cut in half

3 baby artichoke hearts (see page 129) or defrosted frozen artichoke bottoms

½ pound asparagus, hard bottom ends trimmed

Salt

FOR THE *VINAGRETA*

7 tablespoons extra virgin olive oil

2 tablespoons white wine vinegar or fresh lemon juice

Salt and pepper

2 tablespoons finely chopped flat-leaf parsley

2 firm but ripe tomatoes (about 7 ounces), chopped

1 hard-boiled egg, chopped

Bring a large pot of salted water to a boil. Throw in the leeks and potatoes and simmer for 10 minutes. Add the artichokes and cook for 5 minutes, then add the asparagus and cook for 5 to 10 minutes more, until all the vegetables are tender. Drain well and arrange them in a wide serving dish.

While the vegetables are still warm, make the *vinagreta:* Beat the oil and vinegar or lemon juice with salt and pepper to taste in a bowl. Stir in the parsley, chopped tomatoes, and egg. Pour the *vinagreta* over the vegetables, turning them so that they absorb the dressing well.

VARIATION

Add ½ chopped sweet red onion and a few capers and chopped olives to the *vinagreta.*

olive oil—the story

Spain is the biggest producer and biggest exporter in the world of olive oil. Much of its exports have been in bulk, and the main market is Italy, where the oil is either consumed or repackaged in beautiful bottles and exported as Italian or Tuscan extra virgin oil. But a good variety of Spanish extra virgin olive oils are now enjoying a worldwide reputation for quality; twenty have been awarded a *Denominación de Origen* (DO) seal of quality. Olive trees grow everywhere except in the northern regions. Parts of the undulating Andalusian landscape, where once there were wheat, grapes, barley, oats, chickpeas, and all kinds of vegetables, are now entirely covered by olive trees.

The history of olive oil in Spain is ancient. A good deal of what I know about it I learned from my friend Alicia Ríos, who wrote a book on the subject with Lourdes March called *La Cocina del Aceite de Oliva* (*Cooking with Olive Oil*). She is also a *catador,* or master taster, and an official ambassador of olive oil who organizes events and performances.

Olive trees have deep roots and need very little water. They thrive in the Mediterranean climate. It is claimed that some trees in Spain are five hundred or even more than one thousand years old. Could this be true? When I was growing up in Egypt, my Catholic nanny went on a pilgrimage and came back with a small branch from an olive tree under which the pregnant Virgin Mary was supposed to have stopped to rest. The Phoenicians are said to have introduced olive oil in Spain and the Greeks to have planted the first trees, but it was the Romans who planted them on an industrial scale over much of the peninsula. The oil was sent to Rome and throughout the empire for lighting, soap, and cosmetic, medicinal, and liturgical purposes; a top-quality oil, *olio flos,* was for cooking and preserving foods. The Arabs brought more olive tree varieties and ways of cultivating them. The Spanish words for olive, *aceituna,* and for oil, *aceite,* come from the Arabic *al zaitun* and *al zait.* But an alternate Spanish word for olive is *oliva,* an olive tree is *olivo,* and an olive grove is *olivar,* all derived from the Latin *oleum.* Oil mills or presses are *molino,* from the Latin, and *almazara* or *almassera,* from the Arabic.

When I was invited to take part in a conference on olive oil tourism in Seville, I talked about the time when in Seville and cities like Toledo and Córdoba you could tell the religious background of people who lived in every house as you walked through the narrow streets because of the smells of the cooking fats. The Christians used pork fat, the Muslims mostly clarified butter, and the Jews only olive oil. Pork fat was a badge of Christian identity. For a long time after 1492, everyone was afraid of using olive oil for fear of being suspected of being a "secret" Jew and punished for it by the Inquisition.

Speakers at the conference discussed future olive oil "routes," tourist visits to oil producers and olive plantations, harvest festivals, organized tastings, seminars, and cooking demonstrations. We were treated to a trip around the countryside to visit old olive oil mills. Some were really ancient, with massive conical stone grinders and spherical millstones that were once turned by donkeys—relics of another era that may not have changed much since Muslim and even Roman times. A beautifully designed modern museum took us through the different methods of making olive oil. Many of those on the trip were from families that had produced olive oil for generations.

Until the civil war, small family presses could be found all over Spain. Franco's government encouraged the formation of large cooperatives that produced huge quantities of olive oil. The goal of the industry was to produce quantity, without much regard to taste. But, according to José Ramón Guzmán Alvarez, professor at the University of Córdoba, even before that the taste had rarely been good and Spanish olive oil had always had a bad reputation. In an essay entitled "La Génesis de los Paisajes Olivareros: Siglos XVI–XX" ("The Genesis of the Olive Grove Landscape: XVI–XX Centuries"), he explains that because the seigneurial landlords had exclusive milling rights until 1837, and there were not enough communal mills to provide for all the smaller olive growers, they would have to wait their turn for days and maybe weeks for their olives to be pressed, by which time the olives would have gone bad. The big landowners in Andalusia might have produced some good oil for their own personal consumption, but they could always profit from selling the oil for lighting and soap. They also sold it to England as a lubricant for the factories that were operating during the industrial revolution.

You can see why the traditional cooking of Spain was with lard—it tasted better and it was made by families themselves. There were a few producers of decent olive oil by the end of the nineteenth century, especially in Catalonia, which had a prosperous bourgeoisie and French and Italian restaurateurs who liked to use olive oil as well as butter. But even then the cooking in Catalonia was never only with olive oil. It also used lard, often mixing the two. Nowadays, from what I hear from young people in Catalonia, they no longer use lard, for health reasons and because commercial lard is not as good as the home-rendered pork fat of the past (but in the countryside, they still do). The Catalan food historian and gastronome Néstor Luján wrote that some people in Catalonia still think that when olive oil became more common than lard, food lost much of its charm. In the south and along the Mediterranean coast, olive oil continued to be used despite the historical prejudice associating it with "secret" Jews, yet it wasn't until the late nineteenth century that Spanish cookery writers began to extol its virtues over lard. Most of the recipes they featured in their books were French, and by then lard was associated with poor peasant food.

José Ramón Guzmán writes that it was only during the First World War, when Italy's demand for olive oil rose enormously, that olive groves were expanded over the Andalusian hills. And it is only in the last twenty years or so that domestic and world demand increased phenomenally and created the spur for intensive monoculture of olive trees. The European Union has given subsidies to olive plantations, and international campaigns have boosted the consumption of olive oil by promoting the healthful aspects of the Mediterranean diet. Star chefs of the Basque Country and Catalonia started using olive oil rather than pork fat in their dishes, and TV chefs advocated the healthful and gastronomic qualities of the oil while sloshing great amounts into their pans. Enterprising olive oil producers bought the latest state-of-the-art technology from Italy and put all their efforts into creating the best conditions for every aspect of oil production, from growing and harvesting to pressing, blending, and bottling. Many producers of high-quality oils now own their own olive groves. There has been a revolution in olive oil production just as there has been one in wine. It has resulted in extra virgin olive oils comparable in quality to Spain's Iberian pig products.

cream of tomato with tuna
and hard-boiled eggs

{ sopeao—andalusia }

Flame-haired Loli Flores, who was for many years a chef in Seville, remembers sopeao *from the village of Mairena del Alcor near Seville, where she lived as a child with her mother, siblings, grandparents, and great-grandfather. (The famous Gypsy flamenco singer Antonio Mairena was from there.) It was a one-dish summer meal, served with crusty bread to soak up the creamed tomatoes—the name* sopeao *is derived from the word* sopear, *meaning "to soak up with bread." For a big party during the Feria, the Seville spring fair, they made it in a huge deep platter and sometimes added pieces of pigeon and rabbit. They served it with lettuce leaves and followed it with melon or watermelon.*

SERVES 4 TO 6

2 pounds large ripe tomatoes

¼ pound (5 slices) crustless
     firm white bread

1 green or red bell pepper, cored,
     seeded, and quartered

2 to 3 garlic cloves, crushed
     to a paste

1 teaspoon sugar

Salt and pepper

3 tablespoons sherry vinegar
     or wine vinegar

½ cup extra virgin olive oil

4 to 6 hard-boiled eggs,
     quartered or sliced

Two 5-ounce cans tuna in oil,
     drained

There is no need to peel the tomatoes. Cut them into quarters and remove the hard little bits at the stem ends.

Dry the bread under the broiler without browning it, turning the slices once. Grind to coarse crumbs in a food processor and transfer to a bowl. Add the bell pepper to the processor and blend to a paste, then add the tomatoes and garlic and blend to a cream. Add the sugar, salt and pepper to taste, the vinegar, and the olive oil and blend again. Return the bread crumbs to the processor and blend briefly just to fold them in. Taste and adjust the seasoning.

Pour onto a wide platter, and arrange the egg quarters or slices and the tuna, broken into pieces, on top.

spanish olive oils

Olive oils can be light and delicate, or assertive and strong, and their flavors and aromas simple or complex. (They are experienced both up front and as an after-taste.) Flavors range from sweet through fruity, nutty, spicy, and peppery to pleasantly bitter and pungent. Fragrance—fruity, floral, nutty, grassy—can be elusive or intense. Oil from olives from the same tree can vary from one harvest to the next. Some harvests produce exceptional oil, some more ordinary ones. Blended oils hardly vary, because producers achieve consistency by adjusting their mixes. They create styles that marry complementary qualities of different oils and follow both local taste and tradition for stronger-tasting oils, and the preferences for lightness and mildness of the consumer countries newly converted to olive oil.

Oils vary depending on the variety of tree and the soil in which it grows; the weather; when and how the olives are harvested (whether they are picked by hand, or the branches are beaten with poles, or the trees are shaken by machines into inverted umbrellas); how ripe the olives are; how quickly the oil is extracted and by what means; and if the olives are a single variety or a blend. There are more than 260 varieties of olive trees in Spain, including subvarieties that have adapted to different localities or were developed through grafting. Arbequina, Picual, Hojiblanca, Empeltre, and Cornicabra are the most extensively grown for oil. A few, like Manzanilla, are better for table olives than for oil.

The method of production that is now commonly used, called the continuous method, separates the liquid from the solid paste of the crushed olives, and then the oil from the rest of the liquid, by spinning the paste or liquid at high speed in a drum or centrifuge.

Extra virgin olive oils with a low acidity are the finest, with the richest flavor and aroma. When a group of us were invited to rate a few by a producer, small navy blue cups with glass covers had been lined up. The dark glass is so that you are not influenced by the color of the oil—color does not indicate quality or always style, and green oils are not better than yellow ones. However, a dark green oil is more generally characteristic of a fruity, bitter, astringent oil produced from green olives that have not reached maturity, and golden-yellow oils are more likely to have been made from sweet ripe black olives late in the season. We were asked to cradle each cup in our hands to warm it before removing the cover and inhaling the aroma of the oil, then to taste it by dipping in a piece of bread. In between tastes, we chewed pieces of apple to clean our palates.

Olive oils labeled "extra virgin" are produced using only mechanical means and have not undergone any chemical treatment. Oils sold simply as "olive oil" are from second and subsequent extractions, and have been processed chemically and refined to remove their acidity. During the writing of this book, I tasted and brought home some fabulous Spanish extra virgin olive oils. Most memorable were a sweet and fruity Catalan oil made from Arbequina olives and a wonderful Priego de Córdoba from Picudo, Hojiblanca, and Picual olives that had a fruity aroma, a slightly bitter taste, and a piquant aftertaste. An oil I found in Jaén made from Picual and Arbequina olives was strong, fruity, piquant, and slightly bitter. Of the twenty extra virgin olive oils with a DO seal, ten are produced in Andalusia (eighty percent of Spanish olive oil is made in Andalusia), five in Catalonia, and one each in Castile–La Mancha, Extremadura, Valencia, Murcia, and Majorca.

I asked people in different parts of Spain what oils they used. In Seville, Córdoba, and Jaén, the great producing provinces, they told me they used extra virgin oil for cooking everything, even for deep-frying. Top Spanish chefs do the same thing—except for deep-frying. Most other people said they used refined olive oil, which is cheap and bland, for frying, braising, and stewing and for foods such as sweet biscuits and cakes, where they did not want the strong flavor of an extra virgin. They told me that since high temperatures diminish the flavors and the main healthful qualities of extra virgin oils, there was no point in wasting them for deep-frying. Some people said they used sunflower oil because it is cheaper. Many chefs said that for mayonnaise they used a mix of sunflower oil and extra virgin olive oil because too much extra virgin would overpower the taste. A young scientist at an olive oil conference told me that ninety percent of people in Spain use regular olive oil, not extra virgin, because they are not educated enough about quality—and price is an issue too. But everybody said they used extra virgin oil in dressings or to drizzle over a finished dish—a piece of bread, a vegetable, a fish, a soup, a bean stew. The passion for good-quality olive oil is a recent phenomenon, as new as the great Spanish extra virgins that are now being produced.

salad of roasted peppers and tomatoes

{ *pipirrana — murcia* }

Pipirrana, *also called* mojete, *is part of a family of salads based on chopped or pureed tomatoes. In this case, the tomatoes are roasted and turned into a sauce with a sweet intense flavor. These were the traditional foods of agricultural laborers of Andalusia, Murcia, and La Mancha. On festive occasions, tuna, hard-boiled eggs, and black olives would be added.*

SERVES 4

3 red bell peppers

1 pound tomatoes

1 to 2 garlic cloves, finely chopped

3 tablespoons extra virgin olive oil

Salt and pepper

1 teaspoon sugar

Put the peppers and tomatoes on a sheet of foil on a baking sheet and roast in a preheated 500°F oven. Take the tomatoes out after about 15 minutes, when they have softened a bit and their skins have loosened.

Turn the peppers over and continue to roast for an additional 15 minutes, or until they are soft and their skins have blistered and blackened in parts. To loosen the skins further, put the peppers in a sturdy plastic bag, twist it shut, and let steam and cool for 10 to 15 minutes.

Meanwhile, peel the tomatoes, discarding the hard white bits at the stem end, and chop them.

When the peppers are cool enough to handle, peel them, remove the stems and seeds, and cut them into strips about ⅔ inch wide. Reserve their juices to add to the salad.

Sauté the garlic in 1 tablespoon of the olive oil in a large skillet for seconds only, just until the aroma rises. Add the tomatoes, salt and pepper to taste, and the sugar and cook over high heat for about 8 minutes, or until reduced to a sauce. Stir in the peppers.

Serve at room temperature or chilled, sprinkled with the remaining 2 tablespoons olive oil and the juices from the peppers.

VARIATION

In La Mancha, *asadillo* is a similar salad of roasted red peppers simply dressed with fresh tomatoes blended to a cream with extra virgin olive oil and a little crushed garlic.

peppers and paprika
{ pimientos y pimentón }

Franciscan monks returning from the Americas in the sixteenth century brought back seeds of various species of peppers of the *Capsicum* family, both sweet and hot, to plant in their monasteries along the Camino de Santiago in northern Spain and in Extremadura, where the monks of the Yuste monastery are believed to be the first to have planted them. They called them *pimientos,* which is like the word *pimienta,* used for the black peppercorns that had once arrived from the East, because they gave a similar sensation. Fresh peppers quickly became part of peasant cooking all over Spain, and dried and crushed or pulverized peppers became the most loved and indispensable of Spanish flavorings.

The use of peppers is so characteristic of Spanish cooking that an old friend of mine I met again when I was testing recipes for this book was afraid to eat anything at my house because he is allergic to them. Despite my assurances that I would not use any, he always insisted on taking me out to eat. Although there are many Spanish recipes without peppers, they are found in all kinds of dishes. Fresh mild-flavored bell peppers (they ripen from green through yellow to red) are used raw, roasted, fried, stewed, or stuffed. Green peppers are favored for the zing they lend, red ones for their sweetness. Intensively grown bell peppers from Murcia and Almería can be found in all European supermarkets, and throughout Spain, but there are dozens of other varieties that are typically known only in their own localities. A few of these have become known outside Spain. The small elongated green Padrón peppers (*pimientos del Padrón,* also known as *pimientos del Herbón*) of Galicia are usually mild, but the occasional one is extremely hot: the uncertainty attached to biting into one that may be hot adds an element of excitement. The small, pointy, mild, and gentle *pimiento de Gernika* is typical of Basque cooking. Traditionally, it was picked when ripe and left to dry hanging on long strings. Today it is used green and fresh as a tapa or a vegetable accompaniment to many dishes. The *pimiento Riojano,* which grows in La Rioja, cone-shaped with a pointed tip, is used mainly when red and sweet, but it appears in many local dishes when it is half green and half red. The peppers can be seen drying in garlands on village balconies. The small, sweet, bright red triangular *piquillo* peppers, from Lodosa in Navarre, are sold roasted and peeled in tins and jars. They have become fashionable since innovative Basque chefs began stuffing them with meat, fish, or cheese. *Cristal* peppers, smaller than *piquillos* and with a sweet delicate flavor, also from Navarre, are roasted over wood fires and sold in jars or cans.

By the nineteenth century, pepper-growing regions had begun to dry certain types of red peppers and to grind them to a fine powder called *pimentón.* In 1893, the Spanish gastronome Angel Muro wrote in his cookbook, *El Practicón,* that *pimentón* had become for almost all inhabitants of Spain a product of prime necessity, and that in Castile especially not a single food was put on the table that was not seasoned with it. Some called it "the Spanish vice." Today, although many traditional regional dishes are flavored with *pimentón,* some Spaniards hardly use it at all.

Different varieties of peppers are picked when they are red and sun-dried or smoke-dried to be used whole, in flakes, or as ground *pimentón. Pimentón,* now usually referred to abroad as Spanish paprika, comes in three varieties: sweet and mild (*dulce*), bittersweet (*agridulce*), and hot (*picante*), all of which may also be smoked. *Pimentón dulce* is the most widely used; there are few hot dishes in Spain. *Pimentón picante,* which is similar to cayenne or chile powder, is not greatly appreciated except in Galicia, Extremadura, and the Canary Islands. Murcia is known for its *pimentón dulce.* The *pimentón* from the Valley of La Vera, in northern Extremadura, has a smoky flavor. Traditionally, tobacco farmers there dried their tobacco leaves in barns heated by holm oak fires, and they used to hang peppers to dry at the same time, so the peppers absorbed the smell of the smoke. Eventually their flavor became so popular that the farmers moved their production from tobacco to *pimentón.*

Small, round, a dark burgundy color, mild, and sweet, with a delicate flavor, *ñora* peppers are always used dried. They are beloved by Catalans, Valencians, and Murcians, who use them to flavor rice, pasta, fish, soups, and stews. These peppers are used to make sweet *pimentón dulce* in Murcia. The dried *choricero* peppers from the Basque Country, Navarre, and La Rioja are not very different in flavor. A thick red paste made from the soaked pulp of dried *choricero* peppers is sold in jars. *Guindilla* peppers are hot chiles. The Basque *guindillas del norte* are small, long, and thin. When green, they are semisweet and piquant; as they ripen to red, they range from medium hot with a sweet flavor to hot. The red peppers are used fresh, fried in olive oil with garlic. Green *guindilla* peppers are sold preserved in white wine vinegar. Dried red *guindillas* are broken into flakes or pulverized to make *pimentón picante,* sometimes called *pimienta cayena.*

roasted tomato salad
with olives, eggs, and tuna

{ mojete huertano—murcia, andalusia, and la mancha }

This was at the same time a festive peasant dish and a dish de vigilia—*of abstinence. The tuna and other ingredients bathe in the juice of roasted tomatoes. You need ripe tomatoes with a fine taste. Serve this in soup bowls with spoons and accompanied by good country bread.*

SERVES 6

2 pounds tomatoes

6 tablespoons extra virgin olive oil

1 teaspoon sugar

2 tablespoons red or white wine
  vinegar

Salt

About 24 black olives, pitted

3 hard-boiled eggs, quartered

One 5-ounce can tuna in oil,
  drained

Roast the tomatoes to soften them: Place them on a sheet of foil on a broiler pan under the broiler, not too close to the heat, for 10 to 15 minutes, until the skin is brown and they feel soft.

Peel the tomatoes, remove the hard bits near the stem ends, and coarsely chop them. Place them, with their juices, in a wide serving dish, add the olive oil, sugar, vinegar, and salt to taste, and mix very well. Mix in the olives, and arrange the hard-boiled eggs and chunks of tuna on top.

VARIATIONS

- Instead of roasting the tomatoes, you can simply peel them, with a serrated knife; or blanch them briefly and peel them. Chop them, reserving the juices, and proceed as above.

- In Frailes, a village in Andalusia, Manolo (see page 173) adds potatoes to a similar salad he calls *pipirrana.* Cook 6 to 8 medium new potatoes in boiling salted water; drain. When they are cool enough, peel and slice them, and sprinkle them with salt before mixing them into the salad.

- In La Mancha, they add 1 teaspoon cumin to the dressing.

- Add a few anchovy fillets packed in olive oil.

- Add 2 green or red bell peppers, roasted (see page 128), peeled, seeded, and cut into ribbons.

roasted pepper and onion salad

{ mojete manchego — la mancha }

This mojete, *which La Mancha peasants made in the fields over a fire, has a strongly flavored garlic, cumin, and lemon dressing. Serve with good crusty bread to soak it up.*

SERVES 6

6 large red bell peppers

A head of garlic

2 pounds small to medium white or red onions, not peeled

6 tablespoons extra virgin olive oil

3 to 4 tablespoons fresh lemon juice, or to taste

Salt

1 teaspoon cumin, or more to taste

A handful of black olives

Line two baking sheets with foil. Arrange the peppers and garlic on one sheet, and the onions on the other. Place the sheet with the peppers and garlic on the top shelf of a preheated 350°F oven and roast the peppers for 40 to 45 minutes, turning them once, until the skins blister and blacken; take the garlic out after 20 minutes, or when the cloves feel soft. Roast the onions on the shelf below for about 1 hour, or until soft.

When the peppers are done, place them in a couple of plastic bags, twist shut, and steam and cool for 10 to 15 minutes. When the peppers are cool enough to handle, peel them, remove the stems and seeds, and cut them into strips about ½ inch wide.

When the onions are done, let them cool slightly and peel them. Cut each onion in half and then into thick slices. Arrange the peppers and onions on a platter or in a shallow bowl.

For the dressing, separate and peel the garlic cloves. Blend them in a food processor with the olive oil, lemon juice, salt to taste, and cumin.

Pour the dressing over the peppers and onions, add the olives, and mix well. Let the salad sit for a while so the flavors mingle.

roasted peppers and eggplants

{ *escalivada — catalonia* }

In Catalan, escalivar *means "to grill"; another name for this dish is* rustifaci, *which means "roasted." It was usual in Catalonia to cook all kinds of vegetables over wood embers in the fields and on beaches; that is also how they were cooked in the fireplace at home. Some, like onions and potatoes, were wrapped in foil and left in the ashes. This way of cooking gives vegetables a delicious smoky flavor, but today they are most often roasted in the oven. Escalivada, now usually made with eggplants and peppers alone, has become popular throughout Spain. It is dressed simply with olive oil and salt.*

SERVES 6

4 medium-small eggplants

4 fleshy red bell peppers

6 tablespoons extra virgin olive oil

Salt

Put the eggplants and peppers on a sheet of foil on a baking sheet and prick the eggplants in a few places with a pointed knife to prevent them from bursting. Put the tray in a preheated 350°F oven. Take the peppers out after about 45 minutes, when they are soft (leave the eggplants in). Put them in plastic bags, and twist to seal the bag. Let steam and cool for 10 to 15 minutes to make the skin come away more easily. Take the eggplants out after about 1 hour, when they are soft.

When the peppers are cool enough to handle, peel them, remove the seeds, and cut them into 8 strips each. Reserve the juices. Peel them and cut them into similar strips.

Arrange the vegetables in one layer on a serving plate, alternating the peppers and eggplants, and sprinkle with the olive oil and a little salt.

VARIATIONS

• Cook the peppers and eggplants under the broiler or on a grill over glowing embers. Turn them occasionally until they are soft and blackened all over, then continue as above.

• Cook 4 medium onions, not peeled, along with the eggplants and peppers. They will take longer to soften, about 1¼ hours. Peel them, cut them into wedges, and add them to the peppers and eggplants.

- Garnish the dish with black olives and chopped flat-leaf parsley.

- In Aragon, a version of *escalivada* called *frigolla* uses tomatoes. Roast 4 tomatoes for about 10 minutes, until they are slightly soft. Peel them, and cut them into wedges, and add to the other vegetables.

- In Murcia, a similar dish called *ensalada asada* includes roasted eggplants, peppers, onions, tomatoes, and garlic cloves, all cut into small pieces. The vegetables are put in a low oven for up to 1½ hours, and each type is taken out when it is soft. They are dressed with olive oil and lemon juice.

grilled vegetables

{ verduras a la plancha — catalonia

and mediterranean spain }

Grilling vegetables on a plancha, or a griddle, was the way peasants cooked them in the field, and now innovative chefs have made the technique fashionable. Asparagus, scallions, bell peppers, tomatoes, tender baby artichokes, eggplants, zucchini, and mushrooms are turned in olive oil and then cooked whole or in slices on a lightly oiled griddle or on an oiled grill over dying embers. You can do them under the broiler or roast them in a hot 450°F to 500°F oven, turning them once. If you watch them, you cannot go wrong. Serve them with a sprinkling of sea salt and a trickle of extra virgin olive oil, or with vinagreta *(page 135),* salmorreta *(page 138),* alioli *(page 141), or* mayonesa *(page 140).*

ratatouille-like vegetables

{ samfaina — catalonia }

Samfaina *is like the ratatouille of Provence. It is served as a hot accompaniment to fish, chicken, or meat and is also good as a cold starter, with bread. Many countries around the Mediterranean have a similar dish. In Catalonia, they cut the vegetables small and cook them until they are very soft and jammy; they do not usually include zucchini. I too prefer it without. Catalans say the dish originated with them, and that is very likely, since they were the first to put eggplants and zucchini, which came with the Arabs, with the peppers and tomatoes they brought back from the Americas.*

SERVES 4

1 large onion, cut in half and sliced

6 tablespoons olive oil

1 red or green bell pepper, cored, seeded, and cut into ½-inch cubes

4 garlic cloves, chopped

1 eggplant, cut into ½-inch cubes (skin on)

1 zucchini, cut into ½-inch slices or cubes (optional)

2 large tomatoes, halved crosswise and grated, or peeled and chopped

Salt

Sauté the onion in the oil, in a wide skillet, covered, over low heat, stirring often until soft. Add the bell pepper and cook, covered, stirring occasionally, for about 7 minutes, until soft. Add the garlic and stir for 2 to 3 minutes, then add the eggplant and zucchini, season with salt, and cook, covered, stirring and turning the vegetables often, for about 20 minutes, until slightly browned.

Add the tomatoes, season with salt, and cook, uncovered, for 10 to 15 minutes, until the vegetables are so soft they have lost their shape and much of the liquid has disappeared.

roasted red peppers with anchovies

{ pimientos con anchoas—la rioja }

Besides its grapes, La Rioja *is renowned for the vegetables that grow in the fertile plain of the Ebro Valley. The red peppers,* Pimientos Riojano, *have an intense color and flavor. Their sweetness is brought out by the saltiness of anchovies in this popular tapa that is served in the local wineries.*

SERVES 6

5 fleshy red bell peppers

Salt

3 tablespoons extra virgin olive oil

12 anchovy fillets preserved in oil

Place the peppers on a sheet of foil on a baking sheet and roast in a preheated 350°F oven, turning once, for 45 minutes, or until they are soft and the skins are blackened in parts.

Put them in a sturdy plastic bag, twist to seal it, and let them cool and steam for about 10 minutes.

When the peppers are cool enough to handle, peel and seed them. Cut each in half, then cut each half into 4 strips. Spread them on a serving plate, sprinkle with salt and the olive oil, and arrange the anchovies on top.

sautéed peppers and tomatoes

{ *fritada de pimientos y tomates —*
aragon, navarre, and la rioja }

Also known as chilindrón, fritada *is a specialty of the valley of the river Ebro in northeast Spain. It is served hot as a garnish for meat, chicken, or fish or cold as a first course.*

SERVES 4

1 large onion, cut in half and sliced

3 to 4 tablespoons olive oil

2 red bell peppers, cored, seeded, and cut into 8 strips each

2 garlic cloves, sliced

1 pound tomatoes, peeled and chopped

Salt and pepper

1 teaspoon sugar

Extra virgin olive oil

Fry the onion in the olive oil in a large skillet over medium heat until soft, stirring occasionally. Add the peppers and cook, stirring, until they have softened. Add the garlic, and when the slices begin to color, add the tomatoes, salt and pepper to taste, and sugar. Cook until the peppers are very soft and the sauce is reduced to a jammy consistency. Serve at room temperature, with a drizzle of extra virgin olive oil.

VARIATIONS

• Roast the peppers (see page 128), peel and seed them, cut them into squares, and add them when the sauce is reduced.

• For *pimientos* in *chilindrón con jamón*, fry 4 slices of *jamón serrano* or prosciutto, cut into small pieces, with the onion.

• For a wonderful light meal, break 4 eggs over the vegetables when they are done and cook until they set. Serve with bread.

zucchini with onions and oregano

{ *zarangollo — murcia* }

Cooking zucchini with onions and herbs until they are very soft gives them a delicate flavor and pleasing texture. This is good hot or cold.

SERVES 6

1 large onion, cut in half and sliced

3 to 4 tablespoons olive oil

2 pounds zucchini, thinly sliced

Salt

1 tablespoon chopped oregano

Fry the onion in the oil in a very large skillet over very low heat, stirring often, for about 15 minutes, until soft and golden. Add the zucchini and cook over low heat, covered, turning occasionally and sprinkling with salt, for about 30 minutes, until soft.

Add the oregano and cook for 10 minutes more.

VARIATION

When the zucchini are done, lightly beat 5 eggs, stir them in, and cook very briefly, stirring gently, until they set to a creamy consistency.

eggplant fritters with honey

{ *berenjenas con miel — andalusia* }

I have eaten several versions of these eggplant fritters, which are a specialty of Córdoba, and have loved them all. The combination of savory and sweet is sensational. In the town of Priego de Córdoba, which is in the mountains on the Ruta del Califato (the tourist route of old Muslim Spain), where there is an old Moorish quarter, the eggplant slices I ate were very thin and crisp and served with a dribble of honey. I learned from the chef at the restaurant Rio a new way to prevent the eggplant from absorbing too much oil, which is to soak the slices in milk, then drain them and cover them in flour.

These are best eaten as soon as they are done, but they are also very good reheated in the oven.

SERVES 4 TO 5

2 eggplants (about 1¼ pounds)

About 2 cups whole milk

Flour for dusting or dredging

Salt

Olive or sunflower oil for
   deep-frying

Orange blossom honey
   or other aromatic
   runny honey

Peel the eggplants and cut them into slices about ⅓ inch thick. Put them in a bowl, add enough milk to cover, and put a small plate on top to hold them down. Let soak for 1 to 2 hours; drain.

Cover a plate with plenty of flour mixed with a sprinkling of salt. Working in batches, turn the eggplant slices in this so that they are entirely covered with flour, then shake them to remove the excess. Deep-fry in sizzling but not too hot oil, turning the slices over as soon as the first side is brown. Drain on paper towels.

Serve hot with a dribble of honey, and let people help themselves to more honey if they like.

VARIATION

In Córdoba, I had the eggplant slices dipped in batter. The coating was crisp, the eggplant was moist, and they were served with grape juice molasses.

eggplant with béchamel and cheese

{ berenjenas con queso — catalonia }

The sixteenth-century Sevillian soldier and madrigalist Baltazar de Alcazár dedicated a poem to eggplants: he wrote, "Tres cosas me tienen preso/de amores el corazón/la bella Inés, el jamón/y las berenjenas con queso" ("Three things hold my heart a prisoner of love—the fair Inés, ham, and eggplants with cheese"). He was of Jewish descent and was proclaiming his love of ham, the most Catholic of foods, and at the same time his loyalty to an ancestral dish of eggplant and cheese that, according to the archives of the Inquisition, was considered a sign of Judaizing.

I learned from people in Spain to steam the eggplants, which gives them a meltingly soft texture. Even the skin becomes very soft. The sauce is light and creamy, and on top is a crunchy, garlicky crust.

SERVES 4

1 large eggplant or 2 smaller ones (about 1 pound), cut lengthwise into 8 slices (about ½ inch thick)

Salt

1¼ cups whole milk

4 tablespoons (½ stick) butter

2 tablespoons all-purpose flour

3 ounces aged Manchego or aged cheddar cheese, coarsely grated

¼ cup fresh bread crumbs

3 tablespoons chopped flat-leaf parsley

1 garlic clove, crushed

1 tablespoon olive oil

Steam the eggplant slices in a covered steamer over boiling water for about 4 to 5 minutes, until they are very soft. Gently lift them out and arrange them in one or two layers in a baking dish. Sprinkle very lightly with salt.

Heat the milk almost to a boil.

Meanwhile, melt the butter in a medium saucepan. Add the flour and stir vigorously with a wooden spoon over low heat for 3 to 4 minutes. Pour in the milk a little at a time, stirring vigorously, until the sauce has thickened (it will not be very thick) and is smooth. Let cook gently, stirring, for 10 minutes, then gradually stir in the cheese. If necessary, add a little salt. Pour the sauce over the eggplant.

Mix the bread crumbs, parsley, garlic, and olive oil with a little salt and sprinkle over the top of the eggplant. Bake in a preheated 375°F oven for 20 minutes, then put under a hot broiler until the topping begins to color. Serve hot.

sautéed vegetable medley

{ pisto manchego—la mancha and madrid }

I was surprised to find this Mediterranean ratatouille-type dish in the center of Spain. Fried onions, eggplants, and zucchini comprise the old Moorish dish alboronía, *which the Castilians adopted after they conquered Toledo. Peppers and tomatoes were added later. Some versions are without eggplants. Some people peel the eggplants and zucchini. Some add potatoes or drop some eggs on top at the end. I prefer to cook the eggplants separately, because of the way they absorb a lot of oil but then release it.*

The best pisto *that I have eaten was made by Rosemary, my friend Alicia's young Bolivian maid in Alicante. She learned how to cook when she worked at the home of the Spanish architect Antonio Lamela, who built the modern center of Madrid and whose family created the bourgeois style in the exclusive* barrio de Salamanca. *Rosemary swam with us early in the morning, then started cooking fabulous dishes for our large group of family and friends. This is her recipe, slightly adapted.*

SERVES 6

2 large onions (about 1 pound), coarsely chopped

About ⅔ cup olive oil

3 red bell peppers, or a mix of red and green, cored, seeded, and cut into ½-inch cubes

3 zucchini, cut into ½-inch cubes

Salt and pepper

5 to 6 tomatoes (about 1 pound), peeled and diced

1½ teaspoons sugar, or to taste

1 large or 2 small eggplants (about 1 pound), cut into ½-inch cubes

Fry the onions in about ⅓ cup of the oil in a large skillet or paella pan over medium-low heat, stirring often, until they begin to soften. Add the bell peppers and cook until they begin to soften. Add the zucchini, season with salt and pepper, and cook, turning them gently, until they soften. Add the tomatoes, with their juices, and the sugar and cook until the liquid has evaporated.

Meanwhile, fry the eggplant in ⅓ cup oil in another large skillet over high heat, stirring and turning the pieces with a slotted spoon or spatula. It will absorb a lot of oil at first but then gradually release most of it. When the eggplant is well cooked and soft, lift it out and drain on paper towels.

Add the eggplant to the rest of the vegetables, mix gently, and cook for a couple of minutes more.

VARIATION

Rosemary also makes *pisto* with potatoes cut into cubes—they go in after the onions—and flavors it with 1 teaspoon chopped fresh oregano.

winter vegetable medley

{ *menestra de invierno — asturias* }

This winter dish from mountainous Asturias is soupy and heartwarming. Hard-boiled eggs, cut in half, are often served as an accompaniment.

SERVES 4

1 large carrot, cut into bite-sized
  pieces

1 large leek, trimmed, washed, and
  cut into ¾-inch-wide slices

4 new potatoes, quartered

About ½ pound cauliflower
  florets (from 1 small cauliflower)

½ large onion, chopped

2 tablespoons olive oil

2 garlic cloves, chopped

3 slices *jamón serrano*, prosciutto,
  or bacon, cut into small pieces

1½ tablespoons all-purpose flour

Cook the carrot, leek, and potatoes in a large saucepan of boiling salted water for 20 minutes. Add the cauliflower florets and boil for another 10 minutes.

Meanwhile, fry the onion in the oil in a skillet, until soft. Add the garlic and *jamón serrano*, prosciutto, or bacon and stir for 1 to 2 minutes. Add the flour and stir for another minute.

Drain the vegetables, keeping their cooking water, and return to the saucepan. Add 2 cups of the cooking water to the garlic and ham, a little at a time to begin with, then more quickly, stirring vigorously so that lumps do not form. Pour over the vegetables, and cook for 10 minutes more, or until the vegetables are very tender.

medley of spring vegetables

{ *menestra de primavera—navarre and la rioja* }

This marvelous combination of green vegetables is one of the great vegetable dishes of Spain, a specialty of the regions crossed by the river Ebro. In 1837, it was cited in the Diccionarió de la Real Academia *as a soup. Although some modern chefs cook the vegetables al dente, I prefer them in the traditional way, long-cooked and soft, in a delicious soupy wine sauce lightly thickened with flour. You can vary the proportions. It makes a perfect first course but can also be served as a side dish, in which case it is enough for six. Tiny bits of ham lend the usual Spanish touch. Make it with fresh vegetables in the spring, but you will also have a lovely dish using frozen ones.*

SERVES 4 TO 6

3 cups chicken stock (or 3 cups water plus 1 bouillon cube)

1⅓ cups shelled fresh fava beans, or defrosted frozen fava beans

4 fresh baby artichoke hearts (see page 129) or defrosted frozen hearts or bottoms, cut in half

½ pound asparagus, hard bottom ends trimmed

1⅓ cups fresh peas or defrosted frozen peas

Salt

½ large onion, chopped

2 tablespoons olive oil

1 garlic clove, finely chopped

2 thin slices *jamón serrano,* prosciutto, or bacon, chopped

1½ tablespoons all-purpose flour

1 cup dry white wine

Bring the stock (or water and bouillon cube) to a boil in a saucepan. Add the fava beans and artichoke hearts or bottoms and simmer for 10 minutes, then add the asparagus and simmer for 5 minutes. Add the peas and cook just until the vegetables are tender, adding a little salt. Remove from the heat.

Fry the onion in the oil in a medium skillet over low heat, stirring, until soft. Add the garlic and chopped *jamón serrano,* prosciutto, or bacon and stir for 1 minute. Add the flour and stir until it acquires a little color, then gradually add the wine, stirring vigorously. Cook, stirring, until the sauce thickens a little. Add 2 ladles of the stock from the vegetables, stirring vigorously, and cook, stirring, for 8 to 10 minutes.

Pour the sauce over the vegetables, shake the pan, and cook until the vegetables are very tender. Serve hot or warm.

ALICIA RÍOS IVARS

When I arrived in Madrid airport for one of my research trips for the book, Alicia had a vegetable feast waiting for me. Alicia is a friend of many years. She was my mentor in Spain as I worked on the book, arranging invaluable contacts, taking me to visit people, answering endless questions, and sending me recipes and articles. I stayed with her in Madrid, where I used her extensive library of culinary books. You will find her name throughout the book.

Alicia is tall and thin and dresses toreador-style, her clothing fashioned of the exotic silks and colorful cottons she has collected on her travels. She adopted a Vidal Sassoon haircut when she came to London after college in the sixties to improve her English. During her stay, to earn extra money, she cooked at Cranks and other vegetarian restaurants. Alicia taught philosophy and psychology before opening her own restaurant. She is a food historian and an olive oil specialist and is known internationally as a food artist who creates collective performances. I met her at the Oxford Symposium of Food in 1985. The theme was "Food Ways, Science, and Lore." Harold McGee was there. Alicia made a Galician *quemada*, recited a spell, and I helped to light it.

Alone or with Ali&Cia, the EAT Art group she founded with her architect niece Barbara Ortiz, she has created edible hats, edible greenhouses, edible libraries, and, most spectacularly, edible cities and islands in different parts of the world. For the edible cities, they invite the local communities to think of ways to construct a section of their city using their own traditional foods. With columns of spring rolls, palaces built of Indian sweets, parks of green rice, and skyscrapers of bagels, stuffed grape leaves, and sushi, the final edible map reflects the ethnic mix of the population. At the end of the performance, with background music, the public is invited to eat the result. On April 28, 2007, I was in Trafalgar Square with my children and grandchildren and we watched fourteen volunteer teams from community centers and social clubs led by Alicia and Barbara bring their models of different parts of London created with samosas, pakoras, pizzas, and the like. Because of the huge crowd, we did not get to eat any of it.

Alicia has a summer house in Calpe, on the Costa Blanca in the province of Alicante. Her little *casita* is next to her mother Pepa's house. Her maternal grandfather had land in Alicante, and her parents—her father was an internationally renowned geological scientist from Zaragoza—were so taken by a rock in the sea, called El Peñón de Ifach, that they built three little houses overlooking it so that their three daughters would always have a home there. They were the only houses near the little fishing village of Calpe. Now one has been sold and the two houses left are the last Spanish enclave in a world of high-rise buildings and an English, German, and Russian expat population.

I stayed at the *casita* with a group of Alicia's friends. She had suspended hundreds of plastic flowers on strings from the ceilings and strewn many more over the floors and beds. Margarita, Pepa's *dame de compagnie;* young Rosemary from Bolivia, Alicia's maid; and Ana, whose husband is a local fisherman, prepared sumptuous meals for us every day. Many of their recipes are in this book.

On Saturday nights, after it gets dark, Alicia sometimes projects films in the garden on a whitewashed wall that houses the laundry and wood oven and the grill where she makes paella. She has a collection of silent films, Hollywood musicals, old newsreels, Almodóvar films, old Catalan films, blues and rock and roll concert films, documentaries. She calls it the Cantina Visual Cine Club, and everybody is invited, even people she meets on the beach and passersby. Friends and neighbors bring their own chairs and sandwiches. Her mother's friends are in their eighties and nineties. Alicia puts out drinks, cordials of herbs and flowers, on the table, with food nibbles. At the end, everyone is invited to dance to music from a small portable record player.

artichokes with green sauce

{ alcachofas con salsa verde — catalonia }

This recipe was inspired by one in Tía Victoria's Spanish Kitchen *by Victoria Serra, translated by Elizabeth Gili. It was lent to me by Elizabeth, a beautiful blue-eyed lady in her nineties. Her husband, Joan Gili, a Catalan, had come to London in 1933. He ran a Hispanic bookshop in Cecil Court off St. Martin's Lane and translated several of García Lorca's books with Stephen Spender. He also started the Anglo-Catalan Society. Nostalgic for his family cooking, he wrote to his mother for recipes and eventually encouraged her to write a book that was published in Spain as* Sapores *by his father, the publisher Luis Gili.*

I used frozen artichoke bottoms. If you want to use fresh artichokes, see page 129 for how to prepare them.

SERVES 4

8 fresh artichoke hearts or bottoms
    (see page 129) or frozen ones,
    defrosted

½ slice white bread,
    crusts removed

1 to 2 large garlic cloves

2 tablespoons olive oil

1 tablespoon white wine vinegar

½ to ¾ cup chopped flat-leaf parsley

3 tablespoons extra virgin olive oil

Salt

Cook the artichokes in boiling salted water until just tender. Drain and let cool.

Fry the bread and garlic cloves in olive oil in a small skillet over medium heat, turning to brown them lightly all over. Drain on paper towels.

Pour the vinegar over the fried bread, then blend with the garlic in the food processor. Add the parsley, extra virgin olive oil, and some salt and blend to a creamy sauce.

Serve the artichokes at room temperature, spreading a little of the sauce over each one.

artichokes in almond sauce

{ alcachofas en salsa blanca—

navarre, la rioja, and aragon }

I loved a delicate dish of cardoon stalks in an almond sauce that I ate in Navarre. At home, I had trouble finding cardoons, so I was happy to hear that artichokes are also cooked in the same way in Spain, as are ribs of Swiss chard. You may be able to find cardoons preserved in jars; in Spain, you can buy them frozen. If you have fresh cardoons, see the variation. I use frozen artichoke bottoms. It is a dish you can easily make for a lot of people if you have frozen artichokes.

SERVES 8

2¼ cups milk

2¼ cups chicken stock
   (or 2¼ cups water plus
   1 bouillon cube)

2 tablespoons olive oil

2 tablespoons all-purpose flour

2 garlic cloves, crushed to a paste

½ cup ground almonds

Salt

Two 14-ounce packages
   frozen artichoke bottoms or
   three 9-ounce packages frozen
   artichoke hearts, defrosted

Bring the milk and stock (or water and bouillon cube) to a boil.

Meanwhile, heat the oil in a large saucepan. Add the flour and stir vigorously with a wooden spoon over low heat for about 30 seconds, without letting it brown. Stir in the garlic, then stir in the milk and stock mixture a little at a time, stirring vigorously to prevent lumps. Continue to stir until the sauce thickens, then stir in the ground almonds and add salt to taste. Add the artichokes and cook for about 15 minutes, until they are tender. Serve hot.

VARIATION

Use cardoons instead of artichokes, fresh or preserved in jars. Fresh cardoons are sometimes sold with the prickly outer parts of the stems removed. Only the inner part of the stalks are eaten. If the cardoons have not already been trimmed, you will need about 4 pounds. Tear off the leaves and cut the stalks into 3- to 4-inch lengths. Cook in boiling salted water acidulated with the juice of ½ lemon for about 20 minutes. Drain and refresh in a bowl of cold water, then peel off the tough skin and strings from the stems and discard. Drop stalks into the sauce and cook for 15 to 25 minutes, until tender. (If using jarred cardoons, just heat through in the sauce.)

peas and fava beans with ham

{ *guisantes y habas con jamón—catalonia* }

I love the Catalan way of making a grand dish with a symphony of flavors out of ordinary vegetables. The peas and favas are cooked until they are soft, not crisp. Serve them with toasted bread with a drizzle of extra virgin olive oil.

This dish is often made with fava beans alone. Sometimes tomatoes are added. With Catalan sausages or chorizo, it is a main dish. See the variations for all three versions.

SERVES 6

¼ pound thinly sliced *jamón serrano*, prosciutto, or bacon, cut into small pieces

¼ cup olive oil

5 to 6 garlic cloves, chopped

3⅓ cups shelled fresh fava beans or defrosted frozen fava beans (1 pound)

2¼ cups chicken stock (or 2¼ cups water plus 1 bouillon cube)

A sprig of marjoram

A sprig of mint

1 bay leaf

Salt and pepper

3⅓ cups shelled fresh peas or defrosted frozen peas (1 pound)

6 scallions, trimmed and thinly sliced

⅓ cup rum, brandy, or anise-flavored liqueur

Sauté the *jamón,* prosciutto, or bacon in the oil in a large saucepan, stirring, for about 30 seconds if using *jamón* or prosciutto, or until lightly browned if using bacon. Add the garlic and stir for seconds only, until the aroma rises.

Add the beans, the stock or water and bouillon cube, the sprigs of marjoram and mint, and the bay leaf, bring to a simmer, and simmer, covered, for 10 to 20 minutes, until the beans are tender (the time depends on how young the beans are; frozen beans will take about 15 minutes). Add salt, taking into consideration the saltiness of the stock, and some pepper.

Add the peas, scallions, and rum, brandy, or liqueur and cook, covered, for 7 to 10 minutes, or until the peas are soft.

VARIATIONS

• Omit the peas and use 6⅔ cups (2 pounds) fava beans.

• Add 2 tomatoes, peeled and chopped, after the garlic.

• Omit the rum, brandy, or liqueur and add a cinnamon stick along with the fava beans. Stir in 3 tablespoons roughly chopped mint toward the end of cooking.

• Boil 14 ounces semi-cured chorizo in water for 20 minutes; drain. Cut into slices and add to the cooked peas and beans. Or add 14 ounces *morcilla* (Spanish blood sausage), boiled for only 10 minutes and cut into slices.

braised peas and artichokes

{ guisantes y alcachofas —catalonia }

Fava beans, a favorite vegetable in Catalonia, are more often used in this dish than peas, but this version with peas is delightful. (See the variations for the fava version.) Serve it with toasted bread drizzled with extra virgin olive oil.

SERVES 6

1 large onion, chopped

2 tablespoons olive oil

¼ pound sliced *jamón serrano* or prosciutto, cut into small pieces

3 garlic cloves, finely chopped

2 medium tomatoes, peeled and chopped

1 teaspoon sugar

½ cup brandy

1 cinnamon stick

2 thyme or oregano sprigs

3 mint sprigs

14 ounces frozen artichoke bottoms, defrosted, or 6 fresh baby artichoke hearts (see page 129)

About 2 cups chicken stock (or 2 cups water plus ½ bouillon cube)

Salt

2⅔ cups fresh peas or defrosted frozen peas (about 14 ounces)

Sauté the onion in the oil in a wide skillet over low heat for about 20 minutes, stirring occasionally, until it is soft and just beginning to color. Add the *jamón*, prosciutto, or bacon and cook, stirring, for about 30 seconds if using *jamón* or prosciutto, or until lightly browned if using bacon. Add the garlic and cook, stirring, until the aroma rises, then stir in the tomatoes. Add the sugar and cook for about 10 minutes over medium heat, until reduced almost to a paste.

Pour in the brandy and add the cinnamon stick and herb sprigs. Put in the artichoke bottoms or hearts, cover with the stock (or the water and bouillon cube), and add salt. Cook, covered, over low heat for 10 to 15 minutes, until the artichokes are tender.

Add the peas and cook for 5 to 10 minutes, or until the peas are soft.

Serve hot or at room temperature.

VARIATIONS

- Instead of the brandy, add ¼ cup Moscatel or other sweet white wine, *aguardiente*, or grappa.

- Instead of peas, use fava beans, fresh or frozen. Add them at the same time as the artichokes. Cook until very tender.

wild mushrooms

My Catalan friend Pepa Aymami had a huge crateful of wild mushrooms, *setas,* spread out on towels on the garden table on her terrace in Barcelona. You could smell the forest. She cleaned off any bits of earth with a brush and cooked them in a huge skillet over high heat with a little sweet-tasting extra virgin olive oil, a sprinkling of salt, and just a touch of crushed garlic, so that it would not mask the flavors and aromas of the mushrooms.

Wild mushrooms grow in breathtaking varieties in the Basque Country and Catalonia, where people are crazy about them. Catalans have identified a hundred edible species, about fifteen of them of gastronomic quality. The most prized are cèpes, chanterelles, and morels. During the season in September and October, market stalls are full of mushrooms. People go mushroom hunting in the mountains. You can learn to identify the edible ones on organized tours, and you get to cook them and eat them. There are mushroom festivals, and restaurants dedicate their menus to them. They are grilled, sautéed, baked, or scrambled with eggs; used as a garnish for game and meat; and added to sauces and stews.

Wild mushrooms grow in other parts of Spain, especially in the wet northwest, but people there had always been afraid of picking them—until Catalans and Basques came to get them. They were afraid because three or four people are said to die of food poisoning every year. And until recently they did not value them because they were wild and free.

PEPA AYMAMI

*Pepa is a glamorous blond, blue-eyed live wire. I first met her at an interna-*tional symposium on Mediterranean food in Barcelona in 2004; she was director and coordinator. Scholars from various Mediterranean countries came together to discuss the histories, peoples, religions, products, cooking techniques, and shared food heritage of the area, and chefs were invited to demonstrate their dishes using Mediterranean products. Pepa put together chefs from warring countries (they fell into each other's arms) and initiated the project Taste for Peace. She later got the chefs to help compile a database of all the dishes they had in common for her Fundació Viure el Mediterrani, which aimed to establish the gastronomic heri-tage of the Mediterranean and to create a Mediterranean Product brand.

She is also the director of the Fundació Institut Català de la Cuina (page 105). When I stayed with her in Barcelona, I met her colleagues, passionate Catalan gastronomes, over lunch. She sent me a huge book, their archive of recipes col-lected from chefs, farmers, and housewives, most of them in mountain and fishing villages. I keep phoning her for advice and details. How long can I boil the blood sausage before it explodes? What is *vi ranci*? (It is fortified—not rancid—wine.)

Pepa's office is in a flat above her own and she manages to cook lunch every day for everyone. She has four children, two daughters and two sons. Her elder son,

Juan, is unusual in that although he comes from a very Catholic family he became convinced that he was of Jewish origin and wanted to convert to Judaism. When rabbis in Spain would not con-vert him, he went to Israel to study at a yeshiva. His family thought it was a kibbutz. He became Jewish and Israeli and fought in Lebanon. He now lives in Barcelona with his Catalan wife and sons and has joined the Jewish community, which is made up mainly of people from North Africa and Latin America.

mushrooms with garlic

{ *champiñones al ajillo—mediterranean spain* }

Spanish terms for mushrooms can be a bit confusing. All mushrooms are hongos, *but wild ones are referred to as* setas, *and cultivated button mushrooms as* champiñones. *The easiest mushrooms to cultivate and the most common are the* champiñones de Paris, *so called because they were first cultivated near Paris in Napoleon's time (these are our ordinary white button mushrooms). They are highly regarded in Spain. As they do not have the rich flavor and aroma of wild funghi, this way of preparing them, with plenty of garlic, a rich extra virgin olive oil, and a little lemon juice, or wine if you like, suits them well. They are a popular tapa all over Spain, served with crusty bread to mop up the garlicky oil.*

SERVES 4

½ pound button mushrooms

¼ cup extra virgin olive oil

4 to 5 garlic cloves, chopped
    or sliced

½ teaspoon red pepper flakes
    (optional)

Salt and pepper

1 tablespoon fresh lemon juice
    or ¼ cup dry white wine
    (optional)

2 tablespoons chopped
    flat-leaf parsley

Wipe any dirt off the mushrooms. If necessary, trim the stems and rinse them briefly under cold water. Cut them in half, or into quarters if they are large.

Heat the oil in a large skillet. Add the mushrooms, garlic, and red pepper flakes, if using, and sauté over medium-high heat, stirring and turning the mushrooms and adding salt and pepper, until they absorb the oil and then release it and their juices. Add the lemon juice or white wine, if using, lower the heat, and cook until the mushrooms are very soft and the juices have almost evaporated, so that the oil is sizzling. In all, the cooking may take about 15 to 20 minutes.

Stir in the parsley and serve hot or at room temperature.

marinated mushrooms with lemon

{ champiñones marinados — mediterranean spain }

These mushrooms are dry-cooked first so they lose their juices and then better absorb the scent of grated lemon zest in the marinade. They keep well in the refrigerator and make a good little appetizer to nibble with bread and olives.

SERVES 6 TO 8

Grated zest of ½ lemon

Juice of 1 lemon

5 tablespoons extra virgin olive oil

Salt and pepper

1 pound button mushrooms

2 tablespoons chopped
flat-leaf parsley

Mix the lemon zest, lemon juice, oil, and some salt and pepper in a wide shallow bowl.

Wipe the mushrooms clean. If necessary, trim the stems and rinse them briefly under cold running water. Cut them in half, or into quarters if they are large. Heat them in a wide dry nonstick skillet over medium heat, turning them occasionally, for 10 to 12 minutes, until they release their juices and the juices evaporate. Put them in the bowl with the marinade while they are still hot, and mix well. Cover and refrigerate for at least 5 hours; they will keep for many days.

Serve at room temperature, with a sprinkling of parsley.

mushroom flan

{ *pastel de hongos — navarre* }

Navarre has had a long relationship with France, and that is one reason why they cook with cream there. They also have dairy cows. If wild mushrooms such as cèpes and chanterelles are unavailable or too expensive, use cremini or button mushrooms.

SERVES 4 TO 6

1 pound mushrooms,
    preferably wild

½ large onion, chopped

3 tablespoons olive oil

Salt and pepper

3 large eggs

1 cup heavy cream
    or crème fraîche

1 to 2 garlic cloves, crushed

3 tablespoons chopped
    flat-leaf parsley

Wipe the mushrooms clean; wash them briefly if necessary. Trim them and cut them in half, or into quarters if large.

Fry the onion in the oil in a skillet over medium-low heat until soft and just beginning to color. Add the mushrooms, season with salt and pepper to taste, and cook, stirring, until the mushrooms have released their juices and these juices have almost evaporated.

Beat the eggs lightly with a fork, then beat in the cream or crème fraîche, along with the garlic and parsley. Season to taste. Fold in the mushrooms and onions and pour into a wide buttered baking dish or flan mold.

Bake in a preheated 400°F oven for 45 to 60 minutes, until the flan is set and golden. Serve warm.

butter beans with chestnuts

{ judias blancas con castañas — andalusia }

Chestnuts were once a staple in Spain. Peasants dried them for use throughout the year. For this dish, they soaked both chestnuts and dried beans overnight. This easy version made with canned beans is delicious. With a little more liquid, it can be served as a potaje, *or soup; with chorizo, as in the variation, it becomes a substantial main dish.*

SERVES 4

½ large onion, chopped

2 tablespoons olive oil

3 garlic cloves, finely chopped

2½ cups (about 8 ounces) defrosted frozen chestnuts or vacuum-packed chestnuts

1 cinnamon stick

2 cloves

Salt and pepper

Two 15-ounce cans butter beans or navy beans, drained

1½ tablespoons extra virgin olive oil

Fry the onion in the oil in a wide saucepan over low heat, stirring often, until soft. Add the garlic and stir until the aroma rises. Add the chestnuts and water to cover, put in the cinnamon stick and cloves, and season with salt and pepper. Simmer, uncovered, until the chestnuts are tender—10 to 15 minutes if frozen, less if vacuum-packed—and the liquid a little reduced. Stir in the beans and cook for 5 minutes longer.

Serve hot or warm, drizzled with the olive oil.

VARIATIONS

- To thicken the sauce, take out a few chestnuts and mash them with a fork, then return them to the pan.

- Add a pinch of saffron and 1 teaspoon sugar at the start.

- For a main dish, boil 1 pound semi-cured chorizo in water for 20 minutes; drain, cut into thick slices, and add to the chestnuts at the same time as the beans.

- Use fresh chestnuts. To peel them, see page 130.

spinach with raisins and pine nuts

{ espinacas con pasas y piñones — catalonia }

This way of preparing spinach is known throughout Spain as espinacas a la catalana. *It can be served as a starter or as a side dish. You will need a large pot if you use fresh spinach, as the leaves are bulky before they collapse into a soft mass. It is fine to use frozen leaf spinach; see the variation.*

SERVES 4

1½ pounds spinach

2 tablespoons pine nuts

¼ cup olive oil

2 tablespoons raisins, soaked in
    water for 20 minutes
    and drained

Salt and pepper

Wash the spinach thoroughly in plenty of water and remove any thick stems. (If using baby spinach, you don't need to remove the thin stems.) Drain, and put the leaves with only the water that clings to them in a large pot. Cover the pot and put over high heat until the water begins to boil, then lower the heat and steam for a few minutes; the leaves wilt into a soft mass in 2 to 3 minutes.

Sauté the pine nuts briefly in the oil in a large skillet, shaking the pan or stirring constantly, until they just begin to color. Add the raisins and spinach and mix well. Season with salt and pepper and cook for 5 minutes, stirring occasionally.

Note: If you have bought fresh baby spinach ready washed in a bag, you will need to add about ¼ to ⅓ cup of water in the pot to create some steam.

VARIATIONS

• Use frozen leaf spinach instead of fresh. Defrost it and cook it in a little water for a few minutes until soft, then drain.

• Use Swiss chard instead of spinach.

spinach with béchamel and hard-boiled eggs

{ espinacas con bechamel—navarre }

This makes a lovely vegetarian dish. The Spanish-style béchamel is light and creamy and has a special taste and aroma because of the sherry (or wine). I love it.

SERVES 4 AS A STARTER; 2 AS A MAIN DISH

1½ pounds whole spinach

2¼ cups whole milk

¾ cup dry sherry or white wine

½ large onion, finely chopped

6 tablespoons (¾ stick) butter

3 tablespoons all-purpose flour

Salt

A pinch of nutmeg

4 hard-boiled eggs,
    cut into quarters

Wash the spinach thoroughly in plenty of water and remove any thick stems. Drain, and put the leaves with only the water that clings to them in a large pot. Cover the pot and put it over high heat until the water begins to boil, then lower the heat and steam for 2 to 3 minutes, until the leaves wilt into a soft mass. Drain, let cool slightly, and coarsely chop.

Heat the milk with the sherry or wine until warm.

Meanwhile, sauté the chopped onion in the butter in a saucepan over very low heat until soft. Add the flour and cook, stirring, over medium heat for 1 to 2 minutes, until light brown. Gradually add the milk, a little at a time to begin with, and stir vigorously to prevent lumps from forming. Add salt to taste and the nutmeg and cook, stirring, for 15 to 20 minutes over gentle heat, until the sauce thickens to the consistency of light cream.

Add the spinach and mix well. Cook for 3 to 5 minutes, and adjust the seasoning.

Serve hot in little bowls, arranging a quartered egg over each serving.

Note: If using baby spinach, you do not need to remove the thin stems. And if it is prewashed and dry in a bag, you will need to add ¼ to ⅓ cup water to the pot to create enough steam to cook it.

red cabbage with apples, raisins, and pine nuts

{ *lombarda a la madrileña — madrid* }

Red cabbage is a winter dish that is served on New Year's Eve in Madrid. The sweet-and-sour flavor goes well with game and roast pork. It is sometimes made with apples only and no raisins and pine nuts, sometimes with no apples and with raisins and pine nuts. Cook it in a large casserole or pot with a tight-fitting lid.

SERVES 8

1 red cabbage (about 2 pounds)

4½ tablespoons olive oil

½ cup water

2 garlic cloves, crushed
    or finely chopped

2 Golden Delicious or other dessert
    apples, peeled, cored, and
    chopped into ½-inch pieces

¼ cup raisins, soaked in water
    for 20 minutes and drained

5 tablespoons red or white wine
    vinegar or cider vinegar

2 tablespoons sugar, or to taste

Salt and pepper

¼ cup pine nuts

Remove the tough outer leaves and cut the cabbage into quarters through the core. Cut away the hard core, and shred the cabbage.

Put the cabbage in a large casserole or pot, add 4 tablespoons of the oil, the water, garlic, apples, raisins, vinegar, sugar, and salt and pepper to taste, and mix well. Cover, bring to a simmer and steam over very low heat for 45 to 60 minutes, stirring and turning over the cabbage every so often, until it is very soft.

Meanwhile, fry the pine nuts in the remaining ½ tablespoon of oil in a small skillet, stirring, until they just begin to color.

Stir the pine nuts into the cabbage and serve hot.

VARIATIONS

- Sauté ¼ pound bacon, cut into small pieces, in the oil before you put in the pine nuts.

- Fry a chopped onion in the oil before you put in the pine nuts.

- Add ½ teaspoon cloves and ½ teaspoon cinnamon along with the salt and pepper.

- Use red wine instead of the water.

"wrinkled" potatoes
with red and green sauces

{ papas arrugadas y mojos canaries—canary islands }

My daughter Anna brought back a little booklet from a family holiday in Lanzarote in the Canary Islands entitled Papas Arrugadas y Mojos Canaries, *which was subtitled "The Best Recipes from the Canaries." Their hotel had held a cooking demonstration of their famous "wrinkled" potatoes and the accompanying green and red sauces. Potatoes are the most popular food of the islands—they grow twenty varieties, most of them ancient varieties—and the favorite way of cooking them is to boil them in their skins with a huge amount of salt until all the water has evaporated. They come out wrinkled and covered with a white powdery film.*

I ate them in an Irish pub in Seville. They had a firm but tender texture and intense potato flavor. Amazingly, they were not too salty, because the salt in the water has the effect of drawing out their juices rather than being absorbed. I cooked them at home several times—on two occasions they turned out to be inedible because too salty when the skins had been too thin, so look for potatoes with good skins. Serve them in their skins, hot or warm. They can be made ahead and reheated in the oven before serving.

You are supposed to pick up the potatoes with your hands and dip them into the traditional sauces as you take bites. The friends who ate them at my house preferred to put blobs of sauce on their plates or to spoon some onto their cut-open potatoes.

SERVES 6

2 pounds small to medium waxy
  potatoes (in their skins), washed

4 tablespoons coarse sea salt

Put the potatoes in a large saucepan that holds them in one layer, and add just enough water to cover and the salt. Bring to a boil and cook, uncovered, over medium heat, letting the water bubble for 25 minutes, or until the potatoes are very tender and the water has evaporated. Leave them over very low heat for a few minutes, moving them and turning them over in the dry pan, until they are wrinkled and covered with a fine powder of salt. Serve hot or warm, with one or both of the sauces.

>>>

½ green bell pepper,
    cut into large pieces

½ cup coriander leaves

2 garlic cloves, or to taste,
    crushed to a paste

¼ to ½ teaspoon ground cumin

1½ tablespoons white
    wine vinegar

Pinch of fine sea salt, or to taste

½ cup extra virgin olive oil

green sauce with cilantro

mojo verde de cilantro—canary islands

This sauce is also great with fried, grilled, or poached fish. It keeps well in the refrigerator.

Blend all the ingredients except the oil to a paste in the food processor. Gradually add the oil and blend to a light creamy consistency.

4 garlic cloves, or to taste,
    crushed to a paste

¾ teaspoon *pimentón picante*,
    chile pepper, or cayenne

2 teaspoons *pimentón dulce*
    (or sweet paprika)

¼ teaspoon cumin

6 tablespoons extra virgin olive oil

2 tablespoons white or
    red wine vinegar

Salt

spicy red sauce

mojo picón—canary islands

This mojo, *a garlic and chile pepper sauce, is also called* mojo colorado. *In the Canaries, they make it hot or sweet with their own special dried chile peppers that they soak in boiling water, then pound with plenty of garlic. I have had it in Seville with* pimentón, *which makes it very simple.*

Mix the garlic with the *pimentón,* and cumin in a bowl, then beat in the olive oil and vinegar. Add salt to taste.

mashed potatoes with olive oil and scallions

{ *patatas aliñadas — andalusia* }

I love this potato dish, which I first ate in a bar in Seville. It is said that it was a monk, Hieronymous Carda, who brought potatoes to Spain from Peru, and that they were first grown in Málaga. This is a specialty of Málaga, where potatoes are still sometimes called by their early names, papas *or* batatas.

SERVES 6

1½ pounds baking potatoes,
    peeled and cut in half
    or quartered

6 tablespoons (or more)
    extra virgin olive oil

Salt and pepper

6 to 8 scallions, chopped

2 tablespoons chopped
    flat-leaf parsley

Cook the potatoes in boiling salted water until soft.

Drain, keeping about ½ cup of the cooking water, put in a bowl, and coarsely mash. Stir in the olive oil, salt and pepper to taste, and a little of the cooking water—enough to give the potatoes a soft, slightly moist texture. Stir in the scallions and parsley.

Serve at room temperature.

potatoes with fried onions and eggs

{ p a t a t a s   a   l o   p o b r e   c o n   h u e v o s   r o t o s — a n d a l u s i a }

Manolo (see page 173) took me to Embutidos Luque in Fuensanta de Martos in Jaén, where they make artisanal hams and sausages. Hams and sausages hung from the ceiling like stalactites in a cave, and there were huge piles of salted pigs' ears and feet in boxes. One of their new chorizos is made with olive oil instead of pork fat. We went on to the family restaurant Estrella, where three ladies, Loli Luque Peragón, Yolanda Luque Garrido, and Igna López Fernandez, cooked half a dozen local dishes for us. After we finished, we went to the kitchen, and they gave me the recipes. This is one of them. I made double the quantity in my paella pan for a family lunch in the garden. When I explained that the potatoes were called a lo pobre, *meaning "of the poor," my six-year-old granddaughter Nell said, "But we are not poor."*

SERVES 4

1 pound waxy potatoes, peeled

1½ large onions,
    cut in half and sliced

¼ cup olive oil

Salt

6 large eggs

2 tablespoons chopped
    flat-leaf parsley

Cook the potatoes in boiling salted water for 15 to 25 minutes, until tender, then drain. Fry the onions in the oil, in a large covered skillet over low heat, stirring often, until they are soft and their juices have evaporated, so that the oil is sizzling. It can take 25 minutes.

Cut the potatoes into ⅓-inch-thick slices and add them to the onions. Cook, uncovered, over medium to high heat, turning the potatoes and onions with a spatula and adding salt to taste, until they are golden.

Beat the eggs lightly with a little salt. Pour over the potatoes and stir until they have set to a creamy consistency. Serve hot, sprinkled with the parsley.

VARIATIONS

• Add 1 green bell pepper, cored, seeded, and cut into small pieces, with the onions.

• Fry ½ pound cured chorizo, sliced, and about 8 chopped slices of bacon in a little oil in a large skillet, and add them to the potatoes before you pour in the eggs.

• Sprinkle 2 to 3 teaspoons wine vinegar over the potatoes before adding the eggs.

stuffed artichoke bottoms

{ alcachofas rellenas — andalusia }

I ate delicious stuffed artichokes at the Bar el Choto in Frailes. The cook, Caridad Zafra, described the stuffing. I cannot get small artichokes with leaves tender enough to eat, so I made the dish with frozen artichoke bottoms I get from a small Iranian store near me; they come from Egypt. I baked them instead of deep-frying them.

SERVES 6

3 ounces (4 slices) crustless
    white bread

1 cup flat-leaf parsley leaves

6 slices *jamón serrano* or prosciutto

3 large garlic cloves, finely chopped
    or crushed to a paste

2 large eggs

Salt if necessary

Two 14-ounce bags frozen
    artichoke bottoms (about 20),
    defrosted

About 2 cups chicken stock
    (or 2 cups water plus
    1 bouillon cube)

For the stuffing, coarsely blend the bread, parsley, *jamón* or prosciutto, and garlic in a food processor. Mix in the eggs. Add salt if necessary; you may not need any because of the saltiness of the ham.

Spread a heaped teaspoon of the mixture into each artichoke bottom and arrange them in a wide baking dish. Pour in enough chicken stock (or water and the bouillon cube) so that it does not entirely cover the artichokes.

Bake in a preheated 375°F oven for about 30 minutes, until the artichokes feel tender when you cut into them with a pointed knife.

ROSA TOVAR LARRUCEA

I went shopping with Rosa at Madrid's San Martín market and then watched her cook lunch for friends in her charming attic flat. Rosa was born in Salamanca. Her mother was from a Basque shipowning family. Her father, a university professor, was a gourmand who had acquired a varied palate, because his notary father moved the family between northern Castile, Cantabria, Castellón, Alicante, and Madrid. He always had little stories to tell about the dishes that his wife put on the table, and he passed his fascination with the history of food to his daughter.

In 1985, Rosa founded a company that made pastries and frozen sauces. Now she teaches in cooking schools in Madrid, Guadalajara, and Salamanca. She teaches all kinds of people, including chefs, pastry cooks, and butchers. Young people in Spain want to learn about new technology, the latest international trends, and healthy eating and organic foods, as well as how to prepare quick and easy dishes, and more traditional ones to make on weekends. Rosa's cook-

ing shows how traditional foods can be updated and become lighter, healthier, and more pleasing without losing their character. She has written several books, including *Arroces* (*Rice*) and *3,000 Años de Cocina Española* (*Three Thousand Years of Spanish Cooking*), with Monique Fuller. Some of the recipes she has e-mailed me have gone into this book, including two recipes for *berenjenas rellenas,* stuffed eggplants.

bell peppers stuffed with rice in tomato sauce

{ pimientos rellenos de arroz con salsa

de tomates — valencia and murcia }

I like to use sweeter-tasting red bell peppers for stuffing, but others prefer the more peppery green ones. The most common filling is a mix of ground pork and rice, but this one with rice alone makes a beautiful dish for vegetarians. It is best to use short-grain or "round" rice, which is soft and sticks together when cooked. Choose peppers with a good base so they can stand up in the baking dish.

SERVES 6

FOR THE TOMATO SAUCE

2 pounds ripe tomatoes

6 garlic cloves, chopped

½ to 1 red chile pepper, seeds
    removed, finely chopped

3 tablespoons olive oil

2 teaspoons sugar

Salt

FOR THE FILLING

1 large onion, chopped

¼ cup olive oil

3 medium tomatoes

½ teaspoon sugar

2 teaspoons chopped oregano

Salt

>>>

For the sauce, cut the tomatoes into quarters (you do not need to peel them) and remove the hard white bits near the stem ends. Blend them to a light puree in a food processor.

Heat the garlic and chile pepper in the oil in a wide skillet, stirring, for 30 seconds, until the aroma rises, then add the tomatoes, sugar, and some salt. Cook over medium-high heat, stirring occasionally, for 25 to 30 minutes, until the sauce is reduced and thick.

For the filling, fry the onion in the oil in a large skillet over medium heat, stirring often, until soft and golden. Add the tomatoes, sugar, oregano, and a little salt, and cook until the liquid has almost disappeared. Add the rice, stir well, then add the stock (or water and bouillon cubes). Stir in the saffron, and salt and pepper to taste, and bring to a boil, then simmer over low heat for about 15 minutes, until most of the liquid has been absorbed but the rice is still underdone.

>>>

1¼ cups short-grain
    (round) rice or risotto
    rice, such as Arborio
2½ cups hot chicken
    or vegetable stock (or
    2½ cups water plus
    2 bouillon cubes)
Good pinch of saffron
    threads
Pepper

6 red or green bell peppers,
    or 3 of each

Retaining the stalk, cut a circle around the stalk off the tops of the peppers, and keep these to use as caps. Remove the cores and seeds with a pointed spoon, and shave the inside of the lids to make more room for the filling. Using a spoon, fill the peppers with the rice without pressing it down too much, so that there is a little room for it to expand. Replace the caps and arrange the peppers snugly in a baking dish.

Pour the tomato sauce around the peppers, cover with a sheet of foil, and bake in a preheated 400°F oven for 1 hour. Remove the foil and continue to bake for another 15 minutes, or until the peppers are soft and have browned on top; be careful not to let them fall apart. Serve hot.

tomatoes stuffed with tuna

{ *tomates rellenos de atún — murcia* }

These tomatoes can be served hot or cold. I like them best cold, and with the chopped olives in the filling.

SERVES 4 AS A STARTER

8 small to medium tomatoes
(about 1¼ pounds)

1 large onion, finely chopped

2 tablespoons olive oil

2 garlic cloves, chopped

One 6-ounce can tuna in oil

3 tablespoons coarsely chopped
black olives (optional)

Cut a small slice off the stem end of each tomato and keep these to use as lids. Remove the pulp and seeds with a pointed teaspoon, and turn the tomatoes upside down so the juices run out.

Fry the onion in the oil in a skillet until soft, stirring often. Add the garlic and stir until the onion and garlic begin to color. Take off the heat and stir in the tuna and the olives, if using.

Stuff the tomatoes with the tuna mixture and replace the lids. Arrange them snugly in a small baking dish. Pour about ¼ cup water around the tomatoes and bake in a preheated 400°F oven for 20 minutes, or until soft.

tomatoes stuffed with meat

{ *tomates rellenos de carne—murcia* }

These tomatoes can be served as part of a hot main course.

SERVES 4

4 large beefsteak tomatoes
   (about 2 pounds)

½ large onion, chopped

2 tablespoons olive oil

5 ounces ground pork

Salt and pepper

4 slices *jamón serrano* or
   prosciutto, chopped

1 hard-boiled egg, quartered

Cut a small slice off the stem end of each tomato to use as lids. Shave the inside of the lids to leave more room for the stuffing. Remove some of the pulp and seeds with a pointed teaspoon. (You can use this to make *pa amb tomàquet;* see page 154.)

Fry the onion in the oil in a skillet until golden. Add the pork and cook for 5 to 8 minutes, stirring and breaking it up until it is no longer pink. Season with salt and pepper.

Transfer the pork and onions to a food processor, add the *jamón* or prosciutto and hard-boiled egg, and blend to a smooth paste. Taste and adjust the seasoning if necessary. Stuff the tomatoes with this paste, pressing it in firmly, and cover with the lids.

Arrange the tomatoes in a baking dish. Bake in a preheated 400°F oven for 30 minutes, or until the tomatoes are soft; remove them before they start to fall apart.

eggplants stuffed with meat

{ berenjenas rellenas de carne — balearic islands }

Eggplants are favorite vegetables on the Balearic Islands. This dish is not at all greasy, the way some eggplant dishes can be, because the eggplants are not fried. The recipe is Rosa Tovar's.

**SERVES 4 AS A STARTER;
2 AS A MAIN COURSE**

2 medium elongated eggplants
    (about 1 pound)

3 tablespoons olive oil

Salt and pepper

¼ cup fresh bread crumbs

¼ cup whole milk

1 medium onion, chopped

2 garlic cloves, chopped

1 medium tomato, peeled
    and chopped

½ pound ground pork

½ teaspoon cinnamon

¾ teaspoon cumin

1 egg, lightly beaten

Heaping ¼ cup grated cheese—
    Manchego, Mahón, or even
    cheddar

Trim the stem ends of the eggplants and cut them lengthwise in half. Pour ⅔ cup water and 1 tablespoon of the oil into a wide casserole or skillet, and put in the eggplant halves, cut side up. Season with salt and pepper, cover with a tight-fitting lid, and bring to a boil over medium heat. Lower the heat and let the eggplants steam for 5 to 8 minutes, until slightly softened (check with the point of a knife). Add a little water if it evaporates too quickly.

When they are cool enough to handle, hollow out the eggplants with a large pointed spoon, leaving just enough pulp for a thin wall; reserve the pulp. Return the eggplant shells to the casserole, or, if you used a skillet, transfer them to a baking dish, along with any remaining water. Coarsely chop the pulp.

Soak the bread crumbs in the milk.

Fry the onion in the remaining 2 tablespoons oil in a large skillet over medium heat, stirring occasionally, until it just begins to color. Add the garlic and stir for 30 seconds, or until aromatic, then add the tomato and cook for 3 to 5 minutes. Add the pork, season with salt and pepper to taste, the cinnamon, and cumin, and stir, turning the meat and breaking it up, for 5 to 8 minutes, until it changes color. Add the eggplant pulp and bread crumbs in milk and cook, stirring, until any liquid has evaporated. Remove from the heat, add the egg, and mix very well.

Spoon the mixture into the eggplant shells. Sprinkle with the grated cheese and bake in a preheated 350°F oven for 20 minutes. Serve hot.

eggplants stuffed with ground almonds

{ *berenjenas al horno con almendras—balearic islands* }

This surprising recipe with almonds and a gentle sweet-and-sour flavor is from Rosa Tovar. She says it is of Jewish origin. In Majorca, many dishes are. You can use the same filling for fat zucchini.

SERVES 4

2 medium elongated eggplants (about 1 pound)

⅔ cup water

1 tablespoon red or white wine vinegar

1 teaspoon sugar

¼ cup olive oil

½ large onion, chopped

¼ cup fresh white bread crumbs

⅓ cup ground almonds

2 large eggs, lightly beaten

Salt and pepper

1½ tablespoons chopped flat-leaf parsley

Trim the stem ends of the eggplants and cut them lengthwise in half. Pour the water into a wide casserole or a skillet, and stir in the vinegar, the sugar, and 2 tablespoons of the olive oil. Put in the eggplant halves cut side up, cover with a tight-fitting lid, and bring to a boil over medium heat. Reduce the heat and let the eggplant halves steam for 5 to 8 minutes, until they soften but still hold their shape.

When they are cool enough to handle, hollow out the eggplants with a large pointed spoon, leaving just enough pulp to form a thin wall; reserve the pulp. Leave the eggplant shells in the casserole, or, if you used a skillet, transfer them to a baking dish, along with any remaining liquid. Coarsely chop the pulp.

Fry the onion in the remaining 2 tablespoons oil in a large skillet, stirring occasionally until soft and beginning to color. Add the eggplant pulp and cook, stirring and mashing it, for 5 to 10 minutes, until it is very soft and the liquid has evaporated. Add the bread crumbs, ground almonds, and eggs, season with salt and pepper, and mix well.

Fill the eggplant shells with the ground almond mixture. Bake in a preheated 350°F oven for about 20 minutes, or until the stuffing puffs up and collapses. Serve hot, sprinkled with the chopped parsley.

VARIATION

Add 2 teaspoons rose water or 1 teaspoon chopped oregano to the filling.

FISH AND SEAFOOD

{ pescados y mariscos }

Spaniards adore fish and seafood. Despite the depletion of their stock through overfishing, they still have a huge variety caught in the waters of both the Atlantic and the Mediterranean. Hake, monkfish, tuna, and bream are favorites; turbot, skate, sole, red mullet, sardines, and anchovies are popular too. The list of splendid mollusks and crustaceans caught off the coasts sounds, in Spanish, like a magic incantation: *sepia, pulpo, percebes, vieiras, zamburiñas, almejas, berberechos, mejillones, bueyes, centollos, changurros, nécoras, quisquillas, camarones, gambas, carabineros, cigalas, langostinos, langostas, bogavantes, navajas, lapas, bígaros.* Shrimp and clams are much used—sometimes they seem to be thrown into a dish as an adornment.

Traditional fish and seafood specialties, including soups, stews, omelets, and rice dishes, are invariably said to have originated as what fishermen once cooked for themselves on boats or their wives prepared for them at home. And older fishermen say that until the 1960s, when tourism emerged, they fished only for their own consumption, as they could rarely sell their catch. Even including lobster, seafood was considered poor food, because the elites and the aristocracy had only ever valued meat in the past. And due to the high mountains and lack of transport in the Spanish hinterland before roads were built in the 1960s, fresh saltwater fish was hardly ever consumed inland. The only fish available in the interior was from the rivers—trout, salmon, and eels—and salt cod, *bacalao.* As meat was strictly forbidden by the Church on days of abstinence, which amounted to a good part of the year, preserved salt cod became the substitute for meat.

To understand just how important and appreciated the products of the sea have become today in Spain, you have only to visit a market in any big town and see the lines of people at the fish stalls. They watch the fishmonger in anticipation as he or she (the women who sell fish are dressed in elegant white blouses, coiffed, and bejeweled) cleans and prepares the fish and seafood with art and tenderness. Spain consumes more fish and seafood per capita than any other country except Japan.

Many of those old dishes that fishermen cooked in the past must have acquired glamour and sophistication. Did they really use all that wine and brandy as people do now? Did they really make the fantastic sauces? But they certainly would have lavished time and love on what was their major staple. Rural folk were once very suspicious of strange-looking creatures from the sea, but today it is the crustaceans and mollusks thrown together pell-mell into a soup or a paella that lure tourists into quayside and coastal restaurants. Josep Pla, the greatest writer in the Catalan language, complained in the 1960s about the spectacular new dishes that were, he said, a "diabolical combination of fish of all categories . . . a disorder against nature . . . not the integrated symphony that it should be." In the past, fishermen threw anything they did not sell into their soups and stews, but what Pla was complaining about was the kind of dishes that seaside restaurants were inventing to attract customers.

Those spectacular dishes that are a feast for the eye may also be difficult and messy to eat. When you come to cook them, you can choose versions referred to on restaurant menus as "*del señor*," which do not entail using your fingers to crack open shells and pull out morsels as you eat.

You will find more seafood dishes in the chapter on rice.

grilled fish and seafood

{ parrillada de pescados y mariscos }

*The favorite way of cooking fish and seafood on every Spanish coast is a la par-
rilla (on the grill over embers) or on a* plancha *(a large flat griddle). You can cook
one type of fish or seafood alone, or have a selection for a great* parrillada *(mixed
grill). Serve it simply sprinkled with salt, extra virgin olive oil, lemon juice, and
chopped parsley, or with one or more of the following dressings and sauces:* salmorreta *(page 138),* vinagreta *(page 135),* vinagreta de tomate *(page 137),* alioli
(page 141), mayonesa *(page 140),* salsa de romesco *(page 143),* mojo de perejil *(page 139),* mojo verde de cilantro *(page 280), or* mojo picón *(page 280).*

*Grilling is not a precise way of cooking; you have to use your intuition, and
experience helps. Here are some suggestions:*

- *Fish steaks* (monkfish, tuna, swordfish, hake, turbot, cod, halibut, or haddock).
  Brush with olive oil and sprinkle with salt. Place on a well-oiled grill about
  2 inches from glowing embers, or on a medium-hot well-oiled flat griddle, and
  cook for 2 to 4 minutes on each side, depending on the thickness. The fish is
  cooked when the flesh begins to flake away from the bone when you cut into it
  with the point of a knife. *Note:* The best way to cook tuna is to marinate it in
  olive oil for 30 minutes, then just sear it on the outside over high heat and leave
  it rare or medium-rare inside.

- *Thick fish fillets or large whole fish—split open down the belly and the backbone
  removed* (sea bass, bream, hake, or turbot). Leave the skin on. Brush with extra
  virgin olive oil and season with salt. Cook on the skin side only, not too close
  to the fire if on a grill, or on a medium-hot well-oiled griddle. Do not turn
  over; the fish will cook through.

- *For whole fish* (small or medium bream, red mullet, sardines, or flatfish such as
  sole). Have the fish scaled and cleaned, but keep the heads on. Brush with extra
  virgin olive oil and season with salt. Cook for 2 to 5 minutes or so on each side,
  depending on the size; cut into one fish with a pointed knife to see if it is done.

>>>

- *Mussels and clams (in their shells)*. Clean, and test to make sure they are alive (see page 127 or page 304). Put them on a baking sheet over the fire or on a hot griddle. They will open within minutes and be done as soon as they do.

- *Jumbo shrimp (in their shells)*. Sprinkle coarse sea salt on a moderately hot griddle and lay the shrimp on top. Turn them over as soon as the first side turns pink, in about 3 to 5 minutes, and serve as soon as they are pink on both sides.

- *Lobster*. A way of killing a lobster is to put it in the freezer for an hour to put it to sleep, then lay it on its back on a cutting board and chop its head off, then cut it lengthwise in half with a big serrated knife. Lay the lobster halves shell side down on a medium-hot grill, cover with foil, and cook for 10 to 15 minutes, until the flesh is opaque in the thickest part. Provide nut crackers and lobster picks to remove morsels from the jointed claw sections. It's best to avoid the green stuff, the tomalley (the lobster's liver), as any contaminants such as mercury may be concentrated in it. The red bits are the roe in a female; they are a delicacy.

- *Small squid*. To clean the squid, see page 127. Cut the bodies open to make flat pieces. Using a sharp knife, score the inside with parallel lines ½ inch apart, without cutting right through, and crisscross these with other parallel lines. Turn the bodies in olive oil to coat and place them scored side down on a very hot grill or griddle. Cook for 1 to 2 minutes, then turn the pieces over. They will curl up immediately and be done. Alternatively, cut the bodies into slices and put on an oiled griddle, with the tentacles. Throw on some finely chopped garlic and chopped chile pepper.

fried fish and seafood

{ *pescados y mariscos fritos—andalusia* }

Andalusians are the world's best at frying fish and seafood. Here are some of their tips and suggestions:

- Fry one type of fish or seafood or a medley that might include small fish such as red mullet, sole, anchovies, whitebait, and baby hake with baby squid, and jumbo shrimp. Large fish can be used, cut into steaks or fillets or into chunks. If you have squid, clean it as described on page 127 and cut the bodies into rings.

- Use olive oil to deep-fry—refined olive oil, called simply "olive oil," not extra virgin oil.

- Use a large tall pot so that there is no risk of the oil bubbling over.

- When you are ready to fry, heat the oil until it is hot but not smoking. There must be enough to generously cover the fish. The temperature should remain constant, so adjust the heat as necessary.

- Fry fish of about the same size together, since their cooking times will be the same.

- Season the fish inside and out with salt and coat completely but lightly with flour; shake off excess flour.

- Small fish must be fried very quickly at high heat so that they become crisp and brown but are still moist inside. Larger fish take longer and need a lower temperature so they have time to cook inside before the skin gets burnt.

- Fish steaks or fillets are best first dipped in seasoned flour and then in lightly beaten egg for extra protection—or they can be dipped in batter.

- When fish fillets are battered, they are called *buñuelos* (fritters). The art is to have a batter that fries crisp and dry and not at all greasy. For a good one, see below.

- When frying, turn the fish or seafood only once. Lift out and drain on paper towels.

- Serve with lemon wedges and one or more of the following sauces: *alioli* (page 141), *mayonesa* (page 140), *romesco* (page 143), *mojo verde* (page 280), *mojo de perejil* (page 139), *salmorreta* (page 138), *vinagreta* (page 135).

batter for deep-frying shrimp, squid, and fish fillets

Here is a batter for coating raw shrimp to make gambas en gabardina *(shrimp in a raincoat) and squid rings for* calamares en gabardina. *You can also use it for coating fish fillets to make* buñuelos de pescado *(fish fritters).*

½ cup all-purpose flour

Pinch of salt

½ cup cold water

Make the batter quickly, just as you are about to fry. Put the flour in a bowl and sprinkle in the salt. With a fork, beat in the water—the water should be as cold as possible. Do not overbeat, or the batter will be chewy. It's fine if it is slightly lumpy.

Coat the shrimp (shells removed, tails left on if you like), squid, or fish fillets in the batter so that they are well covered all over. To test if the oil temperature is right, drop in a little batter; if it floats back to the surface quickly, the oil is hot enough; if it touches the bottom, the oil is not hot enough; if it turns brown, it is too hot. The oil should never be allowed to smoke. Working in batches, drop the pieces one by one into the hot oil and fry just until crisp and lightly golden, turning them once. Remove with a slotted spoon and drain on paper towels. Scoop any bits of burnt batter from the oil between batches. Serve at once.

shrimp with garlic

{ gambas al ajillo — andalusia }

This is a popular tapa in bars all over Spain. It is very garlicky and a little hot with chile. The amount of garlic and chile is up to you. Shrimp has the flavor of the sea, and there is no need for extra salt. Serve the dish sizzling hot, with a warmed baguette cut into slices to soak up the garlicky oil.

SERVES 4 AS A STARTER

4 to 5 tablespoons olive oil

1 pound medium or large shrimp, peeled

1 teaspoon red pepper flakes or ½ chile pepper, finely chopped

4 garlic cloves, finely chopped

2 tablespoons chopped flat-leaf parsley

Heat the oil in a large skillet over medium-high heat. Put in the shrimp and pepper flakes or chopped chile, and turn the shrimp over in seconds, as soon as the first side becomes pink. Add the garlic and stir over medium heat for a minute or so, just until the shrimp is pink all over and the garlic has just begun to color. Serve immediately, sprinkled with the parsley, in a heated *cazuela* or bowl.

white beans with clams

{ *alubias con almejas — cantabria* }

Along the Cantabrian coast in the north of Spain, clams are large and meaty. You can make this dish with good-quality canned white beans. The beans acquire a delicate flavor from the wine and from the brine in the clams.

SERVES 2

1¼ pounds clams

3 tablespoons olive oil

1 large onion, chopped

3 garlic cloves, finely chopped

One 15-ounce can small white
    beans, drained

⅔ cup fruity white wine
    or cava

Salt

2 tablespoons chopped
    flat-leaf parsley

Wash the clams and throw away any that are not closed or that do not close when you rap them against the counter. Soak them in cold salted water for 1 hour, so that they release any sand they have inside.

Heat the oil in a wide casserole or pan with a tight-fitting lid. Put in the onion and stir over low heat until very soft and beginning to color, then add the garlic and stir for a minute or so. Add the beans, the wine, and a little salt, mix gently, and cook for 2 to 3 minutes.

Put the clams on top of the beans, put the lid on, and cook over medium-high heat for 3 to 5 minutes, until the clams open. Throw away any that do not open, and serve sprinkled with the parsley.

VARIATIONS

• Fry ½ small chile pepper, chopped, with the onion.

• Some cooks add a little *pimentón* (paprika) to the dish.

artichokes with shrimp and clams

{ alcachofas con almejas—andalusia }

This delicately flavored dish is a specialty of Córdoba. Chef Manuel Andrade, who is from Córdoba, cooked it for us in his little restaurant, Porta Gayola, in Seville. It was exquisite, with tiny baby artichokes he called alcahuciles *that he had picked the previous day. It is difficult to find fresh baby artichokes and time-consuming to prepare them, but you can use frozen artichoke hearts if you are lucky enough to find them (they are available in France and hopefully will come here soon) or frozen artichoke bottoms. Manuel says that in Córdoba they use their local Montilla-Moriles sherry-type wine. I have also used manzanilla, a fino sherry.*

SERVES 4

1 pound clams

3 tablespoons olive oil

1 medium onion, finely chopped

2 to 3 garlic cloves, finely chopped

1 tablespoon all-purpose flour

1 cup Montilla-Moriles wine or
 a dry sherry or dry white wine

1 cup fish or chicken stock

Salt

8 frozen artichoke bottoms
 or baby artichoke hearts,
 defrosted and quartered

½ pound small to medium shrimp,
 peeled

2 tablespoons finely chopped
 flat-leaf parsley

To clean the clams, see page 127.

Heat the oil over low heat in a wide casserole, preferably one that you can bring to the table. Add the onion and cook, stirring, until soft. Add the garlic and cook, stirring, until the onion and garlic begin to color. Add the flour and stir vigorously for 1 minute, then gradually add the wine and stock, stirring all the time. Season with salt, add the artichokes, and cook for 10 minutes, or until they are tender.

Put the shrimp and drained clams on top of the artichokes and sprinkle with the parsley. Cover and cook over medium heat until the shrimp turn pink and the clams open. Throw away any that do not open.

baby squid in their ink

{ c h i p i r o n e s   e n   s u   t i n t a — b a s q u e   c o u n t r y }

Many fishmongers and some supermarkets now sell baby squid, not more than 2½ inches long, cleaned and ready to cook; and some also sell little sachets of concentrated squid ink. (When cuttlefish or squid sense predators, they squirt the ink that is stored in sacs to fend off attack, but there is hardly enough ink to cook with.) You can buy good enough ready-made fish stock in gourmet markets, so this dish is easy to make. Rinse and drain the squid, and cut the bodies into slices. If you are using squid that has not been cleaned, see the instructions on page 127.

Serve this dish with fried or toasted bread, or with plain white long-grain rice or vermicelli (see the variation) and with garlic mayonnaise (page 141). The long-grain rice grown in Andalusia and Extremadura has become popular now for making plain rice, as has basmati.

SERVES 4

1 large onion, chopped

3 to 4 tablespoons olive oil

2 garlic cloves, finely chopped

1 large tomato or 2 medium, peeled and chopped

1 cup dry white wine

1½ cups fish stock

½ teaspoon sugar

Salt and pepper

1 or 2 packets (4 grams each) squid ink

1½ pounds cleaned baby squid

Plain rice (optional; recipe follows)

2 tablespoons chopped flat-leaf parsley (optional)

Sauté the onion in 2 tablespoons of the oil in a large saucepan, covered, over low heat, stirring occasionally, for about 20 minutes, until soft and golden.

Add the garlic and cook, stirring, until the aroma rises and it just begins to color, then add the tomato and cook, stirring often, for 5 to 8 minutes. Add the wine, fish stock, sugar, and some salt and pepper. Simmer over low heat for 10 minutes, then add the squid ink. (Some people blend the sauce with an immersion blender, or in a regular blender, but I like it as it is.)

Meanwhile, slice the squid body into rings about ⅓ inch thick. Fry with the tentacles in the remaining oil in a large skillet over high heat for 1 to 2 minutes, stirring and turning the pieces.

Drop the squid with their juices into the ink sauce and cook for 5 minutes, or until tender.

Serve hot, over the rice if serving it, sprinkled, if you like, with the parsley.

>>>

1½ cups long-grain white rice
or basmati rice

4 tablespoons (½ stick) butter

Salt

plain rice

arroz blanco

Bring a large saucepan of salted water to a boil. Throw in the rice and boil for 12 to 18 minutes, until tender. The time depends on the type and quality of rice. (Some new types of basmati take even less time—I haven't been able to discover why that is, so look on the box for instructions.) Drain quickly in a strainer, return to the pan, and stir in the butter, cut into pieces so that it melts more evenly. Add salt if necessary.

VARIATION

Chipirones en su tinta con fideus (baby squid in their ink with vermicelli): This is a wonderful alternative to serving with rice, which I discovered in Andalusia. Break 3 dried vermicelli nests (*fideus*) into small pieces and throw them into the simmering stew a few minutes before you are ready to serve. Cook until al dente.

GASPAR REY I GRIFÉ

Gaspar Rey I Grifé is the founder, editor, and main writer of Cocina Futuro, a magazine for and about chefs, caterers, and restaurateurs. He travels around the country to wherever something of interest is happening and keeps up with all that the chefs are doing in Spain. Gaspar is a cultured and worldly Catalan who left Spain because he found it oppressive under Franco. The Madrid he fled in the 1960s was like a small provincial city. The oil was rancid, the wine rough and acidic, and people did not care. And chefs were never seen out of the kitchen. Since Gaspar came back to live in Madrid in 1994, he has been getting a lot of joy from witnessing—and from being in a position to encourage—the transformation of Spanish products and gastronomy.

A friend gave me Gaspar's telephone number when I decided suddenly to go to Asturias, and he in turn gave me contacts there and in other regions. He took me to some of the best restaurants in Madrid and Toledo and gave me his insider's

views on wine, on small farms that are rediscovering old products (like black tomatoes), on new products (like foie gras and seaweed), on food fashions, and on the ways and techniques of *nueva cocina* chefs. We discussed all kinds of dishes and, in particular, ways of cooking fish.

boiled octopus with potatoes

{ *pulpo a la feria—galicia* }

This is the way octopus is cooked and served at fairs and festivals in Galicia. It is a popular tapa throughout Spain, known as pulpo a la gallega. *Octopus needs to be tenderized before it can be cooked. This used to be done by bashing it or by plunging it in boiling water three times before cooking. But now it is tenderized by freezing. In America, it is commonly sold cleaned and already tenderized by freezing. A traditional way of serving is on a round wooden platter.*

SERVES 6

1 frozen octopus
    (about 2½ pounds), defrosted

1 pound waxy potatoes

Plenty of extra virgin olive oil
    for drizzling

Coarse sea salt

1 tablespoon *pimentón dulce*
    (or sweet paprika) or a little
    pimentón picante (hot paprika)
    or a mixture of the two

If the octopus has not already been cleaned, cut halfway through the muscle that connects the tentacles to the inside of the head and discard the contents of the head cavity: pull or cut out the ink sac, the hard oval "beak," and the gelatinous innards. Cut away the mouth and eyes with the cartilage around them. Turn the head inside out and wash it under cold running water. Remove any scales that may be left on the suckers and wash well.

Bring a large pot of lightly salted water to a boil. Throw in the octopus and simmer, covered, for 30 to 45 minutes, or until tender. To test it, lift out the octopus, cut off a piece of tentacle with kitchen scissors, and try it: it should not be rubbery. (If you are not serving the octopus right away, leave the water in the pot and bring it to a boil again so that you can add in the octopus and heat it through before you serve.)

Cook the potatoes in boiling salted water until tender. Drain and cut them into slices about ½ inch thick. Arrange the potatoes in a wide shallow baking dish. Sprinkle with oil, and turn to coat them all over. Heat through in a medium oven for about 10 minutes before serving.

Lift the octopus out of the water. Using scissors, cut off the head and throw it away—it is not as good as the tentacles. Then cut the tentacles into bite-size pieces, and spread on top of the potatoes. Sprinkle generously with olive oil and coarse salt, and dust with the *pimentón*.

baked crab with cider

{ centollo a la sidra — asturias }

Hard cider is the drink of Asturias. Sidrerías, *cider houses and bars, are everywhere. Asturian cider is hard and dry; I used a vintage cider that was only slightly sweet, and it went beautifully with the fish and crabmeat. In Asturias, this is the filling for their famous spider crab, called* txangurro. *It is more spectacular to bake it in the shell as they do, but it is easier although less dramatic to enjoy it in ramekins, as in this recipe.*

SERVES 4 AS A STARTER

1 medium onion, chopped

2 tablespoons olive oil

1 small tomato,
    peeled and chopped

Salt

Pinch of cayenne or chile powder

½ pound hake, cod, or other
    white fish fillet, without skin

½ pound crabmeat, picked over
    for shells and cartilage

¾ cup hard cider

2 tablespoons chopped
    flat-leaf parsley

2 tablespoons bread crumbs

1 tablespoon butter

Sauté the onion in the oil in a large skillet, stirring occasionally, until soft. Add the tomato, salt to taste, and the cayenne or chile pepper and cook for 8 minutes.

Put in the fish fillet and cook for 5 minutes, or until it begins to flake, turning it once. Flake it in the skillet, then add the crabmeat, hard cider, and parsley, mix gently, and cook for 1 minute.

Oil 4 ramekins and spoon in the crab mixture. Sprinkle the tops with the bread crumbs and dot with the butter. Put under a preheated broiler to lightly brown.

whole bream baked in a salt crust

{ dorada a la sal—andalusia, valencia, and murcia }

Whole fish cooked encased in a sea salt crust is deliciously moist and flavorful. It is a fisherman's way in areas where they have salt pans. They bury the fish in damp salt crystals in wooden boxes and take them to be cooked in the local bread oven. I had trouble producing a firm crust that came away cleanly, taking away the skin with it, as many recipes tell you it should do. José María Conde de Ybarra (see page 412), said that the salt must be wet enough to stick together and that you need thick layers (of three fingers deep) on top of and below the fish. I found it easier, and without using too much salt, to make a crust that comes away relatively cleanly by mixing the salt with egg white. And if the skin does not come off with the crust, it does not matter. The scales will come off.

You can use sea bass or gray mullet instead of bream. Ask the fishmonger to gut the fish through a small incision so that the salt does not get inside and to keep the scales on—this is very important. You must use coarse sea salt or kosher salt, which will draw out moisture from the fish, not fine salt, which would be absorbed by the flesh. This is good served with boiled new potatoes.

SERVES 2

4½ pounds coarse sea salt
    or kosher salt

2 to 3 large egg whites

2 whole bream (14 ounces to
    1 pound each), gutted but
    not scaled

Extra virgin olive oil for drizzling

2 lemon wedges

A small bowl of *Alioli*
    (page 141)

Line a baking pan large enough to hold the fish with a sheet of foil. Mix the salt thoroughly in a bowl with enough of the egg whites so that it feels like wet sand. Make a bed for each fish with about one-third of this mixture on the foil, and place the fish on it. Then cover the fish entirely with a thick layer of the rest of the salt mixture, molding it firmly around each fish so that it is completely covered and making sure that the opening in the belly is closed so that salt does not get in. You can leave the tails uncovered.

Bake in a preheated 400°F oven for 25 minutes. The top layer of salt will form a hard crust. To serve, crack open the crust with a heavy knife and carefully remove it. The skin may come off with it—but for me, it does not. Brush off any bits of salt and peel off any skin, then gently lift off the top fillets and transfer them to a platter or plates. Pull out the backbone and lift off the remaining fillets.

Serve with a drizzle of olive oil, accompanied by the lemon wedges and *alioli*.

sea salt

Sea salt is produced in salt pans *(salinas)* in Cádiz, Murcia, Majorca, and Ibiza as well as in the estuary of the Ebro River in Catalonia and the Canary Islands. The Phoenicians introduced the original techniques for extracting it from the sea and also the way of cooking fish in it. In the last few years, Spain has seen, apart from industrial salt production, the growing harvest of a high-quality gourmet salt called *flor de sal*. This is the crunchy irregular crystallized flakes that form on the surface of special evaporation pools on beaches in hot, sunny, dry, windy conditions. The top layers are collected by hand as they form by skimming them off the surface of the water with a net at the end of a pole. *Flor de sal* has a distinctive taste of the sea, and its high magnesium content makes it a flavor enhancer. When sprinkled over a finished dish, it gives a pleasant taste sensation without being absorbed by the food. It is too good and too expensive to use for baking fish in it.

marinated tuna with tomatoes

{ atún marinado—andalusia }

Off the coast of Cádiz in Andalusia, tuna are caught when they migrate from the Atlantic to the Mediterranean to spawn in the warmer water in the spring and early summer. They are caught by a technique called almadraba, *introduced by the Phoenicians and practiced by the Arabs, in which the fish are led through a maze of nets into a central area. When the last net is raised, the larger adult fish are selectively impaled on hooks by fishermen who jump into the water. They are hauled onto boats, where flaked ice is shoveled over them while they are still flapping. Due to overfishing, the practice has now been drastically reduced, but tuna remains a favorite fish of this coast. You need the freshest, best-quality tuna for this dish, which makes a most delicious first course.*

SERVES 8 AS A STARTER

2 thick slices tuna steak
   (about 1 pound)

Juice of 1 lemon

9 tablespoons extra virgin olive oil

Salt and pepper

1 pound large tomatoes, diced

6 scallions, trimmed and sliced

1 tablespoon red or white wine
   vinegar

½ teaspoon sugar (optional)

1 to 2 tablespoons chopped
   flat-leaf parsley

Cut the tuna into bite-sized, roughly ¾-inch, cubes.

Mix the lemon juice, 6 tablespoons of the olive oil, and a little salt and pepper in a glass or plastic bowl and turn the tuna pieces in this marinade. Cover with plastic wrap and refrigerate for about 6 hours, turning the pieces over in the marinade at least once.

Just before serving, dress the diced tomatoes and scallions with the remaining 3 tablespoons olive oil, the vinegar, and a little salt. Add the sugar if the tomatoes do not seem sweet enough. Mix with the marinated tuna, and serve on a shallow platter, sprinkled with the parsley.

sardines in a pickling marinade

{ s a r d i n a s   e n   e s c a b e c h e — a n d a l u s i a }

Escabeche *was originally a way of preserving game, such as partridge and rabbit, and fish, such as sardines, mackerel, and tuna, that has now become a delicacy to be served cold. The name is said to originate from the Persian word* sikbaj, *which refers to food with vinegar. Foods in escabeche are normally dipped in flour and deep-fried before being marinated, but in Andalusia, they prefer to just poach their sardines very briefly in the marinade. This can be a mix of just olive oil and vinegar (that is too sharp for me) or of olive oil, vinegar, and dry white wine. I did not have enough dry white wine when I made this, so I added some Moscatel, which gave the sardines a lovely sweet touch.*

Ask the fishmonger to prepare the sardines. The sardines should be made at least a day before you want to start serving them as a tapa or starter, and they will keep for a few weeks in the refrigerator. Serve them, if you like, on toasted bread.

SERVES 4 TO 5

2 pounds sardines, heads cut off, gutted, scaled, and backbone removed

⅔ cup dry white wine or a mix of a dry wine with a little Moscatel, or as needed

⅔ cup white wine vinegar, or as needed

⅔ cup olive oil, or as needed

Salt

3 garlic cloves

2 bay leaves

10 black peppercorns

A sprig of thyme or oregano

Arrange the sardines in layers in a wide saucepan.

Mix the white wine, vinegar, and olive oil together and season with a little salt. Stir in the garlic, bay leaves, peppercorns, and sprig of thyme or oregano and pour over the sardines. If the mixture does not cover them entirely, add a little more of the liquids in equal quantities. Bring to a boil and simmer for 3 to 5 minutes. Let cool, then transfer to a glass or ceramic dish, cover with plastic wrap, and keep in the refrigerator.

Remove from the refrigerator 1 hour before serving, as the oil in the marinade almost solidifies when it is cold.

VARIATIONS

- Add ½ teaspoon *pimentón dulce* (or sweet paprika).

- If you don't have Moscatel wine, you can add ½ to 1 teaspoon sugar.

pan-grilled fish with garlic and chile dressing

{ *pescado a la bilbaina — basque country* }

This method of cooking fish keeps the flesh moist and juicy. You can also do it on an outdoor grill. You need thick fillets with the skin left on, and the oil must be a good extra virgin. The dressing is simple and tasty. Serve it with boiled potatoes.

SERVES 2

2 thick monkfish, hake, bream, or other firm-fleshed white fish fillets (6 to 7 ounces each), skin left on

Salt

4 to 5 tablespoons extra virgin olive oil

5 large garlic cloves, sliced

½ to 1 small dried or fresh chile pepper, seeds removed, finely chopped

2 to 3 teaspoons white wine vinegar

1 tablespoon chopped flat-leaf parsley

Season the fish with salt. Grease a large heavy skillet or *plancha* (a flat griddle) with 1 to 2 tablespoons of the oil and heat to just below the smoking point. Place the fillets skin side down in the skillet or on the griddle and cook over medium heat. The fillets will gradually cook through to the top and do not need turning over. They are done when the flesh is opaque throughout and flakes when you cut into it. If the fillets are very thick, this can take up to 15 minutes. (Alternatively, turn the fillets over and cook for 2 to 5 minutes on each side depending on the thickness of the fillet.)

Meanwhile, for the dressing, very gently heat the remaining 3 tablespoons of oil with the garlic and chile pepper in a small pan until the garlic is just lightly golden and crunchy (do not let it turn brown). Take off the heat and add the vinegar and parsley.

Serve the fish hot from the pan, with the dressing poured over.

VARIATION

Have the fishmonger butterfly small bream or other small fish and remove the backbone. Cook them as above, skin side down only.

roasted whole bream with potatoes

{ besugo al horno con patatas—madrid }

This is the great festive Christmas Eve dish of Madrid that is now popular in other parts of Spain. I ate it in Asturias. I was with the American journalist Jane Kramer and the food writer Pepe Iglesias in a restaurant called La Arcea (another name for the becada, *or woodcock), overlooking the sea in Andrin, the port near Llanes. The fish was sensational. They used a wonderful Galician Albariño, but you can use another fruity dry white wine. And you can use sea bass instead of bream.*

SERVES 4

1 large sea bream or sea bass
    (about 4½ pounds), gutted and
    scaled

Salt

1 onion, cut in half and sliced

6 tablespoons extra virgin olive oil

8 to 12 waxy potatoes, peeled

A good pinch of saffron

1 cup Albariño or other fruity dry
    white wine, such as Riesling

1 lemon, cut into thin slices

2 garlic cloves, crushed to a paste
    or through a press

2 tablespoons fine bread crumbs

2 tablespoons chopped
    flat-leaf parsley

Rinse the fish and season inside and out with salt. Line a baking dish large enough to hold the fish with foil.

Sauté the onion in 1 tablespoon of the oil in a skillet over medium heat until soft and golden. Spread in the baking dish.

Cook the potatoes in boiling salted water for 10 minutes; drain and cut into thick slices.

Add the potatoes to the onions. Sprinkle on 3 tablespoons of the oil, add the saffron and a little salt, and mix gently, then pour in the wine.

Rub the top of the fish with 1 tablespoon of the oil and place it in the baking dish, with the potatoes around it. Slash it in 2 places at the thickest part. Cut 1 slice of lemon in half and insert one half in each cut. Put 1 lemon slice inside the fish and the rest on top of the potatoes.

Mix the remaining tablespoon of olive oil with the garlic, bread crumbs, and 1 tablespoon of the parsley, and sprinkle this mixture over the fish. Roast the fish in a preheated 475°F oven for 30 to 35 minutes, or until cooked (test using the point of a knife in the thickest part—the flesh should be opaque right through to the bone) and the potatoes are tender.

Serve sprinkled with the remaining tablespoon of parsley.

hake in green sauce with asparagus

{ merluza en salsa verde con espárragos — basque country }

Fishermen in the north of Spain around the Bay of Biscay caught hake when they went whaling in the northern seas, and Basque chefs gave it a prestigious place in Spanish gastronomy. This is one of their favorite recipes for this long slender fish with a delicate flesh, but you can use other fish, such as monkfish or cod. Parsley is the Basque herb par excellence. The sauce, with olive oil, garlic, and parsley, acquires an unctuous texture from the juices of the fish itself. The skin plays a part, so do not remove it. The asparagus cooking water is also part of the sauce.

SERVES 2

½ pound asparagus, hard bottom
    ends removed

3 garlic cloves, finely chopped

¼ cup mild extra virgin olive oil

1½ teaspoons all-purpose flour

2 tablespoons very finely chopped
    flat-leaf parsley

Salt

2 hake steaks (6 to 7 ounces each)

Cook the asparagus in boiling, salted water to cover until tender. Drain, reserving 1 cup of the cooking water.

Stir the garlic in the oil in a large skillet over low heat for a few seconds; do not let it brown. Add the flour and stir for a minute. Add the parsley, then gradually add the reserved 1 cup asparagus cooking water, stirring vigorously until the sauce thickens. Add salt and simmer gently for about 8 minutes, until the sauce thickens a little more.

Put in the fish steaks and swirl the pan without removing it from the heat, so as to move the fish steaks very gently around. This allows the white liquid they release to mix with the sauce and give it a slightly gelatinous texture. (You can cheat by moving the steaks around with a wooden spoon.) After 5 minutes, turn the fish steaks over, arrange the asparagus around them, and cook for 3 to 5 minutes, until the fish only just begins to flake away from the bone when you cut into it with a pointed knife.

VARIATIONS

• Use peas instead of asparagus.

• Omit the asparagus and use 1 cup fish stock instead of the asparagus water. Add 8 clams (see page 127) when you have turned over the fish, and continue with the lid on to steam them open.

hake cooked in cider

{ merluza a la sidra—asturias and cantabria }

In Asturias, hard cider replaces wine as the local drink, and it is used in many dishes. Serve this one with boiled or roasted potatoes (page 279 or page 430).

SERVES 4

1 large onion, chopped

3 to 4 tablespoons olive oil

5 garlic cloves, finely chopped

1 large tomato or 2 medium
   tomatoes, peeled and chopped

½ teaspoon sugar

1½ cups hard cider

Salt

4 hake steaks, 6 to 7 ounces each
   (see the variations)

Flour for dredging

Fry the onion in 2 tablespoons of the oil in a wide skillet, stirring often, until soft. Add the garlic and stir until the onion and garlic are lightly golden. Add the tomato and sugar and cook until much of the liquid has evaporated.

Add the cider and a little salt and boil over high heat for 5 to 10 minutes to reduce the sauce.

Meanwhile, season the fish steaks with salt and dredge them in flour to coat them well, then shake to remove excess flour. Fry them briefly in another pan filmed with oil over high heat, turning them once, just to give them a little color.

Transfer the fish to the sauce and cook over low heat for 3 to 5 minutes depending on the thickness of the steaks, until the fish is opaque throughout and the flesh begins to flake when you cut into it with the point of a knife.

VARIATIONS

- Use monkfish instead of hake. It will take a few minutes longer to cook.

- Fry ½ to ¾ chile pepper, seeded and chopped, with the onion and garlic.

- Mash the yolk of a hard-boiled egg and stir it into the sauce.

- Add the juice of ½ lemon (about 1½ tablespoons).

- Add a handful of clams to the pan. Put them on top of the fish when you add it to the pan, and cook with the lid on until they open and the fish is done.

PEPE IGLESIAS

I recognized Pepe at the Oviedo airport from the cartoons on his website, which show a round figure with a wide smile emerging from a casserole with a pen and notebook, and the same figure forming out of the vapors from a bottle of wine, like the genie that appeared from Aladdin's magic lamp. Pepe's full name is José Juan Iglesias del Castillo y Díaz de la Serna. I was with Jane Kramer, who was writing about me for *The New Yorker*. We had decided only days before to go to Asturias, and a couple of telephone calls to friends led me to Pepe, the "ambassador" of Asturian gastronomy.

Pepe drove us through the rugged mountains, along the fast-flowing rivers and woodlands of the fantastically beautiful Picos de Europa. We stopped at little shepherds' villages, where we saw sheep and goats and tasted the strong cave-ripened blue cheese, Cabrales, and drank the local still hard cider. We visited the sanctuary of Covadonga in Cangas de Onis, where, according to legend, the Virgin Mary appeared to the chief Pelayo and helped him to fight off the Muslim armies. Pepe gave us a running commentary on the Roman, Gothic, Baroque, and pre-Romanesque architecture of the region, and we ate in restaurants where the chefs did their own exquisite take on local dishes.

Pepe was born and raised in Madrid, among the pots and pans of his parents' restaurant, El Horno de Santa Teresa. When they died in a tragic accident in 1976, he abandoned his veterinary studies to take over the restaurant. In 1990, he retired to a more peaceful life on the beach of Salinas near Avilés in Asturias, where he shares a house with his doctor wife, María, and became a restaurant critic and food and wine writer. People are always sending me recipes they have cut out from Spanish magazines and newspapers that turn out to be his. He has written twenty books, including *Comer con Vino* (*Eating with Wine*), about matching food with wine. He is famous for his virtual *Enciclopedia de Gastronomía*, where he offers recipes and articles and chats about food and wine.

salmon in brandy sauce

{ salmon al brandy — asturias }

The rivers of Asturias, which cut gorges into the Cantabrian mountain range, are full of beautiful wild salmon. This is a recipe sent to me by Pepe Iglesias. It is the way salmon might have been prepared in the homes of wealthy mining families in the first decades of the twentieth century. The sauce was traditionally put through a chino, *a conical sieve; if you want a smooth, creamy sauce, you can blend it. The brandy gives it a rich taste, and the chile pepper adds a little heat. Serve with boiled new potatoes.*

SERVES 4

1 large onion, chopped

3 tablespoons olive oil

3 garlic cloves, finely chopped

2 to 3 tomatoes (8 ounces),
   peeled and chopped

½ teaspoon sugar

1 cup fish stock

½ cup brandy

Salt

1 chile pepper, cut open
   and seeds removed

4 skinless salmon fillets
   (5 to 6 ounces each)

Sauté the onion in the oil in a large covered skillet over low heat, stirring occasionally, until soft. Add the garlic and cook briefly, stirring, until the onion and garlic begin to color. Add the tomatoes and sugar and cook until the sauce has reduced to a jammy consistency.

Pour in the fish stock and brandy, add the chile pepper and salt to taste, and simmer for 5 minutes. Put in the salmon fillets, and simmer, uncovered, over low heat for 4 to 10 minutes depending on the thickness of the fillets, turning them once, until the fish is done to your liking (I prefer salmon slightly underdone). Taste the sauce occasionally and remove the chile when the sauce is only just a little peppery.

If you wish, lift out the salmon fillets and blend the sauce to a light cream with an immersion blender, then return the fillets to the pan to heat through before serving.

salmon with peas

{ salmón con guisantes — asturias }

Asturias is famous for the salmon caught in its many rivers. When the fish return from the Atlantic to their spawning grounds in May, the first big catch of the season is called campanu, *because church bells (*campanas*) have always pealed to signal its arrival. A favorite way of cooking salmon in Cangas de Onis, in the Picos de Europa, is with fresh green peas. Pepe Iglesias (see page 328) explained that the lettuce leaves that cover the peas and the fish produce steam that cooks the peas. Without any added water, the peas have a more intense sweet flavor.*

SERVES 2

½ large onion, chopped

2 slices *jamón serrano* or
    prosciutto, sliced into
    ½-inch-wide strips

1½ tablespoons olive oil

2 tablespoons butter

1⅔ cups fresh peas

Salt

6 to 8 romaine lettuce leaves

2 skinless salmon fillets
    (5 to 6 ounces each)

¼ lemon

Sauté the onion and *jamón* or prosciutto in the oil in a large skillet over low heat, stirring occasionally, until the onion is soft. Add 1 tablespoon of the butter and the peas, stir, and season with salt. Cover with the lettuce leaves, put on a tight-fitting lid so that the peas cook in the steam created by the lettuce, and cook over very low heat for 15 minutes.

Lift up a few of the lettuce leaves and put in the salmon fillets. Season with salt and lay half the remaining butter on each fillet. Replace the lettuce leaves, put the lid on, and cook over low heat for 6 to 10 minutes depending on the thickness of the fillets, or until the fish is done to your liking. The peas will be very soft—that is how they are supposed to be. Serve with a sprinkling of lemon juice, with the lettuce as an extra garnish.

cádiz-style sea bream

{ urta a la gaditana — andalusia }

Urta is the sea bream fished off the Cádiz coast, but you can use other firm white fish, such as monkfish, cod, haddock, or turbot. Cádiz is sherry and brandy territory, and you find them in all kinds of dishes, including this one.

SERVES 4

1 onion, chopped

2 green or red bell peppers, cored,
    seeded, and cut into thin strips

6 to 7 tablespoons olive oil

1 pound tomatoes

¼ cup dry sherry or white wine

Salt and pepper

4 bream fillets (5 ounces each)

Flour for dredging

¼ cup brandy

Fry the onion and peppers in 3 tablespoons of the oil in a large skillet until the onions are golden and the peppers are soft.

Cut the tomatoes into quarters and remove the hard bits at the stem ends. Blend them (unpeeled) to a cream in the food processor.

Pour the creamed tomatoes into the skillet, add the sherry or wine, and season with salt and pepper. Cook over medium-high heat for 10 minutes to reduce the sauce.

Meanwhile, dredge the fish fillets in flour mixed with a sprinkling of salt, and shake off the excess. Briefly shallow-fry the fish in the remaining oil in a large skillet, turning the pieces once, to brown them lightly on both sides. Pour brandy into the sauce and carefully light it with a long match.

When the flames die down, pour the sauce over the fish, and cook for about 3 minutes, until the fish is opaque throughout.

fish in onion and saffron sauce

{ pescado en amarillo—andalusia }

This recipe, used for cooking cazón *(tope shark) on the Málaga coast, is great with other white-flesh fish, such as monkfish, cod, haddock, or turbot. The wine and saffron sauce thickened with ground almonds is exquisite, and the saffron gives the dish its name—*amarillo *means "yellow."*

SERVES 4

1 large onion, chopped

3 tablespoons olive oil

4 garlic cloves, chopped

4 pieces monkfish fillet (about 7 ounces each)

1½ cups dry sherry or white wine

⅓ cup water

A pinch of saffron threads

Salt

¼ cup ground almonds

Fry the onion in the oil in a large skillet or casserole over low heat, stirring often, until it just begins to color. Stir in the garlic and cook until aromatic, then put in the fish. Cook, turning the pieces once, to brown them lightly on both sides.

Pour in the wine and water, add the saffron and some salt, and cook, uncovered, over low heat for 5 minutes. Add the ground almonds and cook for 5 minutes more, or until the fish is opaque throughout and the sauce has thickened.

monkfish with brandy

{ r a p e   a l   b r a n d y — c a t a l o n i a }

Here is another simple recipe for a tasty fish dish. Catalans call it rap al conyac. *In the Catalan region of Penedes, they make a brandy that is heartier than French Cognac and drier than the brandy of Jerez. You can use other fish, such as cod, turbot, or haddock.*

SERVES 2

2 monkfish fillets
   (about 6 ounces each)

Salt

2 tablespoons olive oil

2 to 3 garlic cloves, finely chopped

1 tablespoon tomato puree

¼ cup Cognac or other brandy

2 tablespoons chopped
   flat-leaf parsley

Season the fish fillets with salt. Sauté in the oil in a skillet over medium-high heat until lightly colored, turning them once. Lift the fish onto a plate, add the garlic to the pan, and stir for half a minute, or until the aroma rises and the garlic only just begins to color. Add the tomato puree and about ¼ cup water and stir well.

Heat the brandy in a small pan and carefully ignite it with a long match held over the edge of the pan. When the flames die down, pour it into the sauce. Stir well, return the monkfish to the pan, and cook for about 7 minutes, turning the fillets once, until they are opaque throughout. Stir in the parsley.

monkfish with caramelized onions flambéed with rum

{ rape con cebolla confitada al ron—catalonia }

I ate this dish at a festival in Sitges, on the Costa Brava, at a gastronomic event to celebrate the life of the painter Santiago Rusiñol, who had popularized the beautiful resort. A jazz band played and local restaurants offered their best dishes at stands. I was sitting next to Xavier Mestres, president of the Fundació Institut Català de la Cuina (Catalan Culinary Institute; see page 105). He explained that it was the "indianos," the emigrants who came back home from Cuba and Venezuela in the nineteenth century, who introduced rum into Catalan cooking; they arrived at a time when the local bourgeoisie had adopted the French technique of flambéing. Monkfish is a popular fish in Spain, but you can use other firm white fish such as cod, haddock, halibut, or turbot.

SERVES 2

1 large onion, cut in half and sliced

2 tablespoons olive oil

2 monkfish fillets
(about 6 ounces each)

Salt

2 tablespoons rum

Sauté the onion in the oil in a large skillet covered to begin with, then uncovered toward the end, over low heat, for about 30 minutes, stirring often, until very soft and dark golden brown.

Season the fish fillets with salt and add them to the pan. Cook gently, turning them once, for 8 minutes, or until opaque throughout.

Pour the rum into a small pan and carefully ignite it with a long match held over the edge of the pan. When the flames die down, pour the rum over the fish, and remove the fish from the heat.

fish and seafood in saffron béchamel

{ bechamel de mariscos—catalonia }

I asked Xavier Mestres about dishes of French origin that had been transformed and Hispanicized. I was given béchamel as an example. In Spain, it is sometimes made with white wine or sherry, and sometimes tomato. Here it includes fried onions, grated lemon zest, and saffron. The crunchy topping makes a lovely contrast to the creamy béchamel.

For the fish, you can use cod, haddock, or turbot.

SERVES 6

1 onion, chopped

5⅓ tablespoons (⅔ stick) butter

¼ cup all-purpose flour

2½ cups whole milk, heated

Grated zest of 1 lemon

A good pinch of saffron threads

Salt and pepper

2 large egg yolks, lightly beaten

½ pound scallops, preferably
  with orange roe

½ pound medium to large shrimp,
  peeled

2 tablespoons olive oil

½ pound skinless firm white fish
  fillets (see headnote above)

1 slice of white bread, crusts
  removed

2 tablespoons butter, melted

Sauté the onion in the butter in a medium saucepan over low heat until it is soft but not colored. Add the flour and stir vigorously with a wooden spoon for a minute or so, then add the milk a little at a time, stirring vigorously and taking it off the heat at each addition, until you have a thick, creamy sauce. Add the lemon zest, saffron, and salt and pepper to taste and simmer over low heat for 10 minutes, stirring occasionally. Beat in the egg yolks and take off the heat.

Cook the scallops and shrimp in the olive oil in a skillet over high heat for 2 minutes, turning the shrimp over as they turn pink and the scallops as they are seared. Transfer to a baking dish. Cook the fish fillets briefly in the same pan, sprinkling them with salt and turning them once. They can be slightly undercooked. Transfer to the baking dish.

Pour the béchamel over the fish and shellfish and mix gently.

Place bread under the broiler to dry out; grind to crumbs in a blender. Sprinkle over the béchamel. Drizzle with the melted butter. Put the baking dish in a preheated 400°F oven for 15 minutes to heat through, then put under the broiler to brown the top.

VARIATION

Add 5 tablespoons sherry to the béchamel.

bacalao

When I asked people in Spain what their favorite dish was, they often described one made with *bacalao*, salt cod. In this once fervently Catholic country, until the mid-twentieth century, before refrigeration, when transport into the interior from the sea was by mule, *bacalao* was the traditional choice for penitential dishes, replacing the meat during Lent and on days of abstinence (including every Friday and Wednesday). Spaniards became addicted to its very particular flavor and texture, and it is a much-loved delicacy even in coastal areas. The "pig of the sea," which replaced the ubiquitous ham and chorizo in so many dishes, is the food that evokes memories for everyone.

Cod is not a fish of Spanish waters. During the tenth century, Basque fishermen found a secret source in the high seas off Norway. Eventually they went as far west as Newfoundland to get it. To preserve it for the voyage home, they filleted the fish, stacked the fillets between layers of salt to extract their moisture, and dried them. *Bacalao* was carried to all parts of the Spanish hinterland by mules and in barges along rivers. Every region has its own special ways of cooking it.

Salt cod can be found in many ethnic fish markets and in grocery stores. It needs to be soaked in plenty of cold water for 12 hours to 2 days, depending on the strength of the cure, and the water must be changed four or five times to remove all the salt. You have to taste a bit to see if most of the salt is gone—there should still be a slight taste of salt remaining. In Spain, *bacalao* is often sold soaked and desalted, ready to be cooked.

To produce something of the flavor and texture of salt cod with fresh cod: Put thick cod fillets on a plate and sprinkle very generously with coarse sea salt or kosher salt. Leave them for at least 1 hour, turning them every 15 minutes or so and sprinkling them with more salt. The crystals will draw out the moisture from the flesh and some will be absorbed (do not use fine sea salt, or too much salt will be absorbed). Wipe off the salt and rinse the fillets under cold running water. Then soak in plenty of cold water for 30 to 45 minutes, changing the water three times. Drain and pat dry with paper towels.

creamed salt cod with mashed potatoes and garlic

{ *brandada de bacalao — catalonia* }

Catalans share brandada *with the South of France and the Languedoc. It can be a creamy emulsion of fish with milk or cream and olive oil beaten in, or a thicker puree with mashed potatoes. I prefer the potato version and make it with plenty of garlic, but you may prefer only a touch. Serve* brandada *as a starter or tapa.*

SERVES 6 AS A STARTER

1 large baking potato (about
  7 ounces), peeled and quartered

½ pound salt cod, desalted
  (see bacalao, opposite)

½ cup cream or whole milk,
  warmed

½ cup extra virgin olive oil

2 to 4 garlic cloves, crushed to
  a paste or through a press

Pepper

Salt if needed

FOR SERVING

9 or more thin slices white
  bread, crusts removed, cut
  into triangles, and fried in olive
  oil or toasted and brushed with
  extra virgin olive oil

Cook the potato in boiling salted water until soft; drain.

Put the salt cod in a saucepan of cold water and bring to a simmer, then remove from the heat and let stand for 15 minutes.

Drain the salt cod, carefully remove any skin and bones, and flake the fish into small pieces with your fingers. Put the fish in the food processor and blend to a rough paste. Pour in the cream or milk and the oil, a little at a time, alternating them, and blend to a smooth-creamy puree that retains a little texture. Add garlic and pepper to taste, then add the potatoes and blend briefly to a fluffy puree. If you desalted the fish too much, you may need to add a little salt.

Serve the *brandada* at room temperature, or spoon it into a baking dish and warm it in the oven before serving, accompanied by the fried or toasted bread.

fish soup with mayonnaise

{ gazpachuelo — andalusia }

I love this easy-to-make soup, a specialty of Málaga. The garlicky mayonnaise stirred in at the end gives it a creamy texture and adds to the mysterious, delicate, slightly winey flavor. Hake or another firm white fish can be used instead of monkfish. Small clams are usually added (see the variation), but small or medium scallops are perfect in this soup. Serve with toasted or fried bread.

SERVES 4

½ pound monkfish fillet

2¼ cups fish stock or water

1 cup dry white wine or sherry

1 small onion, finely chopped

2 bay leaves

Salt and pepper

4 waxy or new potatoes
   (about 1 pound), peeled and cut
   into ¼-inch-thick slices

½ teaspoon sugar (optional)

16 medium or large shrimp, peeled

8 small scallops

⅓ cup store-bought mayonnaise
   (I use Hellmann's)

3 garlic cloves, crushed to a paste

2 tablespoons chopped
   flat-leaf parsley

Put the monkfish in a large saucepan and add the stock or water, wine or sherry, onion, bay leaves, and a little salt and pepper. Bring to a boil, then simmer over low heat for 5 to 6 minutes, until the fish is just barely opaque throughout. Lift out and put it aside.

Add the potatoes to the pan and simmer until they are tender but not falling apart. Taste the broth and adjust the seasoning. If the wine is very dry, you might like to add a tiny bit of sugar.

Cut the monkfish into chunks and return them to the pan. Add the shrimp and scallops and cook for 1 to 2 minutes, until the shrimp turn pink and the scallops are no longer translucent.

Put the mayonnaise in a bowl and stir in the garlic. Add a few tablespoonfuls of the fish broth and beat vigorously with a wooden spoon, then pour into the soup, stirring very gently so as not to break up the potatoes and fish, and heat through. Stir in the parsley.

VARIATION

Use ½ pound clams instead of scallops. Wash and soak in cold salted water for 1 hour to clean them (see page 127). Put them in a pan with about ½ cup of water, cover, and steam over medium heat. The shells will open very quickly. Take the clams out of their shells and add them to the soup. Strain the clam cooking water, pour it into the soup, and heat through. Add a drop of vinegar or lemon juice to the broth.

pepa's fish soup

{ *suquet de peix — catalonia* }

This is an everyday Catalan fish soup that is more like a stew. It has several variants, but I love the way my friend Pepa Aymami (see page 267) makes it. Like so many Catalan dishes, it starts with a sofregit *(sofrito in Castilian Spanish) of garlic and tomato, and a picada of ground almonds, garlic, and parsley is stirred in at the end. Use hake, cod, halibut, or other firm white fish.*

SERVES 4

3 tablespoons olive oil

4 garlic cloves, sliced

1 large tomato or 2 small tomatoes, peeled and chopped

1 pound waxy potatoes, cut into ⅓-inch-thick slices

½ cup dry white wine

About 1½ cups fish or chicken stock

Salt

A good pinch of saffron threads

¾ teaspoon sugar

½ pound firm white skinless fish fillets (see headnote)

½ pound medium or large peeled shrimp

FOR THE *PICADA*

10 unblanched whole almonds

1 large garlic clove

1½ teaspoons olive oil

1 tablespoon chopped flat-leaf parsley

Heat the oil in a wide casserole. Put in the garlic and tomato and cook over medium heat, stirring often, until the tomato is reduced to a jammy sauce.

Add the potatoes, wine, and enough stock to cover the potatoes, then add salt to taste, the saffron, and the sugar and simmer, covered, over low heat for about 20 minutes, until the potatoes are just tender.

Meanwhile, for the *picada*, fry the almonds and garlic clove in the oil in a small skillet until both are lightly brown; drain on paper towels. The usual way is to crush and grind these to a paste in a mortar with the parsley, but you can use a food processor; add a ladleful of the stock to dilute it.

Put the fish in the soup and cook for 3 minutes (5 minutes if using monkfish). Add the shrimp and *picada* and cook until the shrimp turn pink and the fish is opaque throughout.

lobster hotpot

{ c a l d e r e t a   d e   l a n g o s t a — b a l e a r i c   i s l a n d s }

This sublime Minorcan specialty can be found in restaurants along the Balearic coast. The spiny lobster, queen of the local seas, was once considered poor food, which only the fishermen who fished it off the rocky coast would eat. The hotpot is in the classic Catalan style, starting with a sofrito *of fried onion, pepper, and tomatoes and ending with a* picada *of almonds, garlic, and parsley to thicken the sauce. Serve it with toasted slices of a good country bread or a baguette to dunk in the sauce. Offer lobster picks or thin forks or skewers for people to extract the lobster meat from the claws and legs, spoons for them to eat the sauce with, and finger bowls.*

Buy your lobsters live, and ask the fishmonger to kill and chop them for you. Have him separate the head, legs, and meaty claws from the tail and cut the tail lengthwise in half or crosswise into four pieces. He can discard the black intestinal vein or not, and the tomalley or liver (the green mass inside the head is considered a delicacy but may contain toxins). The roe, or coral—if the lobsters are female—is both edible and tasty and can go in the sauce. Ask him to crack the legs a little. Or do it all yourself at home with a heavy knife.

SERVES 6

1 large onion, chopped

1 green or red bell pepper,
 cored, seeded, and chopped

3 tablespoons olive oil

¾ pound tomatoes (4 to 5),
 peeled and chopped

1 teaspoon sugar

4½ cups fish stock

½ cup Cognac or other brandy

Salt and pepper

>>>

Fry the onion and the pepper in the oil in a large *cazuela* or casserole over low heat until very soft. Add the tomatoes and sugar and cook until the sauce is reduced and jammy. Use an immersion blender to blend it to a cream directly in the pan, or use a food processor and return it to the pan.

Add the fish stock and brandy and season with salt and pepper. Add the fennel, if using, then add the monkfish and lobster, bring to a boil, and cook for 5 minutes.

Meanwhile, for the *picada:* Fry the almonds and garlic in the oil in a small skillet over low heat for moments only, turning them once, until they are golden. Pound them to a paste with the parsley in a mortar, or blend them to a paste, and add the brandy.

>>>

A few fennel sprigs, torn into
    pieces (optional)

14 ounces monkfish fillet, cut into
    cubes

Two 1½-pound lobsters, cut into
    large chunks (see headnote
    on page 345)

FOR THE *PICADA*

12 blanched whole almonds

3 garlic cloves

½ to 1 tablespoon olive oil

⅓ cup chopped flat-leaf parsley

¼ cup Cognac or other brandy

FOR SERVING

6 slices of country bread,
    lightly toasted

Stir the *picada* into the simmering sauce and cook for 3 minutes more, or until the lobster shells turn a deep red and the meat is opaque, with a firm texture. Serve in bowls and pass around toasted slices of bread.

VARIATION

For a Catalan version, stir 1 to 2 tablespoons grated bittersweet chocolate into the sauce at the end.

fish stew with peppers and tomatoes

{ caldereta de pescados y mariscos — cantabria }

Galicia, Asturias, and Cantabria share similar fish stews and soups. Not long ago, all the men in the little fishing villages dotting the Atlantic coast went out to fish at night. The name caldereta *comes from the pot,* caldera, *in which they cooked some of their catch on board their small boats. Nowadays fishermen take pizza along to sustain them, while their stews have developed into prestigious dishes. Serve this one with sliced and toasted country bread brushed with extra virgin olive oil.*

SERVES 6

1 large onion, chopped

1 red or green bell pepper, cored, seeded, and diced

3 to 4 tablespoons olive oil

4 to 5 garlic cloves, chopped

3 medium tomatoes, peeled and chopped

2¼ cups dry white wine or oloroso sherry

2¼ cups water

1 teaspoon sugar

Salt and pepper

½ cup Cognac or other brandy

14 ounces monkfish or other firm white fish fillets

½ pound shrimp, peeled

7 ounces small scallops

⅓ cup chopped flat-leaf parsley

Fry the onion and pepper in the oil in a large pan over low heat, stirring often, until soft. Stir in the garlic and cook for a minute or so, then add the tomatoes and cook for about 10 minutes, until reduced. Add the wine, water, sugar (to mitigate the sharpness of the wine), and salt and pepper to taste, and simmer for 20 minutes.

Heat the brandy in a tiny saucepan. Carefully ignite it with a long match placed on the edge of the pan, and when the flames die down, pour it into the broth. Add the monkfish and cook for 8 minutes (other fish may take less time). Add the shrimp and scallops and cook for 1 to 2 minutes, turning them once, until the shrimp turn pink and the scallops are opaque.

Serve the soup sprinkled with the parsley and accompanied by toasted bread brushed with olive oil.

VARIATIONS

- For a slightly more substantial version of this stew from Galicia, peel 2 or 3 potatoes, cut them into small pieces or slices, and add them with the wine and water.

- Put ½ chile pepper, seeded, into the broth and take it out when the broth is hot enough to your taste.

POULTRY AND GAME

{ a v e s   y   c a z a }

Peasant farmers in Spain kept hens for their eggs—they ate chicken only on festive and celebratory occasions. That is why Spanish chicken dishes are so special. Although there is now intensive farming, and chicken is very cheap, the memory of those times is still powerful. Turkey was brought back from what is now Mexico by the conquistadores and was adopted by the nobility as their grand dish for great occasions. In Andalusia and Catalonia, turkey is still the grand Christmas dish, with extraordinary stuffings.

Spain is the European country with the greatest tradition of shooting game birds. There are partridge and woodcock, pheasant and quail, duck and pigeon. For centuries, hunting and shooting were noble sports reserved for the aristocracy (laws once made game the preserve of the landed elites), and noble codes of practice still govern the sport. Peasants were not allowed to shoot or even to take birds that had died accidentally, but of course there were always poachers. Now shooting is a national sport, and game cooking has wide appeal. During their season, game birds are on every restaurant menu. Every region has hunting preserves in national parks or on private wildlife estates. There are hunting and shooting clubs and associations, and organized driven-shooting (birds are "driven" over a waiting gun line; a team of "beaters" drives the birds by tapping sticks and using flags to encourage them to fly over the shooters) has become an industry.

Roast Chicken with Apples and Grapes, page 352.

Some farmed birds are raised naturally in their wild environment—they are hatched in nurseries and very quickly allowed into the wilderness.

Recipes for cooking game abound in old Spanish cookbooks and in collections compiled by monasteries centuries ago. Wild birds have a rich, strong flavor, but their meat is tough compared with that of farmed game. They have to be well hung and tenderized. The old aristocratic recipes advocated marinating game in wine and brandy and pot-roasting or stewing it, but innovative restaurants in Spain now serve tender, juicy roasted birds, their meat still slightly pink (sometimes almost raw), accompanied by a sauce. The peasant game dishes, which were once clandestine because the game would have been poached, are hearty soups and stews with beans and vegetables, and rabbit and hare dishes, which are still very popular.

Now that game is on our own supermarket shelves and the prices compare favorably with that of free-range organic chicken, we should be inspired by Spain's ways of cooking it. The season for partridge is from September 1 to February 1 and you can get squab and quail all year round; and all game birds can be bought frozen.

garlic chicken

{ *pollo al ajillo — castile - la mancha* }

Cervantes's seventeenth-century romantic "hero," Don Quixote, kept telling his manservant Sancho Panza not to eat garlic, as it would betray the vileness of his character. And the strong smell of garlic that assailed the knight the first time he saw his beloved Dulcinea del Toboso made him think that an evil magician had disguised her as a coarse peasant woman. Scholars of the period have a possible interpretation—that the smell of garlic was a coded message that she was a Conversa (Christian convert from Judaism), because at the time converted Jews were derided as eaters of excessive amounts of garlic. The Catalan food writer and critic Xavier Domingo, who wrote El Sabor de España *(The Taste of Spain), once commented, "There are many cuisines in Spain, but they all have one thing in common—garlic." However, its lavish use is a particular characteristic of Castilian cooking. If you are fond of garlic, add the peeled cloves of two whole heads—they will become soft, sweet, and mellow. That is how I like it, but I have to say that it is more common to cook the cloves in their skins and to remove them before serving. Serve this with potatoes or with bread to soak up the sauce. Rabbit is also great cooked in this way.*

SERVES 4 TO 6

¼ cup olive oil

1 chicken (about 3½ pounds),
    cut into 6 pieces

Salt and pepper

1 to 2 heads of garlic, cloves
    separated and peeled

3 bay leaves, preferably fresh

1 cup dry white wine or dry sherry

1 cup chicken stock (or 1 cup
    water plus ½ bouillon cube)

Heat the oil in a wide heavy-bottomed casserole or pan. Put in the chicken pieces and brown them all over, turning occasionally and seasoning with salt and pepper. Do them in batches if your pan is not wide enough to hold them in one layer. Remove them and fry the garlic cloves in the same oil over low heat until just lightly golden.

Return the chicken to the pot, add the bay leaves, and pour in the wine or sherry and chicken stock. Simmer, covered, for about 10 minutes, turning the chicken pieces occasionally. When the breasts are done, take them out and continue to cook the thighs and legs, uncovered, for another 10 to 15 minutes, until cooked through and no longer pink when you cut into them with a knife. Return the breasts and heat through.

roast chicken with apples and grapes

{ pollo con manzanas y uvas — asturias }

Apple trees are mentioned in Asturian monastery documents as early as the eighth century. By the twelfth century, smallholders were contracted to plant and tend a certain number of apple trees for the benefit of their landowners. The clergy covered their extensive lands with apple trees. In Asturias today, apples are an important part of the local economy. They are used to make cider and also appear in dishes both savory and sweet. In this dish, the apples are sometimes cooked in the oven with the chicken, sometimes sautéed separately in butter (Asturias is dairy country), sometimes accompanied by raisins, sometimes by white grapes. When my friend Alicia Ríos and her assistant, Simon Cohen, sent out e-mails to their friends asking for their favorite recipes, Ana Isabel Lozano sent me this one, which has become one of my favorites. The apple inside the cavity gives the chicken a fruity aroma and the freshly pressed grape juice gives it a caramelized glaze. In Asturias, they would use Reineta apples, but Golden Delicious are a good substitute.

SERVES 4

5 Golden Delicious apples

Juice of ½ lemon

2 pounds seedless white grapes

1 chicken (about 3½ pounds)

Salt and pepper

3 tablespoons olive oil

⅓ cup (5⅓ tablespoons) butter

Peel and core the apples. Cut one in half or quarters, to fit easily inside the chicken, and cut the rest into 8 slices each. Drop them into a bowl of water with the lemon juice to prevent them from discoloring.

Blend half the grapes in a food processor. Collect their juice by pressing the mush through a fine strainer into a bowl, using a wooden spoon. You should get about 1 cup of juice.

Stuff the chicken with the halved or quartered apple and put it in a baking dish.

Sprinkle with salt and pepper and rub with 1 tablespoon of the oil. Turn the bird breast side down and pour about ½ cup of the grape juice over it.

Roast in a preheated 375°F oven for 45 minutes. Turn the chicken over, pour the remaining grape juice over it, and return to the oven. Roast for another 30 minutes, or until the chicken skin is browned and caramelized and the juices run clear when you cut in between the leg and the body of the bird with a pointed knife.

While the chicken is roasting, heat the butter with the remaining 2 tablespoons oil in a large skillet. Put in the drained apple slices and the remaining grapes and sauté over medium heat, turning the fruit once, until the grapes are soft and golden and the apples tender and caramelized. This can take 20 minutes. Transfer to a baking dish, with their juices, and reheat in the oven when you are ready to serve.

VARIATION

Substitute a handful of dark or golden raisins or 6 to 8 moist pitted prunes, cut into pieces, for the sautéed grapes; add them to the skillet with the apples.

chicken with peppers and tomatoes

{ pollo al chilindrón — la rioja and aragon }

Chilindrón, *also called* fritada, *is a garnish of onions, peppers, and tomatoes that is ubiquitous in La Rioja and Aragon and the parts of northeast Spain where the Ebro River flows. You can use sweet red peppers or green ones, which provide a more peppery flavor, or both. The chicken and the* chilindrón *are cooked separately and come together at the end.*

SERVES 6

1 medium onion, chopped

6 tablespoons olive oil

4 garlic cloves, chopped

4 red or green bell peppers
    (or a combination), cored,
    seeded, and cut into wide strips

1½ pounds tomatoes, peeled
    and chopped

Salt and pepper

1 teaspoon sugar

1 large chicken (about
    4½ pounds), cut into 6 pieces

5 ounces sliced *jamón serrano,*
    prosciutto, or bacon, cut into
    thin strips

½ cup dry white wine

Fry the onion in 3 tablespoons of the oil in a wide skillet or casserole over medium heat, stirring often, until beginning to color. Add the garlic and peppers and cook for 10 minutes, stirring often. Add the tomatoes, season with salt, pepper, and the sugar, and simmer over medium heat for 15 to 20 minutes, or until the sauce is much reduced and jammy.

Meanwhile, brown the chicken pieces lightly in the remaining 3 tablespoons oil, in a large skillet, sprinkling with salt and pepper and turning them over once. Add the *jamón,* prosciutto, or bacon and stir for 2 minutes. Pour in the wine and cook, covered, over low heat for 20 to 30 minutes; remove the breasts when they are done, after about 15 minutes, and transfer to a plate, then return them to the pan when the legs are done. Add the tomato and pepper sauce and heat through.

chicken in almond and egg sauce

{ *pollo en pepitoria — castile - la mancha* }

There are several versions of this dish, which is also called pollo en salsa de almendra. *When it is made with a boiling hen, it is called* gallina en pepitoria. *It is best to use chicken thighs, which can take long stewing. The mix of wine and chicken stock thickened with almonds, garlic, cinnamon, saffron, and egg yolk makes a splendid sauce with a delicate flavor.*

SERVES 4

¼ cup olive oil

6 to 8 chicken thighs (skin on)

Salt and pepper

1 large onion, chopped

2 cups chicken stock (or 2 cups water plus 1 bouillon cube)

1 cup dry white wine

2 bay leaves

½ to ¾ teaspoon cinnamon

2 large hard-boiled eggs

½ cup blanched whole almonds

5 garlic cloves

A good pinch of saffron threads

You will need a wide casserole or pan that will hold all the chicken thighs in one layer. Heat 3 tablespoons of the oil in the casserole or pan over medium heat. Add the chicken thighs, and turn them, to brown them lightly all over, adding a little salt and pepper. Take them out, lower the heat, and put in the onion. Sauté gently over low heat until slightly golden.

Return the chicken pieces to the pot, add the chicken stock, wine, bay leaves, and cinnamon, and simmer gently, covered, over low heat for 25 minutes, turning the chicken pieces and adding a little salt and pepper.

Cut the hard-boiled eggs in half, take out the yolks, and set aside. Finely chop the whites in dice.

Fry the almonds and garlic in a small skillet in the remaining tablespoon of oil, turning them until the almonds are very slightly brown—the garlic will get browner.

Blend the almonds, garlic, and egg yolks to a paste in a food processor (or mash in a mortar), adding a few tablespoons of the stock from the chicken. Stir the paste into the simmering stock, add the saffron, and cook for 10 minutes longer, or until the chicken is done.

Serve sprinkled with the chopped egg whites.

VARIATION

In La Rioja, walnuts are used instead of almonds.

chicken cooked in cider with potatoes and peas

{ pitu a la sidra con patatinas y guisantes — asturias }

Hard cider, potatoes, and peas are major products of Asturias. Pitu *is the word there for the hens seen running around the villages pecking for grains of corn. They are tasty but tough and need a lot of cooking. I use chicken thighs in this dish because breasts become stringy if they are stewed for a long time.*

SERVES 4 TO 6

1 large onion, chopped

3 tablespoons olive oil

3 garlic cloves, chopped

¼ pound sliced *jamón serrano*, prosciutto, or bacon, cut into small strips

6 chicken thighs

Salt and pepper

1½ tablespoons fresh lemon juice

2¼ cups hard cider

1 pound waxy potatoes, peeled and cut in half, or into quarters if large

3¼ cups fresh peas or defrosted frozen baby peas (about 1 pound)

Sauté the onion in the oil in a covered wide skillet over low heat, stirring often until soft. Stir in the garlic and the *jamón*, prosciutto, or bacon, then add the chicken thighs and brown them all over, turning occasionally and adding salt and pepper.

Add the lemon juice and cider and cook, covered, over low heat for 30 minutes, or until the chicken is very tender.

In the meantime, cook the potatoes in boiling salted water until tender; drain.

Drop the potatoes into the pan with the chicken, and add the peas. Check the seasoning and simmer, covered, for 5 to 10 minutes more, until the peas are soft.

chicken and shrimp with almond and chocolate sauce

{ pollo con langostinos — catalonia }

This is a splendid example of the famous mar y montaña *(sea and mountain) Catalan dishes that mix meat and seafood. I asked a Catalan I met at a dinner why they mixed them and was told, "The mountain is right by the sea and we use what we have." My friend Pepa Aymami is famous for this dish. When I asked her for the recipe, she sent me a copy of the book she and her colleagues at the Fundació Institut Català de la Cuina had just published,* Corpus de la Cuina Catalana, *and marked the page with the recipe. Her version was the grand variation, with lobster instead of shrimp and with chocolate in the* picada, *the nutty paste that is stirred in at the end of many Catalan dishes to thicken the sauce and add another dimension of flavor. Putting chocolate in savory dishes was a novelty that came with the Spanish returnees from Mexico in the nineteenth century. Brandy and sherry give another sensational note.*

Catalans grate rather than chop their tomatoes, and that gives the famous sofregit *of fried onion, garlic, and tomato a finer texture. To grate tomatoes, cut them in half and grate on the fatter holes of a box grater until you get to the skin; discard the skin.*

SERVES 6

1 large chicken (about
    4½ pounds), cut into
    6 to 8 pieces

Salt

Flour for dredging

¼ cup olive oil

About 20 jumbo shrimp, peeled

2 medium onions, chopped

3 tomatoes, grated (see headnote
    above and page 129)

Pepper

½ cup Cognac or other brandy

>>>

Season the chicken pieces with salt and turn them in flour to coat them all over, then shake off the excess flour. Brown lightly in the oil in a wide casserole over medium heat, turning occasionally. Remove the chicken.

Fry the shrimp very briefly in the same oil for 2 minutes, turning them once, until they turn pink; then remove them.

Fry the onions in the same oil over low heat, stirring occasionally, until soft and just beginning to color. Add the tomatoes and salt and pepper to taste, and cook over medium-high heat until all the liquid has evaporated and the sauce is reduced to a jammy consistency.

Heat the brandy in a small pan. Carefully ignite with a long match, and when the blue flames die down, pour it into the sauce. Add the chicken pieces and just enough water to almost cover them. Simmer, covered, over low

>>>

FOR THE *PICADA*

½ cup blanched whole almonds

1½ teaspoons olive oil

5 to 6 garlic cloves,
    crushed to a paste

½ cup flat-leaf parsley leaves

1 ounce bittersweet chocolate,
    grated

¼ cup oloroso or amontillado
    sherry

heat for 20 to 30 minutes; remove the breasts after 15 minutes (check to see that they are done), and put them back when the legs and thighs are done.

Meanwhile, for the *picada*, fry the almonds briefly in the oil in a small skillet, stirring and turning them until lightly browned. The traditional way is to crush all the *picada* ingredients together in a mortar, but it is easier and perfectly fine to blend them in a food processor: Finely grind the fried almonds first, then add the garlic, parsley, and grated chocolate and blend to a paste. Add the sherry and blend well.

Stir the *picada* into the sauce and cook for 5 minutes. Add the shrimp and heat through.

VARIATION

Use the cooked meat from 1 lobster instead of shrimp.

duck with pears

{ p a t o   c o n   p e r a s — c a t a l o n i a }

Twenty years ago, when I was working on a BBC television series on Mediterranean cookery, I ate a duck with pears at Remei Martinez's Can Toni restaurant in the port of San Feliu de Guíxols in Catalonia, and I have always remembered it. It is one of the crowning dishes of Catalan cuisine. I have since found other versions, all of them rich and complex, but Remei's is still my favorite. She said that the recipe was originally for goose, but now it is most often made with duck. Other fruits such as peaches, apples, figs, and cherries are sometimes used instead of pears. Remei used wild ducks, which have little fat, are quite tough, and need to be stewed. The ducklings that are now raised in Spain are very tender and, like the ones we buy, very fatty and best roasted.

SERVES 4

1 duck (about 5¼ pounds)

Salt

¼ cup olive oil

12 whole blanched almonds

4 small unripe pears,
    such as Pomice or Conference,
    peeled, cut in half, and cored,
    or left whole

2¼ cups dry white wine

1 onion, finely chopped

2 tomatoes, grated or peeled
    and chopped

1 teaspoon sugar

1¼ cups chicken stock (or 1¼ cups
    water plus 1 bouillon cube)

>>>

Place the duck in a roasting pan. Rub it with salt and 1 tablespoon of the olive oil, and prick the skin in a few places to allow the fat to run out. Turn it breast side down, and roast in a preheated 400°F oven for 1 hour.

Remove the duck from the roasting pan, pour out the fat, and add ½ cup water, then return the duck to the pan, breast side up. Roast for another hour and 10 minutes, or until the skin is nicely browned and the juices run clear when you cut between a leg and the body with a pointed knife.

Meanwhile, for the sauce, put the almonds on a piece of foil on a baking sheet and toast in the oven for 5 to 6 minutes, until lightly browned; set aside.

Put the pears in a saucepan with the wine and simmer, uncovered, over low heat for 15 to 30 minutes, until tender; the time will depend on the type of pears and their degree of ripeness. Watch that they do not fall apart. Remove from the heat.

>>>

1 sprig of thyme

1 bay leaf

4 garlic cloves

3 to 4 tablespoons brandy or
pear brandy

Sauté the onion in the remaining 3 tablespoons of oil in a wide casserole, uncovered, over low heat, stirring occasionally, for about 10 minutes, until soft. Add the tomatoes, some salt, and the sugar and cook, stirring every so often, over high heat for 8 minutes, or until the sauce is jammy. Add the stock (or water and bouillon cube), thyme, and bay leaf, pour in the wine from the pears, and simmer for 15 minutes.

When the duck is cooked, lift it out of the roasting pan and set aside to rest. Ladle off the fat from the cooking juices and add the juices to the sauce.

Make a *picada:* Grind the toasted almonds and garlic cloves into a fine paste with a mortar and pestle or in a food processor, then mix in the brandy. Stir this into the sauce and simmer for about 10 minutes.

Cut the duck into 4 pieces and put them in the sauce. Add the pears, heat through, and serve.

roast guinea fowl with marzipan and dried fruit stuffing

{ pintada rellena de mazapán y frutos secos — balearic islands }

This dish of medieval origin is still cooked in the houses of the Majorcan nobility. Wild guinea fowl disappeared from the island years ago, but they are now farmed. Their flavor is only slightly gamy, less assertive than that of pheasant or partridge. Guinea fowl have little fat and need barding (covering with pancetta or bacon before roasting) so that the flesh remains juicy. The stuffing recipe here makes more than will fill the cavities of the guinea fowl, because it is so delicious you will want to have extra. The extra is cooked separately in foil. Alternatively, rather than stuffing the birds, you can cook all the stuffing separately (see the variations).

SERVES 4

FOR THE STUFFING

5 ounces soft pitted prunes

¼ pound soft dried apricots

½ cup blanched whole almonds

½ cup sugar

1 teaspoon orange blossom water (optional)

1 large egg yolk

>>>

For the stuffing, boil the prunes and apricots in just enough water to cover over low heat for 15 to 20 minutes, until they are very soft; drain.

Finely grind the almonds with the sugar in a food processor. Add the orange blossom water, if using, and the egg yolk and blend to a soft paste, adding a few drops of water if necessary to bind it. Mix the paste with the drained fruit in a bowl.

Rub the guinea fowl with salt and pepper and the oil or butter. With a narrow spoon, fill the cavities of each one with the stuffing. Wrap the extra stuffing in an oiled sheet of foil, and put it in the oven for the last 30 minutes of cooking.

Wrap the birds with the pancetta or bacon. Put them breast side down in a high-sided baking dish that holds them snugly. Pour in the wine, cover loosely with foil, and roast in a preheated 400°F oven for 1 hour.

>>>

FOR THE GUINEA FOWL

2 large guinea fowl (about
   2 pounds each)

Salt and pepper

2 tablespoons olive oil or butter

½ pound thinly sliced pancetta
   or bacon

1 cup dry white wine or fino sherry

Turn the birds over, cover them again with the foil, and roast for 15 minutes. Remove the foil and roast for about 15 minutes more, or until the legs pull away from the body and the juices run clear when the thigh is pierced. The flesh should not be red.

Serve with the pan juices, accompanied by the extra stuffing.

VARIATIONS

- You can cook all of the stuffing separately. Put it in a lightly greased small baking dish. Press it down firmly and cover with foil. Put the dish in the oven with the guinea fowl for the last 30 minutes of cooking. As the birds are not stuffed, they may need only about 1 hour of cooking.

- Soak the prunes and apricots in brandy instead of boiling them in water.

- Instead of the almond paste, add ⅓ cup raisins and ⅓ cup toasted pine nuts.

roast stuffed capon

{ capon relleno — catalonia }

Capons, geese, guinea fowl, and turkeys are Christmas specials in Spain. Capons are especially popular in the north. Every year on December 21, there is a capon fair at Villalba in Galicia, where the birds are raised on a diet of boiled cornmeal and potatoes or chestnuts soaked in milk or white wine. Capons from Villalba also appear in other Spanish markets. Capons are roosters that are castrated by hormone injection and fattened to reach enormous weights. Their meat is more tender, juicy, and flavorful than chicken. Catalans make glorious stuffings with different combinations of dried fruit, nuts, sausage, and brandy (see the variations), which they also use for turkey.

This recipe is based on one from an archive of recipes of the Fundació Institut Català de la Cuina (see page 105). You can also use it for turkey and for very fat chickens. I always cook the stuffing separately. Take the bird out of the fridge 2 hours before you want to start cooking it.

SERVES 8

1 capon (about 7 pounds)

Salt

2 tablespoons olive oil

2 Golden Delicious or Granny Smith apples, peeled, cored, and cut in half

2 onions, quartered

1 head of garlic, cut horizontally in half

2 ripe tomatoes, peeled and quartered

1 cinnamon stick

2 bay leaves

1 cup sweet white wine, such as Moscatel

>>>

Remove the neck and giblets from the cavity of the capon, if there are any, and remove any string or trussing. Rinse the bird inside and out in cold running water. Season generously with salt and rub with the olive oil. Push the apples into the cavity and place the bird breast side down in a roasting pan. Put the onions, garlic, tomatoes, cinnamon stick, and bay leaves around it and pour in the wine. Cover loosely with a foil tent. Place the roasting pan in the middle of a preheated 375°F oven and cook for 1 hour and 10 minutes.

Meanwhile, for the stuffing, coarsely chop the prunes and dried peaches or apricots. Put them in a bowl with the brandy to soak for at least 30 minutes.

Fry the onion in the oil in a large skillet until soft. Add the pork, season with salt and pepper, and cook, breaking up the meat and turning it, until it changes color. Make space for the sausages, put them in, and turn them until they change color. Add the pine nuts and stir for a minute or two, then stir in the ground almonds and cinnamon. Mix the pork mixture with the dried fruits and their brandy and

>>>

½ cup brandy

Pepper

FOR THE STUFFING

½ pound soft pitted prunes

½ pound soft dried peaches
   or apricots

¾ cup brandy

1 large onion, chopped

2 to 3 tablespoons olive oil

½ pound ground pork

Salt and pepper

½ pound thin pork sausages
   or Italian pork sausages,
   skinned and sliced

⅔ cup pine nuts

⅓ cup ground almonds

1 teaspoon cinnamon

place in the middle of a large double sheet of foil. Bring the sides up making a parcel. Alternatively, put the stuffing in a deep baking dish, press down firmly, and cover with foil. Place on a rack below the capon.

Take the roasting pan out, remove the foil, turn the capon breast side up, and roast, uncovered, for another 35 to 50 minutes, until well cooked and golden brown: it is done if you pierce the thickest part of the thigh with a pointed knife and the juices run clear. (For different-sized birds, allow 17 minutes per pound plus 30 minutes.)

Transfer the capon to a serving platter. Remove most of the fat from the pan juices, and place the roasting pan over medium heat. Stir in the brandy and deglaze, scraping up the browned bits from the bottom of the pan. Season with salt and pepper, and pour into a jug.

Carve the bird and serve accompanied by the sauce and stuffing.

VARIATIONS

- Add Golden Delicious apples, peeled, cored, and chopped, to the stuffing.

- Add a handful of dark or golden raisins to the stuffing, or add a dozen coarsely chopped cooked chestnuts.

- Use fresh bread crumbs instead of the almonds.

- An aristocratic dish in Majorca is capon stuffed with sweet potatoes, raisins, apples, almonds, and hazelnuts.

stuffed turkey

{ pavo relleno — catalonia }

In Seville and Córdoba, they eat turkey at Christmas. Sometimes it is simply turkey pieces cooked in sherry or white wine with ground almonds to thicken the sauce. My friend Loli Flores, who has always worked in restaurants in Seville, told me that in their country house they fed brandy to the turkeys and later injected their meat with brandy. Count José María Ybarra (see page 412) told me that his mother had the nuns make the family turkey. They deboned it and injected the meat with brandy. One stuffing was a mix of sausage meat, chestnuts, and brandy; another was dried fruit, pine nuts, and bread soaked in milk. Pavo trufado was layers of turkey and pork tenderloin slices, with slices of jamón and black truffles in between. I am telling you this in case you will be inspired to improvise.

Here is a simple way of roasting turkey that keeps it juicy and flavors it with brandy. The traditional Catalan stuffing for turkey is the same as the one for capon on page 367. Put it in a baking dish covered with foil and place it in the oven for the last hour of cooking.

SERVES 14

1 turkey (about 14 pounds)

Olive oil

Salt

1 orange, cut in half

12 tablespoons (1½ sticks) butter, softened

¾ cup brandy

1½ recipes Stuffing (page 367)

Lay two large sheets of foil in a roasting pan, one of them crosswise and the other lengthwise. Brush with oil and lay the turkey breast side up in the middle. Remove any trussing, sprinkle inside with salt, and push the orange into the cavity.

Blend the butter and brandy. Push it between the breast meat and skin: lift up the skin starting from the neck—gently work your fingers, then your hand, under it—and push in the soft butter and brandy, pressing on the skin to ease it into an even layer over the breasts. Tuck the flap of skin in at the neck to keep it from leaking out.

Wrap the turkey in the foil so that the parcel is roomy but well sealed. Cook in a preheated 425°F oven for 30 minutes, then lower the heat to 335°F and cook for 2 hours.

Open the foil parcel, turn up the oven to 400°F, and roast for another 30 minutes, or until the skin is crisp and brown and the juices run clear when you pierce a thigh.

partridge in white wine

{ *perdiz a la toledana — castile - la mancha* }

The queen of the Spanish skies is the fast-flying red-legged partridge. She has always been the queen. Don Quixote relied on shooting one for a meal. When the season opens at the end of summer in Castile, hunters go out in small groups with their hired entourage—loaders who look after the guns, and beaters who thrash the bushes and flush out the birds shouting, "Vamos! Vamos!" In the past, when hunters brought the birds home, they were cooked and preserved in a vinegar marinade called escabeche, *so that they could be kept and eaten over several months. These days, game butchers are there in the field with refrigerated vans to buy the birds from the hunt organizers.*

Partridge is the item of choice in restaurants in Toledo during the hunting season. El Bohío in Illescas, on the road between Madrid and Toledo, opened just before the Spanish Civil War as a modest meson *(inn) and became famous for its* perdiz. *The restaurant is still owned by the same family; but now Pepe Rodríguez Rey cooks modernized and sensational versions of the old dishes of La Mancha, and his brother Diego is the maître d'. This way of cooking partridge is one of the classics. Serve it with roasted or mashed potatoes (page 430 or page 281).*

SERVES 4

4 small partridges

Salt

3 tablespoons olive oil

1 large onion, chopped

2 large carrots, thinly sliced

6 to 7 garlic cloves, sliced in half

1 cup dry white wine

1 cup water

3 bay leaves

A sprig of thyme

12 black peppercorns

Singe any remaining partridge feathers over a flame and pull off. Rinse the partridges and salt them lightly.

Heat the oil in a wide casserole over medium-high heat and turn the birds in it to brown them all over. Take them out, and sauté the onion, carrots, and garlic in the same oil over medium-low heat, stirring often, for about 10 minutes, until the onion is soft. Add the wine, water, bay leaves, thyme, a little salt, and the peppercorns, put in the partridges, and cook, covered, over low heat, turning them over at least once, as the sauce will not cover them entirely, for about 40 minutes, until when you pierce the thickest part of the thigh with a pointed knife, the meat is no longer pink.

VARIATION

Some cooks like to blend the sauce to a cream. Use a handheld immersion blender after removing the cooked birds.

partridge with grapes and chocolate

{ *perdiz con uvas y chocolate——*
aragon, navarre, and la rioja }

When game birds are shot in the wild, they are tough and need braising or stewing. The amount of chocolate in the sauce is so small that you hardly detect it, but it softens the acidity of the vinegar and wine and lends a mysterious flavor. Don't be tempted to add much more; I overdid the amount once and did not like it at all. Serve with slices of dense country-style bread, crusts removed and fried in olive oil or toasted.

SERVES 4

4 small partridges

Salt

¼ cup olive oil

1 large onion, cut in half
    and sliced

6 garlic cloves

1 tablespoon white or
    red wine vinegar

1½ cups dry white wine

1½ cups chicken stock (or
    1½ cups water plus
    ½ bouillon cube)

2 bay leaves

6 cloves

Pepper

½ pound seedless white grapes

2 teaspoons grated dark chocolate,
    or more to taste

Singe any remaining partridge feathers over a flame and pull off. Rinse the birds and pat dry. Season with salt.

Heat the oil in a wide casserole. Put in the onion and garlic cloves and cook over low heat, stirring often, until they begin to soften. Put in the birds and cook, turning occasionally, until they are lightly browned all over. Add the vinegar, wine, chicken stock (or water and bouillon cube), bay leaves, and cloves and season with salt and pepper. Simmer, covered, over low heat for 30 minutes, turning the birds a few times.

Add the grapes and chocolate and cook for 15 to 20 minutes, or until the grapes are soft and the birds are done. Remove the lid toward the end to reduce the sauce a little.

Serve the partridges on top of fried or toasted bread, with the grapes and sauce poured over.

JESÚS SANTOS
AND THE *BECADA*

Jesús Santos was one of the chefs who pioneered the new Basque haute cuisine. He opened his first restaurant, Goizeko Kabi, in Bilbao in 1982 and now has five across Spain and a cooking school. I was taken to the Goizeko in the Wellington Hotel in Madrid by Gaspar Rey (see page 309). One of the best in the city, it serves exquisite innovative dishes. During game season, King Juan Carlos and Queen Sophia and the local aristocracy can often be seen there.

It was game season, and Jesús had hurt his leg while out shooting, but he stopped to sit with us from time to time to talk about his tasting menu and the methods (steam, *sous-vide*, and so on) now used in modern establishments. We had crab and all manner of seafood, an exquisite eggplant dish, suckling pig, duck, and an absolutely heavenly *becada* (woodcock). The favorite item on the menu is always woodcock, a bird with a strong gamy taste.

Jesús told us that he was from a peasant family of Palencia, a mountain province of Castile and León, and had gone with his brother at a young age to work in the Basque Country, where wealthy families employed cooks. I asked Jesús if he was inspired mainly by the local Castilian gastronomy. "Yes," he said, "and Castilian cooking was influenced by Arab and Jewish traditions—and I am a Converso." I told him that when I came into the restaurant and heard his name, I told Gaspar I was sure he was a Converso. Santos was the name many Jews who fled to Portugal took when they were forced to convert there. Here is the story of the Jews of Palencia: By the fifteenth century, the community was so large that there were two Jewish quarters and Jewish families had spilled out into different parts of the city. After 1492, those who had not converted moved to Portugal, but five years later, they were forced to convert there. In the seventeenth century, many of their descendants found their way back to Spain as Christians.

roast woodcock with brandy

{ *becada asada al brandy — basque country and northern spain* }

The elusive (and expensive) becada *is considered the most desirable of game birds, succulent with the most fat and a strong gamy flavor. It is a migratory bird that winters in the mountain woodlands of northern Spain, where it is stalked by hunters who love the challenge of shooting it. When the bird is apprehended, it bursts out of the grass and soars upward almost vertically before racing to safety in a high, swirling flight pattern. It looks haughty, with its very long beak, and it is always cooked with the head and beak left on except at times when shooting it is forbidden, and it appears illicitly in restaurants unrecognizable, with the beak cut off. It is cooked undrawn—that is, with the liver and entrails still inside, like berry-eating songbirds—so that its full flavor can best be appreciated. The bird's entrails are choice bits. Buy birds with the heads left on and the eyes removed. Woodcock are at their best from October to December but can also be bought frozen.*

I asked Basque restaurateur Jesús Santos for several recipes, which his assistant Martine Beaulieu sent me. A recipe for becada *came with step-by-step photographs showing how the chef prepares it. I tried it, but it was incredibly complex, with too many ingredients and too many steps. Instead, I give a simple traditional way that hunters and gourmets have eulogized in verse.*

Quail are also cooked in the same way. For instructions on roasting quail, see the variations.

SERVES 4

1½ large onions, finely chopped

¼ cup olive oil

¾ cup brandy, or to taste

4 woodcock

Salt and pepper

8 slices pancetta or bacon

4 large slices firm white bread, crusts removed and fried in olive oil or toasted

Sauté the onions in 2 tablespoons of the oil in a large covered skillet or casserole, over low heat, for about 30 minutes, stirring occasionally until very soft. Then cook uncovered over medium-high heat, stirring often, until golden brown and caramelized. Heat the brandy in a small pan. Using a long match, carefully set it alight. When the flames die down, pour it into the onions, stir, and remove from the heat.

For the woodcock, singe off any remaining feathers over a flame. Rinse the woodcock and rub them with salt and pepper and the remaining 2 tablespoons oil. Cover each one with 2 slices of pancetta or bacon. Truss the birds

>>>

by tying their legs together with kitchen twine, and bend the heads around so that the beaks lie to the side. Arrange them in an oiled baking dish and roast in a preheated 450°F oven for 10 to 15 minutes, depending on their size, or until tender and done to your taste. To test, cut into the thickest part of a thigh: the flesh should be pink and juicy. (Many chefs these days like their *becada* almost rare. One told me he turns off the oven after 5 minutes and leaves the birds in for another 5.)

Scoop out the innards from each bird and discard the gizzard. Chop the intestines and liver, add them, with the drippings, to the onion sauce, and heat through.

Serve the woodcock on the fried or toasted bread, with the sauce poured over.

VARIATIONS

- Place a slice of *mousse de foie gras*, or duck liver pâté, on each slice of toast.

- A suggestion from Pepe Iglesias (see page 328): Instead of serving the woodcock on toast, accompany them with chestnuts boiled in milk and sautéed in butter, mashed or left whole (page 408).

- To use quail instead of woodcook, cover each bird with 2 slices of pancetta or bacon and roast in a preheated 425°F oven for 15 to 20 minutes—they must not be rare, only slightly pink.

quail with grapes

{ codorniz a las uvas — galicia }

In some Spanish recipes for quail with grapes, the birds are cooked in grape juice rather than wine; the juice is made by mashing grapes in the blender and then pressing the juice through a strainer or colander with small holes. In others, the grapes are caramelized in sugar syrup that is allowed to brown. I particularly like this old Galician version adapted from a recipe sent to me by Pepe Iglesias. It was once made with lard, but now butter is used in this part of Spain, which is dairy country, and cream makes a luscious sauce. Albariño grapes are used in Galicia, but you can use any flavorful seedless white grapes. You will need to pick up the birds with your fingers when you eat, so provide finger bowls for your guests, as well as paper napkins.

SERVES 4 AS A MAIN COURSE; 8 AS A STARTER

4 tablespoons (½ stick) butter

3 tablespoons olive oil

8 quail

1 pound seedless white grapes, stemmed

⅔ cup dry white wine

½ cup heavy cream

Salt and pepper

Heat the butter and oil in a large skillet. Put in the quail and cook over medium heat, turning them occasionally, for about 8 minutes, until lightly browned all over.

Add the grapes, wine, and cream and season with salt and pepper. Bring to a boil, then simmer, covered, over low heat for about 15 minutes, turning the birds, so that all parts bathe in the sauce, or until the grapes are soft and the birds are done. To test them, cut between the leg and the body of one quail with a pointed knife: the juices must run clear but the flesh should still be slightly pink.

VARIATION

For a version from Mediterranean Spain, use Moscatel grapes and a half-and-half mix of sweet Moscatel wine and chicken stock. Omit the cream.

quail with caramelized onions and brandy

{codorniz al brandy—basque country and northern spain }

In his book Homage to Catalonia, *written in 1937, George Orwell described the way peasants spread out nets over the grass at night and then lay down on the ground making noises like female quail. When male quail came running, they got entangled in the nets. Although European Union rules have made it illegal, it is still a Mediterranean custom to catch migrating birds that fly over the sea in big nets. In Cyprus, where hunting is a large-scale activity, endless tapes of birdsong are played to lure birds into the nets. But in Spain, as in the United States, most quail you find now are farmed.*

The onions take a long time to caramelize; they are delicious with the added brandy.

SERVES 2 AS A MAIN COURSE; 4 AS A STARTER

5 tablespoons olive oil

2 large onions, cut in half and sliced

4 quail

Salt and pepper

½ cup brandy, or to taste

4 slices country bread, fried in olive oil or toasted

Heat the oil in a wide heavy skillet or casserole. Put in the onions, cover, and cook slowly over very low heat, stirring often, for about 30 minutes, until very soft and beginning to color.

Push the onions to one side of the pot, put in the quail, season with salt and pepper, and turn up the heat to medium. Turn the quail to brown them all over, and stir the onions occasionally so that they brown evenly. Add the brandy, and cook over low heat until the onions are caramelized and the quail are done; this will take about 25 to 30 minutes. Pull the leg of one of the quail: if it moves easily, and the juices run clear when you cut in between the body and a leg, they are done.

Serve on the toasted or fried bread.

grilled quail

{ *c o d o r n i z   a   l a   p l a n c h a — m e d i t e r r a n e a n   s p a i n* }

*A good way to cook quail is grilled over hot coals or on a flat griddle (*a la plancha*). You can ask the butcher to spatchcock (butterfly) them, or do it yourself, as described below. Serve with alioli (page 141).*

SERVES 2 AS A MAIN COURSE; 4 AS A STARTER

4 quail

1 to 2 garlic cloves, crushed to a paste

1½ tablespoons fresh lemon juice

3 tablespoons olive oil

Salt

To spatchcock the quail, lay the birds breast side down on a cutting board and, using poultry shears or kitchen scissors, cut down along both sides of each backbone, starting from the bottom all the way up to the neck, and remove the backbone. Open each quail out like a book. Make a small slit in the skin to release the legs, turn the bird over, and press down hard with the palm of your hand along the breastbone until it lies flat.

Mix the garlic, lemon juice, and olive oil in a large dish. Add the quail, turning to coat them well in the marinade, and leave for a couple of hours in the refrigerator, covered with plastic wrap; turn the quail over in the marinade at least once.

Prepare a fire in a grill or heat a flat *plancha*, or griddle.

Oil the grill or *plancha*, lay the quail on it, skin side up, and cook for 7 minutes. Turn over and cook for another 5 minutes, then check to see if they are done by inserting a sharp pointed knife into a bird's thigh. If the juices run clear, the quail are ready. Season with salt and eat with your fingers.

squab with red wine

{ *pichón al vino tinto — castile and león* }

*Young domesticated pigeons, or squab, are an old delicacy of Castile. You see curious ancient clay and straw dovecotes (*palomares*) in wheat fields where the grain was once the ready feed for thousands of birds. At one time, pigeon rearing was a major agricultural activity, and the meat was often pickled or preserved in fat. Squab are birds killed when they are one month old, before they have learned to fly (until then they are fed by their parents). There is little meat on a squab, and most of it is on the breast; it is dark red and very tender and moist. The flavor is fine and delicate, quite different from the tough gamy flesh of wild wood pigeons (*palomas*). It is fashionable now to roast or grill farmed squab and to serve the meat medium-rare, but the traditional way of braising it in a red wine and brandy sauce also suits the delicate meat. Serve them with large slices of fried or toasted bread. Sautéed mushrooms make a good accompaniment.*

SERVES 4

4 garlic cloves

4 tablespoons (½ stick) butter

4 squab (about 12 ounces each)

2 tablespoons olive oil

Salt and pepper

1 medium onion, chopped

1 leek, trimmed, washed,
    and chopped

1 carrot, chopped

2¼ cups dry red wine

½ cup brandy

1 bay leaf

1 sprig of thyme

1 cup chicken stock (or 1 cup
    water plus ½ bouillon cube)

Put a garlic clove and a small piece of butter inside each squab. Heat the remaining butter with the oil in a wide casserole or skillet over medium heat. Brown the birds on all sides, sprinkling them with salt and pepper; then take them out.

Put the chopped onion, leek, and carrot in the casserole and sauté over low heat, stirring occasionally, until soft and beginning to brown. Add the wine, brandy, bay leaf, and thyme, and cook for 15 minutes. Add the stock (or water and bouillon cube), season with salt and pepper, and put in the birds. Cook, covered, turning the squab a few times, for 15 minutes, or until they are cooked. To test if they are done, pull one of the legs; it should move easily.

VARIATIONS

- Sauté 1 Golden Delicious apple, peeled, cored, and chopped, with the vegetables.

- A Catalan version adds 1 tablespoon grated bittersweet chocolate to the sauce at the end.

- Sauté 4 ounces chopped *jamón serrano* or prosciutto with the vegetables.

pheasant with apples

{ *faisán con manzanas—asturias* }

When pheasants have been hunted wild, they are usually no longer young, and while their flavor is richer, they can be quite tough and so need slow cooking. Our own pheasants that are available in autumn, or at other times frozen, are farmed. They are young and relatively tender (hen pheasants are the most tender, with more fat) and are best roasted at high heat for not too long. Asturias is apple country, where they also make an apple spirit that is like Calvados.

SERVES 4

2 young pheasants (about 1½ pounds each)

Salt and pepper

2 tablespoons olive oil

5 Golden Delicious apples

4 tablespoons (½ stick) butter

12 slices pancetta or bacon

½ cup Calvados

Pull off any feathers on the pheasants or burn them off over a gas flame, then rinse the birds. Rub them with salt, pepper, and 1 tablespoon of the olive oil. Put them breast side up in a large casserole or baking dish with a lid.

Peel and core the apples. Cut one apple in half. Push a small piece of butter and an apple half in the cavity of each bird. Wrap each bird in 6 slices of pancetta or bacon.

Cut the remaining apples into 8 slices each. Heat the remaining butter with the remaining oil in a large skillet. Put the apple slices in—in batches if necessary—and cook briefly over medium heat, turning them once, to brown them lightly on both sides, about 8 to 10 minutes. Pour in the Calvados and let it bubble for a moment. Arrange the apples around the pheasants, with their sauce, and cook, half covered, in a preheated 425°F oven for 30 minutes, or until the legs pull away easily from the body and juices run clear. Cut each pheasant in two down the breastbone and serve accompanied by the apples, with the sauce poured over.

VARIATIONS

- Use sweet hard cider instead of Calvados.

- Instead of apples, use 1 pound soft pitted prunes, soaked in 1 cup Cognac or other brandy for 30 minutes.

- Use 1 pound white, red, or black seedless grapes instead of apples with 1 cup brandy.

foie gras and truffles

When the Chernobyl disaster in 1986 left radioactive clouds over Hungary and France, they stopped production of foie gras, and Catalonia, Navarre, and the Basque Country started producing it. Now these regions make some of the best goose foie gras in the world, and innovative Spanish chefs are fond of using it.

Black truffles (*trufa*) are found in woodlands in northern Spain, deep in the soil around oak, hazelnut, and pine trees. About ninety percent of the crop goes to France, the rest to grand restaurants; truffles never had a place in Spanish regional cooking. When the supply of wild truffles decreased, and prices and demand abroad increased, truffle cultivation was started in areas where they never grew before, such as the forests around the town of Sarrión in southwest Aragon. Here a course on truffle cultivation given in 1987 by an agronomy engineering student, Francisco Edo Navarrete, was the initial inspiration for local people to start cultivating.

Locals now use truffles in their cooking. As they keep very well, cooks can use them all year round. Although cultivated truffles do not have the same powerful aroma as wild ones, they are delightful.

pheasant stuffed with duck liver pâté

{ faisán a la moda de alcántara }

The recipe for this mythical dish appears in the memoirs of Laure Junot, Duchess of Abrantès, published in Paris in 1831. According to the duchess, it came from a culinary manuscript her husband, General Jean-Andoche Junot, had salvaged when his soldiers sacked the monastery of Alcántara in Extremadura while serving in Napoleon's army during the Peninsular War. She popularized this way of cooking pheasant, woodcock, and quail, marinated in port wine and stuffed with foie gras pâté with truffles, calling it à la mode d'Alcántara. Auguste Escoffier later commented that the manuscript was the only worthwhile French gain from the war. While stuffing game birds with foie gras pâté has long been part of French haute cuisine, especially with quail, Spanish chefs have only recently pulled the style out of their past and developed their own versions. The pheasant is sometimes braised, but I prefer this version in which it is marinated for 24 hours in port and then roasted. I stuff it with store-bought duck's liver pâté with truffles. In the monastery, they made the pâté themselves and added truffles to the port during the cooking. It is best to use hen pheasants rather than cocks—they have more fat and are more tender. Serve with boiled chestnuts (see page 408).

SERVES 4

2 young hen pheasants
(about 1½ pounds each)

1½ cups port

Salt

5 ounces duck liver pâté
with truffles

10 to 12 slices pancetta or bacon

Marinate the pheasants the day before cooking: Burn off any feathers and rinse the birds. Put each one in a large plastic bag. Pour half the port into each bag and twist the bags so that they are tightly closed around the birds. Marinate in the refrigerator, turning the bags a few times so as to soak the birds well all over.

Remove the birds and pour the port into a large baking dish. Season the birds lightly with salt, inside and out. Fill the cavity of each with half the pâté, and truss them (tie the legs together with kitchen twine). Place them in the baking dish, breast side up, and cover entirely with the pancetta or bacon, to prevent the flesh from drying out.

Cover loosely with foil and roast in a preheated 400°F oven for 45 to 60 minutes, until the legs pull away easily from the body and the juices run clear (a bird takes longer to cook when it is stuffed).

Carve the pheasants and serve with the stuffing and the sauce of port and roasting juices poured over.

braised rabbit with herbs and white wine

{ conejo al vino }

Mercedes Garcia, who lives in the Andalusian village of Frailes, gave me a rabbit trap made with wire, one that her father made for a living. Rabbit was a staple of the rural population in all of Spain. It was also used as currency to pay the doctor. In Corpus de la Cuina Catalana *(see page 105), I found what seemed like a hundred Catalan ways of cooking it: grilled, roasted, and braised with onions, or tomatoes, or mushrooms, bell peppers, snails, prawns, whole heads of garlic, olives, prunes, pine nuts, and with vinegar and sugar, red wine, or white wine—and it goes on. Later I found this recipe written by hand in Spanish, and I cannot remember who it was from.*

SERVES 4

1 rabbit (2¼ to 2½ pounds),
    cut into 6 pieces

5 tablespoons olive oil

1 large onion, roughly chopped

1 head of garlic, cloves separated
    and peeled

Salt

2 cups dry sherry or white wine

3 thyme or oregano sprigs

2 bay leaves

8 black peppercorns

1 to 2 teaspoons sugar (to taste)

Ask the butcher to cut the rabbit into 6 pieces. If you have to do that yourself, here is how: Trim and discard any flaps of skin and the tips of the forelegs. Using a heavy knife or cleaver, cut the rabbit crosswise into 3 parts—back legs, back and rib cage, and forelegs. Cut between the back legs to separate them. Cut the front part into 2 pieces to separate the forelegs. Cut the back crosswise in half, giving you a total of 6 pieces.

Heat the olive oil in a large casserole, add the onion and garlic, and sauté over low heat, stirring occasionally, until soft. Put in the rabbit pieces, season with salt, and cook, turning the rabbit occasionally, until the pieces are lightly browned and the onion begins to color.

Add the white wine or sherry, herb sprigs, bay leaves, peppercorns, and sugar and bring to a boil, then simmer, covered, for about 35 minutes, or until the rabbit feels tender when you cut into a thigh with a pointed knife; turn the rabbit pieces occasionally. Uncover the pot for the last 10 minutes. The sauce should be reduced and a little syrupy. Do not overcook, or the rabbit will be stringy.

A RABBIT LUNCH AT MICHAEL JACOBS'S HOUSE IN FRAILES

Walking with Michael Jacobs and Manolo el Sereno (see page 173) in the village of Frailes, in Jaén, Andalusia, is like walking with Don Quixote and Sancho Panza. Michael is a tall aristocratic-looking Englishman, Manolo a small man of the people. We are stopped by everyone. Michael wrote a book, *The Factory of Light,* about the village and spent a long time interviewing the inhabitants. Now that he lives there, they want to go on telling him everything. In the bar carved into the mountain where men sit playing cards in the dark, one man gives him a rabbit, another offers him an armful of wild asparagus he had just picked. They become part of our lunch in his little house on the hill.

Michael fell for the magic of Spain as a boy and went on to write many learned and witty travel books and guidebooks about the country. He was first drawn to Frailes by the story of the *milagrero,* the healer miracle man known as el Santo

Custodio, who had lived as a hermit with his goats at the top of a mountain. A shrine and a little church built on the spot are a place of pilgrimage where people pin photos, light candles, and leave gifts. Michael stayed because it was a peaceful place for writing and because he was touched by the friendliness and warmth of the people, who adopted him as one of their own. Unlike Gerald Brenan, who wrote about Spain in the 1940s and '50s but said little about the food, Michael is a gastronome who writes about the food and takes groups on gastronomic tours.

MEAT

{ *carne* }

A Castilian adage, "Vaca y carnero, olla de caballero" ("*Cow and ram,* gentleman's stew"), is a reminder that meat was for centuries the food of the nobility. There was a time when most of the population in Spain only ate fresh meat at festivals or at weddings and funerals, and the everyday meat usually consisted of tiny bits of home-cured ham or chorizo in their stews. But today Spain is a country of carnivores.

Lamb is the most common meat. In the Middle Ages, it was the meat of the Muslims and Jews, who could not eat pork, and of the old Spanish nobility who raised sheep for their wool. Pork is ubiquitous in its cured form, but it is still rarely eaten fresh, except in the areas where pig rearing is an industry, such as in parts of Andalusia and Extremadura. Cattle were in the past bred for dairy. The males were slaughtered young to be eaten as veal or were castrated for work in the fields, while fighting bulls were bred for the bullring. But veal was only for feast days or for the rich. Spanish veal, *ternera*, is not the pale pink veal of milk-fed calves; it is the darker meat of animals that have been slaughtered when they are between nine and twelve months old. But generally Spaniards love their meats very young. The high points of Spanish gastronomy are roast suckling pig, baby lamb, and baby kid, traditionally cooked in a bread oven.

Beef was rarely eaten until a couple of decades ago. The change came about when agriculture was mechanized and the oxen, or *buey*, castrated males that pulled the plow (some as old as twenty), became redundant. Then it was discovered that when they were no longer working, their muscle turned to fat and their mature dark, intricately marbled meat, if well hung, had a magnificent rich taste and a silky tenderness. The first *asador* (roaster) to serve ox steaks cooked over coals was Julián Rivas in the Basque town of Tolosa in 1961. The fashion for grilled ox steak swept through the cider houses of the Basque Country and eventually through cattle-raising northern Spain and the entire country. Now that Spain has run out of the old plow oxen and finds it hard to sell its milk because the European Union has milk mountains, it has turned to rearing the indigenous cattle that were spurned in favor of better milk producers during Franco's time. The meat from these mature cows, which are fattened for several months before slaughter, is of a very high quality.

In the past, offal—tripe, heads, brains, ears, tongues, feet, tails—was not appreciated by the social elites. They only ate it on days of abstinence, as it was not considered to be meat. Foreign visitors noted with surprise that despite Church rules of abstention for Wednesdays, Fridays, and Saturdays, Spaniards ate offal on these days. The working-class poor in the cities got it cheap from slaughterhouses and specialty butchers. Nowadays offal is available in every market, and offal dishes are much-loved regional specialties.

You will find other main dishes with meat in the chapters on rice and on substantial dishes.

lamb stew with milk "shepherd's-style"

{ cordero a la pastora — aragon }

In Don Quixote, *Cervantes tells about Andrés, a fifteen-year-old boy who looks after the sheep of one Juan Haldudo, "el rico" (the rich man). His master beats him and withholds wages because, as he explains to Don Quixote, sheep keep going missing and he is certain that the boy has sold or eaten them. Don Quixote believes he is innocent and interferes on his behalf, only to make matters worse. Shepherds ate lamb when they spent months away from home with their flocks. They would have had ewe's milk to cook the meat in, as in this dish. But did they have wine? Perhaps they exchanged cheese for some. I cooked this dish with neck fillet. It become very tender, and the wine, milk, and herbs gave the potatoes a delicious flavor.*

SERVES 4 TO 6

3 tablespoons olive oil

1½ pounds boneless lamb, such as neck fillet or shoulder, trimmed of excess fat, cut into large pieces (about 3½ inches)

4 garlic cloves, chopped

1 cup dry white wine

7 cloves

2 thyme sprigs

2 bay leaves

1 pound medium new potatoes, peeled and cut in half

Salt and pepper

1 teaspoon sugar (optional)

1 cup whole milk

Heat the oil in a wide casserole. Add the meat and brown it lightly on all sides over high heat. Lower the heat, stir in the garlic, and let it just begin to color. Add the wine, cloves, thyme, and bay leaves, then add the potatoes and season with salt and pepper. Simmer, covered, over low heat for about 1 to 1¼ hours, or until the meat is very tender and most of the liquid has been absorbed.

Add a little sugar if the dryness of the wine needs softening. Stir in the milk, add more salt if necessary, and cook for a few minutes more.

lamb stew with peppers and tomatoes

{ cordero al chilindrón—aragon, la rioja, and navarre }

This is a specialty of northern Spain, in the regions where the Ebro River flows. It is good to make for a large party, as it can be prepared well in advance. The peppers are sometimes fried with the onion, but roasting gives them a finer taste and texture.

SERVES 6

1 large onion, chopped

3 to 6 garlic cloves, chopped

½ pound bacon, cut crosswise into thin strips

5 tablespoons olive oil

1½ pounds tomatoes, peeled and chopped

1 teaspoon sugar

1½ pounds boneless lamb, such as neck fillet or trimmed boneless lamb shoulder, cut into large pieces (2½ to 3 inches)

Salt

5 bell peppers, preferably 3 red and 2 green, roasted (see page 128), peeled, seeded, and each cut into 8 strips

½ cup dry white wine

Pepper

Fry the onion, garlic, and bacon in 2 tablespoons of the oil in a wide casserole or saucepan over medium heat, for about 10 to 12 minutes, stirring, until soft and just beginning to color. Add the tomatoes and sugar and cook for 5 minutes. Remove from the heat.

Heat the remaining 3 tablespoons oil in a large skillet over high heat. Add the meat, sprinkle with salt, and turn the pieces to brown them all over. Lift them out and add them to the tomato sauce.

Add the peppers, stir in the wine, and season with salt and pepper. Simmer, uncovered, over low heat for 1 to 1½ hours, until the meat is very tender and the sauce reduced; turn the meat a few times to keep uncovered parts from drying out.

Note: You may prefer to add the roasted peppers to the stew 15 to 30 minutes before the end of cooking.

lamb stew with honey

{ *cordero a la miel — andalusia* }

This is an old Moorish way of cooking lamb with honey that has been rediscovered by modern chefs in Andalusia. The stew has just a touch of honey and a pinch of hot pepper to mitigate the sweetness. The meat should become so tender that it falls apart.

SERVES 5 TO 6

3 tablespoons olive or sunflower oil

1 pound shallots

2¼ pounds boneless lamb shoulder, trimmed of excess fat and cut into 5 or 6 pieces

Salt

1 cup dry white wine

3 tablespoons brandy

A pinch of *pimentón picante* (or hot paprika) or cayenne

1½ tablespoons orange blossom honey or other aromatic honey

Heat the oil in a wide heavy-bottomed casserole over medium heat. Put in the shallots and turn to brown them all over; take them out. Put in the meat and turn the pieces to brown them all over (you may have to do this in 2 batches; if so, return all the meat to the pot after browning the second batch).

Season the meat with salt, add the wine, brandy, *pimentón*, and honey, and cook for 10 minutes. Put the shallots on top of the meat, cover with water, and bring to a boil, then simmer, covered, for 1½ to 2 hours until the meat is very tender; turn the meat a few times, and add water as necessary to keep it covered.

Turn up the heat and simmer, uncovered, for a few minutes toward the end to reduce the sauce.

VARIATION

Add a little more honey and a tablespoon of wine vinegar, for a sweet-and-sour taste.

tiny grilled lamb chops with potatoes

{ chuletitas de cordero a la parilla con patatas — murcia }

The nearest thing we have to the tiny ever-so-tender chops of very young lamb you get in Spain is small rib chops from a rack of lamb. Here they are served on a bed of sautéed potatoes with onion. You can prepare the potatoes ahead and reheat them before serving. It is good served with alioli *(page 141).*

SERVES 2

FOR THE POTATOES

1 large onion, cut in half and sliced

¼ cup olive oil

1 pound waxy potatoes,
    peeled and cut into slices
    about ¼ inch thick

Salt and pepper

½ cup chicken stock, or more
    as needed

FOR THE LAMB CHOPS

1 rack of lamb (7 to 8 chops)

1 tablespoon olive oil

Salt and pepper

For the potatoes, fry the onion in the oil in a large covered skillet over low heat, stirring occasionally, until soft. Add the potatoes and cook over low heat, stirring and turning them with a spatula and adding salt and pepper, until the potatoes and onion are lightly golden, about 10 minutes. Pour in the chicken stock and cook, covered, over low heat for about 15 minutes, until the stock is absorbed and the potatoes are tender, adding more stock if necessary.

Meanwhile, cut the rack of lamb into chops with a heavy knife or cleaver. Brush them all over with the olive oil.

Just before serving, heat an oiled *plancha* (flat griddle) or heavy skillet over high heat and cook the cutlets for 2 to 3 minutes on each side, just until they are browned on the outside but still very pink and juicy inside; do not overcook them. Cut into one to test—they are best served medium-rare.

Season the chops with salt and pepper and serve beside or on top of the potatoes.

VARIATIONS

- For a garlic and vinegar dressing, stir 2 to 3 garlic cloves crushed to a paste in 2 tablespoons extra virgin olive oil in a small pan over low heat for seconds only, until the aroma rises; do not let the garlic brown. Off the heat, add 1 tablespoon vinegar and ¼ teaspoon sugar and mix well. Drizzle a little over each chop.

- Sprinkle the lamb with plenty of garlic slices fried in olive oil until golden and crunchy.

braised lamb shanks with potatoes

{ jarrete de cordero con patatas — aragon }

These slow-cooked lamb shanks have a marvelous melt-in-the-mouth quality, and the wine sauce is enriched by the gelatin they release. They go well with these crunchy roasted potatoes, but you could also serve them with mashed potatoes (page 281).

SERVES 4

3 tablespoons mild olive oil

4 small lamb shanks
  (about 1 pound each)

1 large onion, finely chopped

2 carrots, sliced

5 garlic cloves, finely chopped

4 tomatoes, peeled and
  finely chopped

2 cups dry white wine

¼ cup brandy (optional)

2 cups water

Salt and pepper

1 teaspoon sugar

FOR THE POTATOES

1½ pounds new potatoes, peeled

Salt

Olive oil

Heat the oil in a wide casserole and brown the shanks over medium heat, turning them occasionally. Take them out.

Cook the onion and carrots in the same oil over medium heat until the onion is soft, stirring often. Add the garlic and cook, stirring, until the aroma rises, then add the tomatoes and cook for 8 minutes.

Add the shanks and pour in the wine, brandy if using, and water. Season with salt and pepper and the sugar and cook, covered, over low heat at a bare simmer for 2 hours, or until the meat is so tender you can pull it off the bone; turn the shanks 3 or 4 times and add a little water if necessary to keep them half covered, then let the sauce reduce toward the end. I like to leave the sauce as it is, but if you wish, lift out the shanks and blend the sauce to a cream with an immersion blender (as they now do in Spain), then return the shanks to the pot.

Meanwhile, for the potatoes, cook them in boiling salted water until barely tender. Drain and cut them in half, or into quarters, if large.

Place the potatoes in a roasting pan or baking dish, sprinkle with salt, and pour a good amount of olive oil over them, so that when you turn them, they become well coated all over. Roast in a preheated 425°F oven for 30 to 40 minutes, or until crisp and golden.

Serve the lamb with the potatoes.

marinated leg of lamb

{ *cordero en adobo de guadalajara—castile - la mancha* }

Rosa Tovar (see page 285) sent me this recipe, which is good for goat, venison, and wild boar, as well as for lamb, mutton, and pork. It was of both hunters and shepherds. It is originally from Alcarria in the province of Guadalajara, but there are versions of it found in small towns and villages in central Spain all the way down to Andalusia. Alcarria, an area of river valleys and mountains that abounds with flowers on which bees feed, produces a famous honey, and the best saffron is also from La Mancha. Start making this dish the day before.

SERVES 6

FOR THE MARINADE

2 tablespoons olive oil

1 onion, cut in half

A head of garlic cloves, peeled

6 black peppercorns

3 cloves

1 cinnamon stick

A sprig of thyme

2 bay leaves

2 tablespoons honey

½ cup red or white wine vinegar

1 cup dry white wine

1 large leg of lamb

Salt and pepper

2 to 3 tablespoons olive oil

1 tablespoon honey

2 tablespoons wine vinegar

A good pinch of saffron threads

For the marinade, put all the ingredients in a saucepan and bring to a boil, then simmer for 25 to 30 minutes. Let cool.

Trim the meat of excess fat and put it in a large plastic bag. Pour in the marinade, twist the bag so that it is closed tightly around the meat, and marinate in the refrigerator for 24 hours, turning the bag a few times so as to soak the meat well all over.

Take out the meat, reserving the marinade, dry it with paper towels, and season with salt and pepper.

Heat the oil in a large casserole. Brown the meat on all sides over medium heat. Pour in the honey and let it brown a little, then stir in the vinegar and saffron.

Strain the marinade into the pot and bring to a boil, then simmer, covered, over low heat for 2½ hours, or until the meat is very tender; turn it every 20 minutes or so and add a little water if necessary—there should be a good amount of sauce left at the end.

roast pork belly with baked apples

{ *panza de cerdo con manzanas—asturias* }

As most of the pork we buy these days is from pigs that have been bred to put on lean meat, it is usually dry and tasteless because it is the fat that carries taste and succulence. With pork belly, the crisp crackling and layers of fat keep the meat meltingly succulent as it cooks. You can cut away the fat after it is cooked if you like. Make sure that the butcher has removed the ribs and that he has scored the rind with deep cuts that go right down to the fat. In Asturias, they serve pork with applesauce or roasted whole apples. Golden Delicious are a good substitute for their Reinetas. They also serve it with the chestnut puree (page 408) or mashed potatoes (page 281).

SERVES 6 TO 8

½ pork belly (about 4 pounds)
    with rind

1 to 2 tablespoons olive oil

Salt

8 Golden Delicious apples

1 cup hard cider

Chestnut puree (recipe follows)

Put the pork belly on a rack in a roasting pan (if you don't have a rack, grease the pan with 1 tablespoon olive oil). Sprinkle the belly with salt, rubbing it into the cuts in the rind. Then wipe the rind with paper towels and rub it and the flesh side with 1 tablespoon oil. Turn the belly rind side up.

Roast in a preheated 425°F oven for 30 minutes, until the rind has started to puff up. Reduce the heat to 375°F and cook for about 2 hours, until the crackling is crisp and brown.

Meanwhile, put the apples in a baking dish that holds them snugly and pour the cider into the bottom. When you have lowered the oven heat, place the dish of apples on the rack below the roast and cook until they are tender when pierced with a knife. The time depends on the apples' size and degree of ripeness. Start checking them after about 40 minutes. Then put the apples back in the oven when the pork belly is almost done and heat through.

Let the belly rest for 15 minutes, covered with foil, before cutting it into thick slices. Serve with the chestnut puree.

chestnut puree

1 pound fresh peeled (see page 130) or defrosted frozen or vacuum-packed chestnuts (about 4 cups)

About 1¼ cups whole milk

Salt

2 tablespoons butter

Put the chestnuts in a saucepan, add enough milk to cover them, and cook, covered, over low heat, until they are soft.

Pour off the milk and reserve it. Add salt to taste and the butter, and mash the chestnuts with a potato masher (or blend in a food processor), adding a little of the milk, if you like, for a creamier texture.

VARIATION

In Andalusia, they rub 1 to 2 teaspoons cumin seeds on the pork with the salt.

chestnuts

{ *castañas* }

Chestnut trees are part of many a Spanish landscape. In northwest Spain, chestnuts were a staple before the arrival of potatoes and corn from the New World. They were worshipped by the Celts. In Galicia, they say that carrying a chestnut in your pocket will keep away the *meigas* (witches). Peasants dried them and made them into bread, and they are still used as a side vegetable, to accompany pork, game, and turkey. In Galicia and Asturias, chestnuts are much used in soups and stews and in cakes. For a garnish, they are boiled in water or milk and served whole or mashed. There are chestnut festivals across the chestnut-growing regions at the beginning of November.

roast suckling pig

{ *cochinillo asado—castile and león* }

Cochinillo, or *tostón,* is the most exquisite and aristocratic of foods. It is a newborn pig between fifteen and twenty days old that weighs between 6½ and 10 pounds and serves six to eight people. It should be roasted slowly to such melting tenderness that it can be cut with the edge of a plate—which is what happens dramatically on festive occasions. Within the triangle delimited by the cities of Segovia, Arévalo, and Peñaranda de Bracamonte, the finest roast suckling pigs are cooked. I ate a fabulous *cochinillo* at the Maracaibo—the best restaurant for miles around—in the hilltop city of Segovia. The Romans built a great aqueduct there, and the Moors an *alcázar* (fortress), and the city is full of Romanesque churches and mansions.

In the past, people took their little pigs in clay dishes to be roasted in the baker's communal wood-burning oven. At Maracaibo, as in most grand restaurants today, they are cooked *sous-vide,* but I asked the chef about the traditional way of cooking them in a domestic oven. These are the instructions for cooking a 10-pound suckling pig as sent to me by Oscar Hernando, the owner, head chef, and sommelier at Maracaibo.

Ask the butcher to butterfly the cleaned suckling pig by cutting it open through the belly (leaving the head intact). Salt it inside only and lay it opened out flat, skin side up, on a rack in a roasting pan. Wrap the ears in foil to protect them from burning. Pour in 2 cups water, to create steam in the oven, and put the pig in a preheated 350°F oven for 15 minutes. Reduce the heat to 275°F and cook for 2 hours, then increase the heat to 350°F and cook for another 15 minutes, or until the skin is crisp and golden. Let it rest for a few minutes, and cut into slices.

pork loin cooked in milk with caramel

{ lomo de cerdo con leche y caramelo —

navarre and basque country }

I had eaten pork cooked in milk in Venice, but the idea of caramel seemed strange (there is also a Spanish version of this recipe without it); the beautiful flavor was a delightful surprise. The milk sauce will curdle, but that is how it is. This is good both hot and cold. Serve with sautéed mushrooms.

SERVES 6

3 tablespoons butter

1 tablespoon olive oil

1 boneless pork loin roast
   (about 2 pounds) or
   2 or 3 pork tenderloins

About 6 cups whole milk, heated

Peel of 1 lemon or orange, removed
   in strips with a small knife

2 cinnamon sticks

Salt

6 black peppercorns

6 tablespoons sugar

¼ cup water

Heat the butter and oil in a large casserole, and brown the meat on all sides over medium heat. Pour in enough milk to almost cover it. Add the citrus peel, cinnamon sticks, a little salt, and the peppercorns and bring to a boil—watch it, because it can boil over very suddenly. Put the lid on slightly ajar and cook at a bare simmer for 1 to 1½ hours, until the meat is very tender, turning it so that it cooks evenly. The milk will gradually curdle. Remove the meat, and discard the citrus peel and cinnamon sticks.

To make the caramel, put the sugar and water in a small pan over low heat until the sugar dissolves. As the syrup begins to color, swirl the pan continuously so that it browns evenly, and cook until it turns a deep golden brown and the smell of caramel fills the kitchen. Remove from the heat and pour in a ladleful of the hot milk. Be very careful, as it spits. The caramel will harden. Return the pan to the heat and stir until the caramel has melted and dissolved, adding a little more milk if necessary.

Pour this milky caramel into the milk sauce, stir well, and cook 10 minutes over low heat to reduce the sauce. It will be a milky brown coagulated mass, which is as it should be, but if you like, blend it to a cream using an immersion blender. Remove the peppercorns before blending.

Return the meat to the pot and heat through, adding salt if necessary. Cut the meat into slices, and serve with the sauce poured on top.

JOSÉ MARÍA CONDE DE YBARRA

{ an andalusian grandee }

I had heard a lot on my travels about peasant lives and peasant cooking from people whose parents—or who themselves—had been subsistence farmers or landless laborers. I wanted to hear what the landowning elite had to say about food. I was going to Seville, so my friend Alicia suggested I phone Marina Domecq, a member of the famous sherry family. Marina gave me her cousin José María Conde de Ybarra's telephone number; she said he was the ultimate gourmet and gastronome. We met at the Hotel Alfonso XIII in the center of the city. I recognized the bon vivant, a large man with a beautiful smiling face.

Count Ybarra lives in the prestigious residential development of Sotogrande in Cadiz with his wife and young son, and they also have a home in Seville and an old converted oil mill on their country estate. The Ybarra family company produces and exports all manner of products, from olives and olive oil to mayonnaise and sauces and preserves, all over the world. Count Ybarra inherited his title as the eldest son, but he does not run the company. His main interest is food. He is a member of a gastronomic society, Tercos y sordos (the stubborn and the deaf), in which members cook for one another and compete for excellence; it was nominated the best in Europe. He enjoys cooking for friends and neighbors on the coast, many of them British aristocrats and celebrities. He radiates pleasure when he describes what he cooks. I filled pages and pages with notes about dishes and techniques as we went from one tapas bar to another over three days in Seville.

I asked Count Ybarra if his ancestors had obtained their land by helping to conquer it from the Moors. No, he said, they were a Basque family who became rich from coal and shipping during the industrial revolution in northern Spain. In the 1840s, the eldest son, José María Ybarra Gutiérrez de Caviedes, came to Andalusia and bought Church land that was being sold off. He planted olive trees and started exporting olives and olive oil to Latin America. He also farmed sturgeon for caviar in the Guadalquivir River. He became mayor of Seville and received a title for his philanthropy—he built hospitals and paid for public works, including covering many streets with cobblestones. He is remembered for having initiated the most popular festival of Seville, the spring Feria, when everyone comes out to dance, eat, and drink.

The Andalusian aristocracy doubled during the nineteenth century, when the old aristocracy was joined by newly ennobled industrialists and men grown rich in the Americas. Investors and industrialists from northern Spain and Catholics from other European countries had been invited to settle in Andalusia since the late eighteenth century. The Belgians controlled lead mines, the French the coal mines. British wine merchants settled in an area around Cádiz that produced fortified wines for which there was great demand in England. The production of sherry was in the hands of a small group of families. Among them were the González family and the Barbadillos; the Domecqs, who came from France; and the Byasses, Garveys, and Osbornes, who were all British. These leading dynasties intermarried and formed a wine aristocracy. Around it developed a closed social world of trilingual grandees. Some of them were brought up by English nannies and sent to Irish convent schools. The aristocracy and landed proprietors combined in a class that owned olive groves and vineyards and bred Arabian horses and fighting bulls.

Jacobo Martínez de Irujo, son of the duchess of Alba, to whom Count José María is related, once said that "the [Spanish] aristocracy no longer exists as a class, neither economically, nor socially, nor culturally." Perhaps that is so, but their unique Hispano-cosmopolitan cuisine, with its English and Gallic touches, has not disappeared in Andalusia. Many of the large wineries have been taken over by multinationals, but the bread-and-butter puddings, the stuffed turkeys, and the sauces with sherry and brandy remain within the families, like a secret cuisine. On special occasions, such as horse races on the beach, people can go from one group of picnickers to another and taste the foods of other families. Count Ybarra knows all the best dishes of Spain, but he remembers nostalgically the ones his mother taught their cook, Teresa. Several recipes in this book were inspired by him.

braised veal knuckle

{ *jarrete de ternera — catalonia* }

Veal was the meat of choice of the northern bourgeoisies, and there are many elegant recipes for it. This slow-cooked veal knuckle from the hind leg (the part that is sawed into rounds to make osso buco), with its rich marrow and gelatinous connective tissue, becomes meltingly tender and produces a sumptuous sauce. Ask the butcher to saw off the end of the bone to expose the marrow.

SERVES 4

3 tablespoons olive oil

1 whole knuckle of veal
    (about 3½ pounds)

1 large onion, chopped

2 medium carrots, chopped

6 tablespoons (¾ stick) butter

2 tomatoes, peeled and chopped

1 head of garlic, cloves separated
    and peeled

2 thyme sprigs

Salt and pepper

1 cup dry, fruity white wine,
    medium dry sherry, or port,
    or more if needed

1 cup veal or chicken stock, or
    more if needed (or 1 cup water
    plus ½ bouillon cube)

Heat the oil in a large ovenproof casserole or flameproof roasting pan over medium heat. Brown the veal knuckle on all sides, then remove it. Add the onion, carrots, and butter to the pot and cook over low heat, stirring, for about 7 minutes, until the vegetables are soft. Add the tomatoes and cook for 5 minutes, or until they soften.

Return the meat to the pot, along with the garlic and thyme, and season with salt and pepper. Pour in the wine and stock (or water and bouillon cube) and bring to a boil. Cover with a lid or foil and cook in a preheated 350°F oven for 2½ to 3 hours, until the meat is very tender, turning it at least once and adding a little more wine and/or stock if the liquid evaporates too quickly.

Take out the casserole or roasting pan and turn the oven up to 425°F. Lift out the meat, remove the sprigs of thyme, and pour the sauce and vegetables, into a saucepan. Return the meat to the empty casserole or roasting pan and cook in the oven for 20 to 30 minutes longer, until it is crisp and brown on the outside but still moist inside. Meanwhile, blend the sauce to a cream with an immersion blender, and reduce to a thick glaze over low heat.

Serve the meat with the sauce poured over it.

VARIATION

Instead of roasting the meat, simmer it in the casserole on the stovetop for 2½ to 3 hours. Serve it as it is, without blending the sauce.

beef stew in red wine

{ estofado de buey — asturias }

Young Luis Bertran Bittini Martinez teaches at the biggest cooking school in Madrid. It is part of the Fundación Tomillo (tomillo means "thyme"), an independent nonprofit organization whose aim is to be of service to society in many different fields. It teaches dropouts, adolescents who have been expelled from school, youths in trouble with the police, the unemployed, handicapped people, and elderly people who wish to remain independent. Luis teaches youths between the ages of sixteen and twenty-one who want to be professional cooks. At the time he invited my friend Alicia and me to lunch at his house, many of his students happened to be Latin American, from Bolivia, Ecuador, and Peru. The year before, they had mostly been Moroccan. He said that when he comes into the class, the students jokingly intone, "Right! Onion, garlic, pepper, tomato!" It is the way so many Spanish dishes start. As we watched him prepare the meal, he told us about what he was teaching. While we ate, his father, Rafael Bittini, told us about how it was when he was young, and Luis's wife told us that young people now bought ready-cooked pasta dishes to heat up.

Use boneless beef shin, brisket, or flank, chuck, blade, or skirt steak. Luis cooked the meat in a sweet Spanish white wine but said that we could use port or red wine. I used a cheap port and it made a splendid sauce. If you want to cook the stew in the oven, use a casserole that can go on the stovetop and also in the oven. Serve it with mashed potatoes (page 281).

SERVES 6

6 to 8 tablespoons olive oil

1 large onion, coarsely chopped

1 red or green bell pepper, cored, seeded, and diced

1 carrot, chopped

1 leek, trimmed, washed, and chopped

Salt and pepper

>>>

Heat 3 to 4 tablespoons of the oil in a wide casserole. Put in the onion, pepper, carrot, and leek and sauté for about 25 minutes, first over low heat until softened, then over medium heat to brown and caramelize them a little. Turn them often and season with salt and pepper. Add the tomato and cook for a few minutes more.

Meanwhile, heat 3 tablespoons of the oil and brown the meat on all sides in a large skillet over high heat; do this in batches, adding more oil if necessary—if the meat is crowded, it will stew rather than brown. Lift the pieces out as they are browned and add them to the vegetables.

Pour the wine into the casserole, add enough water to cover and the bay leaves, and season with salt and pepper.

>>>

1 tomato, peeled and chopped

2 pounds boneless beef
    (see headnote on page 417),
    cut into 1¼-inch cubes

About 2 cups sweet red wine
    or port

2 bay leaves

Cook, covered, over very low heat, at a bare simmer, for 2 to 3 hours, adding water as necessary to keep the meat covered, until the meat is very tender, stirring once in a while to make sure that it does not burn at the bottom. If there is too much liquid at the end, remove the lid to reduce the sauce.

Luis lifted out the meat and blended the sauce to a cream with an immersion blender, but he said it is not necessary to do that. I like to leave the sauce as it is.

VARIATIONS

- Alternatively, put the casserole, with the lid on, in a preheated 325°F oven and cook for 2½ to 3 hours.

- For a version from the Pyrenee mountains, use 1 cup red wine and ½ cup brandy instead of the sweet wine. Pour the wine into the pot with the water. Heat the brandy in a small pan and carefully light it with a long match. Let the flames die down, then pour it into the pot. Add 2 cinnamon sticks and 5 cloves.

- For an *estofado de toro con chocolate* from Navarre, add 1 tablespoon grated bittersweet chocolate, ¼ cup red or white wine vinegar, and 2 cinnamon sticks. Toward the end, add 1 pound new potatoes, peeled, boiled, and halved, to heat through.

barbecued grilled steak

{ chuletón de buey a la brasa —basque country }

Churrasquerías, *steak houses where meats are cooked over smoldering wood fires, have become immensely popular in northern Spain. In Tolosa, in the Basque Country, where they first started grilling ox steaks more than forty years ago (see page 394), they have* chuletón *fiestas. (Now they use well-hung meat from indigenous cows that have been specially fattened.) In the more distant past,* maestro asadores *(master roasters) would be hired to roast meats at village feasts. Today many chefs and owners of* churrasquerías *are Argentinian emigrants. At home, men expect to be in charge of the barbecue when they are cooking for family and friends. Buy large, thick T-bone steaks, which includes both fillet and sirloin, and serve with* alioli *(page 141).*

SERVES 6 TO 8

2 large T-bone steaks,
    2 to 2½ inches thick

Olive oil

Salt and pepper

Start the fire, and wait until it is reduced to glowing coals. Take the steaks out of the fridge and let them come to room temperature.

Trim the excess fat and any sinew from the steaks, and brush them lightly with olive oil. Oil the grill well. Put the steaks on the grill, and sear for 1 to 2 minutes on each side. Move the steaks to a cooler part of the fire, or raise the grill rack, and continue to cook, turning the steaks a few times until they are done to your taste: allow 10 to 15 minutes for rare, a little longer for medium. You can judge by feel. If the meat feels soft when pressed, it is rare; if it feels springy, it is medium. If it feels firm, it is overdone. Transfer the steaks to a carving board, season with salt and pepper, cover with foil, and allow to rest for 10 minutes.

To serve, cut the meat off the bones and cut it across the grain into thick slices. Season with salt and pepper.

VARIATION

You can cook the steaks on a heavy cast-iron griddle or in a heavy skillet. Heat it until it is very hot, and lightly oil the pan before you put the meat in. Press the meat down with a spatula to sear it, and cook for 10 to 15 minutes, turning the steaks over a few times.

meatballs in almond sauce

{ albóndigas en salsa con picada de almendras —

catalonia }

In Spain, meatballs and ground meat stuffings are made with a mix of different meats, most commonly a half-and-half mixture of veal and pork. I asked why. The answer was that veal was once the prestigious expensive partner and pork the plebeian one that made the mix cheaper and provided some fat, but you can use one or the other meat alone. The bread soaked in milk or water and the egg make the mix go further and give the meatballs a soft, moist texture. Meatballs are poached in various sauces. Here the sauce has white wine and is thickened and given a characteristic Catalan flavor with a picada—*a paste of fried almonds, bread, and garlic.*

The meatballs are traditionally rolled in flour before frying, but some cooks now omit this step. Meatballs are supposed to be poor man's food, but these are anything but—the flavors are an extraordinary combination.

SERVES 4 TO 6

FOR THE MEATBALLS

1 large egg

1 pound ground pork or veal,
   or ½ pound of each

4 slices firm white sandwich bread
   (scant 4 ounces), crusts
   removed, soaked in water,
   and squeezed dry

½ small onion, finely chopped

2 garlic cloves, crushed to a paste

2 tablespoons finely chopped
   flat-leaf parsley

Salt and pepper

Flour for dredging

Olive or sunflower oil for frying

>>>

For the meatballs, lightly beat the egg in a large bowl. Add the meat, then add the bread, mashing it with your fingers, the onion, garlic, parsley, and salt and pepper to taste. Work with your hands into a soft, well-mixed paste. Shape into balls the size of large walnuts and roll in plenty of flour.

Heat about ½ inch of oil in a wide skillet until it sizzles when you throw in a small piece of bread. Add the meatballs, in batches, and fry briefly, turning to brown them all over; then lift them out with a perforated skimmer and drain them on paper towels. They do not need to be cooked through, as they will cook further in the sauce.

>>>

FOR THE ALMOND SAUCE

1 cup chicken stock (or 1 cup water plus ½ bouillon cube)

1 cup fruity dry white wine

A good pinch of saffron threads

Grated zest of 1 lemon

Salt and pepper

2 teaspoons sugar

1 thin slice firm white sandwich bread, crust removed

¼ cup blanched whole almonds

3 to 4 garlic cloves

3 tablespoons olive oil

For the sauce, pour the stock (or water and bouillon cube) and wine into a wide skillet and bring to a boil. Add the saffron, lemon zest, salt and pepper to taste, and the sugar.

Make a *picada:* Fry the bread, almonds, and garlic cloves in the oil in a small skillet until golden brown. Lift them out and let cool a little, then grind to a paste in a mortar or food processor. Stir the *picada* into the sauce.

Add the meatballs and simmer, covered, over very low heat, turning once, for about 20 minutes, until cooked through, adding a little water if necessary.

---

meatballs cooked in tomato sauce

{ albóndigas con salsa de tomate—catalonia }

SERVES 4 TO 6

FOR THE TOMATO SAUCE

1 medium onion, chopped

2 tablespoons olive oil

1½ pounds tomatoes, peeled and chopped

Salt and pepper

1 bay leaf

1 teaspoon sugar

1 recipe Meatballs (page 421), browned as directed in the recipe and drained on paper towels

For the sauce, fry the onion in the oil in a wide skillet over low heat until soft. Add the tomatoes, some salt and pepper, the bay leaf, and the sugar and cook for 5 minutes.

Add the meatballs and cook, covered, turning once, for about 20 minutes, until cooked through.

roast venison with chestnut puree and pear compote

{ corzo con puré de castañas y confitura de pera — basque country }

In 1180, King Sancho VI of Navarre declared in a code of regulations on hunting that big game and animals of the woodland could only be hunted "by the king, grandees, nobles, and knights." Today in Spain, big game hunting is a macho trophy sport. But venison and wild boar are much less of a gastronomic tradition than game birds. Only a few Spanish restaurants and hunting clubs are known for their venison and wild boar specialties. Deer are hunted in the high mountains of northern Spain—in the Cantabrian range and the Pyrenees. The meat is mostly sold to Germany and France or turned into pâtés and sausages. The meat from older deer needs to be slowly cooked, but that of young farm-raised animals can be roasted briefly. It is dark red meat with little fat. You must start this dish a day before, because the meat needs to marinate for 24 hours.

SERVES 6

2 cups red wine

7 tablespoons olive oil

1 onion, chopped

10 black peppercorns

2 bay leaves

One 1½-pound (young farmed)
   venison tenderloin

Salt

>>>

Put the wine, 5 tablespoons of the olive oil, onion, black peppercorns, and bay leaves in a glass or ceramic bowl or baking dish and mix well. Add the meat, curled if necessary to fit, and cover with plastic wrap. Refrigerate for 24 hours, turning the meat once.

For the chestnut puree, put the chestnuts in a saucepan, add milk to cover and the cinnamon, and bring to a boil. Reduce the heat, cover, and simmer gently for 10 to 15 minutes, until the chestnuts are soft. Pour out the milk; add the butter and salt to taste. Mash the chestnuts with a potato masher, or blend in a food processor. Reheat when ready to serve.

For the pear compote, put the wine and sugar in a wide saucepan, add the pears, and cook, covered, over low heat for 8 to 10 minutes, or until they are tender; turn them once.

>>>

FOR THE CHESTNUT PUREE

1 pound fresh peeled (see
    page 130) or defrosted frozen
    or vacuum-packed chestnuts
    (about 4 cups)

About 1½ cups whole milk

½ teaspoon cinnamon

2 to 3 tablespoons butter

Salt

FOR THE PEAR COMPOTE

1 cup dry red wine

¼ cup sugar

4 unripe pears, such as Comice or
    Conference, peeled, quartered,
    and cored

Salt

Lift out the meat, reserving ½ cup of the marinade, pat it dry with paper towels, and sprinkle with salt. Bring the marinade to a boil in a small saucepan and reduce to about half. Heat the remaining oil over high heat in a large skillet. Add the meat and turn it around to sear it all over. Then put it in a baking dish, with the reserved marinade, and roast in a preheated 400°F oven for 20 minutes, or until it is done to your liking. It is best eaten rare or medium-rare, while still pink and juicy inside (the meat is too dry if well-done).

Serve the meat cut into slices, accompanied by the reheated chestnut puree and pears.

wild boar stew with red wine

{ estofado de jabalí al vino tinto — extremadura }

They eat a lot of game in Extremadura, where every village has its own wild boar recipe. Some of the most sophisticated recipes, with wine and spirits, originated in the monasteries. When I went to buy wild boar for this stew at Borough Market in London, the young Italian butcher who waited on me said, "Use shoulder, because it has some fat—otherwise the meat will get stringy if you cook it for two and a half hours." He removed the thick outer layer of fat and cut the meat into large pieces for me.

Wild boar is common in Spain, where the animals run free in parts of the countryside. I have found recipes from various regions. Sometimes port is used, sometimes a spirit such as Calvados. This recipe was sent to me by Pepe Iglesias (see page 328). Serve it with slices of good bread to soak up the sauce or with mashed or boiled potatoes, or with chestnuts boiled in milk (page 408), or with whole roasted apples.

SERVES 6

2 pounds boneless wild boar
    shoulder, excess fat removed,
    cut into large pieces

3 to 4 tablespoons olive oil

2 large carrots, diced

1 large onion, chopped

A head of garlic, cloves separated
    and peeled

2½ cups dry red wine

2 to 3 bay leaves

2 thyme sprigs

1 teaspoon cinnamon

Salt and pepper

Brown the meat lightly all over in the oil in a wide casserole; remove it. Put in the carrots, onion, and garlic and sauté, stirring, until they are soft and just beginning to color. Add the meat, pour in the wine, and add just enough water to cover the meat. Add the bay leaves, thyme, cinnamon, and salt and pepper to taste. Bring to a boil, then simmer, covered, for about 2½ hours, until the meat is extremely tender, adding water to keep the meat covered and turning the pieces occasionally.

VARIATIONS

- Add 2 to 3 tablespoons red or white wine vinegar.

- Remove the meat and blend the sauce with an immersion blender, then return the meat and heat through.

- For a Catalan version, omit the carrots, and add 2 tomatoes, peeled and chopped, to the onion and garlic once they've softened. Add ¼ cup brandy or port and about 3 tablespoons grated bittersweet chocolate about 10 minutes before the meat is done.

calf's liver with onions and brandy

{ higado de ternera encebollado al brandy — catalonia }

Except for calf's liver, offal was the food of the poor, and consumption of it went down as Spain grew rich. Since immigrants from Latin America have arrived in large numbers over the last decade or two, though, the offal stands that had almost disappeared from city markets have been doing a booming trade. Calf's liver has always been a delicacy. It is important not to over-cook it—it should still be pink inside.

SERVES 4

3 to 4 tablespoons olive oil

2 large onions, cut in half
    and sliced

1 pound thinly sliced calf's liver,
    cut into 1-inch strips

Salt and pepper

¼ cup brandy

Heat the oil in a large skillet. Add the onions and sauté, covered, over low heat until they are soft, stirring occasionally. This can take up to 25 minutes because of the large amount of onions. Then cook, uncovered, over medium heat, stirring often, until golden.

Add the liver to the onions and sauté for 1 minute, adding salt and pepper and turning the pieces just to brown them lightly all over. Pour the brandy over them and cook over high heat for 1 minute to reduce the liquid quickly. The timing for the liver depends on the thickness of the liver. Cut into a piece—it should still be pink inside.

VARIATION

For an Andalusian version, a famous tapa, use chicken livers instead of calf's liver and sauté very briefly, stirring and turning them to brown them all over. Use oloroso sherry instead of brandy.

oxtail stew

{ *rabo de toro — andalusia* }

This recipe for rabo de toro, *"oxtail," was given to me by Manuel Andrade, who was for many years head chef at El Burladero in the Hotel Colón in Seville. Bullfighters have lodged there during the season since the Exposición Ibero-Americana world's fair held in the city in 1929. Manuel now has his own restaurant, the Porta Gayola in Calle Barcelona, where he cooks some of the best food I have eaten in Seville in a tiny upstairs kitchen.*

Manuel's is the classic recipe for this famous dish, the way it was made with the trophy bull's tails that were given to the picadores, *the horsemen who pierce the bull's back with a lance early in the bullfight. There are many estates in Andalusia where bulls are raised for the* corrida. *The dish is served in all the tapas bars in Seville and in Córdoba, where the tails of ordinary cows are used. What we call oxtails in America are not the tails of oxen (castrated bulls that were once used for the plow as work animals) but those of ordinary beef cattle. Butchers sell them cut up into pieces consisting of vertebrae surrounded by meat, fat, and connective tissue. After long, slow cooking, the meat becomes silky-tender and the sauce rich and gelatinous. With the heady flavors imparted by the wine and brandy, this dish is a luxury.*

Serve it with the roasted potatoes on page 430 or with mashed potatoes (page 281). In grand restaurants in Spain, they remove the meat from the bones and serve it up with the sauce atop a little ball of mashed potatoes.

SERVES 6

5½ pounds oxtails, cut into pieces

6 tablespoons olive oil

2 medium onions, chopped

3 carrots, chopped

1 large leek, trimmed, washed, and chopped

4 garlic cloves, chopped

3 bay leaves

>>>

Cut away the excess fat from the oxtails—the larger pieces have the most fat. Leave any skin on; it will disappear during the cooking. Place the pieces on a sheet of foil on a baking sheet and roast in a preheated 500°F oven for 30 minutes, until they have browned and released more fat.

Meanwhile, heat the oil in a large casserole. Add the onions, carrots, leek, garlic, bay leaves, and thyme and cook over medium heat, stirring often, for about 10 minutes, until softened a little. Add the tomatoes and cook for another 10 minutes.

>>>

1 sprig of thyme

6 medium tomatoes, peeled and chopped

2¼ cups dry red wine

1 cup dry white wine

1 cup brandy

Salt and pepper

Add the browned oxtails to the vegetables (discard the fat). Pour in the wine and brandy and season with salt and pepper. Simmer, uncovered, for 10 minutes. Add enough water to cover the oxtails and cook, covered, for 3 to 4½ hours, until the meat is meltingly tender and falls away from the bone. Let the stew rest for about 20 minutes, and remove the fat from the surface with a ladle and paper towels.

It is usual in Spain to lift out the oxtails and the bay leaves and thyme sprig and blend the sauce to a cream with an immersion blender, then return the oxtails and reheat before serving. I like the sauce with all the bits of vegetables and prefer not to blend it.

SERVES 6

3 pounds baking potatoes

Salt

½ cup olive or sunflower oil

roasted potatoes

patatas al horno

Peel the potatoes and cut them in half or into quarters, depending on their size. Put them in a large saucepan with cold water to cover and add salt. Bring to a boil and simmer for about 10 minutes, until the surface of the potatoes is slightly fluffy. Drain off the water and shake the pan to roughen the surface of the potatoes so that they will absorb more oil and become crisper. (Another way to do this is to scratch the surfaces of the potatoes with a fork.)

Arrange the potatoes in a large baking dish or roasting pan and sprinkle with a little salt. Pour the oil over them and turn them to coat them all over. Roast in a preheated 425°F oven for 50 to 60 minutes, turning them once, until crisp and golden.

potatoes with chorizo

{ p a t a t a s   a   l a   r i o j a n a — l a   r i o j a }

This is an earthy, strong-flavored dish that is served as a first or main course. By tradition, the potatoes are cut only halfway through with a wide knife, then snapped apart by twisting the blade—this is meant to release more starch so as to make the sauce thicker and also to allow the potatoes to absorb more flavor. Small pork ribs, shallow-fried or roasted in the oven, are sometimes added to make this a meatier dish. It is usual to add pimentón, *but I did not add any, as there was enough* pimentón *from the chorizo; taste and see what you think. Soft semi-cured or fully cured chorizo can be used.*

SERVES 2 AS A MAIN COURSE; 3 TO 4 AS A STARTER

1 large onion, chopped

3 to 4 tablespoons olive oil

7 ounces cured or semi-cured spicy chorizo, cut into ½-inch-thick slices

2 garlic cloves, chopped

1 pound new potatoes, peeled and cut into 1- to 1½-inch pieces

½ to 1 teaspoon *pimentón dulce* (or sweet paprika; optional)

Salt

Sauté the onion in the oil over low heat in a wide skillet, stirring often, for 20 minutes or longer, until it is really brown, almost caramelized. Add the chorizo and garlic and cook, stirring, for about 2 minutes. Add the potatoes and cook for 5 minutes, turning them over.

Add the *pimentón* if desired and salt to taste, then pour in enough water to cover. Simmer over low heat for about 25 to 35 minutes, until the potatoes are tender and the liquid is very much reduced, turning the potatoes if necessary so that they are well cooked all the way through. You should be left with a sizzling sauce that coats the potatoes and chorizos. If there is too much liquid, increase the heat and let it bubble away.

VARIATIONS

- Chop ½ green and ½ red bell pepper, add them when the onion is soft, and continue to cook until the pepper is lightly browned and the onion is well browned.

- Add 1 tomato, peeled and chopped, to the fried onion.

- Add a whole dried or fresh chile pepper to the onion.

fresh pork sausages

{ *botifarres — catalonia* }

Catalan botifarres *are pure fresh pork sausages with only salt and pepper as seasoning. Catalans have wonderful ways of cooking them, stewed in red or white wine, in sparkling cava, or in hard cider. They accompany them with mashed potatoes or apple puree, caramelized onions or caramelized pears, or white beans. They make a wonderful cheap meal, but you must buy good medium-coarse pork sausages. The recipe names that follow are in Catalan.*
SERVE 2 SAUSAGES PER PERSON.

---

pork sausages cooked in wine, cava, or hard cider

{ *botifarra amb vi o sidra — catalonia* }

Prick each sausage in 2 or 3 places with a pointed knife. Heat 1 tablespoon olive oil in a large skillet, add the sausages, and turn them to brown them all over. Pour out the excess fat, and add enough red or white wine, cava, or hard cider to at least half-cover the sausages, and cook over medium-high heat, turning them occasionally, for 20 to 25 minutes, until they are cooked through and the liquid has almost disappeared.

pork sausages with caramelized pears

{ botifarra amb peres—catalonia }

Prick each sausage in 2 or 3 places with a pointed knife. Fry them in a little oil in a large skillet over low heat, turning them occasionally, for 20 to 25 minutes, until they are cooked through and well browned; or cook them in wine as on page 434. Have 1 slightly unripe pear, such as Comice or Conference, per person. Peel, core, and cut into 6 slices each, and sauté in a little oil over medium heat, turning them, until they are soft and lightly browned all over. Serve with the sausages.

---

pork sausages with apple puree

{ botifarra amb poma—catalonia }

Prick each sausage in 2 or 3 places with a pointed knife. Fry them in a little oil in a large skillet over low heat, turning them occasionally, for 20 to 25 minutes, until they are cooked through and well browned, or cook them in wine as above. Peel, core, and quarter 1 apple per person. Put them in a pan with about a finger of water and cook, covered, over very low heat for about 15 to 20 minutes, until soft. Watch, as the water can evaporate too quickly and they can burn. Remove the lid and continue to cook to evaporate any remaining water, then mash to a rough puree. Serve with the sausages.

pork sausages with caramelized onions

{ botifarra amb cebes — catalonia }

Prick each sausage in 2 or 3 places with a pointed knife. Fry them in a little oil in a large skillet over low heat for about 20 to 25 minutes, turning them occasionally, until they are cooked through and well browned; or cook them in wine as on page 434. For three people, cut 2 large onions in half and slice them. Put them in a large skillet with 3 tablespoons olive oil, cover, and cook over low heat, stirring occasionally, for about 30 minutes, until they are very soft (they will stew in their own juices). Remove the lid and cook, stirring often, over medium heat for 15 minutes more, until they are brown and caramelized.

---

pork sausages with white beans

{ botifarra amb mongetes — catalonia }

Grill or fry the sausages. Drain a can of good-quality white beans and cook them in a little extra virgin olive oil in a skillet, over high heat, adding salt and pepper. Serve them with the sausages, with an extra dribble of oil.

pig's ears and feet

I have tried a few recipes for pig's ears and feet: the ears, *orejas,* gelatinous and crunchy, cut into little squares and stewed in white wine with a touch of cinnamon; the feet, *manos* (they call them "hands"), gelatinous and rich in flavor, cooked in fortified wine and a tiny bit of chocolate, were delicious. But I will not make them again. They are difficult to buy, especially ears; most butchers don't sell them. And they take too long to prepare before you even begin to cook them. You have to singe off any remaining hairs, then scrub them, blanch them, and rinse them in cold water. Then you boil them for 3 hours. I cut up the ears and removed the bones from the feet. They are much-loved delicacies in Spain, but these days people eat them at restaurants and rarely cook them at home.

RICE AND PASTA

{ *arroces y pastas* }

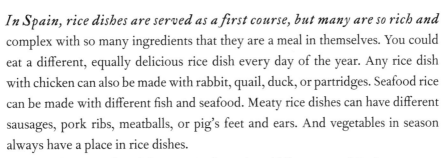

In Spain, rice dishes are served as a first course, but many are so rich and complex with so many ingredients that they are a meal in themselves. You could eat a different, equally delicious rice dish every day of the year. Any rice dish with chicken can also be made with rabbit, quail, duck, or partridges. Seafood rice can be made with different fish and seafood. Meaty rice dishes can have different sausages, pork ribs, meatballs, or pig's feet and ears. And vegetables in season always have a place in rice dishes.

Arabs first introduced the grain in the early Middle Ages, and Berber peasants were brought in from North Africa to grow it. Berbers remained to work the rice fields well into the seventeenth century, and many villages still bear the names of their tribes (see page 536). *Arroz*, the Spanish word for "rice" (it is *arròs* in Catalan and Valencian) comes from the Arabic *roz*.

People eat rice all over Spain, and now many regions grow it. Andalusia and Extremadura are very big producers, and the colder regions of Aragon and Navarre also cultivate rice. But the historical rice-growing regions where rice is a staple are the Mediterranean regions of Catalonia, Valencia, and Murcia. Their high-quality indigenous Spanish rices are protected by *Denominaciones de Origen*: Arroz del Delta del Ebro, Arroz de Valencia, and Calasparra. Rice is classified commercially by the size of the grains and the relationship between their length and width. Indigenous Spanish rice is medium- or short-grain. Long-grain rice was introduced

Seafood Paella, page 450.

recently, mainly for export, but it is now also sold in Spain for cooking plain white rice and for new-style dishes such as rice salad. Some varieties of short- or round-grain make sticky rice that falls apart and is best for stuffing vegetables and some puddings. The special characteristic of Spanish medium-grain rice is that it has a higher starch content than the long-grain (the starch is stored in a white *perla*, or "pearl," that you can see as a white spot), and that allows it to absorb maximum flavor from the stock in which it is cooked and from the other ingredients. It can absorb twice its volume of liquid while still remaining as separate grains.

In her book *El libro de la paella y los arroces* (*The Book of Paella and Rice Dishes*) published in 1985, the celebrated Spanish food writer and broadcaster Lourdes March uses medium-grain rice for all the traditional Spanish recipes except for stuffed vegetables and puddings, for which she uses short-grain. But her book was written before Bomba, an ancient strain of tiny round rice that was nearly extinct, became famous and in demand starting a decade or so ago, after it was acclaimed by celebrity chefs and written about by foreign journalists. Bomba is said to be the rice for "people who can't cook paella or haven't the time to watch it," because it keeps a firm shape and does not easily overcook—it can absorb up to three times its own volume in liquid without falling apart. Bomba has become the rice of choice for chefs and gourmets. It is more than twice the price of other Spanish rices because the yield of the plants is low. It was neglected in Franco's time when high production was required. The three *Denominaciones*

de Origen now produce Bomba, as do some other regions too.

At home, people still cook with the medium-grain rice they are used to (it is considered sacrilegious to use long-grain for paella). The major types of medium-grain are Senia, in the marshlands surrounding the Albufera lagoon in Valencia; Bahia and Montsianell in the flatlands of the Ebro River in Catalonia; and the hybrid Balilla x Sollana in the mountains of Murcia along the banks of the Segura River near the town of Calasparra. Calasparra has become famous for its Bomba rice, because the sowing and harvesting is done by hand on the small terraces where machinery cannot get to, and the irrigation water comes from cold mountain springs; Moorish-type canals, dams, and waterwheels continue to regulate the flooding and draining of the rice paddies, much as they did in the early Middle Ages. Over the last twelve years, both Catalonia and Valencia have cultivated a high-quality Bomba. The growers there are very active in agricultural research to improve varieties and methods of sowing, harvesting, and processing (hand labor, they say, is for tourists). What makes a rice grain different is the *terroir*—the environment and climate in which it grows: humid flatlands, cold mountains, or drylands.

The important thing about cooking Spanish rice dishes is knowing how to handle the grain—how much water it needs, how long to cook it. I have learned most of what I know from Lourdes March, who is a longtime friend. In Spain, rice is never soaked or washed before cooking. Stock is almost always used to cook it, not water, and the stock has to be boiling when it comes in contact with the rice. Different amounts of liquid are required for different types of dishes. "Dry" rice dishes (*arroz seco*) cooked *al horno* (in earthenware casseroles in the oven) need about twice the volume of stock to rice. Rice cooked in wide shallow paella pans needs more liquid because much of it evaporates. Moist *arroces melosos* with a so-called honey texture (*miel* means "honey") are cooked in large saucepans with two and a half times the amount of stock to rice by volume, while the *arroces caldosos* (soupy rice dishes) need three times the amount of stock.

When cooking rice, you add all the stock at once, unlike when making risotto, and you stir only once with a wooden spoon, then leave the rice alone. You do not keep stirring throughout the cooking, because that would break some grains and release the starch that gives Italian risotto its creamy, slightly sticky texture—something that is not desirable in a Spanish rice dish.

None of the cooks that I watched making rice ever measured. They all took handfuls of rice, saying "*un puñado*" (a handful) and added stock "*a ojo*" (by eye). It makes sense, because qualities of rice vary, and even the same type of grain from the same field can behave differently from one harvest to another. And depending on whether it is new or has been hanging around in a shop for ages, it will absorb different amounts of liquid and take more or less time to cook. The amount of water needed also depends on the size and shape of the pan or baking dish, the amount of rice, and the heat of the oven or burner. For soupy rice, the amount of liquid matters less than the cooking time, which is all-important. If you cook it for too long, the rice will be soggy and may fall apart. For paella, where the amount of liquid matters, there is no foolproof method to determine the exact quantity needed. Making paella is an art that is acquired through experience. You have to watch that the rice does not get too dry, adding a little more boiling stock or water if necessary, and that it does not overcook.

The general rule is to allow ½ cup uncooked rice per person. The recommended amount of salt needed is generally given as 1 teaspoon for 2 cups rice, but since in Spain rice is always cooked in stock, you have to take into consideration the saltiness of the stock, and of course salting always has to be a matter of taste. If you cannot find a Spanish rice—these are often labeled simply "paella rice"—you can use a risotto rice such as Arborio or Carnaroli. Do not use long-grain rice for these recipes.

paella

Paella has a strong emotional charge in Spain. It is a Sunday dish, and its preparation is a social affair that takes place in the open air out in the countryside or in the garden. According to my friend Alicia, cooking paella has become a man's job, one that does not bring their virility into question—on the contrary, it is a way of showing off their skill.

Paella valenciana is the iconic food of Valencia, which became the first emblematic national dish of Spain. What was simply *arroz a la valenciana* became known, as it spread around Spain, as *paella valenciana*, after the large shallow double-handled pan with a slightly convex base that is used to cook it (*paella* means "skillet" in the Valencian-Catalan language). The first paella was born in the rice fields around the Albufera lagoon. It was a communal meal, what the laborers cooked for themselves over a wood fire. They put in what they had at hand: eels, snails, green beans, fresh butter beans, and whatever vegetables were in season, and sometimes chicken or rabbit. Eventually every village in Valencia and neighboring Murcia added all kinds of meats, birds, fish, shellfish, and vegetables to their paellas. With the beginning of mass tourism, paella was adopted by seaside resorts and city restaurants, where it was transformed into gargantuan, baroque dishes with a huge number of ingredients that usually did not taste as good as they looked.

The fashion now in Valencia and also in Madrid is to use a very thin layer of rice in paellas, ideally, they say, only the thickness of three grains and certainly no thicker than one finger (*un ditet*) or one centimeter (a scant half-inch). That is why you need a very wide pan. Paella pans come in many sizes, some large enough to feed a hundred people at a festival. You can cook a paella for two to three people in a large 12-inch skillet, but otherwise you will need a paella pan (see page 120). For four to five people, you would need a 16-inch pan, measured across the top; for six to eight people, an 18- to 20-inch pan. However, you could choose to have a thicker layer of rice, as is common in the north of Catalonia, where it can be up to 1½ inches thick.

There are two passionately held ways to cook paella. One is to start by frying a *sofrito* of onion, garlic, and tomatoes, and any bits of pepper, meat, or seafood, then stir in the rice and coat it with the reduced oily sauce before adding the flavorful stock. The other is to pour in the stock when the *sofrito* is cooked and to bring it to a boil before adding the rice. It is perfectly fine, and often better, to cook some of the meat or seafood for a paella separately and then put them on top of the rice to heat through at the end, but it is important not to crowd the pan with too many ingredients (I am afraid I am often guilty of that—my friends expect lots of seafood). It is the rice that is all-important, because it is the rice that carries the flavors of the stock and the *sofrito*, and it should not be covered up and hidden.

Important advice from Lourdes is to always have some boiling-hot stock or water at hand in case you need to add more liquid. Often, at the end of cooking a paella, the rice at the top is a bit hard while it is well cooked underneath. Her tip, in that case, is to cover the finished dish with a damp cloth while it rests for 5 to 10 minutes. The rice needs to cook for 18 to 20 minutes; the grains should be dry and separate when done, and the bottom should have a caramelized crust, called *socarrat*.

Count Ybarra, from whom I learned much about Spanish cooking (see page 412), also had some tips. The stock should never come up higher than the level of the rivets for the handles in the pan, and it should be boiling hot when it is added in. Start over high heat, he said, and then, as soon as tiny "crab holes" appear, lower the heat. If you are cooking a large paella on your domestic stovetop, turn two (or more) burners on, and move the pan around so that the rice cooks evenly and all the way to the edges. In Spain, when a paella is cooked outdoors, a wide, built-in charcoal grill or a special large gas ring with several concentric circles joined to a butane cylinder, which gives the desired spread-out heat, is used. When you hear crackly noises, it means that the famously desirable *soccarat* is forming. Use medium-grain Spanish or paella rice. If it is not available, use a risotto rice such as Arborio or Carnaroli. Most people in Spain add a pinch of yellow coloring (see page 453) instead of or in addition to saffron threads to give the rice a bright yellow color. Try the two.

chicken, rabbit, and bean paella

{ paella valenciana — valencia }

I have a fabulous memory of the original "real" paella valenciana *that I ate more than twenty years ago when I was on reconnaissance for a BBC television series. It was cooked in the open in a field in a giant paella pan. It was fantastic and exquisite. This is Lourdes March's recipe from her* Libro de la paella y los arroces. *She uses* garrofón, *a type of fresh white lima beans, but you can use canned beans. The snails bring a taste of the rosemary they feed on. If you can't find them, you can just use the rosemary. It will not be the paella they cook in the Valencian countryside, but it will be near enough. If you can't find Spanish paella rice, use Arborio or Carnaroli.*

SERVES 6

⅔ cup olive oil

1½ pounds chicken thighs
and drumsticks

1 pound rabbit or lean pork,
cut into chunks

½ pound green beans, trimmed
and cut in half

1 medium tomato, peeled and
chopped

1 teaspoon *pimentón dulce*
(or sweet paprika)

9 cups water

Salt

12 small land snails, cleaned, in
their shells or canned snails

A sprig of rosemary

2 pinches of saffron threads

1 cup canned lima beans, drained

2 cups paella rice or Bomba

Heat the oil in an 18-inch paella pan, and fry the chicken and rabbit pieces over high heat, turning to brown them lightly all over. Add the green beans, tomato, *pimentón* (or paprika), and water and bring to a boil, then turn down the heat, season with salt, and simmer for about 45 minutes, or until the meats are very tender. Much of the water will have evaporated.

Take out about 2 cups of the water and set it aside. Add the snails, rosemary, saffron, and lima beans, turn up the heat, and add the rice, spreading it out evenly in the pan. (Do not stir the rice again.) Add as much of the reserved water as you need to cover the rice. Cook for 10 minutes, then turn down the heat and cook for another 8 to 10 minutes, until the grains are tender but firm, adding a little of the reserved water if the rice looks dry before it is done. The best part is said to be the crunchy and slightly brown part at the bottom called *socarrat*.

VARIATION

Artichoke hearts or bottoms can be used instead of the green beans.

seafood paella without shells

{ arroz del señorito a la marinera—valencia }

*When Alicia e-mailed her friends asking for their favorite recipes, María Ortells sent this one for seafood paella, a specialty of Alicante. It is different from other seafood paellas in that the shrimp are peeled and the clams removed from their shells, so that you do not need to use your fingers to eat it. Presumably it is the way local young noblemen (*señoritos*) liked it. It has now caught on in the rest of Spain, where it is sometimes called* arroz de mariscos limpio *(clean) or* pelado *(peeled). It is less dramatic-looking than other seafood paellas but equally delicious and less messy to eat.*

In Alicante, they use dried ñora *peppers (see page 128), but* pimentón *(or paprika) will do. The* ñoras *are soaked in boiling water for 30 minutes, then drained, cut open, and seeded; then the pulp is scraped from the skin with a spoon. (You only get about 1 teaspoon of pulp from each pepper.) Nowadays I can buy small baby squid less than a finger long, already cleaned. If the squid you buy has not been cleaned, see page 127 for instructions. You can use mussels instead of clams (see the variations) or small scallops. If you cannot buy good fish stock, use chicken stock.*

SERVES 6

24 clams

1 large onion, chopped

5 tablespoons olive oil

4 garlic cloves, crushed to a paste
   or finely chopped

2 tomatoes, peeled and
   finely chopped

Salt

A good pinch of saffron threads

The pulp of 2 *ñora* peppers
   (see headnote above) or
   1 teaspoon sweet *pimentón dulce*
   (or sweet paprika)

>>>

Scrub the clams and soak them in salted water for 30 minutes. Throw away any with broken shells or that do not shut when rapped sharply on the counter. Drain, put them in a pan with about ½ inch of water, cover, and bring to a boil. The clams will steam and open very quickly, and they will be cooked. Discard any that do not open. Take them out of their shells when they are cool enough to handle and set aside. Strain the liquid left in the pan and add it to the fish stock.

Fry the onion in the oil in a 16- to 18-inch paella pan until soft, stirring often. Stir in the garlic and, a few seconds later when the aroma rises, add the tomatoes and a little salt. Cook until the sauce is reduced and jammy and the oil is beginning to sizzle.

Add the saffron, the *ñora* pulp or *pimentón* (or paprika), and the squid to the sauce and stir well. Add the rice, stirring gently so that it gets well coated with the sauce.

>>>

6 cleaned small squid, bodies cut
  into slices about ½ inch wide

2½ cups medium-grain Spanish
  paella rice or risotto rice, such
  as Arborio or Carnaroli

4½ cups fish stock

1 cup dry white wine

18 large shrimp, peeled

2 to 3 tablespoons chopped
  flat-leaf parsley

6 lemon wedges

Alioli (page 141)

Bring the stock and wine to a boil in a saucepan and pour over the rice, add a good amount of salt (the rice will need it, but the amount depends on the saltiness of the fish stock), and stir well, spreading the rice out evenly in the pan (do not stir the rice again during cooking). Bring to a boil and cook over high heat for 3 minutes, then reduce the heat to low and cook for 10 minutes. Move the pan occasionally, rotating it so that the rice cooks evenly.

Put the shrimp on top of the rice and cook for another 8 minutes, or until they have turned pink and the rice is done. Add the clams 3 minutes before the end to heat through. Add a little water if the paella becomes too dry. Remove from the heat, cover with foil, and let rest for 5 to 10 minutes.

Sprinkle the paella with the parsley and serve with the lemon wedges and *alioli*.

VARIATIONS

- I often use scallops seared in oil in a skillet, instead of the clams, along with monkfish, cut into ¾-inch cubes and sautéed until tender.

- You can use mussels instead of clams. To clean them, see page 127.

- For a soupy *arroz caldoso a la marinera del señorito* use 7½ cups fish stock and no wine. Cook for just 20 minutes and serve at once, or the rice will fall apart.

seafood paella

{ *arroz a la marinera — valencia* }

This is the dramatic seafood paella that looks stunning, with crustaceans and shellfish. You can vary the quantities of seafood and also use crab, crayfish, or lobster (boil them separately). Andresito (see page 534), who is collecting reminiscences of people in villages around him in Alicante, told me that on the Alicante coast, fishermen's families made seafood paellas without any vegetables. When they did not go out to fish, they made arroz de piedras *with mollusks from the rocks (*piedras *means "rocks"). The fishermen went around local villages selling their fish on scooters, and people inland added vegetables. In Catalonia, where the tradition of mixing meat and seafood is very old, they had pieces of chicken, pork, rabbit, or duck and sausage in their seafood paellas. Today adding meat and vegetables to seafood paella has become common in other regions, where seasonal vegetables such as green beans, peas, artichokes, or peppers also go in. It is called* paella mixta. *Wine was not added in the past but it is sometimes today. Serve this with* alioli *(page 141) if you like.*

SERVES 4

1 large onion, finely chopped

5 tablespoons olive oil

2 garlic cloves, crushed to a paste or finely chopped

2 tomatoes, peeled and chopped

½ teaspoon sugar

Salt

1 teaspoon *pimentón dulce* (or sweet paprika)

A good pinch of saffron threads

4 cleaned small squid, bodies sliced into ¼-inch-wide rings, tentacles left whole

Fry the onion in the oil in a 16-inch paella pan until soft, stirring often. Stir in the garlic, and before it begins to color, add the tomatoes. Add the sugar, salt to taste, *pimentón* (or paprika), and saffron, stir well, and cook until the tomatoes are reduced to a jammy sauce and the oil is sizzling. Add the squid and cook, stirring, for a minute or so. Add the rice and stir well until all the grains are coated. (You can prepare the dish to this point up to an hour in advance; reheat before continuing.)

Bring the stock and wine to a boil in a saucepan. Pour over the rice, bring to a boil, and add salt to taste (even if the broth tastes a bit salty, it will not be salty when it is absorbed by the rice). Stir well and spread the rice out evenly in the pan (do not stir again). Cook the rice over low heat for 18 to 20 minutes, moving the pan around and rotating it so that the rice cooks evenly. Lay the shrimp on top after 10 minutes and turn them when they have become

2 cups medium-grain Spanish
   paella rice or risotto rice,
   such as Arborio or Carnaroli

3 cups fish or chicken stock,
   plus more if needed

1 cup dry white wine

12 jumbo shrimp in their shells

16 mussels, scrubbed and
   debearded

pink on the first side. Add a little more hot stock toward the end if the rice seems too dry and you hear crackly frying noises before it is done. When the rice is done, turn off the heat and cover the pan with a large piece of foil.

Steam the mussels with a finger of water in a pan with a tight-fitting lid. As soon as they open, they are cooked. Throw away any that have not opened.

Arrange the mussels on top of the paella.

VARIATIONS

- Add 4 quartered small artichoke hearts or bottoms, fresh or defrosted frozen, a good handful of peas, green beans or broad beans cut into short lengths, or roasted red peppers, cut into strips, with the rice.

- In Alicante, they use the pulp of 1 or 2 dried and soaked *ñora* peppers, which they grow, instead of *pimentón;* see page 128.

- Use clams instead of mussels.

- You can make this into an *arroz caldoso,* or soupy rice, by adding 1 more cup of boiling stock, but do not cook it for any longer or the rice will be soggy.

- If you want to use lobster, ask the fishmonger to cut a live lobster into pieces. Boil it for minutes only, until it turns red. Or boil it whole and cut it up.

saffron

{ *azafrán* }

Spanish saffron is of a very high quality. The little red threads that give a slightly bitter flavor, characteristic aroma, and intense yellow color to paellas and many other dishes are the stigmas of a particular purple crocus, *Crocus sativus* (*sativus* means "cultivated," and this crocus does not grow wild). The best quality is Mancha saffron from La Mancha; the Sierra saffron is a lower grade.

The stigmas, which have to be removed by hand, are dried quickly by very lightly toasting them. Two hundred flowers yield only one gram. The plants do not reproduce from seeds, like wild plants—their tiny corms (they look like, but are not, bulbs) have to be dug up and split up into cormlets and replanted by hand. They remain dormant through the summer months, and the pale purple flowers come out in autumn. They must be harvested at dawn, as soon as they open. The Fiesta de la Rosa del Azafrán (Festival of the Saffron Rose) is a great tourist attraction in Consuegra, in the province of Toledo.

Spain was once the world's biggest producer of what was called "the poor man's gold" (the poor man being the farmer). In the 1970s, about 15,000 acres were under cultivation. But production has decreased so much—because it is so labor-intensive and the price is not competitive on the world market—that there are now only 2,800 acres or so. A few hundred dedicated farmers continue the agricultural practices that began when the Arabs first brought the flowers to Spain. Saffron was a popular flavoring among the Al-Andalus elites. The Spanish name of the spice, *azafrán,* is derived from the Arabic. Iranian saffron, which is the biological progenitor of Spanish saffron, is its greatest competitor. Selling at less than half the price, but of the highest quality, Iranian saffron now accounts for more than ninety percent of the market. Some Spanish companies sell Iranian saffron and pass it off as Spanish, a practice that has been in part responsible for Spanish growers giving up.

Saffron threads keep for years if stored in a cool, dry place and out of direct sunlight. You should use very little—only a pinch for a dish for six. If you use too much, the taste will be bitter. Some people actually count the threads and advise 5 to 6 per serving, but I would not go as far as that, especially since the amount also depends on the dish and serving size, as well as the quality of the saffron. I start with a tiny pinch and then add more to taste if necessary.

You can simply throw the threads, as they are, into a stock, sauce, soup, or stew. Some cooks heat them first in a small frying pan (or wrapped in a piece of foil placed on a hot pan lid), then crush them with the back of a spoon, to release more flavor. An alternative is to steep the threads in a little boiling water or stock for about 20 minutes. However, I haven't noticed that either of these procedures makes much difference except perhaps in spreading the color.

Powdered saffron is much used in Spain—although it has lost most of its flavor and aroma—because it is cheap and gives a dish a good uniform color. It is quickly absorbed and can be thrown into the pot a few minutes before serving. A powdered colorant that contains a yellow dye and no saffron is also used by many people to give a brighter yellow color to rice. Only gourmet purists avoid it.

rice with mushrooms

{ arroz con setas—catalonia }

Here is a homey dish made with the cultivated mushrooms that are available all year round. It is easy and delicious. The rice absorbs the flavors of the mushrooms and of the almost cara-melized onions, as well as of the chicken stock and sherry. I like it with the larger quantity of mushrooms, but you may prefer the lesser amount. Use white button mushrooms or the brown creminis, which have a stronger flavor.

SERVES 4 AS A STARTER

5 tablespoons olive oil

10 ounces to 1 pound mushrooms, trimmed and sliced

Salt and pepper

1 onion, finely chopped

2 garlic cloves, finely chopped

1¼ cups medium-grain Spanish paella rice or risotto rice, such as Arborio or Carnaroli

2 cups chicken or vegetable stock (or 2 cups water plus 1 bouillon cube)

½ cup dry oloroso sherry

Heat the oil in a large casserole. Put in the mushrooms and sauté over medium-low heat, adding salt and pepper and turning them occasionally for 8 to 10 minutes, until they have given up their juices. Take them out, leaving the oil and juices behind.

Add the onion and cook, uncovered, stirring often, over high heat for 3 minutes to evaporate the juices, then lower the heat and cook for about 20 minutes, until golden brown and almost jammy. Add the garlic and cook, stirring, for a minute or so, until aromatic. Return the mushrooms, add the rice, and stir so that the grains are well coated with the oily juices. (You can prepare the dish in advance up to this stage and set aside at room temperature; reheat before continuing.)

Meanwhile, bring the stock and sherry to a boil.

Pour the stock mixture over the mushrooms and rice, add salt to taste, and stir well, then cook, covered, over medium heat, without stirring, for 10 minutes. Reduce the heat to low and continue to cook, covered, for another 10 minutes, or until the rice is tender, adding a little boiling water if the rice seems too dry. Let stand covered for 5 minutes before serving.

VARIATION

If you are lucky enough to have wild mushrooms, you can use them, cut in half or in quarters if they are large, instead of the cultivated ones.

black rice with baby squid

{ arroz negro — catalonia }

This has an unusual but delicate flavor and looks dramatic. When fishermen in the Costa Brava and along the Mediterranean coast used the ink from their squid and cuttlefish, there was rarely more than enough for a pale gray rice, so they made it darker by caramelizing the onions. Nowadays you can buy squid ink in tiny plastic sachets, and chefs like to produce an intensely black rice. This recipe is from Corpus de la Cuina Catalana *(see page 105). I added white wine, as some people do; you can omit it and increase the quantity of fish stock by a cup. If you cannot make or buy good fish stock (page 126), use good chicken stock (page 125). Serve* alioli *(page 141) with it.*

SERVES 6 AS A MAIN COURSE; 8 AS A STARTER

2 medium onions, chopped

6 tablespoons olive oil

3 tomatoes, grated (see page 129) or chopped

Salt and pepper

1 pound cleaned baby squid, bodies cut into rings, tentacles left whole

2½ cups medium-grain Spanish paella rice or risotto rice, such as Arborio

4½ cups fish or chicken stock

1 cup dry white wine

4 to 5 (4-gram) packets of squid ink

A handful of chopped flat-leaf parsley

1½ cups *Alioli* (page 141)

Fry the onions in the oil in a 16- to 18-inch paella pan over medium heat, stirring often, until soft and golden. Add the tomatoes, season with a little salt and pepper, and cook until most of the liquid has evaporated and the oil is sizzling.

Add the squid and cook over medium heat, stirring and turning them, for 5 to 8 minutes. Add the rice and stir so that the grains are well coated with the sauce. (You can prepare the dish in advance up to this stage, up to an hour in advance, and reheat before continuing.)

Meanwhile, bring the stock and wine to a boil in a saucepan. Squeeze the contents of the ink packets (I used 4 and liked it that way; 5 give a more intense black color) into a small bowl and stir in a little of the stock to dilute the ink thoroughly, then pour this into the pan and mix very well.

Pour the ink-stained stock over the rice, add salt to taste, and stir, spreading the rice evenly in the pan (do not stir again). Cook over medium heat for 10 minutes, then lower the heat and cook for 8 to 10 minutes more, or until the rice is tender; move the pan around and rotate it so the rice cooks evenly. If the rice gets too dry and you hear crackly frying noises before it is done, pour in a little boiling water.

Serve sprinkled with the parsley and accompanied by the *alioli.*

rice with chicken and red peppers

{ arroz con pollo y pimientos—andalusia }

This is a very special and unusual dish in that the rice is cooked in a glorious mix of creamy onion sauce with chicken stock and sherry and flavored with a touch of saffron. I have roasted the chicken and made a splendid stock with the carcass and juices, and the result was a sensational dish, but that takes too long for most people. A simpler and equally good method is to buy good chicken stock and to mix in the juices and melted fat from the roast, as described below.

SERVES 6

1 chicken (about 3½ pounds)

Salt

5 tablespoons olive oil

3 large onions, halved and sliced

4 garlic cloves, sliced

1 cup amontillado or oloroso sherry
   (I prefer amontillado)

3¾ to 4 cups chicken stock,
   or as needed

A good pinch of saffron threads

2½ cups medium-grain Spanish
   paella rice or risotto rice, such
   as Arborio or Carnaroli

2 red bell peppers, roasted
   (see page 128), peeled, seeded,
   and cut into 6 pieces each

Put the chicken in a baking dish, season with salt, and rub with one tablespoon of the oil. Turn it breast side down, pour in ¾ cup water, and roast in a preheated 375°F oven for 45 minutes. Turn the chicken breast side up, add a little more water if the pan has dried out, and roast for 30 minutes longer, or until the chicken is brown and the juices that run out when you cut between the leg and the body of the bird with a pointed knife are clear.

Meanwhile, sauté the onions in the remaining 4 tablespoons oil in a wide casserole that you can bring to the table. Put the lid on and stir occasionally until the onions are very soft and beginning to color, then cook, uncovered, over medium heat, stirring often, until golden brown. Add the garlic and stir until the garlic is lightly colored. All this can take as long as 45 minutes, because there are so many onions.

Add the sherry and cook for 1 minute more. Blend with an immersion blender or in a food processor, and return the onion sauce to the casserole.

Transfer the roasted chicken to a carving board. Bring the chicken stock to a boil and pour it into the baking dish,

>>>

mixing it thoroughly with the chicken juices and melted fat, then pour this into the onion sauce. Add the saffron and some salt (the rice will need a good amount), taking into consideration the saltiness of the stock.

Cut the chicken into serving pieces—cut each leg and each breast into 2 pieces—and keep them covered. Pick the small pieces of meat off the carcass and wings and add them to the stock.

Bring the onion sauce and stock to a boil, pour in the rice, and stir well (do not stir again). Cook, uncovered, over medium heat for 10 minutes, then lower the heat and cook for another 5 minutes.

Lay the chicken pieces and red peppers on top of the rice, cover with a lid or foil, and cook for another 5 minutes, or until the rice is tender and the chicken is heated through; add a little more stock or water if the rice seems too dry before it is done.

baked rice with currants and chickpeas

{ arroz al horno con pasas y garbanzos—valencia }

In their splendid The Heritage of Spanish Cooking, *Alicia Ríos and Lourdes March say that in the Valencian mountain interior, rice dishes are based on the broth of a* cocido—*a dish of boiled meats (see page 498). The recipe is adapted from one in their book. In Spain today you can buy good* cocido *broth, but here, use beef or chicken stock. Use a* cazuela *or a large shallow casserole that will go both on the stove and in the oven. If you do not have one, start the dish in a deep saucepan, then transfer it to a baking dish. A head of garlic (Valencians call it a "partridge") is placed in the center. Serve it with meatballs or with fried pork ribs and sausages or blood sausages.*

SERVES 8

1 cup dried chickpeas, soaked
(see Soaking Beans, page 487)

Salt

5 tablespoons olive oil

A head of garlic, not peeled

1 cup dried currants or raisins,
soaked in water for 20 minutes
and drained

1 large tomato, peeled and
chopped

1 teaspoon *pimentón dulce*
(or sweet paprika)

5 cups meat or chicken stock
(or 5 cups water plus 1½ to
2 bouillon cubes)

2½ cups medium-grain Spanish
paella rice or risotto rice, such
as Arborio or Carnaroli

Drain the chickpeas, put them in a saucepan with fresh water to cover, and simmer for 1 hour, or until they are soft; add some salt once they have begun to soften. Drain.

Heat the oil in a large *cazuela* or casserole that goes in the oven. Add the garlic and half the currants or raisins and stir over low heat for 2 to 3 minutes. Add the tomato and *pimentón* (or paprika) and stir well, then add the chickpeas, stock, and some salt. Bring to a boil, add the rice, and stir well.

Place the head of garlic in the center of the rice and sprinkle the remaining currants or raisins over the top. Bake in a preheated 400°F oven for 30 minutes, or until the rice is tender.

When serving, give everyone a garlic clove for them to squeeze out the soft inside.

Note: If you do not have a large casserole or a *cazuela*, start the cooking in a large saucepan and just bring to a boil, then pour everything into a large round baking dish, about 14 inches in diameter. Put the garlic head in the center and bake as above.

baked rice with an egg crust

{ arroz con costra — valencia }

This baked rice dish is unusual in that it has an egg topping. Chicken drumsticks, spareribs, and sausages make it a hearty and flavorful meal in itself. You will need a cazuela *or a wide casserole with which you can start cooking on the stove, then continue in the oven. Otherwise you can start in a saucepan and transfer to a baking dish (see Note).*

SERVES 6

3 to 4 tablespoons olive oil

6 country-style pork spareribs or
   6 thin pork loin chops

3 pork sausages

6 chicken drumsticks

4 cups beef or chicken stock
   (or 4 cups water plus
   2 bouillon cubes)

2 tomatoes, peeled and chopped

Salt and pepper

1 teaspoon *pimentón dulce*
   (or sweet paprika)

2 cups medium-grain Spanish
   paella rice or risotto rice, such
   as Arborio or Carnaroli

1⅓ cups canned chickpeas,
   drained (optional)

5 large eggs, lightly beaten

Heat the oil in a wide ovenproof casserole over medium heat. Add the spareribs or chops, sausages, and chicken and brown them, over medium-high heat, turning occasionally. Take out the sausages and ribs or chops as soon as they are lightly browned, but cook the drumsticks for 20 minutes, turning often.

Meanwhile, bring the stock (or water and bouillon cubes) to a boil in a saucepan.

Add the tomatoes to the casserole and season with salt and pepper and the *pimentón* (or paprika); cook 5 minutes over medium heat. Stir in the rice and the chickpeas, if using, with a wooden spoon. Pour in the stock and return the sausages, cut in half, the spareribs or chops, and the drumsticks to the casserole, stirring to distribute the rice and meats evenly. Add salt, taking into consideration the saltiness of the stock. Bring to a boil, then simmer over low heat, without stirring, for 5 minutes.

Bake the casserole, uncovered, in a preheated 400°F oven for 15 minutes, or until the rice is almost tender.

Season the eggs with a little salt and pour evenly over the top of the rice. Bake for another 15 minutes, or until the eggs are firm.

Note: If you do not have a large casserole, brown the meats in a skillet, fry the tomatoes in a saucepan, add the stock and the rice, then pour into a large baking dish. Arrange the meats on top and continue as above.

rice with pork, chestnuts, and raisins

{ arroz con cerdo, castañas, y pasas—andalusia }

The meatballs take some time, but they are worth it. Instead of frying them, you can turn them under the broiler until they are brown all over. Use fresh peeled (see page 130), frozen, or vacuum-packed chestnuts. You can start the dish in advance and continue half an hour before you are ready to serve.

SERVES 4

¼ cup olive oil

8 country-style pork spareribs

1 medium onion, finely chopped

3 garlic cloves, crushed to a paste
   or finely chopped

4 tomatoes, peeled and chopped

A good pinch of saffron threads

1 teaspoon *pimentón dulce*
   (or sweet paprika)

⅓ cup dried currants or raisins

4 cups chicken stock (or 4 cups
   water plus 1½ bouillon cubes)

Salt

2 cups fresh peeled, defrosted
   frozen, or vacuum-packed
   chestnuts

2 cups medium-grain Spanish
   paella rice or risotto rice, such
   as Arborio or Carnaroli

>>>

Heat the oil in a large *cazuela*, or casserole. Sauté the spareribs, in batches if necessary, over low heat for 10 to 12 minutes, turning them once to brown them lightly all over. Remove them.

Sauté the onion in the same oil until it begins to color. Add the garlic and stir for a moment or two, until the aroma rises. Add the tomatoes and cook over high heat until they are reduced to a jammy sauce.

Stir in the saffron, *pimentón* (or paprika), and currants or raisins, and pour in the stock (or water and bouillon cubes). Return the spareribs to the pot, add a little salt, and cook, covered, for about 20 minutes, or until they are tender.

Meanwhile, for the meatballs, put the ground pork, egg, bread crumbs soaked in milk, and parsley in a bowl. Season with the cinnamon, salt, and pepper to taste and work to a soft paste with your hands.

Cover a platter with flour. Roll the meat mixture into balls the size of large walnuts. Roll them in the flour to coat them all over; shake off the excess. Fry them, in batches in about ½ inch of sizzling oil, in a large skillet over medium-high heat, turning them to brown them lightly all over. Drain on paper towels.

>>>

FOR THE MEATBALLS

1 pound ground pork

1 large egg, lightly beaten

6 tablespoons fresh bread crumbs,
    soaked in ¼ cup milk

2 to 3 tablespoons finely chopped
    flat-leaf parsley

1 teaspoon cinnamon

¾ teaspoon salt

Pepper

Flour for dredging

Olive or sunflower oil for frying

Half an hour before serving, bring the stock, with the spareribs, to a boil and add salt to taste. Put in the chestnuts and rice, stir very well, and bring to a boil again (do not stir again). Cook, covered, over high heat for 3 minutes, then reduce the heat to low and cook for another 7 minutes. Now place the meatballs on top of the rice, cover, and cook for 10 minutes, or until the rice is tender and the meatballs are cooked through.

Note: Instead of frying the meatballs, you can put them on a sheet of foil on a baking tray and place them under the broiler, turning them until they are done.

creamy rice with artichokes, fava beans, and peas

{ arroz meloso con alcachofas,

habas, y guisantes — murcia }

Vegetable rice dishes in Murcia are called a la huertana, *meaning "of the vegetable garden."*
Loli Flores, who gave me this recipe and many others, lives in Seville, where she was a chef for
many years. One of her daughters (she has six children) is the chef/owner of a truly vegetarian
restaurant called Habanita (no bits of ham, no lard or chicken stock), something that is very rare
in Spain. We had a great meal there. Use fresh vegetables when they are available, but frozen ones
will do very well. For preparing fresh baby artichokes, see page 129. You could also use cooked
artichoke hearts from a deli counter.

SERVES 6

5 tablespoons olive oil

2 bay leaves

2 medium onions, chopped

1 green bell pepper, cored, seeded,
  and chopped

3 to 4 garlic cloves, chopped

4 cups vegetable stock (or 4 cups
  water plus 2 bouillon cubes)

4 fresh baby artichokes (see
  page 129) or frozen artichoke
  bottoms or hearts, quartered

1⅔ cups fava beans

1⅔ cups peas

1¾ cups medium-grain Spanish
  rice or risotto rice, such as
  Arborio or Carnaroli

Salt

Heat the oil with the bay leaves in a large saucepan. Add
the onions and pepper and sauté, stirring often, over
medium heat for about 20 minutes, until soft. Add the garlic and stir for a minute, or until aromatic.

Meanwhile, bring the stock to a boil in a saucepan.

Add the artichokes and fava beans to the onions and
peppers and pour in the stock. Simmer, covered, for
10 minutes, then add the peas. Bring to a boil again, pour
in the rice, and add salt. Simmer over low heat for 15 to 18
minutes, until the rice is tender. (It should be *meloso*—not
dry, and not soupy, but in between.)

fideos

Various types of dry pasta made of durum wheat, all of them short (about 1 to 1½ inches), are called *fideos* in Spain, or *fideus* in Catalan. The name derives from *fidawsh*, an Arab word for "pasta." Fourteenth-century Catalan cookbooks have recipes for *fideus* and for *aletria*, an alternative word for "pasta" derived from the Arabic *itria*. Fideos come in various thicknesses that are graded from 0 to 4. Size 0 is vermicelli-like, and it is also called *cabello de ángel* (angel's hair). (For this you can use vermicelli nests—break them in your hands into small pieces.) There is also a thin spaghettini and a thicker spaghetti, as well as a small curved macaroni pasta.

Fideos are cooked like rice in a paella pan, in a casserole or earthenware dish, or in a pot, and like rice in Spain, they are cooked in stock or in a sauce, not in boiling water. In Catalonia, they are sometimes first fried in oil—then they are called *rossejats*. Catalonia and Valencia have a variety of pasta dishes. *Fideos* are a legacy of the Arabs. Italian-style pastas such as *caneloni*, *pene*, and *macaroni* date back to the nineteenth century when a large number of Italian cooks opened restaurants or came to work for the newly wealthy Catalan and Basque bourgeoisies. These have become Spanish in style and flavor.

seafood pasta

{ fideuà or fideuada — catalonia and valencia }

In Valencia, I ate a seafood pasta made in a paella pan with short, thin macaroni. Another I had in Catalonia with a vermicelli-type pasta was especially memorable. They were both wonderful, with glorious-looking seafood. This recipe, called fideuà del señorito *(literally, "of the young gentleman"), is less messy to eat because the seafood is peeled or out of its shells, but if you want to make a spectacular one, see the variations.*

You can use either crushed vermicelli or thin spaghettini broken into small pieces instead of fideos *(see previous page). I have used scallops here because they are easier for me to get hold of, but you can put in clams or mussels, which are more commonly used in Spain. If you cannot make or buy a good fish stock (page 126), use a good chicken stock.*

SERVES 6

5 tablespoons olive oil

14 ounces monkfish fillet,
     cut into ¾-inch cubes

Salt

4 cleaned baby squid, bodies cut
     into rings

12 jumbo shrimp, peeled

12 small scallops

5 garlic cloves, crushed to a paste
     or finely chopped

3 tomatoes, peeled and chopped

1 teaspoon *pimentón dulce*
     (or sweet paprika)

A good pinch of saffron threads

5½ cups fish or chicken stock,
     or as needed

>>>

Heat 4 tablespoons of the oil in a 16- to 18-inch paella pan. Add the monkfish, sprinkle with salt, and cook over medium heat for 3 to 4 minutes, turning the pieces occasionally. Add the squid and cook, stirring, for 3 minutes, then add the shrimp and scallops and cook for 1 to 2 minutes, turning them, until the shrimp are pink and the scallops just seared. Transfer the seafood to a platter, and pour the cooking liquid into a small bowl, to add to the fish stock for extra flavor.

Heat the remaining tablespoon of oil in the paella pan, then add the garlic and cook, stirring, until the aroma rises. Add the tomatoes, *pimentón* (or paprika), saffron, and a little salt and cook over medium-high heat, stirring occasionally, for 10 minutes, until much of the liquid has evaporated and the oil is sizzling through (you can do this in advance).

Fifteen minutes before serving, bring the stock with the liquid from the seafood to a boil.

>>>

1 pound *fideos* (size 1 or 2),
     or vermicelli nests or thin
     spaghettini, broken into
     1¼- to 1½-inch pieces

3 tablespoons chopped
     flat-leaf parsley

6 lemon wedges

1½ cups *Alioli* (page 141) for
     serving

Add the pasta to the sauce in the paella pan and cook, stirring, until it is well coated. Pour in the boiling stock, and arrange the monkfish and seafood on top. Cook until the pasta is al dente—from 2 minutes, if using vermicelli, to about 10, if using spaghettini; add a little more stock or boiling water if the liquid dries up before the pasta is done. It should still be moist.

Serve sprinkled with the parsley and garnished with the lemon wedges, accompanied by *alioli*.

VARIATIONS

- Substitute dry white wine or oloroso sherry for 1 cup of the stock.

- For a more spectacular dish, omit the monkfish and scallops and use seafood in their shells.

     Sauté 4 baby squid, bodies sliced into rings, in the paella pan as above; remove from the pan. Sauté 12 or more jumbo shrimp in their shells, turning them once, for 2 to 3 minutes, until they are pink all over; remove from the pan. Put 24 or more clams or mussels (to prepare them, see page 127) in a pan with a finger's depth of water, put the lid on, and bring to a boil; they will open and be cooked in the steam in a minute or so. If you can afford to be lavish, use 6 langoustines instead of the shrimp and boil them in water for 4 minutes. Arrange all the seafood over the pasta to heat through.

pasta with peas, chicken or rabbit, and pork chops

{ *f i d e o s e n c a z u e l a — c a t a l o n i a* }

This heartwarming pasta dish is from the Catalan interior. Small curved macaroni are cooked in an aromatic stock and the meats, sautéed separately, are added toward the end along with the marvelous nutty, fragrant thickener called picada. *You will need a* cazuela *or a wide casserole.*

SERVES 5 TO 6

5 tablespoons olive oil

2 chicken thighs, cut into 1- to
    1½-inch pieces, or 10 ounces
    boneless rabbit, cut into 1- to
    1½-inch pieces

Salt and pepper

6 tiny pork chops

4 pork sausages (about 7 ounces)

1 large onion, chopped

1 red or green bell pepper, cored,
    seeded, and finely chopped

2 garlic cloves, finely chopped

3 tomatoes, peeled and chopped

½ teaspoon sugar

1 bay leaf

14 ounces (about 3½ cups)
    small macaroni

4½ cups chicken stock
    (or 4½ cups water plus
    1 bouillon cube)

⅔ cup fresh or frozen peas

>>>

Heat 3 tablespoons of the olive oil in a large skillet. Add the chicken or rabbit pieces, and sauté over medium heat, turning them and sprinkling with salt and pepper, until lightly browned and cooked through. Take them out and put them on a plate.

Sauté the pork chops in the same oil until lightly browned and cooked through, adding salt and pepper and turning them once. Transfer them to the plate. Sauté the sausages (prick them first with the point of a knife so that they don't burst), shaking the pan and turning them, until done. Take them out and cut them into thick slices.

Fry the onion, pepper, and garlic in a wide casserole in the remaining 2 tablespoons oil over low heat, stirring often, until soft. Add the tomatoes, sugar, a little salt, and the bay leaf and cook over medium-high heat for about 10 minutes.

Bring the stock (or water and bouillon cube) to a boil.

Add the pasta to the sauce and stir well. Pour in the boiling stock and add the peas and some salt. Bring to a boil, then simmer over low heat until the pasta is somewhat softened but a little underdone (about 3 minutes less

>>>

FOR THE *PICADA*

⅓ cup blanched whole almonds or
   hazelnuts, lightly toasted

2 garlic cloves

Pinch of saffron threads

3 tablespoons coarsely chopped
   flat-leaf parsley

than the cooking time on the package). Taste the pasta with a little of the sauce when it begins to soften and add more salt if necessary.

Meanwhile, for the *picada*, blend all the ingredients to a paste in a food processor, and dilute it by adding about ½ cup of the stock from the casserole.

Stir the *picada* into the pasta, along with the rabbit or chicken and the sausage. Lay the pork chops on top, cover, and cook until the pasta is done and the meats are heated through.

VARIATION

Substitute dry white wine or dry oloroso sherry for 1 cup of the stock.

migas

Migas, a dish of fried bread crumbs, is the legendary food of shepherds that was adopted by agricultural laborers along the old transhumance routes that criss-crossed Spain. (These were the routes that sheep took seasonally to reach new pastures.) They cooked on little braziers (*braseritos*). The dish has recently become very fashionable. I ate it in restaurants around the country and at a glamorous party in Madrid. Supermarkets sell it vacuum-packed, ready to heat through. Depending on the region, the bread crumbs are fried in olive oil or lard, or a mixture of both. In La Mancha, Aragon, and Andalusia, they are cooked in olive oil. Again depending on the region, *migas* is eaten with fried bacon and chorizo, or blood sausage, and sometimes also eggs. There are those who eat *migas* with bits of *jamón*, and those who eat it with grapes and chocolate. In Granada, they eat it with anchovies, melon, and orange slices. Some like *migas* with a sprinkling of sugar. In the valley of the Duero River, they eat it like pasta, with a sauce made with fried onion, garlic, a chile pepper, and sweet *pimentón*. In Aragon, they make it with bacon, chorizo, and sweet and hot *pimentón*; in Navarre, with fried onion, garlic, and *jamón*.

My friend Cuqui Gonzáles de Caldas described how olive pickers in Andalusia made *migas* during the harvest. The crumbs were fried in olive oil in a huge shallow communal pan by a *"miguero"*—and they all served themselves from the pan and ate them with olives, raw turnips, and fried or grilled sardines. To finish, they had more *migas* with oranges. Cuqui's mother, who came from Osuna in Andalusia, used to make the dish for her family. There is an art of tearing up bread into very small pieces with your fingers, and Cuqui showed me how to do it on our table at the Sol y Sombra Bar in Seville. It reminded me of a man in a Paris restaurant I saw tearing up bread and making piles; I thought he had an obsessive disorder until I saw him later in the park feeding birds.

migas with bacon

{ *migas con tocino* }

This is the migas *I ate with Cuqui Gonzáles at the Sol y Sombra Bar in Seville (see previous page).*

SERVES 2

½ pound dense country bread, crusts left on

½ cup warm water

Salt

½ teaspoon *pimentón dulce* (or sweet paprika)

A pinch of *pimentón picante* (or hot paprika; optional)

3 to 4 tablespoons olive oil

5 garlic cloves

8 slices bacon

Cut the bread into very thin slices, less than ¼ inch, and then into strips, and then into dice as small as a chickpea. Put them in a bowl. Mix the water with some salt and the *pimentón* (the hot one too, if you wish). Sprinkle this on the diced bread, turning it with your hands so that the pieces are evenly moistened. Leave for a few hours, or overnight, covered with a cloth.

When you are ready to eat, heat the oil in a large skillet (nonstick if you like). Fry the garlic and bacon over medium heat, turning them occasionally. Take out the garlic when it is golden brown and discard it; transfer the bacon to a plate when it is crisp and has released most of its fat. Throw the damp bread into the pan and fry over high heat for about 15 minutes, turning it over continually and breaking it up with a spatula into ever-smaller pieces, until the biggish crumbs are crisp, golden, and crunchy but still soft and slightly damp inside. The fat will be soaked up very quickly, but you can continue to cook, turning the crumbs in the dry pan.

Cut the bacon into small pieces and add them to the pan to heat through at the end.

Comfort food for the stomach and for the soul.

JOSÉ LUIS ALEXANCO'S PORRIDGE

{ *gachas, fariñes, farinetas* }

In a primitive kitchen off his studio and art gallery outside Madrid, the painter, sculptor, and typographer José Luis Alexanco cooked us *gachas* and other foods of the rural poor of La Mancha. Then, feeling happy and satisfied, we went on a tour of his huge white gallery to see his stunning artwork. *Gachas* is a gruel or porridge made with finely ground flour from the legume *almorta* (*Lathyrus sativus*, or grass pea), which was both fodder for animals and eaten by shepherds and peasants. The reliance on and excessive consumption of it during the civil war and the period after was blamed for a neurological disease that caused weakness or paralysis of the legs. But what was once referred to as *gachas de los años difíciles* (*gachas* of the tough years) is now popular, served with vegetables or with pork products such as bacon, chorizo, *salchichón*, or *morcilla* (blood sausage).

José Luis fried lots of garlic with mushrooms and asparagus tips in plenty of olive oil. He removed them and poured in the *gachas*, stirring until the flour acquired a light golden color. Then he gradually added water, stirring all the while. As he stirred the bubbling porridge, he talked about the lives of the peasants of La Mancha, of those who had to give more than half their produce to their landlords and those who waited every day in the village square to be picked for odd jobs; of the women who dyed all their clothes black when somebody in the family died and never again wore anything else. His maternal grandmother kept a goat for milk and cheese, and chickens for their eggs, and she dried her own tomatoes. In the winter, she cooked *gachas* and *caparrones* (mottled brown and white beans) in the fireplace over a wood fire. His paternal grandfather was the butcher in Ojacastro in La Rioja. His pigs tasted better than the pork you get today because they were fed differently. (He only slaughtered during the full moon, and in his sausages he never mixed the meats of male and female swine.)

In other regions, chickpea flour, wheat flour, and cornmeal (polenta) are used to make *gachas* in a variety of ways, sometimes with fried onion and croutons; sometimes with tomatoes and snails or with salt cod. In Andalusia, it is made with wheat flour and colored and flavored with *pimentón* and saffron. In Murcia, they season it with caraway and cloves. In the Canary Islands, they make it with a mix of corn and wheat flours and call it *gofio*. Sweet *gachas* are made with milk and sometimes flavored with grated orange zest and cinnamon or with vanilla. Honey, raisins, and almonds can be sprinkled on. In Asturias, Galicia, and Aragon, *gachas* is made with cornmeal and is also called by the local names *fariñes* and *farinetas*. Grass pea flour is not easy to find outside La Mancha.

spanish polenta

{ *fariñes—asturias and galicia* }

Asturias and Galicia were once the only regions, other than the Canaries and Murcia, where people ate the corn they grew. In the past they dried it and kept it in elevated stone grain stores, then ground it into a fine meal. The rest of Spain fed it to their animals. But in the hungry years during the civil war and afterward, many people made corn bread and ate fariñes, *a cornmeal porridge that is like polenta. Some Spaniards remember nostalgically the way their grandmothers used to make it. They would cook the porridge for an hour or so, stirring it continually. Now we can use instant (precooked) maize cornmeal sold as polenta, which cooks in a few minutes.*

In northern Spain, rural families had milk and butter from their cows and pork products from their pigs. For a treat, they served fariñes *with fried bacon,* chorizo, *and* morcilla *(blood sausage). If you want to use them, slice the sausages and fry them and the bacon in a little oil, then serve them on top of the* fariñes.

SERVES 4 TO 6

6½ cups water

2 teaspoons salt

2 cups instant polenta

2 tablespoons unsalted butter

Bring the water to a boil in a large saucepan. Add the salt, lower the heat, and gradually stir in the polenta with a wooden spoon. Cook, stirring continuously, for 5 to 8 minutes, until the polenta pulls away from the sides of the pan. Stir in the butter.

VARIATION

Serve the *fariñes* in soup bowls and pass very hot milk for everyone to pour on top and let it seep in.

BEAN AND CHICKPEA STEWS

{ *ollas* }

Cocido, olla, puchero, pote, *and* escudella *are all general terms for stews* that rural families kept on the simmer in huge pots hanging in the fireplace, or sitting on a tripod over burning coals. Based mainly on legumes, with some vegetables and tiny bits of ham or sausage, they represented for the peasantry in every region of Spain the main meal of the day almost every day. For special occasions, great quantities were made with a variety of meats and cured pork, including pig's ears, tails, snouts, and trotters. These dishes still appear at festivals where cooks compete for excellence awards.

Beans were characterized in traditional lore as "the meat of the rural poor." In the Basque Country, not so very long ago, the term *babazorro*, bean eater, was an insult meaning "country bumpkin." In the hungry years during the civil war, when there was no meat in the cities, people ate beans, chickpeas, and lentils. In the postwar days of rationing in the 1940s, legumes were part of the one-dish meal, the *plato único*, that people in the cities ate once a day. They ate that at two-thirty in the afternoon, at news time, when children came home for lunch and everybody listened to the radio together.

I have never been to a country that has as great a variety of legumes and as much respect for and pride in them as Spain. You can see displays in shops and markets of more than twenty types of beans, lentils, and chickpeas, with cards giving their provenance, down to the name of the village where they were

Boiled Meats and Chickpeas with Vegetables, page 498.

grown. Beans—small or huge; round or flat; white, black, red, pale green, or speckled—are grown in many different parts of Spain. Apart from black-eyed peas and broad beans, they all came from the New World. By the sixteenth century, farmers were selling the dried legumes at markets. Generally referred to as *alubias* or *judías*, they also have regional names, such as *garrafón*, *judión*, *fabes*, *mongetes*, and *caparrones*. Every region has its beloved favorites. Some, such as the *judiones de la Granja de San Ildefonso*, the *judías del Barco de Ávila*, the *alubias de La Bañeza-León*, the *fabes* of Asturias, and the Galician *faba de Lourenzá*, are covered by a Protected Geographic Identification (PGI). The pale green *lentejas* (lentils) *de la Armuña*, the brown *lentejas Pardinas de Tierra de Campos*, and the *garbanzos* (chickpeas) *de Fuentesaúco* also have the same protected badge of guaranteed quality that links them with the soil and location.

People wonder why the word for beans, *alubia*, comes from an Arabic word and why *judías*, the other general word for them, literally means "Jewish," since beans arrived in Spain after Muslims and Jews were officially expelled. One explanation is that cooking with black-eyed peas was early on associated with Arabs, who called them *lubia*. The Jews cooked black-eyed peas on their New Year as a symbol of plenty and fertility (in my family we still do). The Jewish Sabbath meal-in-a-pot *adafina* (see page 29) contained chickpeas; the Jews who converted and stayed behind in Spain substituted beans from the New World in the regions where chickpeas were not available. The general formula of the Spanish *cocido*, the boiled stew that is found in every region in different forms, follows the pattern of the *adafina*, including the way the broth was traditionally eaten first, with vermicelli or rice.

Despite the traditional importance of legumes in the Spanish diet, consumption and production have dropped dramatically since the 1980s, because people have little time to cook and are concerned with putting on weight. Dried beans and lentils represent hearty traditional fare and rarely feature in modern dishes, except as an accompaniment or garnish for baby kid, partridge, and quail or in salads. Some of the varieties had almost disappeared because they were too expensive to grow, but efforts are being made to restore them as a crop. And now legumes are sold ready-cooked and vacuum-packed. Although they are not eaten very often, the substantial dishes affectionately called *platos de cuchara*—dishes that you eat with a spoon—are loved everywhere in Spain with special nostalgic intensity. But whereas once cooks put everything—meats, sausages, beans, vegetables—in the stew pot at the same time, now, inspired by modern chefs, they put the ingredients in according to how much cooking they need; or they cook them separately, so as to get rid of some of the fat from the pork products, before reuniting them at the end.

I happened to see on YouTube a video of the *gran pucherada* that took place on October 23, 2007, in San Severino in the Basque Country. The main event of the fiesta was a competition of bean dishes—*alubiadas*. Dozens of men (there were no women that I saw) were lined up behind their *pucheros*—tall cylindrical metal pots on tripods with a compartment with glowing embers burning underneath. This type of pot, still used in the area of Las Encartaciones, in the Basque Country in the province of Vizcaya, was famously used by railwaymen who worked on the old coal-fired steam trains and utilized burning coals to cook stews during their long journeys. The background song about beans and *txakoli*—the wine the revelers were drinking—that played as they cooked made me dance in front of my computer.

For us outside Spain, *pucheradas, alubiadas,* and the like might not bring the same joy to our hearts as they do in Spain, but they can provide a great meal in a pot to enjoy with friends in the winter. If we cannot buy the same legumes, we can always find an equivalent. In Spain, I was told that beans should be a year old at most, and that I should look at their age—the date when they were harvested—because the soaking and cooking times depend on age as well as on type. Beans that are less than a year old do not need soaking. But we do not have the privilege of knowing the harvest date—we only know the sell-by date that is written on the packet, so there is no way of telling how long they will take to cook. You just have to bite into one every so often. I was also told that if the water in your area is hard, it will lengthen the cooking time; that is why some cooks advocate using bottled water. A Spanish trick that is supposed to stop the beans from falling apart is to "scare" (*asustar*) them by pouring a little cold water on them from time to time during the cooking, but I am not sure that works, and Spain is the only country I know of where people do that. Some people now use pressure cookers to cook their beans, but as they can so quickly overcook and fall apart, they make purees out of them.

soaking beans

Beans can be cooked without soaking, but they will take much longer to cook. There are two ways of soaking them to reduce the cooking time.

1. Soak the beans in plenty of water for 6 to 10 hours.

2. The quicker method is to boil the washed beans in plenty of water in a large saucepan for 2 minutes, then remove from the heat, cover the pan, and let the beans soak for 1 hour.

Always drain and then cook in fresh water.

beans with cured pork and sausages

{ *fabada — asturias* }

We ate fabada *at Casa Fermín in Oviedo, Asturias. Luis Alberto Martínez Abascal and María Jesús Gil García served us a stupendous avant-garde Asturian tasting menu. At the end, when we thought we could not eat any more, we asked for a taste of a traditional* fabada, *and out it came.* Fabada *is the iconic festive dish of Asturias that has become popular all over Spain. The special Asturian large white beans called* fabes *(*faba *in the singular) that are used to make it have a delicious nutty flavor, a buttery texture, and a thin skin that melts in your mouth. Those of the best qualities from special farms are referred to as* del cura *(of the priest),* del peón *(of the farm laborer), or* del colmillo *(of the sharp tooth). They are expensive and hard to find outside Spain, but you can use other large white beans. We heard more about* fabada *from Jaime Rodriguez, our host at the guesthouse where I stayed in the mountains with the journalist Jane Kramer (see page 554). The family had kept cows, and the rooms where we stayed had been where the cows slept. They used to make* fabada *with smaller white beans that are easier to grow and cheaper than* fabes, *which grow entwined around cornstalks and need careful nurturing. They ate* fabada, *with tiny pieces of home-cured bacon, chorizo, and blood sausage, three or four times a week. The grand version, made years ago for weddings, has plenty of cured pork meats and sausages, blood sausage, pig's feet and ears, and sometimes spareribs or* cecina *(cured beef). The following recipe has the most common combination of ingredients. In Asturias, pork products are always smoked because families cured them in their smoky fireplaces, since it was typically wet outside and damp in their lofts. I prefer them unsmoked. By tradition, all the ingredients are cooked together, but many now prefer to cook the meats separately, as I do, to eliminate some of the fat. Some people also like to present the beans and meats separately.*

SERVES 6

1 pound *fabes* or other large white beans, such as butter or lima, soaked (see Soaking Beans, page 487)

1 small onion

A head of garlic, unpeeled

>>>

Drain the beans and put them in a large pan with enough fresh cold water to cover them by about one fat finger. Bring to a boil, skimming the foam that floats to the top, then add the onion, garlic, and bay leaves. Simmer gently over very low heat, partially covered, shaking the pan occasionally so that the beans do not stick to the bottom, until they are tender. The time depends on the type and age of the beans. It can take from 1 to 2 hours, so

>>>

2 bay leaves

Salt

A pinch of saffron threads
(optional)

½ pound *lacón* (fatty dry-cured
ham from the shoulder) or an
additional ½ pound pancetta,
salt pork, or bacon

¼ pound pancetta or slab bacon,
in one piece

2 semi-cured chorizos

2 *morcillas* (Spanish blood
sausages), about 8 ounces

start trying them as you near 1 hour to see if they are soft, and watch if they begin to break. Add cold water as necessary to keep the beans covered all the time. You should end up with a soupy stew. When the beans have begun to soften, add salt to taste. Add the saffron, if you like, at this stage.

Meanwhile, as soon as you start cooking the beans, put the cured ham and pancetta or bacon in a large saucepan in plenty of water and bring to a boil, then simmer over low heat for 1 hour. Add the chorizos and simmer for 15 minutes. Add the blood sausages and cook for 10 minutes more. Drain, and cut the sausages into thick slices. When the beans are tender, return the meats and heat through.

tolosa red bean stew

{ a l u b i a s   r o j a s   a   l a   t o l o s a n a — b a s q u e   c o u n t r y }

Like many rural bean dishes, this one is a potaje, *or soup, that is transformed on festive occasions into a grand meal with spareribs and all kinds of cured pork meats, blood sausage, and chorizo. But even then the consistency has to be soupy. By tradition, the dish is accompanied by boiled cabbage and small, elongated mild green peppers called* guindillas, *pickled in vinegar.*

The red beans of Tolosa that grew in symbiosis with corn in the steep vegetable gardens of small farmers in the Basque hills have become legendary. They are celebrated during a Semana de la Alubia *(Bean Week) in Tolosa with cooking competitions and communal meals. The beans are dark purple, almost black, and deliciously creamy with a thin skin. The important thing is to cook them so that they are very tender without their skins splitting. You can cook all the different ingredients—the beans, meat, and cabbage—in advance and reheat before serving.*

SERVES 6

1 pound red beans, soaked
   (see Soaking Beans, page 487)

1 small onion, peeled

2 garlic cloves, peeled

6 tablespoons extra virgin olive oil

Salt

8 country-style pork spareribs

½ pound slab bacon, in one piece

About 1 pound semi-cured
   chorizos

About 1 pound *morcillas*
   (Spanish blood sausages)

1 small green cabbage, cut into
   6 wedges

Guindillas (mild green chiles
   preserved in vinegar) for serving

Drain the beans and put them in a large saucepan with the onion, garlic, and 3 tablespoons of the olive oil. Cover with fresh cold water and bring to a boil, removing any foam, then simmer over very low heat for 1½ hours, or until the beans are very tender. Add cold water to cover as necessary, and watch that their skins do not split. When they begin to soften, add salt.

Meanwhile, cook the spareribs and bacon in a large pot of water over low heat for 1 hour. Add the chorizos to the spareribs and simmer for 20 minutes. Add the blood sausages and cook for no more than 10 minutes (or they may burst). Drain and add to the beans when they are cooked.

Cook the cabbage in a large pot of boiling salted water—it will be tender in minutes. Remove the cabbage when it's done, then plunge into the same water, brought to a boil, just before serving.

VARIATION

Caparrones, the small mottled beans that grow in La Rioja, can be used instead of red beans for a Riojan version of the dish.

sausages

{ embutidos }

Nostalgia in Spain has a smell: it is the smell of chorizo hanging in attics and kitchens. The taste and aroma of a piece of chorizo or *morcilla* (blood sausage) evoke powerful ancestral and family memories of the day of the *matanza,* when the pig was killed and the entire family—father, mother, uncles, aunts, grandmothers, and grandfathers—had a part to play in the preparation of the hams and sausages for drying. They cut the pig's throat, drained the blood into a bucket, and salted the hams; they chopped the fat and the rest of the meat and mixed in seasonings for sausages. They washed and scrubbed the intestines, cut them, stuffed them, and tied them. It was hard work, but there was bonding and laughing, and a lavish feast at the end, when the offal was eaten. The cured hams were a luxury that could be used as payment for the doctor or midwife, but the sausages were for the family. For some, these sausages were the only source of meat. Today the ritual of the family *matanza* is in decline, partly because of new hygiene laws that require a veterinarian to test the health of a pig before it can be eaten.

Every region has its own ways of making sausages that have been passed down in families for centuries; Catalonia alone has seventeen special varieties and more subvarieties. Now most sausages are mass-produced in factories, with curing plants where thousands of them hang from rafters like stalactites in musty caves. But there are still family-run artisan concerns that use traditional methods and do not compromise on quality, and some butchers still make their own sausages.

Ana Isabel Lozano, a young woman who lives in Madrid, wrote to me that her family continues to make chorizo and other sausages even though they no longer live in the country or keep a pig. They buy a whole pig from the butcher and have it cut up. They give away half the meat to friends, and the rest they eat throughout the year, some of it from the freezer. They prepare chorizo and other sausages the way her grandmother did and make enough so that they can have sausage to put into all kinds of dishes throughout the year. They make it *a ojo*, by eye, or according to taste. They grind the meat in a food processor with fat and flavorings until it acquires a homogenous reddish color. They fry a little and taste it to see if there is enough salt and *pimentón* (paprika) to preserve it, then stuff it into pig's intestines that they buy from specialty shops. At teatime, they cut semi-cured sausages into slices, cook them in the microwave, and eat them on bread.

Our chances of finding artisanal Spanish sausages are very small at the moment, but hopefully that will improve. In the meantime, there are acceptable mass-produced ones.

Here are the main types of sausages:

- *Chorizo* is a dry-cured sausage made simply with chopped pork and pork fat, seasoned with salt, garlic, and *pimentón,* which gives it a reddish color and distinctive flavor. There are hundreds of regional varieties—long or mini links, thin or thick, or in the shape of a horseshoe; with more or less fat, and more or less garlic; coarse or fine; with sweet *pimentón dulce* or hot *pimentón picante;* smoked or unsmoked; and with additional herbs or other seasonings. *Chorizo blanco* is made without *pimentón.* Hard, fully cured chorizos are ready to eat, sliced for an appetizer or incorporated into a dish. Soft, semi-cured chorizos must be cooked. They can be grilled or fried, whole or sliced. They can also be cooked in wine or hard cider (see page 152). Try this—it is very good.

- *Lomo embuchado* is pork loin that is trimmed of fat, salted and washed, and marinated in a paste of *pimentón,* garlic, oregano, and olive oil (sometimes with wine). Then it is encased in a large sausage skin and air-dried. When it is made from *ibérico de bellota* pork, it is exquisite.

- *Longaniza* is a thin sausage, from Navarre and Aragon, which is made from ground and marinated pork. It is fried or grilled.

- *Salchicha (botifarra* in Catalan*)* is fresh pork sausage seasoned only with salt and pepper. Catalonia's *botifarra dolça,* an unusual sweet pork sausage cured with sugar instead of salt and flavored with cinnamon and grated lemon zest, is eaten as dessert with fried or toasted sweet bread.

- *Salchichón* is like salami; there are many versions across Spain. The Catalan town Vic, north of Barcelona, once the venue of an important pig market, is the charcuterie capital of Spain; one of its specialties is *salchichón.* There is no *pimentón* in their sausage, only salt and pepper; one variety contains wine. A thin one called *fuet* is famous.

- *Morcilla* is blood sausage, made with pig's blood and usually also bread. In Burgos, León, and Valladolid, *morcilla* includes rice and onions. In Asturias, it is smoked and peppery. In Catalonia, *morcilla* is called *botifarra negra;* when it is made with rice and spices, it is called *botifarra negra d'arròs.* The Majorcan *botifarron,* which contains meat and is spiced with cinnamon, fennel seeds, and black pepper, is precooked. In Tolosa, in the Basque Country, the *morcilla* includes minced leeks. In León, there is a smoked blood sausage with bread crumbs and onions. Other versions include pine nuts and flavorings such as nutmeg, oregano, or *pimentón.* A sweet *morcilla dulce* of La Rioja is flavored with sugar, cinnamon, nutmeg, cloves, aniseed, and black pepper. A *morcilla* from Ronda in Málaga is flavored with cloves, oregano, cumin, coriander, and pepper.

- *Sobrasada,* a specialty of Majorca, is a sweetish, peppery, spreadable red paste in a sausage casing: a mix of pork, creamy pork fat, salt, and *pimentón.* There are some inferior commercial varieties, but the good ones are something to discover. The best is the *sobrasada de Mallorca de cerdo negro,* made from the native black pigs (not Ibérico) with large floppy ears that roam free and are fattened in their last three months on figs, legumes, and barley.

white beans with sausages and pig's foot and ear

{ *judiones de la granja de san ildefonso — castile and león* }

On our way to Maracaibo, the best restaurant in Segovia, Ana Lorente, of the wine magazine Opus Wine *(see page 582), took Alicia and me to visit the Palacio Real de la Granja de San Ildefonso, in the nearby hills, where the most famous beans of Spain, the* judiones de la granja, *are from. The palace is like a little Versailles. It was built by Philip V, grandson of Louis XIV of France, and it was the summer residence of the Bourbon kings in the eighteenth century. They came there with their court, cavalry, servants, and cooks. Today, in the tourist shops around the palace, they sell the large oval cream-colored beans, which have a delicious nutty flavor and a buttery texture. The name* de la granja *(from the farm) comes from the farm that was run by the monks from whom the king bought the site. The monks planted the beans, and the gardeners at the palace continued to grow them to feed the horses. I got this recipe from Maracaibo. The pig's ear and foot give the dish a rich gelatinous quality. It is worth making for a lot of people.*

SERVES 12

1 pig's ear

1 pig's foot (cut in half)

2 pounds *judiones de la granja* or other large white beans, soaked (see Soaking Beans, page 487)

½ pound pancetta or slab bacon, in one piece

1 large onion, chopped

4 garlic cloves, chopped

2 bay leaves

Salt

1 pound semi-cured chorizos

1 pound *morcillas* (Spanish blood sausage)

Extra virgin olive oil

Singe any remaining hairs, and scrub the pig's ear and foot under cold running water; then boil them in water for 20 minutes. Drain.

Drain the beans, put them in a large pot, and cover with water. Bring to a boil, removing any scum, then put in the pig's ear and foot, pancetta or bacon, onion, garlic, and bay leaves. Simmer, covered, over low heat, until tender, adding cold water from time to time to keep the beans covered. Once the beans have begun to soften, add some salt.

Judiones de la granja need 2½ to 3 hours to become very tender. (Other beans would need less time, so if you use other beans, boil the pig's ear and foot in the water for 1 to 1½ hours before adding them with some of their cooking water to the beans at the start of cooking.) Cook the chorizos in a pan of boiling water for 30 minutes. Boil the *morcillas* in another pan for 10 minutes—no longer, or they may burst. Drain the sausages and cut them into thick slices.

Add them to the beans to heat through. Serve with a drizzle of olive oil.

boiled meats and chickpeas with vegetables

{ *c o c i d o   m a d r i l e ñ o — m a d r i d* }

Every region has its own version of cocido. *It is the most basic one-dish meal of Spain, served as two or three courses—the broth, or* caldo, *being the first, with added vermicelli or rice, followed by the vegetables, sometimes served as a separate course, and the meats. Although it's likened to the French* pot-au-feu *and the Italian* bollito misto, *it is heavy with its own history and emotional connections. It is said to have evolved from the Jewish Sabbath dish* adafina *(see page 29), and that pork was added in the early period of the Inquisition. One of the best versions of* cocido *is the much-loved Catalan* escudella i carn d'olla, *which includes* pelotas—*large meatballs added to the broth. The Madrid* cocido, *made with the local chickpeas, is the most famous. If you search for* cocidito madrileño *on the Internet, you can find comedy acts about it and hear a popular song from the fifties that translates into something like this: "Don't talk to me about Roman banquets, about the menu at the Plaza in New York, or about pheasant, foie gras, or lobster . . . my sustenance and my pleasure are the touch that a loving woman gives to the* cocidito madrileño.*"*

When the Congressional Club in Washington published their first international cookbook in the early twentieth century, they included a recipe for cocido, *signed by the Spanish king Alfonso XIII. The recipe was from the head chef of the queen's kitchen, Candido Collar. In restaurants in Madrid,* cocido *is on the menu on Wednesdays. At home, a simple version can be cooked any day of the week (paella or* canelones *are eaten on Sundays), while a grand version is prepared for festive occasions. Leftovers are eaten for several days; typical dishes made with them are* croquetas *(page 166) and a hash called* ropa vieja *(literally, old clothes).*

Cocido sounds very complex—it is an event—but it is not difficult, just a matter of many things boiling at the same time in several large pots.

SERVES 6

1 pound beef, knuckle or shin

2 marrow bones (beef, veal, or ham)

½ pound slab bacon or fresh pork belly, in one piece

4 chicken thighs

Put the beef, marrow bones, bacon or pork belly, and chicken thighs into a very large pot, and add enough water to cover by about 1½ inches. Bring to a boil, then reduce the heat and simmer for a few minutes before removing the scum that has formed on the surface. Add the drained chickpeas and the onion and cook for 2 to 3 hours, until the meats are very tender, adding salt to taste after the first hour or so—you will need a good amount. Skim off the scum that comes to the surface occasionally and keep

1¾ cups dried chickpeas, soaked
(see Soaking Beans, page 487)

1 medium onion, stuck with
3 cloves

Salt

3 carrots

8 new potatoes, peeled

½ pound green beans (optional)

2 celery stalks

3 turnips, halved (optional)

½ pound green or Savoy cabbage,
cut into quarters

7 ounces semi-cured chorizo

7 ounces *morcilla* (Spanish blood
sausage), preferably the type
with onions

½ to ¾ cup vermicelli, broken into
small pieces

¼ cup olive oil

2 garlic cloves

OPTIONAL FOR SERVING

1 small baguette, cut into slices and
toasted (for the bone marrow)

Tomato Sauce (page 145)

Extra virgin olive oil

A choice of pickles, such as
gherkins, small onions, and
guindillas (mild green chiles
pickled in vinegar)

adding enough water to keep the meats well covered. You want plenty of broth to serve as soup at the end.

Half an hour before you are ready to serve, cook the vegetables—the carrots, potatoes, green beans, if using, celery, turnips, if using, and cabbage—in a large pot of boiling salted water for about 20 minutes, until tender. Drain, and pour the cooking water over the meat to add to the broth.

Meanwhile, cook the chorizo in simmering salted water for 10 minutes, then add the *morcilla* and simmer very gently for another 10 minutes (be careful—the *morcilla* will fall apart if you cook it too long); drain.

To serve the broth as the first course, strain at least 2 quarts of the broth—reserving the rest to keep the meats moist—into a large saucepan. Bring to a boil, add the broken vermicelli, season to taste, and cook for 5 minutes, or until the vermicelli is soft. Serve the broth and vermicelli.

Then reheat the chickpeas, meats, and sausages in the remaining broth, and transfer them to a deep platter. Cut the meats into pieces and the sausages into thick slices, and arrange on the platter.

Meanwhile, reheat the vegetables, except the cabbage, and arrange on another platter. Reheat the cabbage in the oil, with the whole garlic cloves to give it flavor, and add to the platter.

You can serve the vegetables as a course on their own before the meats and chickpeas, or lay everything out on the table and let people help themselves. If you like, serve the marrow from the bones on toasted slices of baguette. Put the warmed tomato sauce in a bowl, and put a bottle of extra virgin olive oil and plates of pickles on the table for people to help themselves.

DESSERTS AND PASTRIES

{ *postres* }

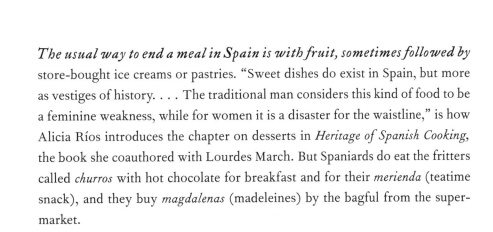

The usual way to end a meal in Spain is with fruit, sometimes followed by store-bought ice creams or pastries. "Sweet dishes do exist in Spain, but more as vestiges of history. . . . The traditional man considers this kind of food to be a feminine weakness, while for women it is a disaster for the waistline," is how Alicia Ríos introduces the chapter on desserts in *Heritage of Spanish Cooking*, the book she coauthored with Lourdes March. But Spaniards do eat the fritters called *churros* with hot chocolate for breakfast and for their *merienda* (teatime snack), and they buy *magdalenas* (madeleines) by the bagful from the supermarket.

A huge range of pastries, including deep-fried doughnuts, raisin and nut breads, and cakes based on almonds, hazelnuts, or walnuts are the "historic" festive foods that celebrate the landmarks of the Christian year—Christmas, the Epiphany, Easter, Ascension Day, the Feast of St. John the Baptist, St. Michael's Day, St. Martin's Day (and so on), and many feasts celebrating the Virgin Mary. Every village honors its own patron saint with parades and fireworks, reenactments of legends, and a special pastry. During the Festival of San Isidro, which lasts for three weeks in Madrid, with processions, music, dancing, and bullfights, bakeries and pastry shops go into a baking frenzy. The traditional pastries once attached to a special day are now made all year round. And many, known as convent sweets, are made by cloistered nuns.

Almond Cupcakes, page 574.

I have a sweet tooth, so I went looking for those sweet dishes that are a "feminine weakness." Every region has its specialties. In the north, which is dairy country, they make puddings, custards, rice puddings, and cheesecakes. The ubiquitous flan we know as crème caramel is everywhere in Spain. Some of the loveliest sweets are made with fruit. There are compotes, flans, tarts, cakes, fritters, and omelets. At an international dessert competition, you would be able to tell the Spanish entries, because they are almost always flavored with lemon peel and cinnamon.

flan

{ crème caramel }

Originally from France, flan spread from the north of Spain and became ubiquitous all over the country.

SERVES 6

FOR THE CARAMEL

½ cup sugar

¼ cup water

FOR THE CUSTARD

2½ cups whole milk

½ cup sugar

1 teaspoon vanilla extract

4 large eggs

For the caramel, put the sugar and water in a stainless-steel saucepan and heat over medium heat. When the syrup starts to bubble and color, swirl the pan to spread the caramel evenly, and then cook until it turns a deep amber, swirling the pan occasionally (watch it, as it can turn too dark very quickly, which would result in a bitter taste). Immediately pour the caramel into a mold that holds at least 4½ cups (it can be metal, porcelain, or Pyrex), turning and tilting the mold to coat the bottom and sides. You have to do this very fast, because the caramel hardens quickly.

For the custard, put the milk, sugar, and vanilla in a saucepan and slowly bring to a simmer, stirring to dissolve the sugar. Remove from the heat and let cool for 10 minutes.

Lightly beat the eggs with a fork or whisk in a large bowl. Gradually beat in the milk, starting with a ladleful, until well blended. Pour into the caramel-lined mold.

Place the mold in a large baking pan and pour in enough boiling water to come halfway up the sides of the mold (this water bath is called a bain-marie). Bake in a preheated 325°F oven for 1 hour, or until the custard has set. Take the mold out of the pan of water and let it cool, then chill in the refrigerator, covered with plastic wrap, for at least 3 hours, or overnight.

Just before you are ready to serve, turn out the flan: Run a pointed knife all around the edges of the mold, place a serving dish on top of the mold (there will be a lot of caramel sauce, so the dish should be deep enough to collect it), and quickly turn upside down. Lift off the mold.

orange flan

{ *flan de naranja — valencia and murcia* }

I love this refreshing, slightly tangy, creamy custard. It is just what you need to end a rich meal. You must use freshly squeezed orange juice or clementine juice, and it is best if you squeeze it yourself.

SERVES 8

2½ cups fresh orange or
    clementine juice

½ cup plus 2 tablespoons sugar

2 large eggs

10 large egg yolks

Heat the citrus juice with the sugar in a saucepan, stirring to dissolve the sugar. Remove from the heat.

Lightly beat the eggs and egg yolks with a fork in a large bowl. Gradually beat in the citrus juice.

Ladle the egg mixture into eight 6-ounce ramekins. Place them in a large shallow baking pan and pour in enough boiling water to come halfway up the sides of the ramekins (this water bath is called a bain-marie). Bake in a preheated 300°F oven for 30 minutes, or until the custard sets (it needs to be cooked at a low temperature to get a perfectly smooth texture without bubbles).

Take the ramekins out of the pan and let cool, then chill in the refrigerator, covered with plastic wrap.

burnt cream

{ *crema catalana — catalonia* }

This creamy custard with a crisp caramel topping is found everywhere in Spain as crema catalana, *but in Catalonia they call it* crema cremada, *which means "burnt cream," and* crema de Sant Josep, *because it is served to celebrate St. Joseph's Day on the nineteenth of March.*

SERVES 6 TO 8

¼ cup cornstarch

4½ cups whole milk

Peel of 1 lemon—removed
   in 1 or 2 long strips

1 cinnamon stick

8 large egg yolks

¾ cup superfine sugar,
   plus about ¼ to ½ cup for
   the topping

Dissolve the cornstarch in ¼ cup of the cold milk in a cup (the cornstarch helps prevent the egg yolks from curdling).

Heat the remaining 4¼ cups milk in a large saucepan with the lemon peel and cinnamon stick until it just begins to boil.

Meanwhile, beat the egg yolks and ¾ cup sugar to a pale cream in a bowl, then beat in the cornstarch mixture. Beat in a ladleful of the hot milk.

Remove the lemon peel and cinnamon stick from the hot milk, and pour in the egg yolk mixture, stirring vigorously. Cook over low heat, stirring continuously, until the mixture thickens. Pour into small *cassoles* or large ramekins. Let cool, then chill.

Just before serving, sprinkle the top of each custard with 2 to 3 teaspoons of sugar, and gently shake the ramekins to spread it evenly. Caramelize the sugar with a mini blowtorch until a dark amber.

crème brûlée with a spanish flavor

Some Spanish chefs now make crema catalana *like crème brûlée, flavored with lemon or orange peel and sometimes cinnamon instead of vanilla. I have to include it, as I just adore the contrast of the light cream (it is silkier than the traditional cream with cornstarch), with its slight orange flavor, and the crisp layer of caramel on the top. To make a good caramel topping, you will need a mini blowtorch. Putting the crème under the broiler to caramelize does not work well.*

SERVES 6

2¼ cups heavy cream

Grated zest of 1 orange

6 large egg yolks

⅓ cup superfine sugar, plus about
    6 tablespoons for the topping

Heat the cream with the orange zest in a saucepan over low heat until almost boiling.

Meanwhile, whisk the egg yolks with the ⅓ cup sugar in a bowl until pale and creamy. Very gradually pour in the hot cream, starting with half a ladleful, so that the eggs do not curdle, whisking constantly.

Ladle into 6 small ramekins so that they are not quite full to the brim. Place them in a large baking pan and pour in enough boiling water to come about halfway up the sides of the ramekins (this water bath is called a bain-marie). Bake in a preheated 300°F oven for about 25 minutes, or until the custards are set but still slightly wobbly in the middle. Remove the ramekins from the water bath and let them cool, then chill in the refrigerator for at least 4 hours, or overnight, covered with plastic wrap.

To serve, sprinkle about 1½ teaspoons of sugar over the top of each chilled crème and very gently shake the ramekin to spread it evenly. Caramelize with a mini blowtorch until a thin layer of amber caramel is formed. Then sprinkle another 1½ teaspoons sugar over the caramel, gently shake the ramekins, and caramelize again to form a thick, crunchy, dark amber caramel. Do not let it get too dark, or the caramel will taste bitter.

almond soup

{ sopa de almendra—extremadura and castile }

In Spain, this is eaten as a first course on Christmas Eve. Although it is unusual to have a soup as a dessert, that is how I like it best. Most recipes use store-bought almond paste, but it is very good and easy to use ground almonds.

SERVES 4

2¼ cups whole milk

½ cup sugar, or more to taste

Grated zest of 1 lemon

1 cup (about 4 ounces) ground almonds

2 slices brioche, crusts removed, cut into 1-inch pieces and lightly toasted

Bring the milk to a boil with the sugar and lemon zest in a medium saucepan. Add the almonds and stir until the sugar is entirely dissolved. Simmer for a minute or two. Remove from the heat and let it rest until it cools and the ground almonds absorb the milk and the soup thickens.

Serve at room temperature in little bowls, over a few pieces of toasted brioche.

VARIATIONS

• Add a pinch of saffron threads to the milk along with the lemon zest.

• Serve sprinkled with lightly toasted pine nuts.

• Sprinkle with cinnamon before serving.

rice pudding

{ *arroz con leche — navarre* }

Rice pudding is popular all over Spain, especially in the north, which is dairy country. It is always flavored with a cinnamon stick and a strip of lemon peel. Most versions are made quite thick. Some are baked in the oven, others made on the stovetop. In Asturias, they sometimes add butter and caramelize the top. My favorite is this very creamy version from Navarre, with the good amount of liquid left at the end thickened with egg yolk. Be prepared for a long cooking time, up to an hour or so; risotto rice will take the longest. Serve it cold, at room temperature, or warm.

SERVES 4 TO 6

6½ cups whole milk

1 cinnamon stick

Peel of ½ lemon—removed
   in 1 or 2 long strips

½ cup risotto rice, such as
   Arborio or Carnaroli

½ cup sugar, or more to taste

4 large egg yolks

Cinnamon for sprinkling
   (optional)

Bring the milk to a boil with the cinnamon stick and lemon peel in a large saucepan. Add the rice and cook gently over very low heat for 45 minutes to 1 hour, stirring occasionally with a wooden spoon so that the rice does not stick at the bottom (especially at the start), until it is very soft.

Stir in the sugar and cook for another 10 to 15 minutes. Remove the lemon peel and cinnamon stick. There should still be a good amount of liquid left.

Beat the egg yolks lightly in a small bowl. Beat in a few tablespoonfuls of the milk and rice so the yolks won't curdle, then pour into the pan, stirring vigorously for seconds only, until the liquid becomes creamy. Do not let boil, or the yolks will curdle.

Pour into a serving dish or little bowls. Serve warm, chilled, or at room temperature, with a light dusting of cinnamon if you like.

VARIATION

Omit the cinnamon. Just before serving, sprinkle the top of the pudding evenly with 3 tablespoons of sugar, and caramelize with a mini blowtorch.

egg and sugar syrup flan

{ tocino de cielo — andalusia }

This flan made with egg yolks originated in monasteries in the wine-producing areas of Jerez de la Frontera and Montilla-Moriles, where, in the late nineteenth century, the bodegas *(wineries) used egg whites to clarify their wines and then gave the leftover yolks to the local convents. The name means "heavenly bacon." It is not as sweet as those you will find in pastry shops in Andalusia, but it is still very sweet, so it should be served in small portions.*

SERVES 8 TO 10

FOR THE CARAMEL

⅓ cup sugar

3 tablespoons water

FOR THE FLAN

2½ cups sugar

2¼ cups water

4 large eggs

10 large egg yolks

For the caramel, put the sugar and water in a stainless-steel saucepan and heat over medium heat. When the syrup starts to bubble and color, swirl the pan to spread the caramel evenly, and then cook until it turns a deep amber, swirling the pan (watch, as it can turn too dark very quickly, which would result in a bitter taste). Immediately pour the caramel into a mold that holds at least 4½ cups (it can be metal, porcelain, or Pyrex), turning and tilting the mold to coat the bottom and sides. You have to do this quickly, because the caramel hardens very fast. Let it cool.

For the flan, make a sugar syrup: put the water and sugar in a saucepan and bring to a simmer, stirring until the sugar has dissolved. Remove from the heat and let cool until warm.

Lightly beat the eggs and yolks with a fork or whisk in a large bowl, then gradually beat in the warm sugar syrup until well blended. Pour into the caramel-coated mold.

Place the mold in a large baking pan and pour in boiling water to come halfway up the sides of the mold. Bake in a preheated 325°F oven for 1¼ to 1½ hours, until set. Take the mold out of the pan, let it cool, then chill in the refrigerator overnight, covered with plastic wrap.

Just before you are ready to serve, turn out the *tocino de cielo*: run a pointed knife all around the edges of the mold, place a serving dish on top of the mold (there will be a lot of caramel sauce, so the dish should be deep enough to collect it), and quickly turn upside down. Lift off the mold.

nougat ice cream

{ *helado de turrón — valencia* }

Turrón, *a kind of nougat confection made of almonds and honey, is produced in Alicante and the neighboring little hill town of Jijona. (It was once sold in the street by Morisco vendors—see page 20.) For this ice cream, you must use the softer* turrón *from Jijona, rather than the harder one of Alicante. At lunch at a men's gastronomic society in the Basque Country, I was offered an instant version—vanilla ice cream topped with crumbled* turrón *and a dash of rum. It was delicious. This recipe is also extremely easy.*

SERVES 6

2½ cups heavy cream

¼ cup superfine sugar

10 ounces soft *turrón* from Jijona

Beat the cream with an electric mixer in a large bowl until it forms stiff peaks (be careful that it does not turn to butter), adding sugar when it begins to stiffen. Crumble the *turrón* with a fork, then beat it into the cream until you have a homogenous cream.

To give the ice cream a dome shape, line a bowl with plastic wrap, pour the cream in, and cover with more plastic wrap. Put in the freezer for at least 6 hours, or overnight.

To serve, remove the top sheet of plastic wrap, turn out onto a serving plate, and peel off the other piece of plastic wrap.

raisin and sweet wine ice cream

{ helado de pasas y vino dulce—andalusia }

This ice cream is fabulous. Because it is a custard, it does not need an ice cream machine or regular beating by hand to prevent crystallization. The base is a rich vanilla ice cream, which is frozen until it is almost firm, and then raisins and the sweet, dark Pedro Ximénez sherry or Málaga Moscatel wine are mixed in.

SERVES 10 OR MORE

¾ cup black raisins

½ cup sweet Pedro Ximénez sherry
    or Málaga Moscatel, plus extra
    for drizzling

2½ cups heavy cream

1½ cups whole milk

1 small cinnamon stick

1 teaspoon vanilla extract

8 large egg yolks

½ cup superfine sugar

Soak the raisins in the sherry or wine in a small bowl.

Meanwhile, heat the cream and milk with the cinnamon stick and vanilla in a large saucepan until almost boiling. Remove from the heat and let stand for 30 minutes to infuse. Remove the cinnamon stick and reheat the milk mixture.

With an electric mixer, beat the egg yolks with the sugar in a medium bowl to a pale, thick cream. Gradually add a ladleful of the hot milk, beating constantly, then pour this into the saucepan, stirring vigorously preferably with a heatproof spatula. Continue to stir constantly over low heat until the mixture thickens enough to coat the spoon. Do not let it boil, or it will curdle. (If it does curdle, you can save the ice cream by beating it with the electric mixer until smooth.)

Pour the custard into a serving bowl and let it cool. Cover with plastic wrap and freeze for 3 to 3½ hours, or until it is firm but not yet hard.

Take the ice cream out of the freezer and thoroughly mix in the raisins, with their sherry or wine. You must do this before the ice cream becomes too hard to mix, but it must be firm enough so that the raisins remain suspended evenly and do not sink to the bottom. If you do not mix thoroughly, there will be little white patches in the ice cream (but that too is lovely). Return to the freezer and freeze until it firms.

>>>

Take the ice cream out of the freezer 10 to 15 minutes before serving, then cut into slices. If it proves difficult to dislodge the pieces from the bottom, dip the bowl in a bowl of hot water for a few seconds.

Pass the bottle of Pedro Ximénez or sweet wine so everyone can drizzle a little over their ice cream.

VARIATION

To shape the ice cream into a dome that is easy to turn out, line another bowl with plastic wrap, pour the semifrozen mixture with the raisins in, cover with another piece of plastic wrap, and freeze overnight. To serve, remove the plastic wrap from the top, then turn out the ice cream onto a serving platter and remove the other piece of plastic wrap.

almond ice cream

{ *helado de almendra — majorca* }

People visit the island of Majorca in January and February for the joy of seeing the almond trees in blossom; a magnificent pink and white spectacle that fills the air with a bittersweet perfume. The trees provide Spain with many of the almonds that are used in the country's famously long repertoire of almond pastries and confections. This ice cream is a specialty of the island and is often served with its famous ensaimada *(see page 111). It is really a water ice, but the almond milk gives it a creamy texture. Adding a few drops of almond extract will give a more pronounced flavor, but be careful not to add too much, as the taste will be overpowering.*

SERVES 8

½ pound blanched
    whole almonds

1½ cups sugar

4½ cups water

3 drops of almond extract
    (optional)

Grind the almonds as fine as possible in a food processor.

Bring the sugar and water to a boil in a saucepan, stirring to dissolve the sugar. Stir in the ground almonds and the almond extract, if using, and bring to a boil again. Remove from the heat and let cool. Then pour into ice cube trays. Cover the trays with plastic wrap and let freeze overnight in the freezer.

Turn out the almond ice cubes (if they are rock-hard, let stand for a few minutes before processing them), drop them into a food processor, in two or three batches, and process to a very fine, creamy slush. (You can serve the slush right away, but crushing the ice cubes in the blender makes such a noise that you may not want to do it when people are there.)

Pour the slush into a serving bowl or individual bowls and return to the freezer, covered with plastic wrap, until ready to serve. If it has frozen hard when you take the ice cream out of the freezer, wait 10 minutes before serving.

VARIATION

To shape the ice cream into a dome that is easy to unmold, line a bowl with plastic wrap, pour in the processed mixture, and cover with another piece of wrap. Freeze overnight. To serve, remove the plastic wrap on the top, then turn out onto a serving platter and remove the other piece.

bread pudding

{ *pudín de pan — andalusia* }

British and Irish wine merchants began setting up business in fortified wines around Jerez de la Frontera in the province of Cádiz in the late eighteenth century. Their names are still on sherry labels. A Spanish version of English bread pudding is still part of the traditional cooking repertoire of an Andalusian elite. The pudding can be served hot or cold, and with or without a crisp caramel topping. Do also try the Ibizan pudding in the variation. It too is quick and easy and delightful comfort food.

SERVES 6

Eight ½-inch-thick slices white bread, brioche, or challah, crusts removed (about 3½ inches square)

⅓ to ½ cup golden raisins

¾ cup blanched whole almonds, coarsely chopped

4 large eggs

5 tablespoons superfine sugar, plus 2 to 3 tablespoons for the optional topping

Grated zest of 1 lemon

1¼ cups whole milk

1¼ cups heavy cream

¼ cup Pedro Ximénez sherry or sweet Málaga wine

Butter a baking dish that will hold the bread in two layers. Arrange the slices in the dish, cutting to fit if necessary, and sprinkle the raisins and almonds between the layers.

Beat the eggs lightly with the 5 tablespoons sugar and lemon zest in a bowl, then beat in the milk, cream, and sweet wine, and pour over the bread. Bake in a preheated 350°F oven for 40 minutes, until golden and risen and lightly set. Serve hot or chilled. If you like, just before serving, sprinkle the top of the chilled pudding evenly with the optional sugar and caramelize with a mini blowtorch.

VARIATION

Greixonera de Ibiza, a pudding made with leftover *ensaimadas*, a specialty of the Balearic Islands made with a kind of puff pastry with lard (croissants are a perfect substitute), is served in all the restaurants on the island of Ibiza. *Greixonera* is the local name for the clay dish in which it is baked and served. Tear 4 small croissants (mine weighed 6 ounces) into pieces, and spread them in a round buttered baking dish, about 10 inches in diameter. Bring 2¼ cups milk and ¾ cup sugar to a boil in a saucepan, stirring to dissolve the sugar. Lightly beat 4 large eggs in a bowl with a fork, add the grated zest of ½ lemon, and lightly beat in the milk. Pour over the croissants and bake in a preheated 400°F oven for 30 minutes, or until set. This is good hot or at room temperature, dusted with cinnamon.

cheese pudding

{greixonera de brossat—balearic islands}

*This very simple and light cheese pudding is from the island of Minorca (*greixonera *is the local name for the clay baking dish it is made in). Brossat *is a fresh cream cheese made with cow's milk (the English brought dairy cows when they occupied the island); fresh ricotta is a good substitute.*

*Chef Miguel Montez Martínez, who cooked in the Balearic Islands for many years during the tourist season, gave me this recipe and also the one for the *greixonera de Ibiza *on page 519. Now back in his home village of Frailes in Andalusia, he is called upon to cook giant stews and paellas for hundreds of people during festivals.*

SERVES 6 TO 8

1 pound fresh ricotta

½ to ⅔ cup superfine sugar

Grated zest of 1 lemon

5 large eggs

Blend the ricotta, sugar, lemon zest, and eggs in a food processor until creamy. Pour into a buttered baking dish about 10 inches in diameter. Bake in a preheated 350°F oven for about 45 minutes, or until it feels firm.

Let cool to room temperature and serve in the dish in which it is baked.

VARIATIONS

- Serve the cheese pudding with fragrant honey. The honey they produce in neighboring Majorca is orange blossom.

- Dust the top with confectioners' sugar and cinnamon.

- For *flaó*, a specialty of Ibiza, a similar cheese mix is the filling for a tart. It is flavored with 3 or 4 mint leaves and 2 to 3 tablespoons of an anise-flavored spirit (you can use pastis, ouzo, or arak). Serve it dusted with confectioners' sugar or a drizzle of honey.

cheese and honey

In the old days, when shepherds traveled far with their sheep and got together during Lent, they toasted bread on the embers of a fire and topped it with slices of aged
hard cheese fried in a little pork fat or olive oil until softened. Sometimes they poured
honey over it, and then they called this *quesomiel,* which means "honey-cheese." Try it
after dinner. Cheese and honey are still sold together by vendors who go around the
mountain villages.

Mel y mató is part of the Catalan, high Aragonese, and Basque shepherds' culture. It is
a popular dessert, a combination of the fresh bland creamy goat cheese of the Pyrenees
called *mató,* served with the local honey (*mel* in Catalan). You can use fresh ricotta; eat it
with a fragrant runny honey. In the Pyrenees, the honey might be chestnut honey.

fried cream

{ leche frita—northern spain }

The leche frita, *literally "fried milk," sold in pastry shops and in supermarkets is made with cornstarch, but I prefer the texture of this homey version that uses flour as the thickener. These creamy pastries can be eaten hot or cold—and can be reheated. When they are straight out of the oil, they are crunchy outside and very creamy inside.*

MAKES 16 PASTRIES

1 cup all-purpose flour

3 cups whole milk

½ cup superfine sugar

Grated zest of 1 lemon or 1 orange

2 large egg yolks

Fine bread crumbs or matzo meal

1 large egg

Sunflower oil for frying

About 4 tablespoons
    confectioners' sugar
    for sprinkling

1 teaspoon cinnamon for sprinkling

Put the flour in a bowl and gradually add 1 cup of the milk, beating with an electric mixer to prevent lumps.

Bring the remaining 2 cups milk, the sugar, and the grated zest to a boil in a medium saucepan. Add the flour-and-milk mixture and cook, stirring constantly, until you have a thick cream. (If lumps form, you can get rid of them by beating with a hand mixer right in the pan.) Continue to cook over low heat, stirring often, for 10 minutes. Add the egg yolks and stir vigorously for a few seconds more; do not let the mixture boil, or the yolks will curdle. Remove from the heat.

Grease a square or rectangular dish with oil. Pour in the milk mixture; it should be about ¾ to 1 inch thick. Let cool, then chill, covered with plastic wrap, for at least 2 hours, until set. The cream should be very firm.

Cover a plate with a layer of bread crumbs or matzo meal. Beat the egg lightly in a soup plate. Turn the cream out onto a large flat oiled platter or work surface, and cut it into 16 squares or rectangles. Lift each piece very carefully and turn it gently in the egg and then in the bread crumbs or matzo meal, so that it is well covered. Heat about 1 inch of oil in a large deep skillet until a piece of bread sizzles when it is dropped in but does not brown too quickly. Deep-fry the pastries in batches until golden brown, turning once. Lift the pastries out and drain on paper towels.

Serve hot or chilled, dusted with confectioners' sugar and cinnamon.

oranges in sweet málaga wine

{ naranjas al vino de málaga—andalusia }

This is a Málaga recipe using the region's own sweet fortified wine and the marmalade made with the bitter oranges of Seville. One of the most extraordinary sights in Seville in January and February is the orange trees bursting with fruit that line the streets.

SERVES 6

8 sweet oranges

1 cup coarse-cut Seville orange marmalade

1 cup sweet Málaga Moscatel or Pedro Ximénez wine

Peel the oranges, removing the white pith entirely. Cut them into ⅓-inch-thick slices and then into pieces, and arrange them in a wide serving dish.

Heat the marmalade in a saucepan with the wine, over low heat until it liquefies, stirring to mix them. Let cool, then pour over the oranges. Let stand for at least an hour before serving at room temperature.

VARIATIONS

- Instead of using marmalade, Murcians dissolve a few tablespoons of honey in the wine and stir in ½ teaspoon cinnamon.

- A Valencian version mixes orange and grapefruit slices with sweet wine or Grand Marnier and is topped with a drizzle of honey and a sprinkling of chopped crystallized lemon or orange peel. Just before serving, sprinkle on toasted sliced almonds.

quince paste

{ dulce de membrillo — mediterranean spain }

I adore everything made with quinces. This soft, creamy, fragrant paste is another thing entirely from the industrial dulce de membrillo, *the firm, dark wine-red, usually overly sweet block that is traditionally served with cheese. It makes a marvelous dessert accompanied by a mild fresh cheese such as ricotta. It keeps for weeks in the refrigerator.*

SERVES 8 OR MORE

4 quinces (about 2¾ pounds)

¾ cup sugar

Wash the quinces and scrub them if they still have the down on their skins. Put them in a baking dish and bake in a preheated 300°F oven for about 2 hours, until soft. Let cool slightly.

When the quinces are cool enough to handle, peel them, cut them in half, and cut out the cores with a sharp pointed knife. Cut into pieces, put in a food processor with the sugar, and blend to a soft, creamy paste.

Pour the quince paste into a wide nonstick saucepan and cook gently for about 30 minutes, stirring with a wooden spoon, until the paste thickens and turns pink. Keep scraping up and stirring in the paste that caramelizes at the bottom of the pan—it will give the paste a stronger color and enhance the flavor.

Pour the paste into a shallow dish, let cool, and chill in the refrigerator.

Serve it with a spoon accompanied by a soft fresh mild cheese such as ricotta.

peaches macerated in wine

{ melocotones al vino — aragon }

The people of Aragon have been growing a special type of sweet yellow-fleshed peach, melocotones de Calanda, *since medieval times. The ones we get in our supermarkets may not be as good, but macerating them in sweet wine as they do in Aragon will give you a delightful dessert.*

SERVES 4

5 large ripe but firm peaches

About 1 cup sweet white or red
    wine, such as Moscatel

To peel the peaches, put them in a bowl, pour boiling water over them, and leave them for a few minutes. Peel them, cut each into quarters, and put into a serving bowl or into four wineglasses. Pour the wine over them (there should be enough to cover them) and leave to macerate for at least 2 to 3 hours, covered with plastic wrap, in the refrigerator.

VARIATION

You can also make this with a dry wine mixed with 2 to 3 tablespoons sugar. Macerate the peaches in a bowl, and add the peel of 1 lemon, cut into strips, and 1 cinnamon stick with the wine.

fresh fruits stewed in wine

{ compota de frutas—navarre }

Navarre is known for its fruits. This compote goes well with the rice pudding on page 511. The fruits turn a beautiful purple red, and their flavor is rich and delicious.

SERVES 6

1 bottle (750 ml) of Rioja or other dry red wine

½ cup sugar plus 2 tablespoons

Peel of 1 lemon—removed in 2 or 3 strips

1 cinnamon stick

3 unripe pears

3 apples

3 peaches

½ cup blanched whole almonds or pine nuts, lightly toasted (optional)

Put the wine, sugar, lemon peel, and cinnamon stick in a large saucepan.

Peel the pears and apples. Cut them through the stem end into quarters, and then into eighths. Cut out the cores and drop them into the saucepan. Bring to a boil, then reduce the heat and simmer for 25 to 30 minutes, until they are just tender. (The cooking time depends on the degree of ripeness of the fruit, and takes longer in the syrup than it would in water.)

Meanwhile, to peel the peaches: drop them into a pan of boiling water for less than a minute; then drain. The skin will come off easily. Cut them into quarters and remove the pits. Add the peaches to the pan when the apples and pears are almost tender, and simmer for a few minutes more, until all the fruits are soft.

Serve the compote at room temperature or cold, sprinkled, if you like, with the lightly toasted almonds or pine nuts.

honey

{ miel }

Beekeeping is an important agricultural pursuit in many parts of Spain. Only about seventy percent is in the hands of professionals and semi-professionals. The majority of professionals are migratory beekeepers, who "follow the bloom" and carry their hives around from fruit groves to hills and mountain forests.

A research group identified thirty-six Spanish honeys. The most fragrant are those that come from bees that feed on the nectars of orange and lemon blossoms (my personal favorites); on rosemary, thyme, lavender, and heathers. There are also chestnut, blackberry, sage, alfalfa, clover, avocado, buckwheat, and eucalyptus honeys. The most common, called *miliflores* (a thousand flowers), are blends from different wildflowers. The most important single-source varieties come from sunflowers. Honeydew "honey" comes from the sweet sticky secretions of aphids and other insects that feed on plant sap. Some honeys have been awarded a *Denominación de Origen* (DO).

dried fruit compote with custard

{ zurracapote con crema pastelera vasca

—basque country and navarre }

Zurracapote, *also called* marmelada de frutos secos, *is a New Year's Eve special in the Basque Country and Navarre. It is great served with this Basque custard, which can be flavored with rum or Cognac; I love it with rum. The recipe is from Carlos Posadas Gomez, a young Basque chef at the Santo Mauro restaurant in Madrid.* Zurracapote *was not on his sensational tasting menu—it came out of his childhood memories when I asked him about traditional Basque dishes.*

SERVES 6

½ pound pitted prunes

½ pound dried peaches or apricots

1 cup Rioja or other dry red wine

3 cups water

⅓ to ½ cup sugar

FOR THE CUSTARD

2¼ cups whole milk

6 large egg yolks

¾ cup superfine sugar

3 tablespoons all-purpose flour

3 to 4 tablespoons rum

Toasted almonds, pine nuts,
    and/or walnuts (optional)

Soak the dried fruits in the wine and water to cover for 2 hours.

Put the soaked fruits, with their soaking liquid, and the sugar in a saucepan and simmer, covered, over low heat, for 20 to 30 minutes, until the fruits are very soft; uncover at the end to reduce the liquid. Let cool, then chill.

Meanwhile, for the custard, bring the milk to a boil in a heavy-bottomed saucepan; remove from the heat. With an electric mixer, beat the egg yolks with the sugar in a bowl to a light, pale cream, then beat in the flour. Gradually pour in the hot milk, a little at a time, beating vigorously until well blended. Then pour the mixture back into the pan. Stir constantly with a wooden spoon or a heatproof spatula over very low heat for about 10 minutes, until the custard thickens. If any lumps form at the start, they will disappear as you work the cream vigorously. Add the rum and mix well. Pour into a bowl and refrigerate, covered with plastic wrap.

Serve chilled or at room temperature in little bowls, the cream at the bottom and the fruits on top with their wine sauce. There will be a lot of custard. Pour some in a bowl for people to help themselves to more. If you like, also pass around a bowl of lightly toasted almonds, pine nuts, or walnuts, or a mix of the three.

pumpkin dessert

{ arnadí de calabaza — valencia }

This is an Easter sweet from the Costa del Azahar (the Orange Blossom Coast) of Valencia, made with sweet orange-fleshed pumpkin. It looks like a pyramid spiked with almonds and has a soft moist texture and an unusual flavor. If you love pumpkin, you will love arnadí, *but it will depend on the taste of the pumpkin. You can use other types of squash. Andresito (see page 534) had lots of huge pumpkins growing in his garden. This is his recipe. He sometimes mixes some boiled and mashed sweet potatoes (* boniato*) with the pumpkin.*

SERVES 8 TO 10

A 2-pound slice of orange-fleshed pumpkin (or 1½ pounds cleaned pumpkin or butternut squash, without peel, seeds, or stringy bits)

About 1¼ cups sugar, or to taste

1¼ cups ground almonds

2 large eggs, lightly beaten

Grated zest of 1 lemon

1 teaspoon cinnamon

½ cup blanched whole almonds

2 to 3 tablespoons confectioners' sugar

To prepare the pumpkin, if necessary, scrape away the seeds or stringy bits. The rind is thin but very hard. It is more easily removed if you first cut the slices into large chunks, then lay the chunks on the cutting board, and cut it away, pressing down with force with a large heavy knife.

Cut the pumpkin flesh into 1¼- to 1½-inch pieces. Put them in a large saucepan with 1 cup water and cook, tightly covered, so that they steam over low heat for 15 to 20 minutes, until the flesh is soft. (Check to make sure that all the water has not evaporated before it is soft, and add a little if necessary.) Drain and mash with a potato masher.

Return to the pan and cook, uncovered, over medium heat for about 5 minutes, until most of the liquid has evaporated. Remove from the heat and stir in the sugar (the amount depends on the sweetness of the pumpkin), then continue to cook, stirring often and making sure that the puree does not burn, until nearly all the moisture has evaporated. This can take 15 to 25 minutes.

Add the ground almonds, eggs, lemon zest, and cinnamon and mix very well. Shape the pumpkin and almond paste into a pyramid in a shallow baking dish. Stick the blanched almonds half in on their pointed ends in lines down the sides. Dust the whole thing with confectioners' sugar. Bake in a preheated 375°F oven for 50 minutes. Let it cool, and serve at room temperature.

ANDRESITO'S BANQUET
IN ALICANTE

We were twenty around the table, wearing straw hats with fresh flowers pinned on.
We ate for hours, laughing and dancing in between courses—conviviality and
alegría de vivir (joy of living) are the spirit of Mediterranean Spain. We started
with marinated anchovies; tiny sweet tomatoes; green olives; *pan con tomate*
(page 154); *cocas* (like pizzas) with tomatoes, peppers, and eggplant (page 209);
and broad beans and artichokes cooked with pancetta. The main course was
chicken and baby lamb chops cooked over embers on the outside grill, and we
finished with fruit and pumpkin fritters. A giant pumpkin filled with honey and
brandy was baked in the outside bread oven. Nearly all the ingredients for the
meal came from the estate.

Our host, Andresito—Andrés Bertomeu—a handsome stocky man with a goa-
tee, had cooked all the dishes with his wife. The rest of us were the houseguests

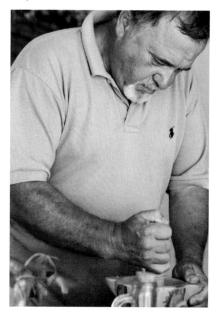

of Alicia and her mother, Josefa, in their
neighboring *casitas* (country houses) by
the sea. Andresito was born on Alicia's
grandfather's estate in Benissa, Alicante,
province of Valencia. His grandparents
and parents were peasant retainers. Alicia's grandmother died giving birth to
Josefa, and Andresito's grandmother,
who had just lost her own baby, breast-
fed her.

Andresito's father planted fruit trees,
tended grapevines, and grew vegetables
on the estate. As a young boy, Andresito
boarded with the Franciscans, who
offered poor children a free education,

but he ran away from the convent after only two years, and that was the only schooling he had. At twelve, he worked in the fields with his father, and as a teenager, he worked in construction, building houses for tourists. After army service, he started his own construction company, with builders, painters, electricians, plumbers, and eventually a secretary, who spoke several languages. Now he is a contractor and multimillionaire with an estate of his own—a grand house with a central courtyard and a swimming pool, vegetable gardens, and every kind of fruit tree imaginable. There are geese, ducks, and turkeys running around. He is an example of the many Spaniards who have done well from the tourist boom. Everybody who owned even the tiniest bit of land by the sea became a millionaire.

Andresito now lets his wife, Maria (her father was the village butcher), run the business while he paints, cooks, collects old recipes, and writes nostalgically about what life was like before tourism in the mountain interior and by the sea. Villages were small. Church bells rang to announce births, deaths, and weddings. People traveled by mule and cart. There was no electricity; they kept food cool in wells. Andresito's grandmother never bought meat or fish, and she cooked chicken only once or twice a year. When a woman gave birth, the villagers boiled a hen and gave the woman the broth, and the men ate the meat. People ate wild rabbits, hares, and wild ducks. They caught small birds in nets and hunted game. Bullets were expensive, so they took used ones out of the game they shot and reused them. They went out at night with oil lamps to find snails in the vineyard.

They ate rice every day. The paella of the interior was made with wild things—rabbit, duck, snails, and water rat—and vegetables in season. Andresito's father kept a pig or two. They cooked the meat, cut into pieces, slowly in its own fat, and kept it in jars. Once in a while, they would bring out a small piece from a jar and divide it among them; his mother always said she did not want any. His father had a milk brother (who was breast-fed by his mother) who kept goats and a few cows. The villagers came to him with bottles and clay jars to be filled with milk. Laborers walked to the fields at sunrise and returned home at sunset. They took their food with them and carried their wine in goatskin bags. Bread was the mainstay, and they used it instead of cutlery to pick up other morsels of food.

On our way from Alicia's to Andresito's estate, we passed through small mountain towns and villages, many of them walled, with the names of Berber tribes and the characteristic prefixes of "Ben" and "Al." There had been a large population of Moriscos (see page 20). When they left en masse in the early seventeenth century, Alicante was repopulated mainly with people from Majorca and Ibiza, who took over their land and houses. The descendants of Moriscos who remained can be recognized today by the names, which came from the jobs—such as Ferrer (iron worker), Fuster (carpenter), Zapatero (shoemaker)—that their forebears took when they converted. The festival of Moros y Cristianos that is celebrated throughout the whole of Spain at different times of the year is, in Alicante, an extraordinary event that takes place in April, with a procession and a dramatic reenactment of battles between Moors and Christians in medieval costume. The area continued to have connections with North Africa, and it shows. When the French were in Algeria, the people of Denia on the Costa Blanca went there to work in the vineyards. More recently, Moroccans have been coming to Alicante to work in construction.

Tourism has not entirely destroyed the old life. The young, like Andresito's sons, eat pizza and fast foods, but in the villages in the interior, they still cook traditional foods. Many families now live in small towns and keep a *casita* (rural house) with a small plot where they have fruit trees and grow vegetables and vines.

apple cream

{ crema de manzana — asturias }

This is a simple dessert that Asturians make with the Reineta apples the region is awash with. It is another sweet that they like to caramelize.

SERVES 4 TO 6

2 pounds Golden Delicious
 or other apples

Juice of ½ lemon

1 to 1¼ cups sugar

5 large egg yolks

⅔ cup heavy or light cream

Peel, core, and quarter the apples, dropping them into a bowl of water with the lemon juice to prevent them from discoloring.

Drain the apples, put them in a saucepan with about ½ cup water, cover, and cook over low heat for about 15 to 20 minutes, until they are very soft.

Mash the apples with a fork or a potato masher. Stir in ⅔ cup of the sugar and cook, uncovered, stirring, over medium-high heat for about 5 to 10 minutes to allow most of the liquid to evaporate.

Beat the egg yolks with the cream in a bowl. Add to the apple puree and cook, stirring vigorously, over low heat for 1 to 2 minutes, until the mixture thickens slightly. Pour into a serving bowl. Let cool, then cover with plastic wrap and chill in the refrigerator.

Just before serving, dust the top of the apple cream with the remaining sugar, and caramelize it with a mini blowtorch. When it cools, it will form a thin, crisp sheet of caramel, with some brown patches.

sweet omelet with rum

{ tortilla al ron—asturias }

This flambéed omelet is delicious and so simple. If you have a mini blowtorch, you can caramelize the top, but it is good without that. Rum was produced in the Caribbean from molasses of the sugarcane introduced there by Spain. A Catalan who emigrated to Cuba, Don Facundo Bacardi Masso, developed a way of refining the rough local product and set up a distillery in 1862. In the late nineteenth century, rum was popularized in northern Spain by the returning emigrants who had grown rich in the Cuban tobacco trade. They, like the newly rich industrial bourgeoisie, adopted French haute cuisine, and so flambéed dishes were in fashion.

SERVES 2 TO 4

5 large eggs

5 tablespoons superfine sugar

4 slices white sandwich bread
   (about ½ inch thick), crusts
   removed

¾ cup whole milk

2 tablespoons unsalted butter

2 tablespoons confectioners' or
   superfine sugar for the topping
   (optional)

2 tablespoons rum

Beat the eggs lightly with the sugar in a medium bowl. Soak the bread in the milk, mashing it with your hand, then add it to the egg mixture, leaving behind any excess milk. Beat well with a fork, or with an electric mixer if you want a very smooth texture.

Preheat the broiler. Heat the butter in a 10-inch skillet. When it begins to sizzle, pour in the egg mixture and cook for 2 to 3 minutes over low heat, until the bottom sets. Then place the pan under the broiler for a minute or so, until the top has set. Slip the omelet onto a serving plate.

If you like, sprinkle it with the 2 tablespoons sugar and caramelize it using a mini blowtorch.

Heat the rum in a ladle or in a small metal cup. Hold a lighted match over the edge, and when you see flames, pour the flaming rum over the omelet. Serve hot.

reineta apples

Pepe Iglesias (see page 328) says there are seventeen varieties of indigenous apples in Asturias, ranging from sweet and semi-sweet to tart and slightly bitter, many of them used for making cider. Their Reineta apples, which seem to be one of the oldest apples around, are used for baking and cooking. According to the British National Fruit Collection, there are at least fifteen different types of Reinettes, most of them in France (the French say there are dozens), but none in Britain and possibly none in America—although there is one type in Canada. I remember eating baked Reinettes and pastries made with them when I was at school in Paris. The smaller children played a game with their fists and sang, *"Pomme de Reinette et pomme d'Api, tapis, tapis rouge; pomme de Reinette et pomme d'Api, tapis, tapis gris."* The Spanish baking Reineta is juicy with a good sweet flavor. When I asked people in Asturias and elsewhere in northern Spain what apples we could substitute, they all said Golden Delicious—how ordinary can you get!

apple omelet

{ *tortilla de manzana — asturias* }

Golden Delicious apples are a good substitute for the Asturian Reinetas. You can cook the apples in advance, but the omelet must be cooked at the last minute.

SERVES 4

4 tablespoons (½ stick) unsalted
    butter

1 tablespoon olive oil

3 Golden Delicious apples,
    peeled, cored, and cut into
    8 wedges each

3 tablespoons superfine sugar

4 large eggs

Melt the butter with the olive oil in a large skillet. Add the apple wedges and sauté over medium-low heat, turning them once, for 15 to 20 minutes, until they are soft and lightly browned on both sides. Sprinkle them evenly with 1 tablespoon of the sugar as soon as they go in, then sprinkle again with the remaining 2 tablespoons sugar when you turn them over.

Beat the eggs lightly in a bowl. Lift the apples out of the pan, leaving the butter sauce in the pan, and gently fold the apples into the eggs.

A few minutes before serving, preheat the broiler. Heat the pan until the butter mixture sizzles. Pour in the egg and apple mixture and cook over medium-low heat very briefly, about 2 minutes, until the eggs set at the bottom. Put the pan under the broiler just to set the top of the omelet; it should still be a little creamy inside. Serve hot.

VARIATIONS

- Add 2 to 3 tablespoons Calvados or Asturian apple brandy to the apples toward the end of sautéing. This is lovely.

- Sprinkle ½ teaspoon cinnamon over the apples when you add them to the butter and oil.

crepes filled with apple puree

{ *frisuelos de manzana — asturias and galicia* }

Thin pancakes like French crepes are a specialty of Asturias, as well as of Galicia, where they are called filloas. *They are commonly served folded and dusted with confectioners' sugar and cinnamon, or drizzled with honey or liqueur, or topped with whipped cream. This version, stuffed with apple puree, is absolutely delicious and elegant to serve. Reineta apples are used in Asturias, but Golden Delicious can be substituted. Calvados is equivalent to the apple brandy made in the region. I add rather a lot to the filling — you can use less. Another equally wonderful version of the same crepes stuffed with custard follows on page 545.*

The crepes can be made in advance, even a day before, and kept, covered with plastic wrap, in the refrigerator.

MAKES ABOUT TWENTY-FIVE 7½-INCH CREPES

FOR THE CREPES

2 cups all-purpose flour

2½ cups whole milk

1¼ cups water

2 large eggs, lightly beaten

1 teaspoon salt

1 tablespoon olive or sunflower oil

1 tablespoon Calvados or brandy

>>>

For the crepes, put the flour in a large bowl. Gradually add the milk and water, beating vigorously with an electric mixer. Add the eggs, salt, oil, and Calvados or brandy and beat until the batter is smooth and free of lumps. Cover with plastic wrap and let rest for 1 hour.

For the filling, peel, core, and quarter the apples, dropping them in a bowl of water with lemon juice as you go, to prevent them from discoloring.

Drain the apples, put them in a saucepan with 4 to 5 tablespoons water, cover tightly, and cook over very low heat for 15 to 20 minutes, until the apples fall apart. Then cook, uncovered, until much of the liquid has evaporated. Mash the apples with a potato masher, then add the sugar and Calvados or brandy and stir until the sugar has dissolved.

To cook the crepes, heat a nonstick skillet with a bottom diameter of about 7½ inches over medium heat, and grease with oil, using a folded paper towel. Stir the batter well and pour about 2 tablespoonfuls into the skillet, tilting the pan quickly until its entire bottom surface is covered; the crepe will be thin. When it releases from the pan and

>>>

FOR THE FILLING

2 pounds Golden Delicious apples

Juice of ½ lemon

6 tablespoons sugar

¼ cup Calvados or other apple
brandy, or to taste

TO FINISH

Sunflower or vegetable oil

¼ cup Calvados or other apple
brandy

¼ cup superfine sugar

the bottom is lightly browned, turn it over with a large spatula (or with your fingers) and cook for a moment only on the other side, until it releases from the pan. Transfer to a plate. Continue this process until all the batter is used up, rubbing the pan with oil each time and stacking the crepes.

To fill the crepes, put a slightly heaped tablespoon of filling in a line across the bottom of each crepe and roll it up. Place the stuffed crepes, seam side down, in two large buttered baking dishes. Finish by sprinkling a little Calvados and a little sugar over each.

Heat through in a preheated 400°F oven for 10 to 20 minutes. I like them when they are very slightly crisp.

VARIATION

For large crepes, use a 9-inch nonstick skillet and pour in about ¼ cup batter for each one.

crepes filled with custard

{ *frisuelos con crema pastelera—*
asturias and galicia }

Make the crepes as on page 543 and fill them with this custard instead of the apple puree. My favorite flavor for the custard is rum, but see the variations for other options.

MAKES SIXTEEN 7½-INCH CREPES

¾ cup plus 2 tablespoons sugar

5 large egg yolks

3 tablespoons all-purpose flour

2¼ cups whole milk

3 tablespoons rum

16 crepes (page 543)

2 to 3 tablespoons superfine sugar to finish

For the custard, with an electric mixer, beat the sugar with the egg yolks in a large bowl to a smooth, pale cream. Beat in the flour.

Bring the milk to a boil in a heavy-bottomed saucepan. Pour into the egg mixture, a little at a time, beating constantly until well blended. Pour this back into the pan and stir constantly over low heat with a wooden spoon or a heatproof spatula until the cream thickens. If lumps form, they will disappear as you work the cream vigorously. Beat in the rum, remove from the heat, and let the cream cool before filling the crepes.

Fill the crepes and arrange in a buttered baking dish as directed on page 544. Sprinkle a little sugar over each and heat in a preheated 400°F oven for 15 minutes.

VARIATIONS

- Omit the rum. Add 1 teaspoon of vanilla extract to the milk when you bring it to a boil.

- Omit the rum. Add the grated zest of ½ orange to the milk when you bring it to a boil.

apple and ladyfinger pudding

{dulce de manzana con bizcocho—asturias}

There is a big tradition of making sponge cake in Spain, and it is often eaten dipped or soaked in sweet wine. Here layers of ladyfingers soaked in sweet wine alternate with layers of apple puree. You can use sweet hard cider instead of wine.

SERVES 6 TO 8

2 pounds Golden Delicious or
 other sweet apples

Juice of ½ lemon

About 2¼ cups sweet white wine,
 such as Moscatel

¼ cup sugar or to taste

A package of ladyfingers (*boudoirs;*
 about 6 ounces)

Peel, quarter, and core the apples, putting them as you go into a large bowl of water acidulated with the lemon juice to prevent them from discoloring.

Drain the apples, put them in a saucepan with ½ cup of the white wine, and cook, covered, over low heat for 15 to 20 minutes, until the apples are soft. Mash the apples with a potato masher, add sugar to taste, and continue to cook, uncovered, stirring often, over medium to high heat for 15 to 20 minutes, until all the liquid has evaporated (the bottom of the pan should look dry). Let cool.

Pour the remaining wine into a wide soup plate. Line a 9- to 10-inch round mold or cake pan with plastic wrap so that it overhangs generously all the way around the edges. Spread half the apple puree in the bottom.

Moisten the ladyfingers in the sweet wine, a few at a time, leaving them in for seconds only (if they absorb too much wine, they will become soggy and fall apart). Arrange a layer of ladyfingers on top of the apple puree, trimming them to fit. Cover with the remaining apple puree and a second layer of ladyfingers dampened in sweet wine.

Cover with the overhanging plastic wrap and another piece of wrap. Chill in the refrigerator for at least 3 hours, or overnight.

To serve, remove the plastic wrap from the top, turn the pudding out onto a platter, and remove the second piece of plastic wrap.

almond cake

{ *tarta de santiago — galicia* }

This is a splendid cake. I have eaten almond cakes in other parts of Spain, but this one is special. Pilgrims and tourists who visit the great Cathedral of Santiago de Compostela in Galicia, where the relics of the apostle Saint James are believed to be buried, see the cake in the windows of every pastry shop and restaurant. It is usually marked with the shape of the cross of the Order of Santiago. I have watched the cake being made in many sizes, big and small, thin and thick, over a pastry tart base at a bakery called Capri in Pontevedra. This deliciously moist and fragrant homey version is without a base. There is sometimes a little cinnamon added, but I find that masks the delicate flavor of orange and almonds and prefer it without it.

When I suggested to a man associated with the tourist office in Galicia that the tarta *was a Jewish Passover cake, I was dragged to a television studio to tell it to all. The hosts thought the idea made sense. The Galician city of Coruña is on the Jewish tourist route, because of its synagogue and old Jewish quarter. Jews from Andalusia, who fled from the Berber Almohads' attempts to convert them in the twelfth and thirteenth centuries, came to Galicia, where they planted grapevines and made wine.*

The cake is normally made in a wide cake or tart pan and so comes out low, but it is equally good as a thicker cake.

SERVES 10

½ pound (1¾ cups) blanched whole almonds

6 large eggs, separated

1¼ cups superfine sugar

Grated zest of 1 orange

Grated zest of 1 lemon

4 drops almond extract

Confectioners' sugar for dusting

Finely grind the almonds in a food processor.

With an electric mixer, beat the egg yolks with the sugar to a smooth pale cream. Beat in the zests and almond extract. Add the ground almonds and mix very well.

With clean beaters, beat the egg whites in a large bowl until stiff peaks form. Fold them into the egg and almond mixture (the mixture is thick, so you will need to turn it over quite a bit into the egg whites).

Grease an 11-inch springform pan, preferably nonstick, with butter and dust it with flour. Pour in the cake batter, and bake in a preheated 350°F oven for 40 minutes, or until it feels firm to the touch. Let cool before turning out.

>>>

Just before serving, dust the top of the cake with confectioners' sugar. Or, if you like, cut a St. James cross out of paper. Place it in the middle of the cake, and dust the cake with confectioners' sugar, then remove the paper.

VARIATIONS

- Add 1 teaspoon cinnamon to the egg yolk and almond mixture.

- Majorca has a similar almond cake called *gató d'ametla*, which is flavored with the grated zest of 1 lemon, 1 teaspoon cinnamon, and sometimes a few drops of vanilla extract.

- In Navarre, the cake is covered with apricot jam.

puff pastry filled with almond custard

{ *costrada con crema franchipán—navarre and basque country* }

This is a Spanish take on the French gâteau Basque, *a flaky-crust pie filled with custard. It is both easier and more delicious, with its combination of crisp, light puff pastry and luscious* crema franchipán—*almond custard. The flavoring for the filling can be vanilla or grated orange zest, but my favorite is rum. I used a store-bought puff pastry sheet weighing 13 ounces and measuring about 13¾ by 8¾ inches. The pastries are best eaten warm. You must try them. Another name for them is* milhojas caliente *(hot millefeuilles).*

MAKES 8 PASTRIES

FOR THE CUSTARD FILLING

¾ cup superfine sugar

5 large egg yolks

¼ cup all-purpose flour

2¼ cups whole milk

¾ cup blanched whole almonds,
  coarsely ground in a food
  processor

3 tablespoons rum

FOR THE PASTRY

13-ounce sheet of puff pastry
  (measuring 13¾ × 8¾ inches)

1 egg yolk, beaten with 1 teaspoon
  water, for egg wash

Confectioners' sugar for dusting
  (optional)

For the custard, with an electric mixer, beat the sugar with the 5 egg yolks in a large bowl to a smooth, very pale cream. Beat in the flour until thoroughly mixed.

Bring the milk to a boil in a heavy-bottomed saucepan. Very gradually pour into the egg mixture, beating constantly until well blended. Pour this back into the pan and stir constantly over low heat with a wooden spoon until the cream thickens. If lumps form at the start, they will disappear as you work the cream vigorously. Remove from the heat and stir in the almonds and rum.

Unroll the pastry and cut it into 8 rectangles. Place them on a lightly oiled sheet of foil on a baking sheet, and brush the tops with the egg wash. Bake in a preheated 400°F oven for 20 to 25 minutes, until the pastries have puffed up and are golden brown.

When the pastries have cooled a little, cut each horizontally in half with a serrated knife and fill each one with about ⅓ cup of the custard. (If you make the pastries in advance, you can heat them through briefly in a low oven before serving.) If you like, dust with confectioners' sugar.

VARIATIONS

- Omit the rum and add 1 teaspoon vanilla extract to the milk.

- Omit the rum and stir the grated zest of 1 orange into the custard.

pastry rolls filled with walnuts

{ *casadielles — asturias* }

In Asturias, I stayed with the New Yorker *journalist Jane Kramer in Jaime Rodríguez and his wife Marichu's farmhouse in Llenín, near Cangas de Onis. We had met Jaime in the street and he had invited us to stay. It is a little mountain paradise with a sweeping view of the Picos de Europa mountains. Once upon a time, cows slept on the ground floor in the winter and Jaime went to school with the donkey cart that took their milk to town. Now the farmhouse has been transformed into a beautiful and welcoming* casa rural, *a family guesthouse, called Heredad de la Cueste. We sat beside the fire as Jaime told us how life had been in the Asturian mountains not long ago. Rural tourism is now the basis of the economy. Marichu works as a guide in the Picos de Europa national park. Her mother cooks traditional food, using local produce, for the guests. We had* casadielles, *fried pastry rolls filled with walnuts, for breakfast.*

At home, I tried several different pastry doughs. This one with olive oil worked best. It can be rolled out easily to make a thin crisp crust for the soft, moist, aromatic walnut filling. In Asturias, it is usual to fry the pastries, but I find they are better baked.

MAKES 12 CASADIELLES

FOR THE DOUGH

½ cup olive oil

½ cup warm water

½ teaspoon superfine sugar

About 2⅓ cups all-purpose flour

For the dough, mix the oil, water, and sugar in a bowl, beating vigorously with a fork. Then gradually work in enough flour to get a soft, smooth, malleable dough that is not sticky: begin by stirring in the flour with the fork, then work it in with your hands and knead briefly. You can use the dough right away or keep it wrapped in plastic wrap, at room temperature, not in the refrigerator, until you are ready to use it.

For the filling, grind the walnuts a little coarsely with the sugar and butter in a food processor. Add the liqueur and blend very briefly.

Divide the dough into 2 pieces, to make rolling easier. Roll each piece out into a large rectangle about ⅛ inch thick; do not flour the surface or the rolling pin—the dough is oily and will not stick. Cut each sheet of dough into 6 rectangles about 3½ by 5 inches.

FOR THE FILLING

1¾ cups walnuts

½ cup superfine sugar

2 tablespoons unsalted butter

3 to 4 tablespoons anise-flavored
   liqueur (you can use ouzo,
   pastis, or arak)

1 egg yolk, beaten with 1 teaspoon
   water, for egg wash

Confectioners' sugar for dusting

Take a lump of filling the size of a walnut, shape it into a loose sausage, and lay it along the edge of a long side of a dough rectangle. Using your little finger or a cotton swab, paint a thin line of the egg wash along the other remaining 3 sides (this is to make the dough stick better), then roll up like a cigar and pinch the ends firmly together. Repeat with the remaining dough rectangles and filling, and arrange the *casadielles* on an oiled baking sheet. Brush them with the egg wash, and bake in a preheated 300°F oven for about 30 minutes, or until slightly golden. Let cool before moving the pastries to a serving plate and dusting them with confectioners' sugar.

walnut cake with brandy

{ tarta de nuez con brandy — asturias }

The lower slopes of the Asturian mountains are covered with walnut and chestnut trees, and walnut cakes are common there. This version, with a syrup poured over, is sensational; it has a marvelous texture and a pure walnut taste, with a touch of brandy. Make sure the walnuts you use are good and fresh.

SERVES 8 TO 10

1 pound (4 cups) walnuts

4 large eggs

1 cup superfine sugar

6 tablespoons (¾ stick) unsalted
   butter, melted and slightly
   cooled

3 tablespoons Spanish brandy
   or Cognac

FOR THE SYRUP

½ cup sugar

1 cup water

1 tablespoon Spanish brandy
   or Cognac

Grind the walnuts in a food processor, not too fine.

With an electric mixer, beat the eggs with the sugar in a large bowl to a pale thick cream. Add the melted butter and the brandy, and beat well. Fold in the walnuts.

Pour the batter into a buttered and floured 11-inch springform cake pan. Bake in a preheated 350°F oven for 45 minutes, or until the cake feels firm.

Meanwhile, for the syrup, put the sugar and the water in a saucepan and boil, stirring until the sugar has dissolved, for about 5 minutes. Add the brandy.

As soon as the cake comes out of the oven, pour the syrup all over the surface. Let stand for at least 1 hour, still in the pan, before serving.

walnut cake

{ *pastel de nuez — asturias* }

I have tried an Asturian walnut cake made only with egg whites, beaten until stiff, but I prefer this one with yolks too because it is moist. These measures give a small, thin cake. I make it in a 9-inch round cake pan and it comes out ¾ inch thick. It is quick and easy to make.

SERVES 4 TO 6

1 cup walnuts

2 large eggs

2 large egg yolks

⅔ cup superfine sugar

Grated zest of 1 orange

Confectioners' sugar for dusting

Grind the walnuts in a food processor, not too fine.

With an electric mixer, beat the eggs and egg yolks with the sugar in a large bowl to a pale, thick cream. Add the grated orange zest and the walnuts, mixing well.

Pour the batter into a greased and floured 9-inch round cake pan. Bake in a preheated 400°F oven for 40 minutes, or until firm. Let cool before removing the cake from the pan. Serve dusted with confectioners' sugar.

rice cake

{ *pastel de arroz — navarre* }

A rice pudding or cake is always homey. But this one is elegant enough to serve at a dinner party. Navarre is famous for its candied fruits. Try to get a variety.

SERVES 8 OR MORE

⅔ cup short-grain (round) rice

6¼ cups milk

3 large eggs, separated

¾ cup sugar

3 tablespoons unsalted butter

⅓ cup raisins

½ to ¾ cup candied fruit, cut into small pieces

Cook the rice in the milk in a large saucepan over very low heat for 45 minutes, or until the rice is very "bloated" but there is still quite a bit of liquid left. Remove from the heat.

Lightly beat the egg yolks. Add the sugar, butter, egg yolks, raisins, and candied fruit to the rice.

Beat the egg whites until stiff peaks form, and fold them into the rice mixture.

Pour the mixture into a buttered mold and bake in a preheated 350°F oven for 1 hour. Cover with foil for the first 30 minutes so that the top does not become too brown.

chocolate cakes and desserts

According to legend, the Spaniards first encountered chocolate as a drink in Mexico in 1519, when the conquistador Hernando Cortés met the Aztec ruler Montezuma, and it was Cortés who introduced the drink to the Spanish court. Chocolate was known only as a drink in Spain until the nineteenth century, and it was always something that only the rich could afford. It was also associated with the Church, because monks in the Americas sent beans to their monasteries back home. The clergy encouraged its use during Lent, believing the drink to have restorative and medicinal properties; in the mid-seventeenth century, Pope Alexander VII declared that liquids, including chocolate, did not break the fast.

The first Spanish cocoa factory was in Astorga in León, and there is now a chocolate museum there. The Maragato muleteers (see page 94) transported the powder all over Spain. A Basque trading company, the Real Compañía Guipuzcoana de Caracas, held the monopoly on the Venezuelan cocoa trade in the eighteenth century. Cocoa beans arrived in the Basque ports and were then shipped to cities all over Europe. One of these was the French Basque city of Bayonne, where Spanish and Portuguese Converso families started a chocolate industry, the first in France. That is where the Basque and Catalan bourgeoisies first got the solid block chocolate they used to make cakes and other desserts.

Chocolate cakes and desserts are part of the bourgeois cuisines of Spain that developed in the late nineteenth and early twentieth centuries in the industrialized north. This was the period when Spain gradually lost its colonies, and many Spaniards who had become rich in the colonies came back to settle in large numbers in Asturias, the Basque Country, and Catalonia, and in ports like Cádiz and Santander. They built fabulous houses, painted pink, orange, mauve, blue, and green, that were inspired by the colonial houses in Mexico, and they invested in the emerging industries. The newly rich local bourgeoisies and these *indianos* employed cooks and demanded from them a refined, mostly French style of cooking and baking.

chocolate and almond cake

{ pastel de chocolate y almendras — catalonia }

This is a moist cake that is good served with whipped cream. The recipe comes from a little book that Carolina Zendrera, my Spanish publisher, gave me, entitled Recetas Tradicionales: La Ermitaña de la Cocina Burguesa del Siglo XX *(*Traditional Recipes: The Hermit of the Bourgeois Kitchen of the Twentieth Century*), published by Zendrera Zariquiey in 1999. The recipes are those of Agueda Bienzobas, who cooked for Carolina Zendrera's grandparents and parents in Catalonia for fifty years. Agueda was born in a village in Navarre in 1907 and went to work in the Martí-Codolars' kitchen in Barcelona as a young girl. The Martí-Codolars, Zendrera's grandparents, were an illustrious family involved in shipping. On their farm, they kept rare animals, including an elephant that was donated to Barcelona Zoo. What Agueda learned from the family cook, and what became her repertoire gathered over the years, which her husband wrote down, is a distinctive mix of Spanish and French haute cuisine. A family friend of the Martí-Codolars called her "the hermit" because she spent so much time alone in the kitchen.*

SERVES 10

5 ounces bittersweet chocolate

3 tablespoons water

11⅔ tablespoons (1⅓ sticks) unsalted butter, cut into pieces

4 large eggs, separated

½ cup superfine sugar

1 cup (4 ounces) ground almonds

1 teaspoon baking powder

¼ cup rum

FOR THE OPTIONAL TOPPING

2 ounces bittersweet chocolate

¼ cup sugar

2 tablespoons unsalted butter

Break up the chocolate and heat with the water in a double boiler or in a Pyrex bowl placed on top of a pan of gently boiling water until almost melted. Add the butter and let them both melt. Remove from the heat.

With a fork, beat the egg yolks, sugar, ground almonds, baking powder, and rum in a large bowl until well mixed. Add the melted chocolate and butter and mix well.

With an electric mixer, beat the egg whites in a large bowl until stiff peaks form. Fold them into the chocolate mixture.

Pour the batter into a greased and floured 9-inch springform cake pan, preferably nonstick. Bake in a preheated 325°F oven for about 55 minutes, until firm. Let cool, then turn out the cake.

For the optional topping, melt the chocolate with 2 tablespoons of water in a double boiler or a Pyrex bowl placed on top of a pan of gently boiling water. Add the sugar and butter, let the butter melt, and mix well.

Spread the topping over the cake.

chocolate and walnut cake

{ *tarta de chocolate con nueces — asturias* }

There were no chocolate cakes in Spain until they first appeared in Catalonia and the Basque Country in the late nineteenth century. This cake is extremely rich, so serve it in small portions. It has two layers—a firm and nutty cake with a light and creamy topping.

SERVES 12

1½ cups (7 ounces) walnuts

4 ounces bittersweet chocolate, broken into pieces

6 large eggs, separated

¼ cup Spanish brandy or Cognac

¾ cup sugar

FOR THE TOPPING

5 ounces bittersweet chocolate

2 tablespoons rum

1¼ cups heavy cream

Coarsely chop the walnuts in a food processor (some will be finely ground in the process).

Melt the chocolate in a double boiler or in a heatproof bowl placed over a pan of gently boiling water. Remove from the heat.

Beat the egg yolks with the brandy and sugar in a large bowl. Using a fork, mix in the chocolate, then fold in the walnuts.

With an electric mixer, beat the egg whites in a large bowl until they form stiff peaks. Fold them into the egg yolk, chocolate, and walnut mixture.

Pour the batter into a greased and floured 10-inch springform cake pan. Bake in a preheated 350°F oven for about 45 minutes, or until firm. Let cool completely in the cake pan.

For the topping, melt the chocolate in a double boiler or in a heatproof bowl placed on top of a smaller pan of gently boiling water, add the rum, and let cool slightly.

Beat the cream in a medium bowl until it forms stiff peaks. Fold in the melted chocolate.

Remove the cake from the pan when it has cooled completely, and spread the topping evenly over it.

chestnut and chocolate truffle cake

{ *trufas de castañas y chocolate—catalonia* }

This cake has a smooth trufflelike texture. It is very rich, so serve only small portions.

SERVES 12 OR MORE

½ pound fresh peeled (see page 130), defrosted frozen, or vacuum-packed chestnuts

1 cup whole milk

1 teaspoon vanilla extract

½ pound bittersweet chocolate, chopped

10 ounces (2¼ sticks) unsalted butter

½ cup superfine sugar

4 large eggs, separated

3 tablespoons Spanish brandy or Cognac

Boil the chestnuts in the milk in a saucepan over low heat for about 10 minutes, until they are soft. Remove from the heat and stir in the vanilla.

Melt the chocolate and butter in a double boiler or in a heatproof bowl placed over a pan of gently boiling water.

Blend the chestnuts and milk to a puree in a food processor. Add the sugar, the melted chocolate and butter, the egg yolks, and brandy and blend until smooth and homogenous.

With an electric mixer, beat the egg whites in a large bowl until they form stiff peaks. Fold in the chocolate and chestnut mixture. Line a 9-inch springform pan with foil and butter the foil, then pour in the batter. Bake in a preheated 325°F oven for 30 to 35 minutes, until just set but still slightly wobbly in the center. The cake will firm as it cools.

Note: For a rougher texture, mash the chestnuts with a potato masher and mix them thoroughly by hand with the other ingredients.

chestnut and chocolate flan

{ flan de castañas y chocolate — andalusia }

Chestnut trees and forests are found all over Spain, and chestnuts were a staple of the peasantry before the arrival of potatoes and corn from the Americas. In the time of the Bourbons, cooks in the homes of the aristocracy made marrons glacés *and chestnut puddings. This one is splendid.*

SERVES 10

FOR THE CARAMEL

½ cup sugar

3 tablespoons water

FOR THE FLAN

7 ounces fresh peeled (see page 130), defrosted frozen, or vacuum-packed chestnuts

4½ cups whole milk

1 cup sugar

1 teaspoon vanilla extract

5 ounces bittersweet chocolate, chopped

6 tablespoons Spanish brandy or Cognac

7 large eggs

For the caramel, put the sugar and water in a saucepan over medium heat. When the syrup begins to bubble and color, swirl the pan to spread the caramel evenly, then cook until it turns a deep amber, swirling the pan occasionally (watch it, as it can turn too dark very quickly). Immediately pour the caramel into a heatproof mold about 9 to 10 inches in diameter and at least 2½ inches high, moving and tilting the mold to coat the bottom and sides well. Do this very fast, because the caramel hardens quickly.

Cook the chestnuts in 2¼ cups of the milk in a pan over low heat for 10 minutes, until they soften. Drain and discard the milk. Put the remaining 2¼ cups milk, the sugar, and the vanilla in a pan and slowly bring to a simmer, stirring to dissolve the sugar. Remove from the heat.

Grind the chocolate as fine as possible in a food processor. Add the drained chestnuts and blend to a soft paste. Gradually add the warm milk and then the brandy.

Beat the eggs with a fork in a large bowl, then beat in the chestnut mixture. Pour into the caramel-coated mold. Put the mold in a large shallow baking pan and pour in enough boiling water to come about halfway up the sides of the mold. Bake in a preheated 325°F oven for 1 to 1¼ hours, or until the flan feels firm. Let cool, then chill in the refrigerator for 2 to 3 hours, covered with plastic wrap.

Just before serving, run a pointed knife around the edges of the flan, place a serving dish on top of the mold (the dish should be deep enough to collect the caramel sauce), and turn upside down. Lift off the mold.

almond cream

{ bienmesabe — canary islands }

Bien me sabé means "tastes good to me." This is a thick, dense almond cream—more like a soft paste—that is served to accompany pastries and ice cream and is spread on toast. It keeps for several days in the refrigerator. Use blanched almonds, and grind them finely, or buy them already ground.

This is very rich, so it's best in small amounts. Serve it with sponge cake or ladyfingers, dipped, if you like, in sweet wine—it can be the Canary Islands' Malvasia or a sweet Málaga wine—or in rum.

SERVES 8

1¼ cups sugar

1 cup water

1 cinnamon stick

2⅓ cups (8 ounces) finely ground
    almonds

2 drops almond extract (optional)

Grated zest of ½ lemon

9 large egg yolks

Malvasia or sweet Málaga wine
    for dipping (optional)

Sponge cake or ladyfingers
    for serving

Bring the sugar and water to a boil with the cinnamon stick in a saucepan, stirring with a wooden spoon until the sugar has dissolved. Remove the cinnamon stick, add the ground almonds, and cook, stirring constantly, over low heat for about 7 minutes, until the mixture thickens. Stir in the almond extract, if using, and the lemon zest, and take off the heat (be very careful not to add too much almond extract, or it will overpower the sweet cream and give a nasty taste). Let cool a little.

Beat the egg yolks vigorously, then stir them into the almond paste. Put the pan back over low heat and stir constantly until you see one or two bubbles come up to the surface, then take off the heat.

Serve the cream at room temperature. Pour a little sweet wine into people's glasses and pass around sponge cake or ladyfingers to dip in at the same time.

DULCES DE CONVENTO

{ pastries and confectionery from the hidden world of cloistered nuns }

I rented a room at El Monasterio de Santa María del Socorro, the convent of a Conceptionist Franciscan order of nuns on the Calle de Bustos Tavera, in the old quarter of Seville. From the outside, it looks like an ordinary house on a narrow street. Inside, the decor is Mudéjar—blue and white tiles line the walls and there is an interior patio. A picture of the Virgin Mary looked down on my bed. I thought of the room I'd shared with my Slovene Italian nanny, Maria, in Egypt. She had been a novice Catholic nun but was convinced by her family that it would be better for her to find work in Egypt, as many Slovene women did at the time, and to send money home. A crucifix, images of the Virgin, and icons of saints hung on our walls, and there was a branch from the "Virgin's Tree" in Matariya, under which Joseph and Mary are believed to have rested.

I had hoped to see the nuns at Santa Maria del Socorro making pastries, not realizing that it would not be possible, because they are cloistered. I only saw Sister Inmaculada Romero, who is in charge of the rented rooms, and an older, very cheerful nun who passed the pastries through a hatch on a wooden *torno* (lazy Susan). The monastery was founded in 1522 by Doña Juana Ayala for women of the nobility who wished to live a contemplative life. Today the nuns spend their time in prayer and silent contemplation and make pastries to support themselves and maintain the convent. Seville has more monasteries and churches than any city in Spain and is famous for its convent pastries. Santa María del Socorro has the widest range—a list of sixty is pinned near the hatch where the orders are given and the pastries appear. Sister Inmaculada says their secret ingredient is *alegría*—joy. They have published their own cookbook (see page 575).

The only time the closed world of Seville's cloistered nuns interacts with the outside world is when the nuns come out to sell Christmas specialties in the great patio of the baroque Palacio Arzobispal on the eighth of December, the feast of the Immaculate Conception, *la Purisima, la Inmaculada*. In the old days, nuns came to Seville from all over Spain. Now they are most likely to be from Latin America, Africa, and India. The new nuns learn to make the old traditional pastries whose secrets have been handed down for centuries.

Some of the convents have their own specialties. At the Monasterio de Santa Paula, an Indian nun sold me jasmine and orange blossom jams, tomato marmalade, chestnut cream, chiles in syrup, and quince paste. San Leandro is famous for its *yemas*—egg yolks cooked in sugar syrup. I adore them, but they are so rich I could only eat one. The nun who served me remained unseen behind the door but answered my questions. She said that by ancient tradition, convents had always made pastries to thank their noble protectors and sponsors. After the civil war, they started selling them to support themselves. A nun in a convent in Toledo once told me that convent pastries were Moorish because long ago, when mosques and synagogues were first converted into churches and monasteries, aristocratic nuns came to the convents with their Morisco maids of Muslim descent.

Around the corner from El Socorro, the Convento de Santa Inés also sells pastries. It contains the remains of its founder, Doña María Coronel, a Sevillian noblewoman who disfigured herself by throwing boiling oil on her face to escape the persistent amorous advances of Pedro I the Cruel (see page 27).

Here are some of the traditional pastries that figure on the menus of convents: *mazapanes, yemas, piñonates, mantecados, mostachones, empanadillas, pestiños, roscos, rosquillas, bizcochos, cocos, hojaldres, milhojas, bollo maimón, glorias, turrones, marquesitas,* and *torrijas*. And here are some with colorful names: *huesos de santos* (saints' bones), *orejas de fraile* (friar's ears), *tetas de novicias* (novice nuns' breasts), *suspiros de monja* (nun's sighs), *borrachuelos* (drunkards), *tocinos de cielo* (heavenly bacon), and *polvorones* (*dust cakes*). Some convents, inspired by the creativity of modern innovative chefs (they can see them on the Internet), have added pastries of their own invention to the traditional ones.

toledan marzipan

{ *mazapán de toledo — castile - la mancha* }

Toledo, the old capital of Visigothic Spain and the capital of La Mancha, is also the world capital of marzipan. It is known as the "City of Three Cultures" because Christians, Muslims, and Jews coexisted there for centuries. I was there with María Rosa Menocal, a medieval scholar who wrote The Ornament of the World: How Muslims, Jews, and Christians Created a Culture of Tolerance in Medieval Spain. *She made me aware of the Mudéjar architecture and design in churches, palaces, and synagogues. A specialty of Toledo, the inlaying of gold, copper, and silver thread into metal, is called* damasquino, *referring to the city of Damascus in Syria.*

Rosa Tovar (see page 285), who sent me this recipe, says there are two ways of making marzipan in Spain. This one, which is used in the two Castiles and in Andalusia, is her favorite. For the other one, common in Catalonia, a sugar syrup is boiled down, then ground almonds are added with a little orange blossom water and the paste is cooked and stirred until it comes away from the sides of the pan. My relatives who came from Aleppo in Syria made marzipan in the manner of Toledo, and those who came from Istanbul made it in the Catalan way.

Marzipan keeps for weeks. You can get your children to roll it into shapes. In Toledo, they shape the marzipan into figuritas, *such as fish, snails, shells,* huesos de santos *(saints' bones).*

MAKES ABOUT 26 BALLS

2 cups (7 ounces) ground almonds

1½ cups confectioners' sugar

3 drops almond extract

2 to 3 tablespoons water

FOR THE GLAZE

1 egg white

1 tablespoon confectioners' sugar

Blend the almonds and sugar in a food processor. Add the almond extract (be careful not to add more, or the taste will be overpowering). Add the water a tablespoonful at a time and blend to a thick paste (I needed only 2 tablespoons); the oil from the almonds will hold the paste together. Blend to a smooth, soft paste.

Shape the paste into balls about 1¼ inches in diameter by rolling lumps between the palms of your hands until they are firm and compact. Lay them on a baking sheet and let stand in a cool, dry place for 12 to 24 hours.

For the glaze, beat the egg white with an electric mixer until firm, then add the sugar and beat until thick and shiny. Brush the marzipan balls with the glaze and put them under a preheated broiler for 1 minute, until the tops are lightly browned, or bake in a preheated 400°F oven for 2 minutes. Let cool.

almond cupcakes

{ marquesas—castile }

This too is Rosa Tovar's recipe (see page 285). Marquesas *(marchionesses) or* marquesitas *are little cupcakes that are most typical of Sonseca in the province of Toledo, where they are made at Christmastime. They are soft and moist and lemony.*

MAKES 24 TO 30 MINI CUPCAKES

3 large eggs, separated

¼ teaspoon fresh lemon juice

1 cup superfine sugar

2 large egg yolks

Grated zest of 1 small lemon

¼ cup cornstarch

3¼ cups (10 ounces) ground almonds

Confectioners' sugar for dusting

With an electric mixer, beat 2 of the egg whites with the lemon juice and ¼ cup of the sugar in a medium bowl until they form stiff peaks.

Beat the 5 egg yolks and the remaining egg white with the remaining ¾ cup sugar in a large bowl to a pale cream. Beat in the grated lemon zest and the cornstarch. Mix in the ground almonds until thoroughly blended. The mixture should be a thick paste that holds together; if it is too dry, add 1 to 2 tablespoons water. Gently fold in the whites.

Spoon the batter into small cupcake liners, filling them three-quarters full. Arrange on a baking sheet and bake in a preheated 350°F oven for 10 to 13 minutes. The cakes will be very soft when you press the tops lightly with your finger. They will harden a little as they cool but will still be very soft and moist.

Dust the hot cupcakes with confectioners' sugar and let cool.

egg yolk sweets

{ yemas de santa teresa }

These famous sweets are named after the mystic Carmelite nun of Ávila, who was canonized in 1622. They are made in monasteries all over Spain. According to legend, in the early seventeenth century, King Philip III obliged wineries, which used egg whites to clarify their wines, to give their yolks to the nuns, and that remained the custom for centuries. This recipe is from Los Dulces del Convento—Recetas del Monasterio de Santa María del Soccoro *(Convent Sweets: Recipes from the Santa María del Soccoro Monastery), written by the nuns at the convent where I stayed in Seville. They say that* yemas *are their favorite sweets and warn you that they do not always come out right when you first attempt to make them. They encourage you to try again, since "hens are not about to die out and there are plenty of eggs." Sor Jesús María, the* maestra repostera *(head pastry chef), said the secret is to arrive at a thick enough syrup, so that the sweets are firm. Making them is a fiddly matter of rolling the very soft, slightly sticky mass into small balls on a bed of fine sugar.*

MAKES ABOUT 9 SWEETS

½ cup sugar

¼ cup water

6 large egg yolks

Superfine or confectioners' sugar

Bring the sugar and water to a boil in a small nonstick pan (if the corners at the base are rounded, it will be easier to work the paste without leaving some behind), then simmer over low heat for about 10 minutes, until the syrup is thick enough to coat a spoon. (If it is not thick enough, the sweets will not firm up.) Let cool a little.

Beat the egg yolks vigorously with a whisk or a fork, then pour them into the syrup, beating with a wooden spoon or a heatproof spatula. Put the pan back over low heat and keep stirring vigorously until the mass thickens to a paste that comes away from the sides of the pan. This will take about 10 minutes. Let cool, then chill in the refrigerator, preferably overnight.

Cover a large plate with superfine or confectioners' sugar. Using a teaspoon, drop small lumps of the chilled paste, the size of a large quail's egg, one at a time in the sugar and roll them into balls about 1 inch in diameter, covering them lightly all over with the sugar. Dampen your hands slightly so that the paste does not stick. Put the balls into little paper candy cases.

pine nut and marzipan sweets

{ *panellets de piñones — catalonia* }

Panellets *are the traditional sweets of All Saints' Day in Catalonia, when they are eaten with roasted chestnuts and sweet wine. Mashed potatoes or sweet potatoes are commonly added to the mixture when they are made commercially, because almonds are expensive. But they are best made using ground almonds alone for the marzipan paste. In reality, it is the labor that makes them expensive: the tricky part is pressing the pine nuts into the marzipan balls and making them stick. It is the kind of sweet that you would make as a special Christmas gift. It is best to make the marzipan paste ahead, even the day before.*

MAKES ABOUT 20 SWEETS

2 cups ground almonds

1 cup superfine sugar

Grated zest of 1 lemon

2½ tablespoons water

1 egg white

1 cup pine nuts

Put the ground almonds, sugar, and lemon zest in a food processor, add the water, and blend to a paste. You should not need any more water to produce a paste, but you will have to blend for a long time until the oil from the almonds is released and binds the ingredients into a firm soft paste. Wrap the paste in plastic wrap and refrigerate for at least 1 hour, preferably overnight.

Take small lumps of the marzipan paste and roll them into small balls, about 1 inch in diameter, between the palms of your hand. When you have shaped them all, lightly beat the egg white in a small bowl. One at a time, roll each ball in the egg white, then take a handful of pine nuts and press them into the ball, holding it in your hand. It is not easy to make them stick—you will have to push them in with your finger. Then roll the pine nut–encrusted ball in the palm of your hand so as to cover it with a film of egg white. Place the balls on a baking sheet lined with parchment paper.

Bake the balls in a preheated 400°F oven for about 10 minutes, until they are slightly golden. Do not try to take the *panellets* off the baking sheet while they are hot—they will be too soft. Wait until they have cooled and firmed.

DRINKS

{ bebidas }

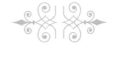

Drinking places in Spain are tavernas *and* tascas (*wine bars*), *cervecerías* (beer houses), and *sidrerías* (cider houses). Brandy distilled from fermented grape juice is produced mainly by the sherry houses of Andalusia and in Catalonia. Strong alcoholic spirits called *aguardientes,* made from fermented and distilled fruit and grain musts, are produced in different parts of Spain. Many refreshing fruity alcoholic and nonalcoholic drinks and heartwarming ones are a part of Spanish tradition that is worth adopting.

the emergence of
spanish wines

A wine-making revolution has turned the country with the greatest amount of land under grapevines in the world, which was once known for producing cheap, undistinguished, anonymous wines to be sold in bulk, into the most promising and exciting country for high-quality wines. This surprised the world, and it surprised Spain.

Fifteen years ago, only sherry and Rioja wines were appreciated abroad, and most Spaniards did not really know about wine. They knew Rioja, were used to drinking their own rough, acidic local wines, and used sherry for cooking. Small farmers made their own wine, usually in a primitive way. They dried grapes on their terraces or in their attics to make sweet wine, and they distilled grape skins and seeds to make *aguardiente* (eau-de-vie) or brandy. Large vineyards were owned by members of the aristocracy and by monasteries. In Franco's time, big *bodegas* (wineries), some of them cooperatives run by the Church, bought grapes from peasant growers, whom they exploited, and produced oceans of cheap bulk wine for export.

Today, every region except Asturias makes wine with a distinctive character, and many of these wines are astonishing. There is wine tourism, with wine routes that include visits to wineries and vineyards. Restaurants pride themselves on their wine lists. At a cooking school I visited in Galicia, the Centro Superior de Hostelería de Galicia, they place great importance on training sommeliers.

I heard about what was happening in the wine trade mainly from three people who write about wine and food: Ana Lorente, Gaspar Rey (see page 309), and Pepe Iglesias (see page 328). Lorente, editor of the magazine *Opus Wine*, explained the phenomenon that has swept the country over the last fifteen years as she drove my friend Alicia and me through the spare landscape from Madrid to Segovia. When Spaniards became wealthy and discriminating in their tastes, and domestic and foreign demand for high-quality wines increased, it became worthwhile for wineries to invest in and make the effort to achieve higher standards. The *Denominación de Origen* (DO) classification that aims to guarantee quality was a spur that rewarded their achievements, and the European Union helped with subsidies.

There is enormous enthusiasm and competitive vitality in the trade today. The old *bodegas* and some new ones adopted state-of-the-art technology and sophisticated practices with the help of oenologists who had learned from French and New World winemakers. At first, they started growing fashionable foreign grape varieties, such as Syrah, Cabernet Sauvignon, Merlot, and Chardonnay, and tried to emulate French styles. Then they went back to their native grapes, Tempranillo, Verdejo, Graciano, Monastrell, Garnacha, Prieto Picudo, and many others, and focused on improving viticulture, from making the most of their *terruño* (land) and irrigating it, to training and pruning the vines and deciding when to harvest. Grapevines carpet many different terrains with different soils and climatic conditions, on mountains and in river valleys, on vast dry plains and on volcanic islands. It is not surprising, then, that Spain has one of the widest range of distinctive wines in the world. Most winemakers blend varieties, and some include foreign grapes to achieve their characteristic color, flavor, and aroma; alcohol content; and aging properties. There are now seventy wines with a *Denominación de Origen* and fifty-five *Vinos de la Tierra* with regional names. The *Vino de la Tierra* system was started as a rebellion against the stricter system of classification, and to get around it. But such wines can be of excellent quality.

There are stars and heroes in the trade, pioneers who started the revolution twenty-five years ago and entrepreneurs who continue to create wines and to improve their wines. Previously little-known areas have produced superstar wines. A few wineries are rated by American wine writers as extraordinary. The map of Spanish wine can change so fast that wine writers find it hard to keep up with the ever-growing number of emerging wines. There is a lot to choose from, among both cheaper everyday wines and the more expensive Reservas and Gran Reservas. I mention some in the chapters on the regions (pages 67 to 118). Try what you find in your stores.

red wine sangria

{ *sangria — andalusia* }

Bits of chopped apple and orange floated in a large bowl of sangria in a little bar in Seville. The barman said it was wine, brandy, rum, and fizzy lemonade. It is something people make to taste, and different fruits can be added, such as peaches. It is a wonderfully refreshing festive drink to serve on a hot day.

SERVES 6 TO 8

2 apples or peaches, or 1 of each, peeled, cored or pitted, and diced

3 to 4 tablespoons sugar

Juice of 4 oranges

A strip of lemon peel

Juice of 1 lemon

½ cup Spanish brandy or Cognac

½ cup rum

1 bottle (750 ml) red wine, chilled

2 to 3 cups chilled soda water

Ice cubes for serving

Put the diced fruit, sugar, orange juice, lemon peel, lemon juice, brandy, and rum in a pitcher or large bowl. Stir, and leave to macerate for an hour or so.

Just before serving, pour in the chilled wine and chilled soda water and stir well. Let people help themselves to ice.

white wine and fizzy lemonade

{ *rebujito — andalusia* }

Served in tall glasses over ice, this is the thirst-quenching summer drink of Seville. Tourists ask for sangria, but this is what the locals want. You can see everybody drinking rebujito *from a jug filled with ice in their* casetas *(tents) during the Feria de Abril, the fantastic April festival. A mix of fino sherry and fizzy lemonade, it is light and refreshing. Cities such as El Puerto de Santa María, Jerez, Córdoba, and Sanlúcar de Barrameda all have their own versions with their own dry sherry and their favored proportion of wine and lemonade. Bottled Casera, which is like 7-Up, is typically used, but plain soda water or sparkling water mixed with freshly squeezed lemon juice and sugar tastes so much better. Experiment with the proportions of the wine and soda water, and with the amounts of lemon and sugar.*

SERVES 4

2 cups fino or manzanilla sherry or dry white wine, chilled

2 cups soda water or sparkling water, chilled

¼ cup fresh lemon juice, or to taste

¼ cup sugar, or to taste

Ice cubes

Mint leaves

Pour the sherry or wine and soda or sparkling water into a large glass jug or pitcher. Add the lemon juice and sugar and mix well to dissolve the sugar. Add ice cubes.

Serve in tall glasses filled with ice, and add 2 or 3 mint leaves to each.

VARIATION

For *tinto de verrano* (summer red wine), another refreshing drink that is very popular in Andalusia, use a chilled medium-bodied red wine instead of the sherry or white wine. Two to 3 tablespoons of rum may also be added.

valencia water

{ *agua de valencia — valencia* }

Agua de Valencia *started as a cocktail in Madrid. The late Constante Gil, an artist and bar owner who painted the people who came to his* Café Madrid de Valencia, *created it in 1959, and it caught on as a drink throughout Valencia. Gil made it with cava, orange juice, and vodka. Nowadays bars make it with vodka, gin, or rum, or the orange liqueur Cointreau. I prefer it as a simple mix of cava and orange juice, but you might like to experiment with other spirits. I drank too much when I experimented and had to lie down and take a nap.*

Mix 2 parts chilled cava and 1 part fresh orange juice, or the same amount of both, in a large glass jug or pitcher. If you like, add sugar to taste, stirring well to dissolve it. Add a good handful of ice. Serve in wide cocktail glasses or wineglasses.

thick hot chocolate

{ *chocolate a la taza* }

Thick, creamy rich hot chocolate served with churros, *the long ribbed crisp fritters of dough, is a popular breakfast in Spain.* Chocolaterías *specialize in the chocolate drink, which is made with bittersweet chocolate and a little cornstarch to thicken the milk. The amount of sugar depends on the sweetness of the chocolate.*

SERVES 2

2 teaspoons cornstarch

2 cups whole milk

4 ounces bittersweet chocolate, grated or finely chopped

2 to 3 teaspoons sugar, to taste

Dissolve the cornstarch in 2 tablespoons of the cold milk in a small cup.

Bring the rest of the milk to boil in a saucepan. Pour in the cornstarch mixture, stirring constantly with a wooden spoon, and cook over low heat for 2 to 3 minutes, stirring, until the milk thickens to the consistency of cream. Add the chocolate and keep stirring until the chocolate has melted entirely. Stir in the sugar to taste.

tiger nut milk

{ h o r c h a t a   d e   c h u f a — v a l e n c i a }

I adore this drink, made with chufas *(tiger nuts) in Valencia, where the nuts grow. The village of Alboraya is famous for its* horchata *and it is full of* horchaterías. *The drink was adopted from the Muslims in the area. It is made in the same way that we made almond milk in Egypt. You can find tiger nuts in health food stores.*

SERVES 4

½ pound tiger nuts

4½ cups water

¼ cup sugar, or more to taste

Wash the tiger nuts, then soak them in cold water for 12 hours. Throw away any that float on the surface—they are likely to be bad.

Drain and rinse the nuts again, then put them in a food processor with about ½ cup of the measured water and blend to a soft paste. Add another ½ cup or so of the water and blend again, then pour into a jug or pitcher. Add the remaining water and mix well. Refrigerate for 2 to 3 hours.

To strain the milk, line a colander or sieve with cheesecloth, set it over a bowl, and pour in the milk. Extract as much liquid as possible from the ground nuts by squeezing them in the cloth. Add sugar to taste and more water if you want to dilute the drink further. Serve chilled.

VARIATION

I like this best just as it is, but some people put a strip of lemon peel in the milk and sprinkle a little cinnamon into the glasses when they serve the *horchata*.

flambéed rum and coffee

{ *ron cremat — catalonia* }

Cremat is a festive drink that was brought back from Cuba by returning sailors in the nineteenth century. It is served during habaneras, *concerts of songs that have roots in Cuba. The songs are romantic and nostalgic, about lost loves, faraway lands, and sailing ships with cargoes of rum. Once they were sung by fishermen in taverns; now the concerts are held on the beaches of the Costa Brava. At such events, the* cremat *has a higher proportion of rum than coffee and is served flaming (*cremat *means "burnt") in earthenware* cazuelas. *For us in our city kitchens and dining rooms,* cremat *made with a greater proportion of coffee makes for a sumptuous and spectacular after-dinner drink. You can burn off all of the alcohol content or as little as you like—by dousing the rum sooner, before the flames die down, with the hot coffee, or by covering it with a lid (be careful not to spill it and start a fire). You can make this with brandy instead of rum.*

SERVES 6

2 cups rum

2 to 3 tablespoons sugar

2 cinnamon sticks

Peel of 1 lemon, removed in 4 large strips

4 cups freshly made hot strong coffee

Put the rum, sugar, cinnamon sticks, and lemon peel in a *cazuela*, shallow casserole, or skillet (I use a fondue dish), and stir over low heat to dissolve the sugar. Ignite the rum with a long match, being careful, as long blue flames will flare up. Let the flames almost die down, for a minute or so, then pour in the coffee—it will put them out. Ladle into cups to serve.

laced coffee

{ *carajillo* }

Drinking coffee laced with rum began in Cuba. *Carajillo* is now made in northern Spain with brandy or orujo—the fiery alcohol from the residue of wine grapes—as well as with rum. For each person, fill a small cup three-quarters full of strong black coffee, sweeten it, if you like, with sugar, and add a tablespoon or more of rum, brandy, or orujo.

MOSCATEL
6 6L
de
CHIPIONA

ÑEZ

AMONTILLA
6 6L
muy
VIEJO

acknowledgments

Much of what is in this book fills me with nostalgia about people.

I asked everybody I met in Spain during the five years I took to research this book to tell me about their favorite dishes. Some gave recipes; some spent hours, even days, talking to me about food and life, about the history of their country, and about the produce. Friends cooked for me and took me to restaurants and on *tapas* crawls; many were always available to answer questions by telephone or e-mail; colleagues gave me their books and sent me recipes; and mentors made contacts for me in different regions.

So many people helped me that I cannot thank them all, but I do remember them all—every recipe reminds me of somebody. I am immensely grateful to the following: Alicia Ríos, Pepa Aymami, Rosa Tovar, Gaspar Rey, Angelita García de Paredes Barreda, Pepe Iglesias, José María Conde de Ybarra, Lourdes March, Cuqui Gonzáles, Lolí Flores, José Luis Alexanco, Andres Bertomeu, Manolo Ruiz López, Michael Jacobs, Ana Lorente, Luis Bertran Bittini Martinez, Jaime Rodríguez, Sister Inmaculada Romero, and Carolina Zendrera. I have written about them in the book. I am much indebted to Simon Cohen and Vicky Hayward, to food historians Xavier Medina and Antoni Riera Melis, to Josep Lladonosa and the architect Miquel Espinet who is president of the Catalan Academy of Gastronomy and Jose Alba Mendoza of the Instituto de la Grasa de Sevilla (Institute of Fats); and I owe special thanks to Rosa María Esteva Grewe, Martine Beaulieu Gracia, Marion Maitlis, and María Rosa Menocal; to Hilary Pomeroy and Edith Grossman, Elena Santonja, Encarna Vicente, and Sonia Ortega.

I thank my publisher and editor, Daniel Halpern, a poet and a true gourmet, who initiated the book and gave his enthusiastic support and valuable advice throughout. I am grateful to Judith Sutton for her intelligent and painstaking editing; to Jason Lowe for the splendid photographs; and to my agent, Lizzy Kremmer, for her unceasing encouragement.

bibliography

I have consulted a large number of old and new regional Spanish cookbooks. Among the books in English that I have consulted are those of writers Colman Andrews, Teresa Barrenechea, Penelope Casas, Sam and Sam Clark, Don Harris, Clarissa Hyman, Elizabeth Luard, Janet Mendel, Marimar Torres, and Steve Winston. I have learned much about Spanish culinary history from *El Libro de la Cocina Española—Gastronomía e Historia* by Néstor Luján and Juan Perucho (Ediciones Danae, 1970); *El Buen Gusto de España* edited by Ana Letamendia and Lourdes Plana for the Ministerio de Agricultura Pesca y Alimentation (1991); *Sabores de España* by Ismael Diaz Yubero (Pirámide, 1998); Xavier Medina's *Food Culture in Spain* (Greenwood, 2005); and *Spain Gourmetour,* the food, wine, and travel quarterly magazine published by ICEX in Madrid.

Of the general books about the history of Spain not mentioned in the text, the following have been especially helpful:

- Bolens, Lucie. *La Cuisine Andalouse, un Art de Vivre, XIe–XIIIe Siècles.* Albin Michel, 1981.
- Braudel, Fernand. *La Méditerranée et le Monde Méditerranéen à l'Époque de Philippe II.* 1949.
- Carr, Raymond, editor. *Spain: A History.* Oxford University Press, 2001.
- Casey, James. *Early Modern Spain: A Social History.* Routledge, 1999.
- Kamen, Henry. *Spain in the Later Seventeenth Century, 1665–1700.* Longman, 1980.
- ———. *Empire: How Spain Became a World Power, 1492–1763.* HarperCollins, 2003.
- Kedourie, Elie. *Spain and the Jews: The Sephardi Experience, 1492 and After.* Thames and Hudson, 1992.
- Marin, Manuela, editor. *The Formation of Al-Andalus.* Part 1. *History and Society.* Ashgate Variorium, 1998.
- Medina, F. Xavier. *Food Culture in Spain.* (Food Culture Around the World series.) Greenwood Press, 2005.
- Menocal, María Rosa. *The Ornament of the World: How Muslims, Jews, and Christians Created a Culture of Tolerance in Medieval Spain.* Back Bay Books, 2003.
- Meyerson, Mark D., and Edward D. Meyerson, editors. *Christians, Muslims, and Jews in Medieval and Early Modern Spain: Interaction and Cultural Exchange.* University of Notre Dame Press, 2000.
- Morris, Jan. *Spain.* Faber and Faber, 1964.
- Read, Jan. *The Catalans.* Faber and Faber, 1978.
- Ruiz, Teofilo. *Spanish Society, 1400–1600.* Longman, 2001.
- Thomas, Hugh. *Rivers of Gold: The Rise of the Spanish Empire.* Reprint, Random House, 2003.

sources

These three companies specialize in Spanish ingredients and products:

Despaña Brand Foods
888-779-8617
www.despanabrandfoods.com (NYC store: www.despananyc.com)

La Tienda
800-710-4304
www.tienda.com

The Spanish Table
505-986-0243
www.spanishtable.com

The following sources also offer a range of Spanish and other Mediterranean ingredients:

www.amazon.com

www.igourmet.com

Kalustyan's
800-352-3451
www.kalustyans.com

Penzeys Spices
800-741-7787
www.penzeys.com

Zingerman's
888-636-8162
www.zingermans.com

index

Note: Page references in *italics* indicate photographs.